Counseling
Older Adults

Counseling Older Adults

John Blando

Routledge
Taylor & Francis Group
New York   London

Routledge
Taylor & Francis Group
270 Madison Avenue
New York, NY 10016

Routledge
Taylor & Francis Group
27 Church Road
Hove, East Sussex BN3 2FA

© 2011 by Taylor and Francis Group, LLC
Routledge is an imprint of Taylor & Francis Group, an Informa business

Printed in the United States of America on acid-free paper
10 9 8 7 6 5 4 3 2 1

International Standard Book Number: 978-0-415-99051-6 (Paperback)

Visit the Taylor & Francis Web site at
http://www.taylorandfrancis.com

and the Routledge Web site at
http://www.routledgementalhealth.com

To Brian, my big love, and Rudi, my little love.

*To Manuel, my father; Beverly, my mother; Al, my brother;
Barbara, my sister-in-law; and Apollonia, my niece.*

To my aunts, my uncles, and my cousins.

*To my grandparents and my great-grandparents,
who ventured into a new world with hope for a
better life for themselves and their families.*

To my family through all generations: past, present, and future.

Contents

Preface   ix

Acknowledgments   xv

About the Author   xvii

Chapter 1   Theories of Aging and Later Life Development   1

Chapter 2   Attending and Listening Skills in Work With
             Older Adults   33

Chapter 3   Stages of Counseling Older Adults   53

Chapter 4   Psychodynamic and Existential Foundations
             in Counseling Older Adults   77

Chapter 5   Transference and Other Counseling Processes
             With Older Adults   107

Chapter 6   Approaches to Counseling Older Adults   131

Chapter 7   The Culture and Context of Old Age   159

Chapter 8   Spirituality and Counseling Older Adults   179

Chapter 9   Multicultural Gerontological Counseling   209

Chapter 10   School, College, and Career Counseling
             and Older Adults: Grandparenting, Reentry
             Students, and Retirement   235

Chapter 11   Health and Rehabilitation Counseling With
             Older Adults   265

Chapter 12   Alzheimer's Disease and Other Dementias   285

Chapter 13   Family Issues in Counseling Older Adults   297

Chapter 14   Psychological Issues in Community and
              Mental Health Counseling   313

Chapter 15   Future Trends in Aging and Counseling   347

References   377

Index   407

Preface

This book is an introduction to gerontological counseling—that is, counseling older persons. As such, it covers theories of aging and their practical application in counseling older adults; basic counseling skills and the counseling process in the context of work with older adults; contextual factors of race/ethnicity, social class, religion and spirituality, and so forth; and social justice and other issues in work with an aging population.

RATIONALE

Having taught courses in gerontological counseling and having been coordinator of gerontological counseling within the counseling department at San Francisco State University, I have found no text that specifically addresses the training needs of counseling students, paraprofessionals, or professionals who work with diverse populations of older adults.

This textbook is not about psychotherapy with older adults; there already is an extraordinary book on that topic.[1] It is about the unique field of counseling and its application to older adults. Counseling differs from psychotherapy in at least two major ways. First, counseling tends to be strengths based; that is, it works with clients to build on their strengths rather than focuses on pathology. Second, counseling is broad and includes working with clients around issues found in schools and colleges, career and retirement, disability and rehabilitation, mental health and community services, couples and families, and of course older adults.

The current textbook is unique in that it discusses counseling skills and process knowledge as well as clinical treatment issues present but often not addressed in meeting the counseling needs of an increasingly diverse group of older clients. In *Counseling Older Adults*, we focus on counseling skills and process within the context of work with older adults.

THEME AND OBJECTIVES

Counseling older adults is not equivalent to counseling the general population, and specialized skills and knowledge as well as sensitivity to the contexts in which older adults live are essential in working successfully with this population. Furthermore, counseling older adults differs from psychotherapy or social work by its focus on helping clients address the normative difficulties and challenges of aging rather than focusing on psychopathology or the particulars of case management. *Counseling Older Adults* addresses the biopsychosocial-spiritual contexts of older adults as well as the counseling skills and process interventions that maximize counseling success within those contexts. The objectives of the book include the following:

- elucidation of major theories of aging,
- presentation of a set of basic counseling skills relevant for use with older clients,
- discussion of major counseling process issues relevant to work with older clients,
- presentation of contextual issues in working with older adults (race/ethnicity, sexual orientation, gender, social class, spirituality, and disability),
- discussion of specific counseling issues in work with older adults (e.g., career counseling, rehabilitation counseling, mental health counseling, family counseling, college counseling), and
- discussion of social justice issues implicit and explicit in counseling older adults.

ORGANIZATION

I organized this book into three sections. The first section, composed of Chapters 1 through 6, addresses theory, practical skills, and some of the deeper dimensions of work with older adults. The second section, comprising Chapters 7 through 9, considers contextual issues of elders. The third section, made up of Chapters 10 through 15, explores various issues that present in later life, including those related to career, college, school, rehabilitation, mental health, and family counseling; this section ends with an invitation to look forward by discussing the positive psychology of aging and the impact of globalization on an aging population.

Chapter 1, "Theories of Aging and Later Life Development," presents major theories of aging and later life development. There is a discussion of implicit theories of aging and an invitation for you to articulate your implicit theory of aging. In an attempt to begin to provide a multicultural and international perspective (where possible), we consider aging from a Hindu perspective and from a classical Greek perspective. We attend to other theories—modern and contemporary—that inform our understanding of the process of aging.

In Chapter 2, "Attending and Listening Skills in Work With Older Adults," we begin the chapter with a discussion of wellness and counseling, following our strengths-based counseling orientation. We explore some of the practical issues of working with older adults. We learn to use basic attending and listening skills that we can draw on when working with older adults. These include nonverbal and verbal skills.

Chapter 3, "Stages of Counseling Older Adults," describes the three stages of counseling: the beginning, middle, and end stages. We learn a set of advanced counseling skills to complement basic attending and listening skills. We also learn a five-step model to efficiently organize our counseling with older adults and their families.

In Chapter 4, "Psychodynamic and Existential Foundations in Counseling Older Adults," we review basic Freudian psychoanalytic concepts and explore three major intellectual streams of psychodynamic theory—ego psychology, object relations, and self psychology. We also are introduced to existential theory. We learn about the application of these theories to aging. We learn about existential anxiety, a particular manifestation of this—death anxiety—and defenses that individuals, including older clients, use to psychologically protect themselves.

Chapter 5, "Transference and Other Counseling Processes With Older Adults," explores some of the deeper elements of the process of counseling, drawing on understandings rooted in psychodynamic theory. We explore the phenomena of transference and countertransference, especially as they relate to younger counselors working with older clients, and look closely at the forms that transference and countertransference take when working with older clients. We also address the therapeutic alliance, resistance, working through, and termination.

Chapter 6, "Approaches to Counseling Older Adults," considers specific ways in which counseling is applied to work with older adults, including individual and group interventions. We briefly review psychodynamic approaches and interpersonal therapy, and we address in greater depth cognitive behavioral approaches as well as reminiscence, including the structured life review and guided autobiography approaches.

Chapter 7, "The Culture and Context of Old Age," begins our discussion of the culture of old age. We consider older adults as a unique cultural group, with particular ways of being, specific shared histories, distinct needs, and discrete strengths. We consider issues of spirituality, diversity, and social justice. We explore the differences between spirituality and religion, address issues of cultural diversities in elders, and touch on some social justice issues as they relate to later life.

In Chapter 8, "Spirituality and Counseling Older Adults," we continue our discussion of culture by addressing spirituality, religion, aging, and counseling. We survey the major world religions, spiritual traditions, and philosophical systems. We look at the role of the counselor when facing issues of spirituality or religion in work with older clients and their families, especially as they relate to illness, aging, and death.

Chapter 9, "Multicultural Gerontological Counseling," introduces us to the concepts of cultural competence and cultural humility when considering issues present in the culturally diverse world of older adults. We explore some issues facing older African Americans, Latino and Latina Americans, Asian and Pacific Islander Americans, First Nations elders (Native Americans), and lesbian, gay, bisexual, and transgender (LGBT) Americans.

Chapter 10, "School, College, and Career Counseling and Older Adults: Grandparenting, Reentry Students, and Retirement," explores the role of older adults as custodial or near custodial grandparents for their grandchildren, the experience of elders who return to school (reentry students), and issues related to the retirement years. These issues are most relevant to school, college, and career counselors, respectively.

In Chapter 11, "Health and Rehabilitation Counseling With Older Adults," we explore some of the physical changes in the body—especially those of hearing, vision, and dual sensory impairment—that can result in differing abilities for some older adults—differences that impact their personal, social, and work lives. We also look at vocational rehabilitation and older adults.

With Chapter 12, "Alzheimer's Disease and Other Dementias," we discuss the demographics of dementia and look at the particulars of Alzheimer's disease and vascular dementia. We review dementia classifications and differentiate dementia from other disorders. We discuss risk factors for dementia, symptoms of dementia, and common behavioral challenges found in persons with dementia. We end our discussion with treatment considerations for dementia.

Chapter 13, "Family Issues in Counseling Older Adults," considers two specific family issues faced by clients who interact with community and mental health counselors: caregiving issues and bereavement. We discuss psychoeducational and family systems approaches to working with families with older adults, especially within the context of caregiving and bereavement in families.

Chapter 14, "Psychological Issues in Community and Mental Health Counseling," addresses the fact that older adults may suffer from a range of mental health issues, including but not limited to depression, anxiety disorders, and alcohol and drug (especially prescription drug) abuse. After discussion of each of the mental health issues' risk factors and client symptoms and signs, we address counselor responses to those older clients who present with these issues.

Finally, Chapter 15, "Future Trends in Aging and Counseling," addresses two issues in contemporary gerontology. In this chapter we look to the future of counseling older adults and consider positive psychology as it relates to later life and healthy aging. We end our discussion by exploring issues in globalization that affect older adults and note some of the relationships between positive psychology, globalization, and aging.

FOUR CAVEATS

This book was designed as an introduction to counseling older adults. As such, the information presented in this book is of a general instructional nature and may or may not be relevant to or appropriate for any given client. Information in the book was not intended to be used for diagnosis or treatment of any mental or physical disorder. For that, you should consult a supervisor, physician, or other licensed health care (including mental health) provider.

Each chapter in the book ends with a case study. All case studies are fictional and designed to illuminate the concepts discussed in each chapter. Any resemblance to any person—living or dead—is strictly coincidental.

To the best of my knowledge, the information in this book is accurate as of the time of printing; however, information changes over time, and I encourage you to supplement what is in this book by doing your own research on those topics that are of interest and relevance to you. I heartily encourage you to read this book not only with an open mind and heart but also with a critical eye. Use that which is useful; discard that which is not useful.

Finally, any errors in this book—whether of omission or commission—are unintentional and presented without malice. I am committed to correcting any errors. You may send corrections and other feedback to me at jblando@sfsu.edu.

Warmest wishes.

—John
San Francisco, CA

NOTE

1. I am referring to Bob Knight's *Psychotherapy With Older Adults* (3rd ed., Newbury Park, CA: Sage, 2004).

Acknowledgments

This book would not have been possible without the assistance of Dana Bliss, Fred Coppersmith, Michael Davidson, and Chris Tominich, all of Routledge Mental Health. I thank Brian de Vries, who is an endless source of inspiration both personally and professionally. I am indebted to all of my friends and colleagues, especially Wanda Lee, who demonstrated that textbooks can be written while working full-time; Rob Williams, who inspires the best in everyone whose life he touches; George Baccay, one of the nicest guys I have ever met; and Deanne Samuels, for her support and insightful feedback on earlier drafts of the manuscript. Thanks too go to Michael Kay, who has yet to have an unkind word about anyone, and to Gary Dorothy, who has allowed so many people to see the world in all its beauty.

About the Author

John A. Blando is associate professor of counseling at San Francisco State University. He is the coordinator of gerontological counseling and of marriage and family therapy in the Department of Counseling. He received his Ph.D. in educational psychology from Stanford University in 1990 and subsequently received training in clinical psychology. He is the author or coauthor of articles and chapters on aging, spirituality, and lesbian, gay, bisexual, and transgender counseling. He is the coauthor (along with Lee, Mizelle, and Orozco) of the popular *Introduction to Multicultural Counseling for Helping Professionals* (2nd ed.) (New York: Routledge, 2007). He is a practitioner of tai chi and is very fond of miniature pinschers.

CHAPTER 1

Theories of Aging and Later Life Development

A person is not a problem to be solved, but a mystery in which to dwell.

—Daniel P. Sulmasy (2002, after Marcel, 1949)

Old age, especially when it has enjoyed honors, has an influence worth all the pleasures of youth put together.

—Marcus Tullius Cicero (106–43 BCE)

CHAPTER OVERVIEW

In this chapter, you will learn some basic information about the major theories of aging and later life development. You will learn about implicit theories of aging. You also will learn two perspectives on aging from two very different cultures—a classical point of view from the ancient city-state of Athens and a Hindu outlook from India. Finally, you will learn a number of modern and contemporary theories of aging, including those of Carl Jung, Erik Erikson, Paul Baltes, Johannes Schroots, and others.

The first time I, as a clinician-in-training, sat down with an older adult client—an 80-year-old who was recovering from a stroke—I thought to myself, "What do *I* really know about growing old?" I was lucky enough to have spent cherished time with my grandparents and to have taken wonderful courses in aging and psychology, but I did not have an experiential understanding of aging. The longer I thought about this, the more I realized that what I did have was a *personal* theory of aging. I did not label it as a theory per se; rather, I thought of it as a set of beliefs. As I reflected on my theory, I came to understand that my personality;

the culture in which I live; my age; my education; my experiences in childhood, adolescence, and adulthood; and a number of other factors influenced my theory.

I came to believe that each of us has a personal theory of aging and later life development. I have one, you have one, and older clients have one. We may not have articulated our theories, but we have them. Like those that influence my theory, many factors influence your theory and older clients' theories: personality, culture, gender, age, cohort, lived experience, and so forth. These factors affect beliefs about development over the life span and into old age. Furthermore, as we change over time, so do our theories of aging and later life development.

You might be thinking, "What relevance does a theory of aging have in my day-to-day life or that of older clients?" I argue that theories of aging do matter. What you believe about aging influences how you perceive and interact with older clients. Furthermore, older clients' beliefs about aging influence how they perceive themselves and how they interact with others. Whether one is counselor or client, one's theory of aging influences one's perceptions and how one lives one's day-to-day life.

Aging, as an area of study, is unique in that there is no single overarching theory. In other words, there is no unified theory of life span development and aging. There are many different theories—some of them biomedical, others sociological, psychological, philosophical, economic, or spiritual. In this chapter, we will look at two philosophical-spiritual perspectives, as well as major psychosocial theories. We will explore how they are similar to and how they differ from one another, focusing particularly on those factors most relevant to counseling.

Older people have sets of beliefs about how personal attributes change over the life course, and they use these beliefs to construct stories of what they were like when they were younger (McFarland, Ross, & Giltrow, 1992). These sets of beliefs are *implicit theories of aging*. That is, each of us has a set of beliefs, even if we do not explicitly articulate it to others or even to ourselves.

Attributes found in these implicit theories take one of three forms: attributes that are perceived as *increasing* with age (e.g., understanding, affection, life satisfaction, pride, or physical discomfort), attributes that are perceived as *decreasing* with age (e.g., activity level, ruggedness, or the ability to remember names or phone numbers), or attributes that are perceived as *neither increasing nor decreasing* with age (e.g., involvement in politics, mood swings, or the importance of being attractive) (McFarland et al., 1992). An older adult may believe that athletic ability decreases with age, happiness decreases with age, and assertiveness increases with age. This is one implicit theory of aging. Another older adult may believe that memory decreases with age but that wisdom increases with age and that common sense stays the same. This is another implicit theory of aging. An individual's set of beliefs compose, then, his or her implicit theory of aging.

Older adults' remembrance of attributes that they believe increase with age are biased, in that they recall themselves as possessing less of a particular attribute when younger than is actually possessed by younger adults. Likewise, older adults' remembrance of attributes that they believe decrease with age are biased in that they recall themselves as possessing more of a particular attribute when younger than is actually possessed by younger adults (McFarland et al., 1992). This suggests either that older adults have implicit theories of aging that are biased—in that the theories demand more change in attributes than what is actually experienced—or that the theories are not biased but older adults' current assessments of changes in the attribute *are* (McFarland et al., 1992). What is clear is that older adults' memories are influenced by their intrinsic theories of aging, namely, in the changes experienced as one gets older, whether the changes are positive or negative, and independent of how self-serving is the memory (McFarland et al., 1992).

Aging is "the transformation of the human organism after the age of physical maturity ... so that the probability of survival constantly decreases and there are regular transformations in appearance, behavior, experience, and social roles" (Birren, 1988, p. 159). This means that upon birth, and for a period of years, we develop toward sexual maturity, reaching an age at which we are most successful at sexual reproduction. After this age begins a period in which we, at an increasing rate, are more likely to die and a period in which changes continue to occur in how we look, how we act, what we experience, and the roles we are given or that we take in our families and culture. One thing is as certain as our birth: If we are so lucky, we shall mature, grow into old age, and die.

What follows is a broad overview of theories of aging and later life development. We will start with two diverse theoretical foundations: that of the city-state of ancient Athens expressed in Plato's perspective on aging and that of India expressed in the Hindu life stage concept of ashrama. We then will explore modern theories of aging, including Carl Jung's perspective, Havinghurst's activity theory, Erikson's eight stages of psychosocial development, Cumming and Henry's disengagement theory, and Neugarten's perspective on personality and successful aging. Finally, we will address some of the major contemporary theories, including Baltes and associates' theory of selective optimization with compensation, Salthouse's resource-reduction theory, Costa and McCrae's personality trait model, Levinson's personality development theory, Tornstam's gerotranscendence theory, Schroots's gerodynamics theory, Atchely's continuity theory, and Rowe and Kahn's theory of successful aging. Though not without their critics, these theories will help you broaden and deepen your understanding of later life and aging.

As we address the theories, consider the degree to which each of them has relevance to clients or is helpful in conceptualizing clients' challenges or in developing therapeutic interventions. Ask yourself, "Are Plato's theory or Hindu ashrama theory relevant to my clients? Are either of these theories helpful to them in conceptualizing their challenges or in developing more adaptive responses? Does gerotranscendence theory have relevance to me? Is it helpful to me in conceptualizing my clients' challenges or in developing therapeutic interventions?"

ANCIENT FOUNDATIONS

We will begin by discussing as examples of the diversity of theories of life span development and aging a theory based on an ancient Western tradition—a classical Athenian perspective on aging presented by Plato—and a theory based on an Eastern tradition—a theory of life span development that evolved in India's Hindu tradition. These two perspectives are offered as example theories of aging. You will find other early theories in the writings of the ancient Romans, Chinese, Persians, and other civilizations.

Plato's Theory of Aging

Plato explicated a theory of aging in at least three of his major works— *Republic*, *Apology*, and *Crito*—and in doing so anticipated three major issues in theories of aging: dialectic between theories, the life review, and the nature of wisdom (McKee & Barber, 2001) (see Table 1.1).

Dialectic Between Theories. A theory of aging can be conceptualized as being either an activity-continuity theory or a disengagement-gerotranscendence theory (McKee & Barber, 2001). An *activity-continuity* theory of aging is one that proposes that in late life, adults continue to seek out those activities, relationships, and values that were of importance to them in midlife (McKee & Barber, 2001). Any theory with this viewpoint fundamentally proposes that we think, feel, and do in late life that which we think, feel, and do in midlife unless something (such as illness) interferes with it. It is a belief in continuity in adulthood. A **disengagement-gerotranscendence** theory of aging is one that proposes that in late life adults develop a perspective different from what they had in midlife. Furthermore, this different perspective is marked by a lesser interest in the beliefs, feelings, and activities common in midlife and

TABLE 1.1   Plato's Theory of Aging

Issue	Description
Dialectic between theories	The dynamic tension between old age as a time of activity-continuity and old age as a time of disengagement-gerotranscendence
Life review	Retrospective evaluation of life prompted by temporal movement toward death
Nature of wisdom	Cognitive, affective, and volitional dimensions of an older person that are useful in responding to life's problems

Note: McKee, P., & Barber, C. E., "Plato's Theory of Aging," *Journal of Aging and Identity,* 6(2), 93–104, 2001.

a greater interest in looking inward and considering one's relationship to the transcendent (McKee & Barber, 2001). Both of these theoretical orientations are present in Plato's writings.

In the *Republic,* Plato describes an interaction in which Socrates asks an old man, Cephalus, the secret of happiness in late life. Cephalus states that happiness in late life is found in qualities that allow one to detach from the values of youth and midlife (especially those of material gain) and "to transcend the many painful aspects of age," especially those of physical decline (McKee & Barber, 2001, p. 94). Furthermore, Plato reflects on several concepts found in disengagement-gerotranscendence theory (discussed below): a movement from materialism to transcendentalism (in the allegory of the cave, represented by the desire to escape from darkness into the light), "identification with prior generations" (in stories of Socrates' respect for the customs and laws of civil society), "responsibility for future generations" (in the allegory of the cave, the wise one's return to the cave as mentor), and a decreased fear of death (in stories of Socrates' gracious acceptance of the inevitability of death) (McKee & Barber, 2001, p. 97). Through these stories, Plato appears to be at the disengagement-gerotranscendence end of the spectrum.

Yet Plato does not stop there. He considers whether older adults who want to disengage have a responsibility not to do so and to remain actively engaged (McKee & Barber, 2001). In the allegory of the cave, Plato comes to the conclusion that older adults have a moral obligation to return to the cave where others remain, to stay engaged, and to share the pains and joys of the younger generations (McKee & Barber, 2001). Plato, in his telling of the story of Socrates' trial, suggests that continuity of thoughts, feelings, and behaviors is present in late life, even in the face of severe circumstances, including the prospect of death (McKee & Barber, 2001). These stories reflect an activity-continuity perspective.

What are we to conclude? For Plato, aging may be a time of activity-continuity or of disengagement-gerotranscendence *or both*. This suggests the possibility that, in terms of theories of aging, what is needed today is an integration of theories from each end of the spectrum (McKee & Barber, 2001).[1]

Life Review. Robert Butler (1963, cited in McKee & Barber, 2001) developed the concept of **life review**[2] to describe why older adults reminisce. He posited that elders review their lives in order to evaluate the decisions they made and the relationships they had over their life course (McKee & Barber, 2001). Butler suggested that older adults reminisce more because they are closer to death, that in reminiscing they may change their judgments, and that life review varies from one person to another and varies over time even within the same person (McKee & Barber, 2001). Plato tells many stories that revolve around life review. In one story, Cephalus not only recounts his past actions and considerations but also analyzes them, eschewing a romanticized nostalgia of the past and emphasizing a "retrospective evaluation" prompted by his realization of the "reality of death" (McKee & Barber, 2001, p. 99). In another story, Socrates, during his trial, tells the jury about his life, detailing its major events and insights—insights that are accessible only to the old (McKee & Barber, 2001). To Plato, life review was a common phenomenon of late life and even more so a process that produced "knowledge and understanding" (McKee & Barber, 2001, p. 100).

Nature of Wisdom. Plato explored the nature of wisdom, a central consideration in many theories of aging (McKee & Barber, 2001). Plato portrayed Socrates as the "wise elder" (McKee & Barber, 2001, p. 100). He believed that wisdom comprised "cognitive, affective, and volitional" (i.e., thinking, feeling, and free choice) dimensions (McKee & Barber, 2001, p. 100). In the *Apology*, Socrates describes wisdom in its affective element and also its cognitive element. In the *Republic*, the wise guardian feels "sorry for" the prisoners (a feeling, that of empathy) and is committed to live in a new way through choosing a life of public service (a volitional behavior) (McKee & Barber, 2001, p. 100). In his writings, Plato prefigured the conception of wisdom as a response to life's problems (Baltes & Smith, 1990, cited in McKee & Barber, 2001).

As counselors, what can we learn from Plato? An overarching question is whether Plato's theoretical formulation is relevant or helpful to our clients. If it is relevant or helpful, we can contemplate several considerations. First, we can conceptualize aging as a dialectic between activity-continuity and disengagement-gerotranscendence. As we listen to our client's stories, we can ask ourselves if our clients continue to seek out those activities, relationships, and values that were important to them in midlife or if they have a greater interest in looking inward and considering their relationship to the transcendent. Furthermore, we can ask ourselves if it would be more therapeutic for our clients to seek out those activities, relationships, and values that were important to them earlier in life or to look inward and consider more transcendent issues. Second, we can ask ourselves whether our older clients would benefit therapeutically from retrospective evaluation or life review. The answer to this question will be based on our theoretical orientation (e.g., psychodynamic versus behavioral), the nature of our clients' issues, the context in which the issues present themselves, and so forth. Third, we can consider the relationship between our clients' wisdom and their presenting issues. We may consider what the relationship is between wisdom and being able to address life's challenges, including those challenges for which clients elicit the help of counselors.

Hindu Theory of Life Span Development and Aging

An alternative to considering theories of aging along the continuum of activity-continuity to disengagement-gerotranscendence is instead to consider them as belonging to one of three broad models—social, medical, and success theories (Crawford, 2003). The **social model** of aging, developed as a response to ageism, seeks to discover and promote positive images of aging and counteract negative images of aging that are so prevalent in North American culture (Crawford, 2003). The social model posits that quantity—that is, length—of life is less important than is quality of life, that with age comes wisdom and other positive qualities, and that negative social attitudes toward old age are the result of social intolerance and not of age-related physical decline (Crawford, 2003).

The **medical model** of aging promotes the idea of aging as disease or illness and posits that aging is a medical problem to be solved. The medical model emphasizes eradication of the disease state of old age and, in its most radical form, suggests that an objective of medicine should be to extend life indefinitely (Crawford, 2003).[3]

The **success model** of aging suggests that successful aging comprises three factors: avoiding disease and minimizing disability, sustaining high levels of both mental and physical functioning, and remaining actively engaged in life (Rowe & Kahn, 1998, cited in Crawford, 2003). Active engagement means that successful older adults engage in "happy activities" (Crawford, 2003, p. 180).

From a Hindu perspective, social, medical, and success models of aging are lacking and are discordant with Hindu ethics (Crawford, 2003). The specific incompatibilities revolve around both the social and the medical models' rejection as repugnant of physical decline, their position that aging and death are unacceptable and that life is not a "brief candle" but can and should be extended indefinitely, and their suggestion that aging necessarily results in loss of power, abandonment, and treatment by indifferent providers (Crawford, 2003, p. 181).

Hindu scriptures exhort old people to go into the forest to live, exposed to the elements, reciting the Veda, abandoning attachment to the material, and attaining liberation (Crawford, 2003). This has much in common with the success model's emphasis on minimizing disease and disability and encouraging high levels of physical functioning and mental performance (Crawford, 2003). Indeed, to live in the forest in old age requires that one "be at low risk for disease and disease related disability" especially given the physical challenges of an environment that contains wild animals, monsoons, and other challenges (Crawford, 2003, p. 184). Existence in the forest is not a retreat from life, though. Furthermore, life in the forest requires reciting holy scriptures, the Veda, an immense and complex text that calls for tremendous concentration and mental activity (Crawford, 2003). Hence, life in the forest requires a high degree of physical as well as mental performance.

Where the success model and the Hindu model of aging diverge is in regard to active involvement with and participation in life. In successful aging models, living life means physical fitness, mental acuity, and social involvement (Kahn & Rowe, 1998, cited in Crawford, 2003); the Hindu model of aging focuses on the "primacy of the transcendent," that is, union with the infinite and eternal reality (Crawford, 2003, p. 185). This goal is met through **ashrama** (or asramadharma), "the progressive unfolding of values through separate stages of the human life cycle" (Crawford, 2003, p. 185).

In the Hindu worldview, there are developmental stages—ashrama— for the realization of the human longings that differ over time: student, householder, forest dweller, and ascetic (Ashrama, 2008; Firth, 2005). The *student* stage is marked by the celebration of early life, and the *householder* stage is marked by the responsibilities of marriage and caring for a family. The *forest dweller* and *ascetic* stages are marked more by detachment and movement toward realization of the essential self— Atman (Saraswathi, 2005). In later life, then, one may move toward abstaining from sex and toward renunciation as a means of beginning to loosen the obligations of family and community and to develop greater autonomy to attend to spiritual matters—namely, the realization of Atman (Saraswathi, 2005). That is, early in life one learns self-control and responsibility (student stage); in midlife, one learns to express one's sexual being and even to acquire material goods—but always with self-control and responsibility (householder stage); in late life, one learns to

TABLE 1.2   Ashrama: A Hindu View of Life Span Development

Stage	Description
Student	Celebration of childhood
Householder	Marriage and care for family
Forest dweller	Movement into the forest of detachment in order to move toward recognition of essential self
Ascetic	Recognition of temporality of inhabited body and the reality of the subtle body

Note: Crawford (2003), Saraswathi (2005), Firth (2005), Whitman (2007).

attend to the transcendent (forest dweller stage and, subsequently, ascetic stage) (Crawford, 2003) (see Table 1.2).

In this view, the good life is one that allows "a capacity to flourish when its time has come" and does not long for it "when its time has gone" (Crawford, 2003, p. 186). If earlier stages of life, then, allow for the fulfillment of dreams, abilities, and wishes, so too does old age. It is just that in old age, the dreams, abilities, and wishes are different from those early in life or in midlife. Furthermore, humans can take comfort in the reality that each stage—including old age—is or can be *ne plus ultra* (the highest point). If it is not, it is only because one longs after the dreams, abilities, or wishes of some other stage—a sign of immaturity (Crawford, 2003).

Finally, an old adult's move to the forest is not retirement as we conceptualize it in North America; rather, it is a movement away from *horizontal* social pursuits and toward a *vertical* transcendent quest (Crawford, 2003). It is only through engagement of this transcendent quest that one is able to reach that state of union with the infinite and eternal reality (Crawford, 2003). The disengagement from the social, then, allows one to more fully engage the transcendent. Crawford (2003) called engagement of the transcendent "life's most difficult [task], requiring all of one's resources of body, mind, and spirit ... reserved for the last part of the journey ... an image of old age that is strenuous, optimistic, and full of joy ... not in spite of old age but because of old age" (p. 187).

There are clear differences between Hindu and non-Hindu attitudes toward dying and death (Vatuk, 1996, cited in Crawford, 2003). In contrast to North American attitudes, the Hindu approach to dying and death is marked by acceptance and by active preparation for the inevitable (Vatuk, 1996, cited in Crawford, 2003; see also Whitman, 2007). Hindu literature is filled with exhortations for long lives and also recognition of karma as well as a recognition of the responsibility of the individual related to his or her future rebirths (Crawford, 2003).

In Hindu tradition, the *essential self*, Atman, is the core of being, though because of ignorance and desire, it attaches to an *empirical self*, an individual body–mind–intellect (Crawford, 2003; see also Saraswathi, 2005). The essential self then is locked into a cycle of life–death–rebirth (i.e., samsara) unless and until it is liberated. Furthermore, the empirical self comprises both a physical body and a subtle body. The subtle body (itself composed of mental and intellectual elements) continues after death and moves from the deceased corporeal body to the next corporeal body into which it is reborn. Death is not liberation; rather, it is merely the disintegration of the corporeal body when the subtle body withdraws. Through the forces of karma, and upon rebirth, the subtle body inhabits a new specific body in a specific environment. The *ascetic* stage of ashrama is that in which one recognizes the temporality of the inhabited physical body and explicitly acknowledges the subtle body.

We can consider counseling older adults from the perspective of Hindu life span development. We can consider at what stage of life span development is an older client—student, householder, forest dweller, or ascetic—and whether that stage is normative (i.e., developmentally appropriate) or nonnormative (i.e., *off time*). If a client is trying to experience a stage off time, we may ask the extent to which that contributes to or is the cause of the client's difficulties. Furthermore, we may consider if it is possible for the client to adopt a more normative stage and if so, how.

MODERN AND CONTEMPORARY THEORIES

We have considered that theories may fall along a continuum from activity-continuity to disengagement-gerotranscendence or that theories may be classified as medical, social, or success models. A third way in which theories of aging may be conceptualized is whether they can be classified as a psychology of *the aged*, a psychology of *age*, or a psychology of *aging* (Schroots, 1996a). Psychology of the aged theories are those that attend to particular behaviors, roles, or activities at a stage of later life (i.e., in a particular **cohort**); these include, for example, theories of retirement or widowhood (Schroots, 1996a). In contrast, psychology of age theories tend to be based on **cross-sectional studies** that look at people at different ages and from different stages in life and are likely to address issues in age-related change over the life course; these include theories that attend to processing speed or attention (Schroots, 1996a). Psychology of aging studies integrate psychology of the aged and psychology of age perspectives into **longitudinal studies** that look at how people evolve over the life course (Schroots, 1996a).[4] It is from a psychology of aging

TABLE 1.3   Modern Theories of Aging

Theory	Description
Gompertz's law	As age increases, so does rate of death.
Hall's hill metaphor	Life as a voyage: As one grows up, one goes up the hill; as one grows old, one goes down the hill.
Jung's perspective	The first half of life is marked by social achievement, conformity, and preparation for living; the second half of life is marked by personal coherence and completeness, preparation for dying.
Havinghurst's activity theory	Life span development comprises six stages and emphasizes the importance of maintaining a meaningful and productive life into old age.
Erikson's stages of psychosocial development	Life span development comprises eight epigenetic stages, each marked by its own dialectic; the final stage is old age, marked by integrity versus despair.
Cumming and Henry's disengagement theory	In midlife and late life, one increasingly turns inward and withdraws from one's social environment.
Neugarten's personality and successful aging theories	Life comprises a series of transitions from one stage to another; adults respond to the stresses of transitions in one of eight ways.

Note: Schroots (1996a), Biggs (1998), Belsky (1999), Moraglia (1994), Reker and Wong (1988), King (1974), Whitbourne (2005), Erikson (1987).

perspective that we will look at modern and contemporary theories of aging (see Table 1.3 and Table 1.4).

MODERN THEORIES

Modern Foundations

Modern theories have their foundations in the 19th- and 20th-century work of such individuals as Benjamin Gompertz (Schroots, 1996a). Gompertz's contribution was the publication of a report indicating a relationship between age and mortality; specifically, he noted that for people, starting at about age 10 and continuing through the end of life, the *rate* of death increased with increasing age (Schroots, 1996a). What became known as Gompertz's law has prompted considerable research into aging and death (Schroots, 1996a). Subsequently, Quetelet posited

TABLE 1.4   Contemporary Theories of Aging

Theory	Description
Baltes's et al. selective optimization with compensation theory	In later life, one becomes more *selective* in choosing in which activities one will invest one's energies; one *optimizes* one's abilities by working harder, practicing, or getting more experience; and one *compensates* for age-related limitations.
Salthouse's resource-reduction theory	As one ages, one's cognitive processing resources decline, resulting in decreased performance of cognitive tasks.
Costa and McCrae's personality trait model	The five personality factors of neuroticism, extraversion, openness to experience, agreeableness, and conscientiousness are traits and do not change much over time.
Levinson's personality development theory	Adult life span development comprises three stable phases of adulthood—early, middle, and late—interrupted by transitional phases.
Tornstam's gerotranscendence theory	As one ages, one has a lesser attraction to the material and rational and a greater affinity for the transcendent and universal.
Schroots's gerodynamics theory	Aging comprises a series of transformations into structures that are either higher or lower ordered.
Atchley's continuity theory	One's identity, when one is an older adult, is influenced by one's lasting perceptions of oneself, as well as by environmental factors that mediate the firmness of one's view of oneself.
Rowe and Kahn's theory of successful aging	Rather than a period of decline, old age can be a period of time invested in minimizing disease and illness, maximizing good physical and cognitive health, and maintaining an active social life of connection to others.

Note: Schroots (1996a); Hill (2006); Tornstam (1997); Sadler and Biggs (2006); Braam, Bramsen, van Tilburg, van der Ploeg, and Deeg (2006); Belsky (1999); Whitbourne (2005); Rowe and Kahn (1997).

that changes over the life span are law bound. He recognized Gompertz's law and also noted there were somewhat reliable age differences in people's physical characteristics and behaviors (Schroots, 1996a). As a mathematician, Quetelet translated his findings into the concept of "the average man"; that is, the normative human (Schroots, 1996a).

G. S. Hall published *Senescence: The Second Half of Life* in 1922, in which he summarized what was known at the time about the psychology of aging (Schroots, 1996a). Hall contributed to the study of aging the **hill metaphor:** Life essentially is a voyage up the hill as one matures and then down the hill as one grows old (Schroots, 1996a). Another author, Charlotte Buhler, laid the groundwork for life span developmental psychology through her book on the life course, in which she emphasized the psychology and biology of development and aging (Schroots, 1996a).

Carl Jung's Perspective of Life Span Development

According to Jung, adults mature throughout the life span. He differentiated between the first and second halves of life (Biggs, 1998). Unlike his fellow psychoanalysts, Jung thought that the second part of life was more important than the first (Mattoon, 1981, cited in Belsky, 1999; Moraglia, 1994).

For Jung, the first half of life is marked by a striving for "social achievement and conformity," whereas the second half of life is marked by a wish for "personal coherence and completeness" (Biggs, 1998, p. 432). "The first half of life is spent in preparation for living ... the second half is spent in preparation for old age and death" (Reker & Wong, 1988, p. 232). The first half of life is lived in terms of "a family, a comfortable lifestyle, a successful career, a respected place in society"; the second half of life is lived not being satisfied with the norms of early adulthood but moving toward something more, ultimately approaching "meaningfulness in the face of death" (Moraglia, 1994, pp. 66, 67).[5]

Jung noticed that beginning in midlife (roughly, age 40) and continuing into later life, an individual's personality characteristics may change (Moraglia, 1994). This change may manifest in a transition from extraversion to introversion (i.e., an increasing inward focus) and a move toward increasing androgyny (i.e., men develop more feminine qualities and women develop more masculine qualities than they had earlier in life). There is evidence for increased introspection as a feature of the second half of life (Neugarten, 1968, and Rosen & Neugarten, 1964, cited in Moraglia, 1994), even if broad personality features remain stable throughout adulthood (Costa, McCrae, et al., 1986, 1988, and 1989, cited in Moraglia, 1994). Likewise, there is evidence of movement toward greater androgyny in older adults with women tending to "recognize and accept their aggressive impulses" and men becoming "more appreciative of nurturant and affiliative" expressions (Neugarten & Gutmann, 1958, cited in Moraglia, 1994, p. 59), though not always acting behaviorally on these changes (Moraglia, 1994). Even with equivocal research results, one can deduce that later life is not merely a continuation of earlier life but a period that is marked by its "own purpose and significance" (Schroots, 1996a, p. 588).[6]

For Jung, a life span developmental perspective became the measure by which one could judge healthy functioning (King, 1974). To Jung, older adults have different priorities than younger adults. When strivings for social achievement and conformity no longer bring meaning, Jung suggested that meaning arises from turning toward the goals of personal coherence and completeness. In other words, when the goals of the first half of life no longer have meaning, Jung believed it was time to attend to other goals—those of the second half of life. When the objectives of early adulthood—settling into one's station in life—are resolved, then it is time to turn inward and begin to focus more on introspection, contemplation, philosophizing, and generativity (Belsky, 1999). This transition was thought to begin sometime between ages 35 and 40, what Jung called *Sturm und Drang* (*storm and stress* or *storm and urge* in German) and what we might call midlife crisis. In fact, Levinson and his colleagues (1978, cited in Moraglia, 1994) found that an overwhelming majority of the middle-aged men they studied were in a period of transition; they were reevaluating their work, relationships, and beliefs about life.

Jung believed that psychoanalysis was not suited to the goals of the second half of life and instead recommended a therapy that focused on expanding one's internal experience and experiencing a sense of flexibility, change, and evolution where anything is possible (see Biggs, 1998). Jung felt this could occur through the use of nondirective work using the technique of something akin to a daydream (Biggs, 1998).

Robert J. Havinghurst's Activity Theory

Havinghurst posited a six-stage theory of life span development, each stage associated with a particular developmental task (Schroots, 1996a). This came to be known as **activity theory** (in contrast to disengagement theory) because of its emphasis on the importance of maintaining meaningful and productive life activity into old age (Schroots, 1996a; Whitbourne, 2005). Havinghurst posited that there are particular developmental tasks associated with different ages (or stages) in life. According to Havinghurst, success in the task results in happiness and facility in subsequent developmental tasks, whereas failure results in unhappiness and problems with subsequent tasks (Schroots, 1996a). Havinghurst's six stages are infancy and early childhood, middle childhood, adolescence, early adulthood, middle age, and later maturity (Schroots, 1996a). Each of the six stages comprises particular physical, psychological, and social elements. Later maturity is the stage of life after age 60. Its developmental tasks are to learn to deal with the physical changes brought about by aging, to devote one's energies to different roles than one had in the past (e.g., as a retiree, or grandparent, or widow), to accept one's own life, and to develop a philosophy about death (Schroots, 1996a).

Erik Erikson's Eight Stages of Psychosocial Development

Erikson was trained as a psychoanalyst, though he believed not that sexual and aggressive urges were what drove people's lives but instead that psychosocial issues were of primary concern (Belsky, 1999). By psychosocial issues, he meant issues related to identity and relationship development (Belsky, 1999). He is best known for creating an epigenetic eight-stage theory of life span psychosocial development, covering infancy through late life (Erikson, 1963/1987). An epigenetic theory is one in which each stage is built on or is dependent on a previous stage. Erikson believed that each stage of development was precipitated by a crisis born from conflict between complementary forces (Erikson, 1963/1987; Schroots, 1996a). In other words, he believed that each of us experiences crises that are based on the conflicting pull we feel to move in two different directions. Our task, then, at each stage is to resolve the crisis by balancing our needs with those of society (Erikson, 1963/1987; Schroots, 1996a). By resolving a crisis in a positive way, we acquire a new virtue (Erikson, 1987; Schroots, 1996a). Conversely, by resolving a crisis in a negative way, we are left with a quality (one might even call it a vice) that makes life more difficult. In other words, in each developmental stage there is a task that can be completed "in a healthy self-integrative way that is ego syntonic" or can be responded to "in a negative, rejecting and self alienating way" (King, 1974, p. 28). In Erikson's theory, the final stage is old age, the stage in which a person is pulled in the direction of integrity or despair. If one has fought off the despair that comes from a belief that one's life ultimately was meaningless and if one has embraced a sense that one's life has been meaningful (integrity), then one is poised to acquire the virtue of wisdom (Erikson, 1963/1987; Schroots, 1996a).

The first stage of Erikson's theory is *infancy*, occurring roughly from birth to age 1. (Erikson would not have been rigid about ages.) Psychosocially, infancy is marked by a struggle between trust and mistrust, and when resolved in favor of trust, it results in the virtue of hope. The second stage, *early childhood*, occurs between the ages of 1 and 6. The main challenge is between developing autonomy or doubt and shame about oneself. When resolved in favor of autonomy, it results in a strong sense of will. Erikson's third stage is *play age*, ages 6 through 10. The main struggle during this stage is between initiative and guilt, and when resolved in favor of initiative, it results in the acquisition of a sense of purpose. *School age*, the fourth stage, occurs from ages 10 to 14. It is during these years that a child struggles between feelings of industry and inferiority. If these feelings are resolved in favor of industry, the child will gain a sense of personal competence. *Adolescence* is the stage from ages 14 to 20. The struggle during this stage is between identity and role confusion; when resolved in favor of identity, the resulting virtue is fidelity. The remaining three stages are those of adulthood. *Young adulthood* lasts from ages 20 to 35 and is marked by the struggle between developing intimacy and feeling isolation. In developing intimacy, one can acquire the virtue of love. *Adulthood* covers the years of midlife, 35 to 65. The task at this stage is to resolve the struggle between generativity and stagnation and in doing so developing the virtue of care. The final stage and the one most germane to our discussion, *old age*, covers those age 65 and older.

As we have seen, *old age* is marked by a struggle between integrity and despair, which is hoped to be resolved in favor of integrity and with the virtue of wisdom. Here, *integrity* refers to a sense of being whole or self-coherent even in the face of diminishing physical powers or cognitive abilities. With integrity, one accepts one's positive and negative qualities (Whitbourne, 2005); one understands that one's life has meaning (Belsky, 1999). *Despair* results from a lack of a sense of wholeness or integrated self; it is a sense that one's life ultimately is meaningless. For a person in despair, death is coming far too quickly for one to right the wrongs in one's life (see Whitbourne, 2005). Wisdom is the concern for life in the face of death; Erikson contrasts wisdom with its antithesis, disdain—that feeling of helplessness, confusion, and sense of being finished with life (Erikson, 1982). Old age's integrity is marked by something of a "*grand*-generative function," (Erikson, 1982, p. 63), that is, a more global, philosophical sense of generativity, a generativity whose object is the whole of humanity.

One of the great strengths of Erikson's theory is that it suggests that across the whole of one's life and even into old age, one can change (King, 1974). Furthermore, each stage of life has the ability to influence a future stage of life (King, 1974). That is, how we resolve our present stage influences how we deal with future stages (King, 1974). We can even say that how we resolve our final stage of life influences our death. The counseling implication is that people can resolve developmental conflicts, perhaps with help from a counselor, and can change for the better. Counseling a person in early adulthood or in adulthood may help that person even into old age; helping a person in old age may contribute to an ability to die with meaning and dignity and grace.

Elaine Cumming and William Henry's Disengagement Theory

In 1961, Elaine Cumming and William Henry proposed that beginning in midlife and continuing through the remainder of life, people begin to turn increasingly inward (Belsky, 1999). They suggested that this turning inward is marked by a "withdrawal ... from previous roles or activities" (Schroots, 1996a, p. 562). They believed that this process of withdrawal was natural (i.e., it was normative) and resulted in an increasing focus on the self and decreasing connection to other people (Schroots, 1996a). According to Cumming and Henry, successful aging was marked by withdrawal from one's social environment (Belsky, 1999). Cumming and Henry believed this phenomenon was universal across all people in all cultures. This theory often has been criticized as being one-sided and myopic in light of the fact that many older adults do not withdraw socially (Schroots, 1996a).

Bernice Neugarten's Perspective on Personality and Successful Aging

Bernice Neugarten made two significant contributions to theories of aging. First, she and her colleagues developed a life cycle theory of life span development[7] that focused on normative and nonnormative transitional events. Common, normative transitional events (i.e., events that signal a transition from one stage of life to another) include marriage and parenthood in early and middle adulthood, retirement in early old age, and widowhood in late life (Schroots, 1996a). These are events that occur at the time one normally expects for them to occur. Normative events are those typically expected to occur in a particular order (e.g., attending college, getting a job and getting married, having children, buying a house, and so forth) and during a particular age in life. Nonnormative transitional events are those that occur out of sequence or at an age in which they are not expected to occur. These can include such events as the death of a child (even an adult child), widowhood in early adulthood, or parenthood in late life (perhaps through marriage to a younger adult). Neugarten believed that our expectations for normative events influence our behaviors at those times in our lives (Schroots, 1996a). She also believed that nonnormative events (i.e., those that are not expected) can cause personal crises (Schroots, 1996a).

Neugarten's second contribution arose from her observation that older adults have varying abilities to cope with stress and to deal with aging; that is, she saw that aging required adapting to changing life circumstances (Schroots, 1996a). She believed that older adults responded in different ways to challenging life circumstances. She identified eight different personality types or ways of responding: "the Reorganizers, the Focused, the Disengaged, the Holding-on, the Constricted, the Succorance-seeking, the Apathetic, and the Disorganized" (Schroots, 1996a, p. 562). She believed that older adults adapt to changes in later life and also can develop patterns that lead to more life satisfaction at the end of life (Schroots, 1996a).

Summary

Modern theories of aging provide the foundation for contemporary thinking about later life and aging as distinct from earlier life and midlife. Jung suggested not only that the second half of life was distinctly different from the first half but also that it was more important than the first half. Havinghurst posited a stage theory of life span development and recognized that late life could be a time of meaning, activity, and productivity. Erikson's eight-stage theory of psychosocial development emphasized the successful resolution of one stage in order to lay the groundwork for the next stage and acknowledged that there was a discrete developmental task in late life. Cumming and Henry believed that the second half of life was marked by social withdrawal and turning inward. Neugarten's life cycle theory addressed both normative and nonnormative events, and her personality theory proposed that older adults' need to adapt to maneuver the challenges of later life.

As a counselor, you can consider whether and to what extent each of these theories inform your views of aging. Ask yourself, "Do I believe that the second half of life substantially differs from the first half, and if so, how does it differ? Can old age be a time of activity, or is it a time of withdrawal? Is life span development linear? Can an individual move backward as well as forward in life span development? Are there specific developmental tasks that are common to older adults, and if so, what are they?" Also, you may ask these questions about your clients:

- Are my clients active or withdrawing in later life?
- Is their development linear?
- Are they experiencing common developmental tasks?
- Are their late-life experiences normative or nonnormative, and how does that impact their presentation?

CONTEMPORARY THEORIES

Paul Baltes's et al. Selective Optimization With Compensation Theory

Paul Baltes and his colleagues' theory of selective optimization with compensation arises out of seven propositions about aging: Aging may be normal, pathological, or optimal; there is considerable variability between individuals in the course of aging; older adults have a reserve capacity that is dormant; crystallized intelligence enhances one's mind and can make up for decreases in fluid intelligence; adaptivity decreases because of aging; over the course of time, the balance between gains and losses favors losses; and older adults are resilient and can continue to survive and preserve integrity (Schroots, 1996a, 1996b).

Baltes considered these seven propositions in developing his theory of successful aging. In Baltes's theory, three processes interact with one another: selection, optimization, and compensation. Selection means making choices given an increasing limitation in the areas in which one can function because of constraints brought about by aging. That is, one becomes more selective in choosing in which activities one will invest one's energies (Hill, 2006). It is a "restriction of one's involvement to fewer domains of functioning" (Baltes & Carstensen, 1999, p. 218), selecting those activities that are "more satisfying and highly valued" (Hill, 2006, p. 44).

Optimization is the process of maintaining one's abilities by working harder, practicing more, or getting more experience at a task or activity (Hill, 2006). An example would be using memory training programs to maintain one's intellectual abilities (Hill, 2006).

Finally, compensation refers to making up for limitations due to aging. Consider the well-known example of the master pianist Rubinstein who altered his piano playing to make up for limitations he experienced as a result of aging (Baltes & Carstensen, 1999; Schroots, 1996a). What Rubinstein did was select a fewer number of pieces to play (selection); he practiced this smaller number of pieces more frequently (optimization); and he slowed down his speed of playing prior to fast passages, giving the appearance of speed in the fast passages (compensation) (Baltes & Carstensen, 1999; Schroots, 1996a).

Timothy Salthouse's Resource-Reduction Theory

Salthouse and others have noted that as people age, their cognitive processing skills decline (Schroots, 1996a). In other words, there is a reduction of cognitive processing resources, and this reduction results in decreased performance of cognitive tasks (Schroots, 1996a). This may manifest as more limited ability to attend, reduced working memory capability, or reduced cognitive processing speed (Schroots, 1996a). Salthouse posited that cognitive processing resources have three qualities: There is a finite amount of resources that increase in the earlier part of life and decrease in the latter part of life (something akin to the hill metaphor); devoting more resources to a cognitive task improves one's performance of that task; and resources can and are used in a multitude of varied cognitive processes. If there is a decrease in space available for processing, a restriction of energy available for processing, or a time constraint, then one may observe a reduction of resources (Schroots, 1996a).

Paul Costa and Robert McCrae's Personality Trait Model

Costa and McCrae posited that the personality factors of neuroticism, extraversion, openness to experience, agreeableness, and conscientiousness are traits (Schroots, 1996a). That is, for any given individual, these five factors do not change much over time. For the most part, what you are early in life so too you will be in later life. Further research suggests that although personality traits remain stable over the course of one's life, other qualities—"goals, values, coping styles, and control beliefs"— may change (Schroots, 1996a, p. 564). For example, one may be an extrovert who, early in life, has goals of developing a successful work life as a talent agent; in late life one likely will still be an extrovert, but one's goal may be to surround oneself more with a large activity-based circle of friends. In this example, one's extroversion early in life was expressed through one's work life and later in life through one's social connections with friends. Across the life course one's extroversion was expressed, though, in different ways.

Daniel Levinson's Personality Development Theory

In contrast to Costa and McCrae, Levinson posited a theory of personality development across the life course (Schroots, 1996a). He believed that each man (his theory arose from his research on men) progresses through a series of stable phases interrupted by transitional phases. He posited three major phases of adulthood: early adulthood (from age 17 to 45), middle adulthood (from age 40 to 65), and late adulthood (age 60 and older) (Schroots, 1996a). The transition from one stage to the next occurs during a 5-year transition period in which a previous stage overlaps with the subsequent stage (Schroots, 1996a). Levinson further believed that there were individual differences in the timing and length of each period, based on biological, psychological, and social factors (Schroots, 1996a).

Lars Tornstam's Gerotranscendence Theory

Lars Tornstam believed that the Western ethic of work productivity has affected our perceptions of aging in that, in the West, aging is seen as a time of decline precisely because it is a time of diminished material productivity (Jonson & Magnusson, 2001). He proposed a new paradigm in which aging is recognized as having qualities that are different from, though no less valuable than, those found in midlife. These qualities are marked by an increased cosmic consciousness, a decreased self-centeredness, and a greater selectivity in the social sphere, emphasizing depth of relationships over breadth. Tornstam contrasted the materialism that is endemic to the West with non-Western values reflected in, for example, Zen Buddhism. In this view, individuals naturally move toward gerotranscendence unless they are constrained by cultural expectations, demands, or structures.

Tornstam believed that each of us contains the potential for *gerotranscendence*—a cosmic, transcendent perspective on life that can arise in late life and in contrast to the materialism and pragmatism that often is the basis of earlier adult experience (Schroots, 1996a; Tornstam, 1997). According to Tornstam, the experience of gerotranscendence generally results in greater wisdom and life satisfaction (Sadler & Biggs, 2006; Schroots, 1996a; Tornstam, 1997). Tornstam believed that gerotranscendence is the last stage in a person's growth toward maturity and wisdom (Tornstam, 1997). It is that time when a person moves away from the goals and values that are normative in early life or midlife and toward goals and values that are markers of late-life maturity.

Gerotranscendence manifests itself on three levels: the cosmic, the self, and the social and individual relations levels (Sadler & Biggs, 2006; Schroots, 1996a; Tornstam, 1997). The cosmic level is marked by a number of qualities, including having changed experiences of "time, space, and objects"; greater feelings of kinship with previous and subsequent generations; a different perception of life; decreased fear of death; greater acceptance of mystery; and a greater sense of connection with "the spirit of the universe" (Schroots, 1996a, p. 566). Cosmic transcendence is associated with meaning in life (Braam, Bramsen, van Tilburg, van der Ploeg, & Deeg, 2006), such as having a sense of meaning, a life purpose, a feeling of fulfillment, and a sense of significance (Almond, 1973, cited in Braam et al., 2006). People experience this cosmic level in feelings of connection with the whole of humanity; a sense of time as circular, not linear; increased recollection of childhood memories; and feelings of connection with earlier generations (Tornstam, 1997)—a sense that one is part of something bigger than oneself. Sometimes this is manifest in an interest in genealogy (Tornstam, 1997). This cosmic dimension may be indescribable through language alone, and understanding may be more tangible through music or visual arts (Tornstam, 1997). For those experiencing this cosmic dimension, the transcendent experience of seemingly minor, everyday activities such as enjoying nature and gardening is what brings joy (Tornstam, 1997).

There will be discovery of previously hidden parts of the self, decreased self-absorption, greater selflessness, an appreciation for one's childlike qualities, and ego integrity (Schroots, 1996a; Tornstam, 1997). The self-understanding acknowledges that the self is not changeless; rather, it is in a continuous state of change, development, and growth. This is manifest in gerotranscendence by greater self-awareness of positive and/or negative qualities of which one formerly was unaware (Tornstam, 1997). It may also manifest in redefinition of qualities of which one is aware; one older man, for example, who in adulthood experienced himself as engaged and empathic, in late life redefined his motivation as performance anxiety (Tornstam, 1997).

Social and personal relations are marked by a reduced interest in superficial relationships, greater desire for time spent with oneself, understanding the difference between one's self and one's roles, decreased materialism, and increased need to reflect (Schroots, 1996a; Tornstam, 1997). Persons experiencing gerotranscendence seek out fewer but deeper relationships, experience an increased desire for solitude, and delight in breaking role expectations and social conventions that in the past have been constricting—what Chinen (1989a, cited in Tornstam, 1997) called *emancipated innocence*. For the gerotranscendent, it is acceptable to acknowledge the limits of one's knowledge (Tornstam, 1997). Furthermore, wisdom is manifest by a sense that right and wrong are not so easily differentiated, which results in restraint in advice-giving (Tornstam, 1997).

Tornstam (1997) differentiated gerotranscendence from disengagement theory and also from Erikson's stage of ego integrity versus despair. Although being more selective in personal and social relations might be perceived as disengagement, gerotranscendence argues that this represents a desirable developmental occurrence (Tornstam, 1997). Erikson's stage of ego integrity versus despair, when resolved positively, results in an integration of life experiences and a coming to terms with the life one has lived—a past-oriented integration; gerotranscendence is more forward directed (Tornstam, 1997).

Gerotranscendence theory is not without its critics. Jonson and Magnusson (2001) argued that gerotranscendence theory suffers from empirical weakness, connections to New Age philosophies and romantic Orientalism, and an attempt to reenchant aging. Jonson and Magnusson (2001) faulted gerotranscendence theory for positioning itself as subjectivist (based on older people's subjective experiences) while relying on objectivist criteria (particularly quantitative research) for validation. They argued, too, that gerotranscendence theory to some degree idealizes those essential values supposedly lost to Western societies yet present in Eastern cultures (a perspective known as romantic Orientalism) (Jonson & Magnusson, 2001). Finally, they believed that gerotranscendence theory attempts to reenchant aging by focusing on the nonrational and spiritual and away from reason and secular pursuit of knowledge about aging (Jonson & Magnusson, 2001).

Johannes J. F. Schroots's Gerodynamics Theory

Schroots's gerodynamics theory finds its basis in complementary concepts from general systems theory and dynamic systems theory (Schroots, 1996a). From general systems theory it takes the concept of **entropy**— that is, that over time, there is an increase in disorder. From dynamic systems theory it takes the concept of **chaos theory**, that fluctuations in dynamic systems can pass a crucial point at which order is created out of chaos. In other words, over time organization can develop where it previously did not appear to exist. Schroots (1996a) argued that aging comprises "a nonlinear series of transformations into higher and/or lower order structures and processes" marked by entropy and resulting in death (p. 566). At various points in the life course, then, a person will branch into a higher- or a lower-level structure (particularly related to mortality, morbidity, and quality of life) (Schroots, 1996a). A diagnosis of diabetes may result in a lower-order structure (greater likelihood of degeneration and death), whereas not smoking may result in a higher-order structure (lesser likelihood of lung cancer and death).

Robert Atchley's Continuity Theory

Atchley's **continuity theory** essentially states that continuity or lack of continuity influences one's perception of oneself as an older adult (Hill, 2006). Namely, one's perception of oneself as an older person is influenced by internal continuity and external continuity. Internal continuity refers to the sense of oneself in the here and now that is rooted in the sense of a historical self (Hill, 2006). It refers to traits that one possesses—changeless, consistent, and reliable indicators of one's self. That is, unless there is a change or maturation over time, how one is earlier in life becomes a predictor for how one will be in late life. If you are a complainer earlier in life, you are likely to be a complainer in old age; if you take things in stride earlier in life, you are likely to do so later in life. But this is not written in stone, and in fact subtle changes, almost imperceptible changes, can occur over the life course allowing one to adapt to situations one formerly would have found difficult (Hill, 2006).

External continuity refers to the environment in which one exists. It manifests in the environments we create for ourselves. An example of maintaining external continuity is that of many older people's preference for spending the holidays in their own homes (Hill, 2006). Another example is that of many older people retaining their driver's licenses even after they no longer drive as a symbol of their potential to have power over their environment and be independent (Hill, 2006). Both internal continuity and external continuity can be called on in times of stress or crisis or difficulty related to aging (Hill, 2006).

The flip side of continuity is discontinuity, a break in internal or external continuity (Hill, 2006). Discontinuity manifests in unexpected events and, whether positive or negative, interrupts one's sense of a stable self. In itself, discontinuity is not necessarily bad, for it may prompt an individual to grow even more and to develop a broader and more nuanced sense of self.

John Rowe and Robert Kahn's Theory of Successful Aging

John Rowe and Robert Kahn have strongly criticized much of the research dealing with older adults and aging as being negativistic and inaccurate (Belsky, 1999). They believed extreme physical deterioration does not necessarily have to occur in later life and can be moderated or tempered. In fact, they distinguished between normal and impaired aging (Rowe & Kahn, 1987, cited in Whitbourne, 2005). Normal aging (also called primary aging) is the "universal, intrinsic, and progressive" process of aging—that is, the process that occurs in all persons, independent of disease (Whitbourne, 2005, p. 6). Impaired aging (also known as secondary aging) is the process of aging that is the result of disease states and, therefore, is not universal (Whitbourne, 2005). In Rowe and Kahn's theory, successful (or healthy or optimal) aging comprises physical, cognitive, and social components.[8]

Specifically, they posited that successful aging is marked by a lack of disease and a relatively high level of physical functioning (physical component), undiminished cognitive functioning (cognitive component), and active involvement in life (social component) (Aldwin, Spiro, & Park, 2006; Crowther, Parker, Achenbaum, Larimore, & Koenig, 2002). That is, for Rowe and Kahn, successful aging requires minimizing risk and disability, maximizing physical and mental abilities, and engaging in an active life (Crowther et al., 2002). Rowe and Kahn's theory, too, is hierarchical; that is, good physical health is essential to cognitive well-being, which is necessary for the ability to maintain activities of daily living, which is itself needed for one to be socially engaged and productive (Aldwin et al., 2006; Rowe & Kahn, 1997).

Crowther et al. (2002) criticized Rowe and Kahn for not attending to the literature on the positive associations between spirituality and health and for ignoring the reality that spirituality plays a large part in the lives of many older adults, particularly older ethnic and minority adults. They expanded Rowe and Kahn's model to include positive spirituality. According to Crowther et al. (2002), a comprehensive model of aging comprises biological (biomedical), psychological, social, and spiritual dimensions, a view shared by Sulmasy (2002). It is argued that spirituality can foster social interactions (e.g., by promoting attendance at religious services) and is associated with lower levels of disability and disease, though the causal mechanisms for these are poorly understood (Sadler & Biggs, 2006). Assessment of older adults' spirituality in addition to assessment of their biomedical, psychological, and social well-being broadens the definition of holistic care and could be incorporated into health care work with older adults (Sadler & Biggs, 2006).

It should be remembered, too, that one's definition of successful aging may be culture dependent (see Torres, 1999). That is, what is considered successful aging in one culture may not be considered successful aging in another culture. In one cross-cultural study, older adults' conceptualizations of successful aging were found to vary depending on their culture: To older Americans, successful aging meant being independent and self-sufficient; to older Hong Kong Chinese, it meant being successfully dependent on family members who would care for them (Torres, 1999).

Even the focus on *success* in aging may be a cultural artifact and may reflect a uniquely North American application of a general cultural emphasis on success to something as organic and fundamental as aging (see Torres, 1999). People in other cultures might not even conceptualize aging in terms of success or lack thereof. Successful aging is a social construct (Torres, 1999).

Instead of thinking in terms of a simple model of successful aging, Torres (1999) recommended a more subtle theoretical framework underlying one's conceptualization of successful aging that takes into consideration political, economic, and religious systems that impact values related to

1. human nature (i.e., whether humans are inherently good, evil, or somewhere in between),
2. the relationship between humans and the natural world (i.e., whether humans are masters of, mastered by, or coharmonious with nature),
3. social relations (i.e., whether ideal human relations are linear, collateral, or individual),
4. time (i.e., whether one's culture primarily is past, present, or future oriented), and
5. activity (i.e., whether one's culture is primarily that of being, being-in-becoming, or doing).[9]

Summary

Salthouse proposed that as older adults' cognitive processes decline, so do their performance of cognitive tasks, whereas Baltes and associates suggested that older adults are more selective in choosing activities, optimize their success through specific strategies, and compensate for age-related weaknesses. Costa and McCrae believed that personal dispositions are traits, not states, and that people who earlier in life were neurotic, extraverted, open to experience, agreeable, or conscientious would remain that way in later life. Levinson posited a three-stage life span developmental model. Tornstam proposed that, similar to the latter stages of ashrama, late life is marked by gerotranscendence or a turning away from the material and a turning toward the transcendental. Schroots took a nuanced view of later life in which adults transform in ways that are higher or lower ordered. Like Costa and McCrae, Atchley believed in the continuity of self—unless there is something that intervenes. Finally, Rowe and Kahn proposed that later life, rather than being a time of decline and disengagement, can be a time of taking good care of oneself, good health, and social connection.

When thinking about each of these theories from the perspective of counseling, you may consider whether and to what extent the theory resonates with or informs your view of aging and of change in later life. You also can consider how and to what extent the theory impacts your work as a gerontological counselor. For example, you may ask, "To what extent can our older adult clients compensate for decline in a specific ability? Are older adults' personalities states that are changeable or traits that are unchangeable? Should older adult clients be less interested in the material and more interested in pursuit of the transcendent? Can older clients engage in activities that lead to good health and social connectedness?"

Theories of aging, whether ancient, modern, or contemporary and whether implicit or explicit, have a tangible impact on what we think about older adults, what we think about aging, and what we believe is possible in the context of counseling. For this reason, it is important to consider and recognize our theory and to explore how it influences our work as a counselor. If we believe that later life is just a period of decline, then our work with clients will be filled less with hope and more with resignation. If we believe that the life span in later life, like that in earlier life, proceeds in stages, then we may try to help our clients successfully navigate the stage at which they are. If we believe that older adults naturally move toward gerotranscendence, then we may be more open to providing a therapeutic space in which our clients can explore their spirituality.

CHAPTER SUMMARY

In this chapter, we discussed implicit theories of aging and why it is important to be able to articulate one's implicit theory. As an introduction to cultural variation in theories, we looked at two culturally diverse perspectives on aging. Finally, we explored some of the major psychosocial-spiritual theories of aging and later life development, both modern and contemporary. Throughout the chapter we considered how theories and theorizing impact the counseling of older clients. In Chapter 2, we will learn about basic attending skills to use with older adult clients, including nonverbal and verbal skills. These skills will be useful to develop a good client–counselor relationship and to help a client articulate his or her needs and work toward resolution of counseling issues.

CASE STUDY

Rudy is a 67-year-old White male who has come in for counseling 2 years after his retirement. His wife of 30 years died 7 years ago; he has no children. He states that his health is good, that he plays golf three times a week even though his game is not what it used to be, and that he has an active sex life. He describes his golfing companions as acquaintances and states that his best friends all passed away in the past few years. His complaint is that he is not entirely comfortable in retirement, and he is thinking about getting a part-time job, "just to get out of the house." He expresses that he is torn about this, as his whole work life was oriented toward retirement, and he actually thought he would enjoy his "alone time" in retirement. Instead, he at time finds himself bored and unmotivated. He wonders if it is just because he is "getting older and having less energy."

Questions

1. Speculate on Rudy's implicit theory of aging.
2. Discuss Rudy from the perspective of successful aging.
3. Discuss Rudy from the perspective of gerotranscendence. Speculate, if necessary.
4. Choose another theory and discuss Rudy from that perspective.

CHAPTER QUESTIONS

1. What is your implicit theory of aging? (Make it explicit.) Does it follow a cultural script?
2. Informally interview an older adult and try to understand those attributes that compose his or her implicit theory of aging. In which attributes does your interviewee expect an increase in later life? Decrease? No change?
3. In your theory of aging, do you fall more along the activity-continuity or the disengagement-gerotranscendence continuum? Explain.
4. How does Plato's description of wisdom differ from that of Tornstam?
5. Explain the four stages of ashrama and how they impact one's perspective on aging.
6. What would you say was Carl Jung's contribution to our under-standing of aging?
7. Compare Jung's perspective on aging with that of ashrama. How are they similar? How do they differ?
8. Trace your life through each of Erikson's stages up to the present. To what extent have you successfully resolved the crises of each of the stages you have experienced?
9. Describe the task of Erikson's final stage. What virtue is acquired when this task is resolved in a positive way?
10. Defend Cumming and Henry's disengagement theory.

11. Take one of Neugarten's eight personality types and speculate on the qualities of the person who is of that type.
12. Give an example, different from what is in the text, of an older adult's use of selective optimization with compensation. Identify each of the three components.
13. Deeply consider, then compare and contrast gerotranscendence theory with disengagement theory. In what specific ways do they differ?
14. Deeply consider, then compare and contrast gerotranscendence theory with Erikson's stage of ego integrity versus despair. How are they similar? How do they differ?
15. Define Rowe and Kahn's theory of successful aging. Describe two criticisms of the theory.
16. Consider your or your family's culture of origin. What does (or what did) successful aging look like in your cultural tradition? How is it similar to or different from the values of the dominant culture?
17. What is your favorite theory of aging? Why?
18. What is your least favorite theory of aging? Why?

GLOSSARY

Activity theory: posits that older adults, in order to maintain self-esteem, actively must be engaged in new social roles to compensate for those roles lost to old age (e.g., that of the worker) and that constraints placed on them to prevent their engaging in these meaningful activities are harmful.

Ashrama: a Hindu theory of four stages of life through which one passes: student, householder, forest dweller, and ascetic.

Chaos theory: states that random fluctuations in a dynamic system can reach a critical point at which the system self-organizes and creates order where once there was chaos.

Cohort: refers to a group of people who share the same experience. For example, 90-year-olds are not only in their 90s but also in a group who, in North America, experienced World War II, the Great Depression, and so forth.

Continuity theory: states that an older adult's identity is influenced by one's lasting perceptions of oneself, as well as by environmental factors that mediate the firmness of one's view of oneself.

Cross-sectional studies: compare groups of people; for example, people in their 40s might be compared on a number of dimensions with people in their 60s.

Disengagement theory: posits that as adults age, they increasingly withdraw from their social world and turn inward.

Entropy: is the phenomenon of increasing disorder in a system that naturally occurs over time.

Gerotranscendence: is the theory that states that as one ages, one has a lesser attraction to the material and rational and a greater affinity for the transcendent and universal.

Hill metaphor: states that life is the voyage of development up the hill and aging down the hill.

Life review: is a process or technique in which one systematically examines one's life.

Longitudinal studies: follow the same set of people over a period of time.

Medical models: of aging promote the idea of aging as disease or illness, a medical problem to be solved.

Social models: of aging take the perspective of the social environment as a starting point for discussing aging and age-related change.

Success models: of aging state that old age need not be a time of negative and gloomy decline but be a time invested in minimizing disease and illness, maximizing good physical and cognitive health, and maintaining an active social life of connection to others.

FURTHER INFORMATION

1. For a wonderful, comprehensive overview of modern and contemporary theories of aging, I strongly recommend Johannes Schroots's "Theories of Aging: Psychological" in Jim Birren's *Encyclopedia of Gerontology* (Vol. 2) (New York: Academic Press, 1996).

2. I highly recommend reading the classics, such as Plato's *Republic*, for insight into fundamental philosophical issues, including those of aging. An excellent translation is found in G. M. A. Grube and C. D. C. Reeve's *Plato: Republic* (Cambridge, MA: Hackett, 1992). The *Republic* also may be found online free at the Massachusetts Institute of Technology's Internet Classics Archive, http://classics.mit.edu/Plato/republic.html. You also might be interested in reading Cicero's *Treatises on Friendship and Old Age* (Champaign, IL: Project Gutenberg, 2001) available from http://www.gutenberg.org/dirs/etext01/tfroa10.txt.

3. Further discussion of Hindu perspectives on aging can be found in S. Tilak's *Religion and Aging in the Indian Tradition* (Albany: SUNY Press, 1989) and also in S. Vatuk's chapter "Withdrawal

and Disengagement as a Cultural Response to Aging in India" in C. L. Fry's *Aging in Culture and Society: Comparative Viewpoints and Strategies* (New York: Praeger, 1980).

4. Consider reading Erik Erikson's *Childhood and Society* (New York: Norton, 1963/1987) or *The Life Cycle Completed* (New York: Norton, 1982) for a deeper understanding of his eight-stage theory, the best known of all theories of life span development.

NOTES

1. Later in the chapter, you will see that modern and contemporary theories of aging tend to fall along a continuum from activity-continuity to disengagement-gerotranscendence.

2. Life review is discussed in detail in Chapter 6.

3. There are over 300 medical, biological, or evolutionary theories of aging (Medvedev, 1990)! Most of the medical or biological theories posit a particular physical mechanism of aging, with aging seen as an undesirable progression to disease, disability, and ultimately death. Evolutionary theories are intriguing in that they posit that there may be an adaptive function to aging, with some theorists suggesting that the very factors that cause aging later in life may be factors that maximize the likelihood of success early in life.

4. One could argue that the Hindu theory of ashrama is a psychology of aging theory.

5. Notice the similarity of this to the later stages of ashrama.

6. This bears a resemblance to disengagement-gerotranscendence.

7. The life cycle theory, true to its time, was heteronormative and culture bound. Today we might expand the theory to include lesbian, gay, bisexual, and transgender (LGBT) and other cultures whose normative and nonnormative transitional events may differ from those of the dominant culture.

8. The concept of successful aging may have its roots in Ancient Rome and the writings of Cicero, who wrote about the essential features of good aging (see Bowling, 1993, cited in Torres, 1999).

9. These five value orientations are from Kluckhohn and Strodtbeck and are described in Torres (1999).

CHAPTER 2

Attending and Listening Skills in Work With Older Adults

All speech ... is a dead language, until it finds a willing and prepared hearer.

—**Robert Louis Stevenson (1850–1894)**

When people talk, listen completely. Most people never listen.

—**Ernest Hemingway (1899–1961)**

CHAPTER OVERVIEW

In this chapter, you will learn the importance of working with older clients from a place of strength, and so we will begin the chapter with a discussion of wellness and counseling. You will learn about some of the practical issues of working with older adults, including how to address older adults and issues of language and communication. You also will learn basic attending and listening skills that you can use with older adults. These include nonverbal skills related to body language, vocalization, and visual communication, as well as the verbal skills of asking questions, giving directives, using verbal encouraging techniques, using keywords, using restatements, paraphrasing, and summarizing, acknowledging feelings, identifying themes, pointing out discrepancies, and addressing a client's story from multiple perspectives.

WELLNESS AND COUNSELING OLDER ADULTS

As you will see in this book, counseling older adults can be a rich, valuable experience—not only for your clients but also for yourself. Although the common stereotype of later life is one of decline, in reality later life can be a time of great wellness (Myers, 2005). Even though there are challenges in later life, to be sure (including poverty, especially among ethnic minority elders and among women, lesser life spans for men, issues of divorce, and chronic medical conditions that may impact activities of daily living), over two thirds of community-residing elders describe their health as good or very good—roughly the same percentage as adults under age 65—though this is less true of African Americans or Latino and Latina Americans than of European Americans (see Myers, 2005).

There are a number of factors that contribute to wellness (broadly defined) in later life. One meta-analysis[1] found that there was a positive relationship between socioeconomic status, social networks, personal competence, and elders' subjective well-being (Pinquart & Sorensen, 2000, cited in Myers, 2005). In other words, elders with higher socioeconomic status, with stronger social networks, and with higher levels of personal competence were more likely to report feelings of well-being. Other studies have found relationships between social relations and life satisfaction (Bowling et al., 2003, cited in Myers, 2005) and lack of chronic medical conditions and successful aging (Strawbridge, Wallhagen, & Cohen, 2002, cited in Myers, 2005). Although much literature on aging has embraced a medical model focus on deficits, counseling is one discipline that rightfully can work from a position of wellness when addressing the needs of older adults.

In this chapter, we will review some practical issues as well as basic attending and listening skills that will be useful when working with older adults. It is important to keep foremost in your mind the value of working from a client's strengths and building on them when counseling.

PRACTICAL ISSUES IN COUNSELING OLDER ADULTS

Before we study particular attending and listening skills in working with older adults and their families, there are two practical issues that we first shall consider: how to address older adults and how to listen for and communicate with your client around central themes common in late life.

Addressing Older Adults

Here's one big tip. When you are working with older adults, address them as *Mr.*, *Mrs.*, *Miss*, or *Ms.* Addressing older adults by using a title is a way of demonstrating respect, not only for them personally but for their age and wisdom. In some cultures, too, it is especially important to demonstrate respect by using a title when addressing older adults. If older adults want to be addressed in some other way, say, by their first name, they will let you know (e.g., "Please call me Bob").

Themes and Communication

David Solie (2004), in his book *How to Say It® to Seniors*, argued that older adults have a different schema than do younger adults. Specifically, older adults want some control over their lives and want to be remembered. You might be thinking, Who does *not* want some control over their lives, or who does *not* want to be remembered? Agreed. With older adults, however, these two issues have particular salience.

In terms of control, older adults face issues that younger or middle-aged adults typically do not face. These issues include losing mobility when they are no longer able to drive safely, decisions about whether to move into extended or nursing care, and issues related to health and end of life. In terms of remembrance, leaving a legacy for future generations likely has more salience for elders as they move toward the end of their lives than it does for younger people. Solie (2004) believed these are the essential themes in later life: "holding on" (control) and "letting go" (legacy) (p. 20).

He argued that the theme of control is omnipresent in later life because older adults face multiple losses, including loss of physical strength, peers, being sought out for consultation, identity, physical space, and financial independence (Solie, 2004). He argued, too, that experiencing multiple losses can increase the likelihood that older adults may interact with others in a contrary manner. In other words, being oppositional may be a technique that some elders use to exercise control (as in, "At least I have control to say, 'no.' "). How might you respond to an oppositional elder? Perhaps by backing off a bit and stating concerns in a way that allows the elder to demonstrate control (Solie, 2004).

Solie (2004) argued that the desire to leave a legacy also influences the presentation of older adults. Leaving a legacy implies that an older adult has acquired wisdom and wants to pass it on to others. It requires an elder to review his or her life and, in doing so, to gain a greater appreciation of life and its lessons, struggles, and joys. Leaving a legacy implies as well a desire to pass this understanding down to others. Why would it be important to listen to your client's theme of control or legacy? Not only will identifying a theme help you organize the material being presented, it also may give you insights into how a client may act in the future or how a client may interact with you in the here and now.

Counseling skills are about communication. In the following section, we will discuss basic listening and attending skills that can be applied when clients bring up issues of control or legacy. One can use these skills to strengthen communication and the relationship between the counselor and an older client.

ATTENDING AND LISTENING

Imagine yourself talking to a friend, telling a story that is near and dear to your heart. But while you're telling your story, your friend is looking out the window or intermittently says, "Did you say something?" How would you feel? Probably unheard. The same is true in counseling. If your client is telling his or her story, it is important for you to attend, to listen. You can attend and listen by using the discrete skills discussed in this chapter. By attending and listening skills, we mean the particular, concrete skills you use to most fully understand the story and the issues that bring an older client (whether an individual, a couple, or a family) to counseling. These skills are foundational in that they provide counselors with some of the basic building blocks on which to shape a session and, unlike conversational skills, have as their focus the client, are driven by goals, and are used to further the client's welfare (Moursund & Kenny, 2002).

Attending and listening skills comprise both nonverbal activities (such as minimal encouragers) and verbal activities (such as paraphrases, summaries, or questions) (see Ivey, Ivey, & Zalaquett, 2009; Kottler, 2000; MacCluskie, 2010; McHenry & McHenry, 2007; Moursund & Kenny, 2002; Murphy & Dillon, 2008) (see Table 2.1).

TABLE 2.1   Nonverbal and Verbal Skills

Skill Set	Skills
Nonverbal	Body language, nonverbal vocalizations, visual communication
Verbal	Asking questions, using directives, using verbal encouraging, using keywords, using restatements, paraphrasing, summarizing, acknowledging feelings, identifying themes, exploring multiple perspectives

NONVERBAL SKILLS

There are a number of nonverbal behaviors that potentially can encourage clients to talk more. As a counselor, in addition to nodding your head, you might smile, lean forward, offer direct eye contact, or say, "Uh huh." This latter encourager, by the way, is *vocal* without being *verbal*; in other words, it is making a sound but not using a word. These **nonverbal behaviors** have as their objective an increase in client talk time, especially about relevant material.

Nonverbal skills are minimal encouragers that include everything except verbal language; they comprise body language (e.g., leaning forward in your seat or nodding your head), nonverbal vocalizations (e.g., saying, "Hmmm"), and visual communication (e.g., maintaining eye contact). In and of themselves, none of these behaviors necessarily act as an encourager. How do you know which ones will be encouragers? Monitor your client's response. Signs of effective encouragers are that your client is talking more, opening up more, or appearing more comfortable in the session.

Culture is a major factor that influences whether any particular behavior is an encourager. In some cultures, for example, direct eye contact is perceived negatively, possibly as being rude, disrespectful, or aggressive. This is true for some Asian cultures as well as for some First Nations (i.e., American Indian and Alaska Native) cultures. For this reason, it is essential that you become familiar with the culture of your client.

Body Language

Body language comprises the behaviors you do with your body—leaning forward, fidgeting, stroking your hair, smiling, grimacing, and so forth. Each of these behaviors may encourage your client either to talk more or to talk less. Generally, we desire a client to talk more rather than less. Suppose a client says, "You won't believe what happened when my daughter came over." If, in response to that, you *lean forward* ever so slightly, your client is likely to elaborate because by leaning forward you have communicated an interest in hearing the story. Suppose a new client walks into your office, unsure of him- or herself or why he or she is there. You *smile*, and your smile puts the client slightly more at ease. Body language is culture specific. Some cultures allow, for example, more physical contact with others when communicating than do other cultures.

Nonverbal Vocalizations

Nonverbal vocalizations are sounds you make that are not words. For example, your older client says, "My daughter says she loves me, but she rarely comes to visit." In response, you vocalize, "Hmmm" or "Uh huh." Your vocalization, if used genuinely, acts as a minimal encourager in that it can communicate to your client that you are listening and are interested in what he or she has to say.

Nonverbal vocalization also refers to the dimensions of speech rate (slower or faster), pitch (higher or lower), volume (softer or louder), and inflection (statement, question, or underlining) (see MacCluskie, 2010). Each of these dimensions is influenced by culture—including language of origin, region of the country, rural or urban community, and other factors. In absolute terms, in some regions of North America, the average rate of speech is faster than in other areas. The same may be true for regions outside of North America. In relative terms, what you the counselor consider to be faster or slower likely is determined relative to what you consider to be an average rate of speech. Like speech rate, pitch, volume, and inflection may be influenced by culture; environment; context such as gender identity, social influence, or power; family history or dynamics; and other factors.

Visual Communication

Visual communication comprises behaviors engaged in with your eyes, including maintaining direct eye contact, squinting, enlarging or shrinking of pupils, and so forth. Say, for example, while your older client is telling you about a medical problem, you are looking at some papers on your desk. What does that communicate to the client? Possibly that you are not that interested in what he or she has to say. If that is what is communicated, your client may be more likely to talk about something else (just to get your attention) or may feel unheard and pull away, in which case you and your client will lose or not develop the warm, collaborative relationship that is the hallmark of counseling. But, say, when your older client is telling you about a medical problem, you maintain a moderate amount of direct eye contact. What does that communicate? Possibly that you are interested in your client and in his or her welfare.

Like other minimal encouragers, direct eye contact is *culture specific*. In other words, in some cultures, such as that of North America and of Europe, direct eye contact may be interpreted as a behavior that facilitates communication. In other cultures, such as some Asian cultures or some First Nations cultures, direct eye contact may be interpreted as aggressive or as disrespectful.

What is true of *your* level of eye contact with your client conversely is true of your *client's* level of eye contact with you. Namely, your client's level of eye contact is at least in part the result of his or her cultural background (see MacCluskey, 2010). This means that you need to attend to the cultural dimension of your work with older clients when you interpret your client's level of eye contact (or other behaviors) as being either appropriate or inappropriate. In other words, older clients from some cultures may avoid direct eye contact, not because they are disengaged from the counseling process but because, for them, that is the culturally appropriate behavior in which to engage.

VERBAL SKILLS

As with nonverbal skills, verbal skills cover a broad range. Next we will discuss those of asking questions, using directives, using verbal encouraging, using keywords, using restatements, paraphrasing, summarizing statements, acknowledging feelings, identifying themes, pointing out discrepancies, and looking at multiple perspectives.

Asking Questions

Oftentimes, beginning counselors believe that the process of counseling is all about the counselor asking questions and the older client answering those questions. Although using questions when counseling clients can be of value, it is only one of a number of skills that contribute to the counseling process. Also, questions, if asked too frequently by the counselor, can result in a counseling session that looks and feels more like an interrogation—an atmosphere that is likely to interfere with the development of a warm, respectful, and helpful counseling relationship. In fact, counselor educator Jeffrey Kottler (2000) recommended asking questions only if information cannot be acquired any other way.

The technique of asking questions can take one of two forms: either open-ended or closed-ended. Open-ended questions help clients open up and speak more about the issues they bring into counseling. Closed-ended questions oftentimes result in clients speaking less or giving the counselor a specific piece of information.

Open-Ended Questions. **Open-ended questions** are those that encourage clients to tell more of their story, to elaborate, or to give more information about the issues that brought them to counseling. The objective of an open-ended question is to have the client talk more. Consider the question, "What brings you here today?" or "How did it come to be that you became the matriarch?" Each of these questions begs for a story, an elaboration, a giving of more information.

Closed-Ended Questions. **Closed-ended questions** are those that encourage clients to give brief responses or to focus more on a particular portion of their story or on a specific piece of information related to the issue that has brought them into counseling. Consider the questions "Where was he when you found him?" or "Who helps you with your housework?" or "When was the last time you saw a doctor?"

Before we go further, try to indentify which of the following are open-ended questions and which are closed-ended questions:

- "What happened next?"
- "How did you feel?"
- "What would you like to talk about?"
- "Who was there?"
- "When did he first begin wandering?"
- "Where were you when you heard the news?"
- "What did she say?"
- "Are you pleased with the outcome?"
- "Why did she end up in nursing care?"
- "What else?"
- "What would you like to be different?"
- "How did he look?"

"Why" Questions. I recommend, as a general rule of thumb, against asking many "why" questions. "Why" questions may be well intentioned, in that you may want information from your older clients about their motives. But clients may perceive "why" questions as evaluative or critical.

Consider the question "Why did you do that?" How would you respond if a counselor posed this question to you? You might be defensive, thinking, "Well, I did it because at the time it seemed like the right thing to do" or "If you were in my shoes, you'd certainly understand why I did that." In fact, the counselor might just have been interested in understanding how a client came to choose one course of action over another. Kottler (2000) reminded us that we need attend not only to our intention in asking a question but also to the recipient's interpretation of the question and the fact that a question may be interpreted in any of a number of ways.

Using Directives

An *open-ended* **directive** is like an open-ended question except that it is phrased as a command. An example of an open-ended directive is "Tell me more." A *closed-ended* **directive** is like a closed-ended question except that it is phrased as a command. An example of a closed-ended directive is "Tell me what you said to her at that point." Like open-ended and closed-ended questions, in general, you will use open-ended directives to gain a broader, deeper, and more extensive story, and you will use closed-ended directives to elicit a specific piece of information.

Using Verbal Encouraging

Verbal **encouraging** techniques are those that result in clients speaking more. They can be in the form of single words or phrases, the repetition of a client's keyword(s), a restatement, a paraphrase, or a summarization (see Ivey et al., 2009). An example of the use of a single word or short phrase as an encourager is saying, "Yes" or "I see" in response to what your client says. Your client may say, "It's been so hard for me since my husband passed away." As counselor, you respond by saying, "Yes" or "I see." Your client then continues to articulate his or her story.

Using Keywords

A **keyword** is a word that your client uses through his or her verbal interactions with you that gives you an indication of the central issue, theme, or topic. You may have a female client, for example, who says the following:

> It's unfair to me when my mother asks me to do some little thing for her on short notice. She doesn't seem to realize that I have a husband and children that require attention too. I don't mind doing things for her. It's just that I can't be on call for minor things. Like yesterday … she called me at 7:00 in the morning and said that one of the light bulbs in her kitchen burned out and could I come over and change it. I was right in the middle of getting the kids ready for school. I told her that I could be over as soon as the kids left for school, but she acted as if I had just told her to drop dead. I thought to myself, "That's so unfair."

Through careful listening to the client, you identify *unfair* as the keyword and you respond, "Unfair." If you are on target with your keyword, the client will respond with a statement such as, "Yes, it's so unfair. I can't seem to get it through to her that I have all sorts of responsibilities." She then may continue to elaborate on her feelings and thoughts about this part of her life.

Using Restatements

A restatement is a short statement of the essence of what a client has said. In response to a client saying, "I was glad to be back in my house after that stay in the hospital. You know, I've never been fond of hospitals," a restatement might be, "It felt good to be back home." Suppose your client then says, "At Christmastime when I was about 8 years old, I had an extremely high fever, and my parents brought me to the hospital. They thought I was going to die, but I pulled through, and my family was the stronger for it." As a counselor, what might be your restatement?

Paraphrasing

The function of a **paraphrase** is to demonstrate that you understand what your client is saying by "reflecting or giving back the message" (McHenry & McHenry, 2007). A paraphrase is a restatement of a longer portion of what a client has said, using your words rather than the client's exact words. In response to a client saying, "I felt so angry after he slammed the door and left. I'm not kidding, I thought I was going to scream right then and there," a counselor might paraphrase by saying, "You were so mad after he did that, you could've screamed" or "You were so irate when he stormed out that you felt like screaming."
    Imagine your client says the following:

> I got into a little fender bender last week. It wasn't a big deal. The damage to the other car was minor, and so I offered to pay for the repair out of pocket in order to avoid going through the insurance company. Now my son is saying that I should think about giving up my license. That's outrageous. There's no way I'm giving up my license.

What might be an appropriate paraphrase?
    Paraphrasing differs from *parroting* (an undesirable technique) in that parroting is the near-exact repetition of what a client has said, typically substituting second person for first person. In response to a client saying, "I felt so angry after he slammed the door and left, I thought I was going to scream," a counselor who is parroting might say, "You felt

so angry after he slammed the door and left, you thought you were going to scream." Imagine yourself as a client who is on the receiving end of parroting. You likely would feel unheard, that the counselor lacked empathy, and perhaps that the counselor was not even listening to the real message that you were trying to communicate. A paraphrase of this would be, "You were so mad when he left, you felt like screaming." The difference between paraphrasing and parroting may be subtle, but a paraphrase is more likely to be received by the client as a response by an understanding counselor, whereas parroting is more likely to be received by the client as a response lacking in empathy or understanding.

Summarizing

Think of **summarizing** as more extensive paraphrasing, covering more of the client's material (Ivey et al., 2009). Summarizing typically is used to articulate the main points or a large portion of a counseling session. Summarizing can be used either at the beginning of a session, at midsession, or at the end of a session (Ivey et al., 2009).

At the beginning of a session, summarizing is useful for bringing into consciousness what transpired in the previous session or previous set of sessions (see Ivey et al., 2009). Summarizing at the beginning of the session usually begins with a statement like, "Last week you were telling me how you came to meet your wife." One limitation of using summarizing at the beginning of a session is that it is leading. That is, the client might feel that he or she must continue talking about what was addressed in the previous session(s), even if he or she has a more pressing issue.

Midsession, summarizing may help consolidate what has gone before, pull together different threads of a story, and offer guidance for the remainder of the session (Ivey et al., 2009). Summarizing midsession may begin with a statement like, "Let me see if I understand so far. Your best friend had told you about this person whom he thought you might like. You agreed for him to set up a blind date. When you met your wife-to-be, you ..."

Summarizing at the end of a session may be particularly valuable in combining the feelings, contents, and direction of the session into a more coherent whole (Ivey et al., 2009). As a general rule of thumb, it is preferable to have the client rather than the counselor provide a summary at the end of a session. You can elicit this summary by asking your client, "When you look back over today's session, what are the main points that you made?" or "Looking back on our session, what are the things that are most important?" or "What can you take away from today's session?" or "What will you take away from today's session?"

Acknowledging Feelings

Acknowledging feelings requires listening carefully to the client, grasping his or her essential feelings, and naming these feelings back to the client in a manner that demonstrates the counselor's empathy and understanding. You can conceptualize acknowledging feelings as a paraphrase that focuses on the essential or underlying feelings being expressed by your client. Typically, when you acknowledge feelings, you include the phrase "You feel" or "You felt" followed by a feeling word (*scared, angry, sad, happy,* and so forth). You might also follow this with a check-in ("Is that right?" or "Am I right?") (see Ivey et al., 2009). Also, when acknowledging feelings, you may use the same feeling word that the client used or an equivalent feeling word (McHenry & McHenry, 2007).

A client may say the following:

> I don't know what I'm going to do. I'm too young for Medicare, and my medical bills are piling up. I have some savings, but at this rate, I'm afraid that within a year I'll go through everything I have. I feel tense and on edge all the time, just waiting for the other shoe to drop.

As a counselor, you may acknowledge this client's feelings by saying, "You feel tense and edgy" or "With all this going on, you feel anxious. Is that right?" or "It's scary spending down your savings and not knowing if something more is going to happen."

Identifying Themes

Identifying themes is parallel to acknowledging feelings, except that instead of focusing on the essential feelings an older client is having, the counselor focuses on the essential meaning behind the story the older client is telling. A way of thinking of the essential meaning of a client's story is to think about the central, recurrent, and pervasive idea that lies under the stories the client tells. Although a client may be aware of his or her theme or core issue, frequently a client's theme becomes apparent to the counselor before it does to the client (Murphy & Dillon, 2008).

Central themes for older adults may include such issues as control, legacy, love, loss, death, meaning, survival, unfairness, or faith.[2] A client, for example, may come to you as a counselor and describe herself as formerly "vibrant, engaged, a hard worker, and socially active." She may then compare her past self with her current self, which she describes as "crippled, useless, and good for nothing." In response to this client, you might say, "You value being active" or "For you, the importance of life is in being active."

A client may say, "My children are adults now, but I still take care of them. I pay for my son's apartment. I bought my daughter a new car. I just paid to have my youngest one (she's 55) get her teeth capped. I have money, yet here I am being careful about what I spend on myself." What would you hypothesize the underlying theme to be? What would you say to the client to reflect that underlying theme?

Pointing Out Discrepancies

This is a therapeutic technique in which the counselor, after working with a client, identifies discrepancies (or conflicts) in the client. Discrepancies can take one or more of many forms (see Ivey et al., 2009), including those that occur within the client and those that occur between the client and another person, group of people, or situation. **Intrapersonal discrepancies** are those that occur within the client. **Interpersonal discrepancies** are those that occur between the client and an external entity.

Intrapersonal discrepancies include mismatches between what a client says or mismatches between what a client says and does, says and feels, or feels and does. A client may laugh while telling a very tragic story (a discrepancy between what a client says and does). A client may look depressed while saying that she is feeling fine (a discrepancy between what a client says and feels). A client may love his spouse yet behave in ways that sabotage the relationship (a discrepancy between what a client feels and does).

Interpersonal discrepancies include conflicts, discord, or differences between a client and another person or group of people, a situation, or the counselor. A client may say, "My husband and I argue a lot more than we used to. I don't know if it's because we're not intimate anymore or maybe we're not intimate because we're so irritable with each other" (conflict between client and another person). A client may say, "There's no way I am going into assisted living; I am staying in my house until I die" (conflict between client and a situation). An older client may say to a much younger counselor, "You look like my granddaughter. What do you know about life? How could *you* possibly help *me*?" (conflict between client and counselor).

As a counselor, if you choose to do so, how do you address these discrepancies? Typically by making a statement that points out the inconsistency. You might say, "On the one hand you're telling me how painful your arthritis is, whereas on the other hand you're laughing about it. Help me understand." Or you might say, "You said it didn't bother you that I was late for our session today, but you seem especially quiet, and I'm wondering if there's a connection."

Exploring Counseling From Multiple Perspectives

Working with a client from **multiple perspectives** means that a client and counselor explore together the intrapersonal and interpersonal dimensions of the issue being discussed (see Ivey et al., 2009). Intrapersonal perspectives refer to the exploration of thoughts, feelings, and behaviors within the individual client, that is, phenomena internal to the client. These include exploration of the self, congruence between thoughts, and congruence between thoughts, feelings, and behaviors. Interpersonal perspectives refer to exploring the relationships between people, specifically between your client and his or her family, your client and others, your client and a situation, and your client and yourself.

Ivey et al. (2009) in their excellent discussion called this exploration from multiple perspectives "focusing the interview," a technique that allows a client to offer retellings of the story from different perspectives and assists a client in forming new, more adaptive narratives. They identified seven potential perspectives: individual, problem, other, family, mutual, interviewer, and cultural/environmental/contextual (Ivey et al., 2009) (see Table 2.2).

From an *individual perspective*, you concentrate on the client and his or her feelings, thoughts, or behaviors. Addressing counseling from an individual perspective often begins with the counselor saying "You" followed by an expression of the client's feelings, thoughts, or behaviors. With this perspective, the counselor will make such statements as "You feel proud of your son," or "It sounds like you thought you didn't belong there," or "You stopped taking your medication because of the side effects."

A *problem perspective* highlights the central theme or issue. With this perspective, you might assert, "It sounds like the issue is that once again your basic medical needs are not being met."

An *other perspec*tive addresses the people in your client's environment that are significant to his or her story, issue, or challenge. You might say, "For years, your best friend ignored your requests to help you out financially, and now her children want to be included in your will" or "As your husband's dementia worsens, friends are avoiding contact."

A *family perspective* delves into the client's family, broadly defined and including family history. You might ask, "Do you see a connection between your father's relationship with you and *your* relationship with your children?" or "Tell me how family fits into the big picture."

TABLE 2.2   Ivey, Ivey, and Zalaquett's Counseling Perspectives

Perspective	Example Statement
Individual	You felt sad and also relieved when you thought about moving into an assisted living facility.
Problem	No longer being able to drive, you feel like you've lost your freedom.
Other	You got angry when the podiatrist ignored your complaints.
Family	What do you think your sister's motive was when she asked to move in with you?
Mutual	Let's see if we can connect you with the regional Area Agency on Aging.
Interviewer	My father also suffered from Alzheimer's disease.
Cultural/environmental/ contextual	It sounds like your experience during the Korean War really had an impact on how you have lived your life.

Note: Adapted from Ivey, A. E., Ivey, M. B., & Zalaquett, C. P., *Intentional Interviewing and Counseling: Facilitating Client Development in a Multicultural Society* (7th ed.), Brooks/Cole, Pacific Grove, CA, 2009.

A *mutual perspective* looks at the relationship between the counselor and the client in the here and now. You might say, "Let's look at this problem and see if we can figure out a solution that works for you" or "How does it feel working with a counselor who's younger than you?"

An *interviewer (or counselor) perspective* in essence is information- or advice-giving based on the counselor's personal experiences. You may make such a statement as "From my perspective, what's going on is ..." or "Based upon my experience ...."

A *cultural/environmental/contextual perspective* identifies contextual factors that impact a client's story, such as a client's cultural background or the particulars of his or her environment (Ivey et al., 2009). In addressing this perspective, your twofold objective is to get a deeper understanding yourself and allow your older client to acquire a deeper understanding of how culture, environment, and context impact his or her issue, presentation, and response. Culture, environment, and context should be defined broadly, including (but not limited to) age, cohort, racial identity, ethnic identity, religion or spiritual tradition and beliefs, immigration status, national origin, gender identity, sexual orientation identity, marital status, disability, region of country, urban/suburban/ rural community, and socioeconomic status. From this perspective, you may state, "You mentioned that your church helped get you through the tough time after your wife's death. Can you tell me more about that?"

or "What do you mean when you said that growing up during the Great Depression made you who you are today?"

CHAPTER SUMMARY

In this chapter, we addressed wellness and its place in counseling older adults. We also focused on some practical issues related to addressing older adults, as well as identified two common themes in later life. Finally, we discussed basic attending and listening skills that are designed to facilitate counseling sessions. Nonverbal skills include those of body language, nonverbal vocalizations, and visual communication. Verbal skills include asking questions, using directives, using verbal encouraging, using keywords, using restatements, paraphrasing, summarizing, acknowledging feelings, identifying themes, pointing out discrepancies, and exploring counseling from multiple perspectives.

In Chapter 3, we will explore how to utilize these skills by considering the course of counseling—including the initial, middle, and termination sessions—as well as consider a procedure for helping an older client identify his or her central issue and then begin to work through that issue by building on his or her strengths.

CASE STUDY

Jeannette and her husband, Allan, were financially well-off and had a number of friends with whom they were not particularly close. They tended to depend on one another for emotional support. Allan died 3 years ago, shortly after the two of them moved into a high-end assisted living residence, and Jeannette, now 80 years old, was encouraged by her children to enter counseling. Jeannette has been living by herself since Allan's death, receiving support services for health, personal care, cooking, and house cleaning. Her children have noticed that she has become increasingly depressed and irritable. When the counselor asks her why she came into counseling, she replies, "I don't know. My children think I'm depressed. But who wouldn't be depressed? I've lost my husband, and I live alone in this building with all of these old people. I've lost my independence. I need this walker all of the time. I can't stand in front of the stove to cook. I can't even take a bath by myself anymore."

She continues, "My brother just died; he was the last of my family. As a child during the depression, we didn't have a lot of money, but at least we had each other. Billie Holiday used to sing a song about money and how when it disappears, so does everybody around you. Me, I have money, and still nobody comes to visit—not my children, not my grand-children, nobody. If you think you can fix things, go ahead and try."

Questions

1. As a counselor, what is a keyword that you might use to encourage this client to continue her story?
2. What restatement might you make?
3. What paraphrase might you make? What might she say in return? What might you say?
4. Are there any discrepancies? Are they internal or external? At what point would you, if at all, point out a discrepancy to Jeannette? How do you predict she might respond? On the basis of your prediction, do you think pointing out a discrepancy would be therapeutic?
5. What do you suspect to be the underlying feeling in your client?
6. What is the essence of your client's story? That is, what is the central theme of your client's story?
7. What would you say to your client from an individual perspective? An other perspective? A family perspective?
8. What would you say to your client from a cultural/environmental/contextual perspective?
9. What is the song reference that Jeannette makes? If you do not know about the song and the singer, find out about them and speculate why the client made this reference and what the singer and the song might mean to her.

CHAPTER QUESTIONS

1. What is your definition of wellness?
2. Describe two central issues that are salient for older adults. How do these issues differ from those faced by younger adults?
3. What is the relationship between culture and the use of nonverbal and verbal skills when counseling clients?
4. What are some nonverbal encouragers? What is the effect of using an encourager when interacting with someone else?
5. What are the differences between stating a keyword, a restatement, a paraphrase, and summary comments? Which of these have you used? What were their effects on the interaction?
6. What is the difference between an open-ended question and a closed-ended question? Give an example of each.

7. What is the rationale behind not using too many "why" questions when interviewing a client?
8. What might be the therapeutic value of a counselor pointing out client discrepancies?
9. What is meant by counseling that is attentive to multiple perspectives?
10. Name each of the "multiple" perspectives and give an example.
11. Which of the listening and attending skills have you used in your day-to-day life when you are interacting with others? Which have you used when working with clients?

GLOSSARY

Closed-ended questions: are questions that are designed to produce a specific piece of information.

Directives: are instructions given by the counselor to the client.

Discrepancies: are interpersonal or intrapersonal conflicts (e.g., between what a client says and how a client feels).

Encouraging: is a technique, whether verbal or nonverbal, that results in clients continuing to tell more of their story, to elaborate, and to talk about their issues.

Interpersonal: refers to relationships that occur between a person and another person or other people.

Intrapersonal: refers to processes that occur within the individual.

Keywords: are words used by a client regularly over a session or across sessions that represent a central or key issue for that client.

Multiple perspectives: refer to the importance of addressing interpersonal and intrapersonal factors that influence the client.

Nonverbal behaviors: are those behaviors that do not include verbal language such as body language or nonverbal vocalizations.

Open-ended questions: are questions that allow a client to elaborate on his or her story.

Paraphrasing: is the restating of the ideas expressed by a client. Paraphrasing is to be distinguished from parroting, which is the exact repetition of a client's statements.

Summarizing: can be conceptualized as an extended paraphrase, in which a larger block of material is restated.

FURTHER INFORMATION

1. To learn more about listening skills, I encourage you to read Allen Ivey, Mary Ivey, and Carlos Zalaquett's exceptional text *Intentional Interviewing and Counseling* (Belmont, CA: Brooks/Cole, 2009).
2. To learn more about the counseling process overall, take a look at Jeffrey Kottler's *Nuts and Bolts of Helping* (Needham Heights, MA: Allyn & Bacon, 2000) or Moursund and Kenny's *The Process of Counseling and Therapy* (4th ed.) (Upper Saddle River, NJ: Prentice Hall, 2002).
3. For a discussion of cultural diversity, multicultural issues, and multicultural competence in counseling, see Lee, Blando, Mizelle, and Orozco's *Introduction to Multicultural Counseling for Helping Professionals* (2nd ed.) (New York: Routledge, 2007).

NOTES

1. A meta-analysis looks at results from across a large number of studies to determine if there are overarching findings or themes.
2. This is not an inclusive list.

CHAPTER 3

Stages of Counseling Older Adults

A journey of a thousand miles begins with a single step.

—Chinese proverb

No problem can stand the assault of sustained thinking.

—Voltaire (1694–1778)

CHAPTER OVERVIEW

In this chapter, you will learn about the three stages of counseling: the beginning, middle, and end stages. You will learn a set of advanced counseling skills to complement the attending and listening skills you learned about in Chapter 2: pros and cons, feedback, interpretation, self-disclosure, and advice-giving. You also will learn a five-step model to organize your counseling in a way that will allow you to work efficiently with older adults and their families: build the therapeutic alliance, explore, determine direction, work–feedback–rework, and terminate.

THE THREE STAGES OF COUNSELING

Counseling, like life itself, proceeds in stages. In counseling's most basic form, we can conceptualize any endeavor as having a beginning, a middle, and an end. One of the differences between effective and ineffective counseling is one's understanding of the stages of counseling and utilization of this knowledge.

TABLE 3.1   Hermann von Helmholtz's Three Stages of
Problem Solving

Stage	Characteristics of Stage
1. Saturation	Awareness of a seemingly unsolvable problem
2. Incubation	Unconscious *working on* the problem
3. Illumination	Solving the problem; enlightenment

Note: Edwards, B., *Drawing on the Artist Within: How to Release
Your Hidden Creativity*, HarperCollins, London, 1986.

We are born, we live our lives (no matter how short or long), and we
die. This idea that everything unfolds in stages is not unique to the Western
world or unique to counseling. This idea is found in Eastern philosophical
traditions, in Abrahamic traditions, in indigenous philosophies, and in the
sciences—in psychology and biology, for example, and even in physics.

There are many, many examples of stage theories or stage perspectives, enough in fact to fill a library. For one example, Hermann von
Helmholtz, a German physician, physiologist, mathematical physicist,
and philosopher of science (Patton, 2008), believed the act of scientific
discovery occurred in three stages, which he called saturation, incubation, and illumination (Edwards, 1986). Saturation refers to being filled
with a problem that seems unsolvable, incubation refers to working
on the problem unaware, and illumination refers to becoming *enlight-
ened*—becoming aware of the solution to the problem (see Academy of
Achievement, 2008) (see Table 3.1).

As another example, in Tibetan Buddhist tradition, the idea of stages
is applied to the act of meditation. In Tibetan Buddhism a common
activity—meditation—can be conceptualized as having a beginning, a
middle, and an end (Rinpoche, 1994) (see Table 3.2). Effective meditation—in this tradition, meditation that brings enduring wisdom rather
than temporary comfort—is that which is "good in the beginning, good
in the middle, and good at the end" (Rinpoche, 1994). "Good in the
beginning" is the stage marked by *motivation* and inspiration (Rinpoche,
1994). It is the stage that the 14th-century Tibetan teacher Longchenpa
called the *heart* of practice (Rinpoche, 1994). "Good in the middle" is
the stage marked by *attitude shift*, realization, a new and clearer perspective, and a change in one's metaphoric *posture* (Rinpoche, 1994).
Longchenpa called this the *eye* of practice (Rinpoche, 1994). "Good at
the end" is the stage marked by *dedication* to the enlightenment and
well-being of all beings (Rinpoche, 1994). It is the stage Longchenpa
called the *life force* of practice (Rinpoche, 1994).

In counseling, not only do individual sessions have a beginning, a
middle, and an end, so too does the course of counseling (see Table 3.3)

TABLE 3.2   Tibetan Buddhist Three Stages of Meditation

Stage	Characteristics of Stage	Longchenpa's Conceptualization of the Practice
1. Good in the beginning	*Motivation* and inspiration to practice	Heart
2. Good in the middle	*Attitude shift*, realization, clearer perspective, changed posture	Eye
3. Good at the end	*Dedication* to enlightenment	Life force

Note: Rinpoche, S., *The Tibetan Book of Living and Dying*, HarperOne, New York, 1994.

TABLE 3.3   Three Stages of Counseling

Stage	Characteristics of Stage	Aspect of Client Experience Addressed in Stage[a]
1. Beginning	*Identification or awareness* that there is a problem; *motivation* to change	Emotional
2. Middle	*Working through* challenge, issue, or difficulty; *incubation*; marked by attitude shift, *insight*, clearer perspective to create new narrative and/or new thoughts, feelings, or behaviors	Cognitive
3. End	*Dedication* to new narrative or to *incorporating* new thoughts, feelings, and/or behaviors into one's life; *problem resolved*	Behavioral

[a] Emotional, cognitive, and behavioral aspects are present in *every* stage of counseling, but oftentimes one or another of these aspects may be dominant in a particular stage.

(see also Moursund & Kenny, 2002). In this chapter, we will focus on the stages of the course of counseling and will explore the forms and content of each of these stages.

Beginning Stage

The beginning or first stage of counseling is, naturally, that which occurs initially. In addition to discussing the beginning stage generally, we also will discuss the particular considerations of the first session.

The beginning stage focuses on developing a therapeutic alliance. By *therapeutic,* we mean that the relationship between the counselor and the client is one that focuses on *healing* and on collaboration intended to bring about a greater goodness of thoughts, feelings, behaviors, and relationships beyond that found only within the bounds of counseling. By *alliance* we mean a bonding or association. This therapeutic alliance is identified by the development of a good, solid, working relationship. This first of three stages typically (but not always) is shorter in length than the middle stage and oftentimes is roughly the same length as, or a bit longer than, the end stage.

First Session

The first session is when one first meets with the client. It is important to attend to several matters regarding this first session: universal design for access to counseling, comfort of client, discussion of parameters of counseling, and learning what to say to your client.

Universal Design for Access. The principle of universal design[1] (Center for Applied Special Technology [CAST], 2009b) for access means that one organizes one's practice so that it is as equally accessible to those with disability as it is to those who are abled. More specifically, universal design means that one (a) represents information in a variety of ways so that clients receive the information they need, (b) allows clients a variety of ways to express themselves (e.g., verbally or in writing), and (c) uses a variety of ways to engage clients in the counseling endeavor so that the client's motivation remains strong (CAST, 2009a).

Disability comes in many forms in later life—eyesight may become weaker, hearing may worsen, walking or climbing stairs may become more difficult, or there may be cognitive or emotional impairment. In addition, older adults with disabilities may have acquired those disabilities earlier in their lives or may have experienced congenital disabilities.

As a counselor, you should ensure that your office space and procedures are accessible. This could take the form of ensuring that your office is barrier free, for example, by verifying that there are ramps and/ or elevators for those who have mobility impairments and cannot use stairs. Universal design could take the form of ensuring that office numbers are written in braille. It could take the form of providing counseling practice materials—for example, consent to treatment forms, confidentiality forms, Health Insurance Portability and Accountability Act forms—in plain language and in formats other than standard print (e.g., large print or oral). It could take the form of ensuring that your office is quiet and free of distraction (an important consideration when working with persons with hearing impairments).

Comfort of Client. Murphy and Dillon (2008) offered what is probably the best advice when it comes to counseling offices: "Offices should be private, soundproof, and as free of interruptions as possible" (p. 60). Privacy and ability to communicate comfortably and without being disrupted certainly contribute to the development of a good working relationship with the client.

There are other factors, too, that can facilitate the counseling process. For example, the furniture and its arrangement can have an impact on the quality of the counseling experience (Murphy & Dillon, 2008). Arrange furniture so that there is an unobstructed space between the counselor and the client. The last thing you should do is conduct counseling from behind a desk. Likewise, furniture should contribute to a sense of equality between the counselor and the client. After all, you are engaged in a collaborative endeavor. One way that this can be demonstrated is by ensuring that your seating and your client's seating are at the same height. You do not want to be sitting, for example, in a chair that is higher than that of your client; this subtle arrangement could communicate to your client that you consider yourself more important or "the expert."[2] Even if your work is only with individuals, you should have available to you enough seating to accommodate other family members if and when they accompany your client and intend to participate in his or her session (Murphy & Dillon, 2008). This can be accomplished by having additional seating in your office or by having stored furniture that can be retrieved and put in your office.[3]

Office décor and accessories should be sensitive to your clients' cultural backgrounds (Murphy & Dillon, 2008). If, for example, you work with clients who are from cultures that are modest about bodies, you probably would not want to display in your office paintings or sculptures of nudes. Working with older adults, you will want some publications in your waiting room of interest to older adults: If they are LGBT, have some LGBT periodicals; if they are non-English speaking (and reside in an English-speaking culture), have some periodicals in their language. Know your clients, and adapt your office décor and accessories so that you demonstrate sensitivity to and respect for your clients' cultural background.

Parameters of Counseling. When you first meet with your clients, you will want to describe what they should expect in counseling—the length and frequency of sessions, what likely will transpire in sessions, confidentiality, and so forth—and to clarify the parameters of counseling.

You might say, "I would like to tell you a little about how this works. I meet with clients typically for 50 minutes and usually once per week. During the sessions, you and I will talk about what is going on with you, identify your goal, and then work toward achieving that goal. The goal we work on will be something with which I can help you—for example, it may be about how you are feeling, about a relationship, about learning a new way of behaving, about getting connected to social services, or about most anything else you want to talk about. However, there are some issues that I am not qualified to help you with. For example, I am not a physician, so I cannot diagnose or treat medical problems. Also, I am not a financial consultant, so I cannot give you advice about financial matters."

It also is during this explanation of the parameters of counseling that you will introduce and discuss confidentiality and limits to confidentiality. Confidentiality generally means that you—the counselor—will not reveal to others the content of counseling (or even the fact that the client is seeing you) without the express permission of the client, within some limits. Discussing confidentiality and the limits to it allows the client to make an informed decision about what information he or she chooses to share with you. Common limits to confidentiality are danger to self, danger to others, elder abuse, child abuse, partner abuse, subpoena by a court of law, and so forth; the specifics will vary from community to community.

What to Say. How do you begin a session? How do you end it? Typically a first session will begin by showing the client to his or her seat and acknowledging him or her by name. Make sure to inquire how the client would like to be addressed, and if there is any doubt, ask the client to correct your pronunciation of his or her name.

This typically is followed by some small talk (e.g., "Did you have any difficulty finding the office?" or "How was the traffic getting here?"). The purpose of small talk is to help put the client at ease and to create a bridge or transition to counseling. You will discuss the parameters of counseling and will clarify anything about which the client has questions.

You will then likely offer a nondirective opening line (Murphy & Dillon, 2008), such as, "Tell me what brings you in today," "Where would you like to start?" or "Tell me what's going on." You the counselor should use your own words when opening the session. Talk to the client the way you normally talk, using the language you use, to the extent that it serves the client.

A first session may end with the counselor acknowledging that the session is coming to a close, possibly a brief summary of the session, and arrangement for the next session. For example, the counselor may say, "Our session is almost over. Today you talked about your memory problems in spite of the absence of a diagnosis of dementia and your continuing anxiety that you may have Alzheimer's disease. I discussed some steps to take: speaking again with your physician, maybe getting tested by a neuropsychologist, and maybe working on reducing that anxiety to a more manageable level. We should talk again. How about next week at the same day and time?"

Subsequent Sessions

Subsequent sessions in this beginning stage of counseling focus on you getting to know the client and the client getting to know you as a counselor. In these sessions, you will work with clients on elaborating their stories, helping them identify their needs, and getting them to commit to counseling if that is called for. You will make either a formal or an informal assessment of your client and his or her situation, and you will develop an initial analysis, formulation, or diagnosis.

Your initial assessment (which may comprise information gleaned from more than one session) likely will include most or all of the following:

- identification of the precipitating event that brought the client into counseling,
- awareness of multicultural factors that are present,
- information gathering about organic or medical conditions that may be present,
- consistency or lack thereof between what the client tells you and what others tell you about the client,
- identification of your client's personality style,
- consideration of whether the client's problem is developmental,
- your client's subjective level of distress,
- your client's degree of impairment in daily functioning,[4]
- your client's history (family, legal, educational, vocational, medical, and so forth), and
- assessment of potential danger to self or others (see MacCluskie, 2010).

In addition to this more traditional perspective on assessment, you may wish to assess your client from a developmental, wellness perspective. From this perspective you would assess your client's overall wellness and satisfaction in five domains: the essential self, the coping self, the social self, the creative self, and the physical self (Ivey, Ivey, Myers, & Sweeney, 2005). The essential self concerns itself with spirituality, gender and culture identity, and self-care. The coping self focuses on the presence of realistic beliefs, management of stress, sense of self-worth, and leisure activities. The social self comprises the experiences of friendship and love. The creative self has to do with thoughts, emotions, control, humor, and work. The physical self is concerned with nutrition and exercise. What questions might you ask that would help you understand your client's spirituality, leisure activities, friendships, emotions, and physical health? You can use insights gained from this assessment to help identify a focus for counseling.

Middle Stage

The middle stage of counseling is where the client does much of the work him- or herself—acquiring new information, identifying goals, gaining insights, trying out new behaviors, and so forth. The middle stage focuses on the client's challenge, issue, or need and its resolution (however that may be conceptualized). In working through, your client may experience a shift in attitude, a realization, or a clearer perspective that impacts his or her thoughts, feelings, and/or behaviors. It is in this middle stage that the great bulk of the work of counseling—within the counseling relationship—is completed. This middle stage of counseling most often is the longest stage.

End Stage

The end stage of counseling typically comprises two activities. The first is the client consolidating the new adaptive skills learned, the insight gained, or the new feelings acquired and using them in his or her day-to-day life outside of counseling. The second is termination of the counseling endeavor. I say endeavor rather than relationship because once someone becomes your client he or she is always potentially your returning client. Furthermore, even if you never see or hear from the client again, you still have a relationship, even if it is historical, with him or her.

This end stage focuses on solidifying a new narrative, consolidating new ways of being (whether these relate to thoughts, feelings, and/ or behaviors), bringing these new stories and ways of being into one's life outside of counseling, and of course terminating the counseling endeavor. This end stage oftentimes is relatively briefer compared to the middle stage or even the beginning stage. When we discuss the five-step model for counseling, we will address at greater length both consolidation and termination.

ADVANCED COUNSELING SKILLS

In Chapter 2, we discussed some basic and universally used counseling skills. These skills included those related to encouraging clients to tell more of their story, reflecting clients' thoughts or feelings, asking questions, and using slightly more directive interventions. To encourage clients to tell more of their story, we addressed the use of nonverbal and verbal encouragers in counseling. To reflect clients' thoughts or feelings, we looked at using keywords, using restatements, paraphrasing, and summarizing, as well as acknowledging feelings and identifying themes. In terms of asking questions, we addressed open- and closed-ended questions as well as their parallel directives. We also explored the use of pointing out discrepancies.

In this chapter, we will discuss some additional skills—more advanced skills—that may be used with clients. We will divide this group of skills into lower risk and higher risk interventions. Risk, in this case, refers to the potential of doing damage to the therapeutic alliance versus potential benefits gained by using the intervention. Lower risk interventions include exploring pros and cons and giving feedback. Higher risk interventions include interpretation, self-disclosure, and advice-giving.

Pros and Cons

Pros and cons is a commonsense technique perfected by cognitive-behavioral counselors, but it is useful to most any client in most any situation. The objective of this technique is to help a client draw out the pros and cons of potential courses of action to come to a decision that is in his or her best interest. One can do this vocally (e.g., "Tell me, what are some of the advantages of ... ?") or by writing on paper (e.g., "In this column let's list the pros and in this column the cons of ..."). Think about an older client who, after a few years of retirement, is considering going back to work. There will be benefits and trade-offs to being in the workplace versus remaining retired. For this person, looking at the pros and cons might help him or her make a decision that feels most comfortable and best meets his or her needs and desires. As a counselor, you might say, "Let's look at this. You're thinking about going back to work. What are some of the pros of going back to work?" Your client might respond by enumerating the benefits, such as supplementing one's income, having social interaction with coworkers or the public, getting out of the house, and so forth. As your client is identifying the advantages, you might—with your client's permission—list these in a column labeled "Pros" on the left side of a sheet of paper. You could do the same with disadvantages, by saying, "What are some of the cons of going back to work?" These could be written on the right side of that sheet of paper under a column labeled "Cons." Remaining retired could be explored using the same pros and cons structure. Once this occurs, you and the client could explore together the pros and cons of each potential course of action (see Figure 3.1).

Reenter Workforce			Remain Retired	
Pros	**Cons**		**Pros**	**Cons**
1. Increased income	1. Less free time to devote to hobbies		1. Wake up late	1. Lonely
2. Socialize with coworkers and with public	2. Might need to wake up and get ready early in the day		2. Lots of free time	2. Less money to spend on "splurge" items
3. …	3. …		3. …	3. …

FIGURE 3.1   Pros and cons examples.

Feedback

Giving clients **feedback (whether verbal or nonverbal) about their behaviors is a technique that conveys to clients some information about how others see them** (see McHenry & McHenry, 2007). Giving feedback means telling the client how you—the counselor—experience him or her. For example, you might say,

- "You face lights up whenever you talk about your marriage";
- "You don't seem to be very engaged today";
- "Whenever the conversation comes around to love and sex, you tend to change the topic"; or
- "I noticed that you don't appear to be very comfortable talking about your daughter."

Interpretation

Interpretation is a therapeutic intervention that has its roots in Freudian psychology. In the psychoanalytic tradition, the therapist decodes or deciphers the client's underlying issue, motivation, or historical family dynamic that resulted in the client's pathological presentation. In contemporary counseling, interpretation—when used judiciously—can be an effective intervention to help a client come to an understanding or insight into the basis of his or her core issues. McHenry and McHenry (2007) believed that interpretation can assist clients in creating new stories by shedding light on their experiences.

To interpret, the counselor looks for themes—behavioral, cognitive, or emotional—with which the client presents; looks for clues regarding the essential issue, motivation, or dynamics behind the theme; and expresses that to the client. Some examples of interpretation are as follows:

- "Could it be that your anger toward your children reflects the anger your mother had toward you?"
- "Is your anxiety over moving into assisted living related to what you have told me is your need to feel in control of your life?"
- "Given the interpersonal challenges you and your partner face, do you think that maybe you are avoiding intimacy with your partner by deciding to go back to work and develop an 'encore' career?"

Self-Disclosure

Self-disclosure means telling the client something about yourself, your thoughts, your feelings, or your behaviors. Why would you self-disclose? You might self-disclose in order to help develop a therapeutic alliance, to illustrate the common humanity of your client and his or her situation, or to encourage a client to develop insight and greater wisdom (see McHenry & McHenry, 2007).

Though this intervention may be useful at times, it should be used carefully and infrequently. It is important for you to remember that self-disclosure is not really about you (after all, counseling is not about you), nor should it be. It is about helping your client. Some examples of self-disclosure are "I went to Catholic school, too" or "My father died recently" or "I also have a chronic medical condition."

Advice-Giving

Many beginning counselors believe that they have an obligation to tell clients how to solve their problems. Oftentimes this belief is manifest through **advice-giving** (e.g., "You should call your daughter and talk about this issue today as soon as you get home" or "You should find a new doctor"). As tempting as it may be to give advice to your client, resist the urge.

Advice-giving has two major drawbacks. Think about this: You give advice to your client, your client takes your advice, but your advice fails. Who is perceived as being responsible for the failure? The client? No.

The counselor? Yes. If you—the counselor—are responsible for the failure, when the failure occurs you will lose credibility and maybe irreparably damage the counseling relationship.

Consider this: You give advice to your client, your client takes your advice, and your advice succeeds. Who is perceived as being responsible for the success? The counselor? Yes. After all, it was you—the counselor—who had the advice. The client? No, or maybe only partially; after all, the client was only following the counselor's advice. The counselor's advice may have resolved the immediate problem, but it likely did not result in a client experience of agency or responsibility. As such, when similar problems occur in the future, the client again may look for someone outside of him- or herself for the answer to his or her problems.

In contrast, when a client generates his or her own response to a challenge, carries out that response, and is successful, then he or she rightfully can take ownership of the success and is more likely to see him- or herself as an agent of change. When a client generates his or her own response to a challenge and carries out that response and it fails, then he or she rightfully can acknowledge the importance of trying, receiving feedback, and altering his or her response based on that feedback.

Advice-giving is not information-giving. If a client asks for some concrete information (e.g., "What organizations provide services to families with a member with Alzheimer's disease?"), give that client the answer if you know it. This is not giving advice; it is giving information.

All said, though, there may be times when giving advice is called for. One example is when it is clear that a client plans to engage in a behavior that is unhealthy. An example is "Your doctor told you to stop smoking immediately or you risk having another heart attack. You should listen to your doctor."

A FIVE-STEP MODEL FOR ORGANIZING COUNSELING

A number of counselor educators (Ivey, Ivey, & Zalaquett, 2009; Kottler, 2000; MacCluskie, 2010; Welfel & Patterson, 2005) have explicated multiple-step structures to guide a counselor. These structures can be used when conducting counseling and also in conceptualizing the work that occurs throughout the course of a counseling endeavor.

Both MacCluskie (2010) and Welfel and Patterson (2005) conceptualized counseling in terms of a three-step model, whereas Kottler (2000) and Ivey et al. (2009) each described five-step processes (see Table 3.4). Although these models have in common the three phases we have discussed—beginning, middle, and end—they differ in the number of steps associated with each phase. Depending on the author, the beginning

TABLE 3.4   Stages and Models of Counseling

Author and Model			
MacCluskie (2010)	Welfel and Pattterson (2005)	Kottler (2000)	Ivey, Ivey, and Zalaquett (2009)
Beginning Stage			
1. Intake and assessment	1. Initial disclosure	1. Pretreatment	1. Initiation of the session
Middle Stage			
2. Working	2. In-depth exploration	2. Exploration	2. Gathering data
		3. Insight	3. Mutual goal-setting
		4. Action	4. Working
End Stage			
3. Termination	3. Commitment to action	5. Evaluation	5. Termination

stage can be conceptualized as containing one or more of the following activities: intake and assessment (MacCluskie, 2010), initial disclosure (Welfel & Patterson, 2005), pretreatment (Kottler, 2000), and initiation of the session (Ivey et al., 2009). The middle phase may be composed of working (MacCluskie, 2010); in-depth exploration (Welfel & Patterson, 2005); exploration, insight, and action (Kottler, 2000); and gathering data, mutual goal-setting, and working (Ivey et al., 2009). The end stage comprises commitment to action (Welfel & Patterson, 2005), evaluation (Kottler, 2000), and termination (Ivey et al., 2009; MacCluskie, 2010).

Looking at the commonalities across models, we can constitute the following five-step model:

1. Build the therapeutic alliance
2. Explore
3. Determine direction
4. Work–feedback–rework
5. Terminate

Step 1. Build the Therapeutic Alliance

Your initial time with your client is one of forging a strong working relationship, a strong therapeutic alliance. A therapeutic alliance is a fancy term for having a strong, collaborative working relationship—a relationship marked by understanding, trust, consistency, growth, and compassion. This relationship does not just occur; it must be cultivated, attended to, and nurtured. Carl Rogers (1961/1995), the consummate counseling professional, developed strong working relationships by being genuine and empathic and offering his clients unconditional positive regard.[5] Virginia Satir, widely recognized as a distinguished, particularly gifted, and influential family therapist, was known for her clinical success, in large part because of her warmth toward her clients, her sincere interest in their well-being, and her strong ability to make an authentic connection with them.

The quality of the relationship you develop with your client is influenced by your nonverbal and verbal behaviors. No matter how insightful you are, if you are checking your cell phone while you are with your client, it is likely that the relationship will not be as strong as it might be if you had turned your cell phone off and focused on your client. Likewise, it likely would not strengthen the working relationship if you were leaning forward and looking at your client during the session, but you spent the entire session asking your client only closed-ended questions. In the first case, there is an incongruity between your overt behavior and a client's expectations; in the second case, there is a discrepancy between your nonverbal and your verbal behaviors. In each case, you are communicating lesser warmth, interest, and engagement with your client.

Step 2. Explore

The exploration step is one in which you listen to your client talk and try to understand your client's predicament, your client's concern. It is the step where you support your client—through nonverbal and verbal encouragers, through open- and closed-ended questions, and through other interventions—in telling his or her story, identifying his or her maladaptive behaviors, or articulating his or her maladaptive thoughts. It is the step where your client will come to a clearer understanding of precipitants, current experiences, and future expectations regarding his or her life circumstance; will more clearly identify problematic behaviors; and will articulate those thoughts that interfere with leading a less painful existence.

The precise form of exploration engaged in will be determined in large part by the counselor's theoretical orientation. Psychodynamic counselors may encourage clients to talk about their families of origin and childhood precipitants of current themes that drive a client. Behavioral counselors would be interested in learning about the specific behaviors that are maladaptive. Cognitive counselors may encourage clients to articulate their irrational thoughts. Gestalt counselors would be interested in exploration of the here-and-now process, that which is transpiring and unfolding in the consultation office. Narrative counselors may encourage a full telling of the client's story.

Step 3. Determine Direction

Effective counseling proceeds from identifying a direction to move and an objective to work toward. A client always has a direction in which he or she wants to move. It may be implicit and not verbalized, but it is there. Most clients want something in their lives to be different, they want a problem to be solved, they want to *feel better*—or they have some variation on this theme. After all, they would not be coming to counseling if they did not have a problem, issue, consideration, pain, or suffering of one sort or another. Given that clients have goals, it makes sense to help them articulate them and make them manifest. A client who articulates his or her challenge or issue is a client who has taken the first step toward resolution. Furthermore, a client who articulates his or her challenge or issue is a client who has taken a step toward collaboration with his or her counselor. It helps the counselor and client develop a mutually agreeable goal toward which to work.

From a counselor's perspective, some general goals (that would take specific expression) are to make conscious those unconscious motivations and desires that impact a client's life, to identify the secondary gains that reinforce problematic behaviors, to challenge irrational thoughts, to confront discrepancies in the client's behavior, or to make manifest unacknowledged feelings (see Kottler, 2000).

Step 4. Work–Feedback–Rework

Once the direction of counseling is clarified and an objective or set of goals is mutually agreed on, it is time to engage in the next step: work–feedback–rework. Work refers to the client engaging in the task or tasks called for by the direction and goals of counseling. For some clients, work means engaging in a real struggle to come to some greater insight or understanding of their own situations and what brought them to this point in life. For other clients, work means identifying new ways of behaving and trying out those new behaviors, first within the context of counseling and then in their world outside of counseling. For yet other clients, work may mean learning new ways of thinking that result in a change in emotions. The work that is conducted in counseling is an interaction between what arises from the client's direction and goals and the counselor's understanding of change, rooted in his or her theoretical orientation. For some counselors change means insight, for others it means new behavioral sequences, and for others it means acquisition of new cognitions.

It is during the work–feedback–rework stage that counselors may rely on the relationship to promote change,[6] not only within the counseling hour but also in the client's outside life. Real-life changes mean that the client implements in his or her own life—outside of counseling—the new behaviors learned, the new insights gained, and/or the new thoughts or new ways of feeling acquired.

Role-play. Subsequent to insights or new thoughts, a client and counselor may engage in role-play. Role-play offers a client an opportunity to try out new behaviors and in doing so experientially understand new ways of thinking and new ways of feeling. Role-plays can be conceptualized in terms of four components: the client playing a role, the counselor playing a role, a situation in which the two *actors* (client and counselor) interact, and critique of the client's *performance* (Hackney & Cormier, 2005, cited in Erford, Eaves, Bryant, & Young, 2010). Ideally, role-plays should be of current, not historical, experiences (Erford et al., 2010). In other words, role-plays should be used to help a client practice new skills to solve a current problem.

One very effective way of utilizing role-plays is to divide it into a two-step process. In the first step, the counselor plays the client, and the client plays the challenging person in the client's environment. In the role-play, then, the counselor can *model* for the client adaptive behaviors around the challenging issue and person in the client's environment. In the second step, the client plays him- or herself and the counselor plays the difficult person, even in an exaggerated way. In this second step, the client has an opportunity to try the new adaptive behaviors previously modeled by the counselor. After this second step, the client can self-critique, and the counselor can offer valuable feedback.[7] The client then goes out into his or her world and uses the new behavior that was practiced within the counseling session; at the next session the client reports to the counselor about the real-life encounters experienced.

Consider the following example: The client is a 75-year-old woman who lives on her own in an apartment in a continuing care community. She currently is able to take care of her personal needs and to live independently, but she has a difficult time communicating with her physician. As she states, "My doctor should figure out what's wrong—that's her job; why should I have to tell her?"

Counselor: "So let's try this. I will play you, and you will play your doctor. You say what your doctor usually says, and I will respond."

Client (role-playing the doctor): "Okay. 'Hello, Mary. How can I help you today?' "

Counselor (role-playing the client): " 'I'm not feeling well.' "

Client (role-playing the doctor): " 'Not feeling well? Tell me what's going on.' "

Counselor (role-playing the client): " 'Well, I am in a lot of pain.' "

Client (role-playing the doctor): " 'Where is it? Can you show me by pointing?' "

Counselor (role-playing the client): " 'It's on my left leg. From here to here. What do you think it is?' "

Client (role-playing the doctor): " 'I'm not sure. Let me take a look. I might also order an X-ray.' "

Counselor: "Okay. Let's stop. How was that?"

Client: "Not so bad. I think maybe I can do that."

Counselor: "Let's switch roles. You be yourself, and I will be your doctor. 'Hello, Mary. How can I help you today?' "

Client: " 'I'm not feeling very good today. My leg has been hurting. It's my left leg. I've been having this pain for the past week. Do you know what it is?' "

Counselor: " 'Let me take a look. No, I don't know what it is. I think it would be good to get your leg X-rayed, then I'll have a better idea of what is going on.' Okay. Let's stop. How was that?"

Client: "It wasn't as hard as I thought. I have a doctor's appointment on Friday. I will tell her what I'm feeling. It will be good for her to know, and it will be good for me, too."

Counselor: "You did a great job. I look forward to hearing how it goes when we meet again next week."

Once the new skills are learned in session, they can be applied to the outside world. It is at this point that a client is given *homework* (though the counselor need not label it as such) to go into his or her life and relationships, try out the new skills, and report back to the counselor.

This latter step—reporting back to the counselor—is the point at which feedback takes place. It is at this point that the counselor can offer reinforcement if application of the new skill was successful or can candidly offer feedback and recommendations if the skill was not successfully applied.

Once this feedback is given and received, the client is encouraged to again work (i.e., rework)—to go back out into his or her environment and try out the new skills again. The counselor can then offer reinforcement when the client eventually succeeds and can encourage the client to consolidate his or her learning and apply it as a matter of routine in his or her life.

Step 5. Terminate

The fifth and final step of the counseling session comprises termination of the counseling endeavor. The termination session should be different from the other sessions you have had with your client. One way to conceptualize the termination session is as a trip down memory lane.

The structure and content can be expressed thus: "You [the client] came into counseling [number of weeks or months] ago with [specific problem or issue]. You decided to work toward the goal of [specific goal or direction of counseling]. Over the course of our work together, you [identify major achievements of the client]."[8]

In the termination session you might engage in a little more self-disclosure than you did during the course of counseling, focusing on your experience of the client. You might say, for example, "When you first came into counseling, I noticed that you [describe an asset that the client was able to use in resolving the issue]. I felt honored to act as a witness to the hard work you engaged in to transcend [describe the challenge]. I've been happy to see how your life has changed by [describe the change], and I wish you well. I also want you to know that you can come back in the future if you so wish."

Of course, this trip down memory lane is most appropriate when the ending of counseling is natural (i.e., when the work of counseling has been completed) and when it is planned (i.e., when the client and counselor mutually agree that it is appropriate to end the counseling endeavor).

Clients can respond to termination in a number of ways: They may begin to repeat their problematic repetitive themes; they may try to hang on by bringing in new problems or intensifying their old problems; they may feel sad, angry, anxious, or guilty; they may feel happy, joyful, or excited (see Moursund & Kenny, 2002); they may try to turn the counseling relationship into a friendship; or they may devalue counseling (see Teyber, 2005). Likewise, a counselor can respond to termination in a number of ways. The counselor may try to manipulate a client into remaining in counseling to satisfy some of the counselor's unmet needs, the counselor may feel sad or angry, or the counselor may feel proud or disappointed. What is important is not that the counselor not have feelings but that the counselor cultivates self-awareness around the feelings and uses those feelings to the benefit of the client. The client's (as well as the counselor's) behaviors and feelings around termination may be

influenced by termination itself and whether it represents a natural and/
or planned ending or unnatural and/or unplanned ending.

Natural Ending Versus Unnatural Ending

Here, **natural ending** refers to ending counseling at a point in the process
that is mutually agreed on by the client and counselor. It occurs typically
once the client has resolved his or her challenge (whether through learning new ways of behaving, having insights, or creating a new story of a
healthier, stronger self) or once it is clear to the client and counselor that
their work together will not result in more improvements. An **unnatural
ending** is one that occurs because of an external factor. An external factor might be having reached the maximum number of sessions allowed
by a social service agency or a managed care corporation, the client moving away, or some other situation that interferes with what otherwise
would have been continued counseling.

Planned Ending Versus Unplanned Ending

When we speak of planned endings versus unplanned endings, we are
looking at termination from the perspective of the counselor. That is,
was this termination planned in coordination with the counselor, or was
it a termination decided on exclusively by the client and (whether or not
this is expressed to the client) contrary to what the counselor believes is
in the client's best interest? A client, for example, may come to a session
one day and announce, "This is my last session; I'm not coming back."
This type of client may be called the "Abrupt Stopper" (Moursund &
Kenny, 2002, p. 118).

Likewise, a client may drop out of counseling unannounced;
Moursund and Kenny (2002) call this the "No-Show" (p. 116). A *no-
show* oftentimes is difficult for a counselor who may attribute the dropout
to *failure* on his or her own part. However, although the counselor plays
a role in the dropout just by virtue of the fact that there was a relationship
with the client, this may not be whole story or even the biggest part of the
story. I like to remind counselors-in-training that counseling is a two-way
endeavor that requires commitment on the part of both parties (i.e., both
counselor and client). I also like to remind counselors-in-training that clients have free will and are free to exercise their will in whatever way they
choose, including dropping out of counseling unannounced.

CHAPTER SUMMARY

In this chapter, we looked at the stages of counseling—beginning, middle, and end. We explored some advanced counseling skills—including

pros and cons, feedback, interpretation, self-disclosure, and advice-giving. We also reviewed a five-step structure for organizing counseling: build the therapeutic alliance, explore issue(s), determine the direction of counseling, work–feedback–rework, and termination. With a foundation in theories of aging and later life development, knowledge of basic attending and listening skills, and an explication of the stages of counseling, we will turn our attention in Chapter 4 to deeper issues in work with older clients and focus on psychodynamic and existential aspects of counseling.

CASE STUDY

Joel is an 80-year-old man who arrives in your office in a wheelchair, wearing thick glasses and a hearing aid in his right ear. His health has been declining steadily over the past 10 years. He was referred to you by his physician and was brought in by his oldest daughter one and a half years after his wife of 50 years had passed away. Joel was originally from Sicily; he immigrated with his wife to North America shortly after the end of World War II, stating, "It was really bad during the war, and my wife and I weren't sure what was going to happen in Europe after the war. We thought we'd be safer here than there." Joel had two siblings— one now deceased—who remained in Sicily. He would see them on his nearly annual trips to Europe. These trips ceased several years ago when his health became so compromised that travel became difficult. Joel has two adult children, neither of whom speaks Sicilian. Joel explains, "I wanted a new life for them. They were in America, and I wanted them to be American."

Joel was self-employed nearly all of his entire adult life as owner and proprietor of a small neighborhood bakery. "I worked hard, with my wife by my side," he says, "6 days a week, but my bakery was good to me, and I loved it." Joel states that it was difficult to adapt to retirement. He adds, though, "It's been especially hard since my wife died. I feel so lonely." Joel states that he is in constant pain because of arthritis. He was diagnosed with arthritis a number of years ago, but only recently has it progressed to the point of pain and mobility impairment. He reports having tried different medications—some over-the-counter and others prescription—none of which help. He states that he is "envious of people who can take a medication and who a half hour later are feeling better." His doctor recommended he try acupuncture, a recommendation he immediately rejected. Joel does not appear to have any noticeable cognitive impairment, though given his presentation, you are considering the possibility that he suffers from depression, is experiencing bereavement, and/or is having difficulty with phase-of-life issues.

Joel also states that he has been estranged from his one remaining sibling—his sister—for the past 10 years and is not sure whether he should try to reestablish contact and his relationship with her. He wants your advice, saying, "You're the expert. ... What would you do if you were me?" Unbeknownst to Joel, as it turns out, you too suffer from arthritis and you too have been estranged from your sibling for many years and have no intention of reestablishing contact. Joel has indicated that he is unsure that he will return for a second session.

Questions

1. What are some potential universal design issues in this case?
2. As a counselor, what would you do during the first stage of counseling with this client?
3. What do you anticipate or predict will compose the middle stage of counseling?
4. Would you share with the client that you have been estranged from your sibling? Why or why not?
5. Would you give advice to the client? Why or why not? If you would give advice, what advice would you give?
6. Give an example of what using the pros and cons technique might look like with this client.
7. Would you use self-disclosure around your medical issue with this client? Why or why not? If so, what would you say?

CHAPTER QUESTIONS

1. Identify and define the three stages of counseling. What are the hallmarks of each stage?
2. Explore in a cultural tradition other than your own the concept of change through stages.
3. What is universal design for learning? What are its three features? What is its relevance to counseling?
4. Describe some of the issues related to furnishing and decorating a counseling office.
5. Identify and describe the five-step structure of counseling.
6. What are the disadvantages of giving advice as a therapeutic intervention?
7. What are the four facets of a role-play?

8. What is the difference between planned endings and unplanned endings in counseling? Between natural endings and unnatural endings?

GLOSSARY

Advice-giving: is an intervention in which a counselor tells a client what to do; generally, this intervention is not recommended.

Feedback: refers to an intervention in which a counselor articulates an observation about the client regarding how others may perceive the client.

Interpretation: is a technique in which a counselor decodes a client's underlying issue, motivation, or family dynamic.

Narrative: is a story. It represents one way of conceptualizing counseling, namely, changing, challenging, or broadening the story the client tells about himself or herself to include healthier, more adaptive functioning.

Natural ending: occurs when the client and counselor mutually agree that the course of counseling should end.

Pros and cons: is a technique in which the counselor prompts the client to identify the advantages and disadvantages of possible courses of action.

Self-disclosure: refers to a counselor sharing something about his or her own personal life with his or her client.

Termination: means the end of a course of counseling.

Universal design: is the philosophy that activities should be accessible to all individuals, regardless of ability or disability.

Unnatural ending: is when the end of counseling occurs because of some force external to the counseling endeavor (such as managed care limits on the number of counseling sessions paid for).

FURTHER INFORMATION

1. To learn more about Tibetan Buddhist philosophy, see Sogyal Rinpoche's modern classic and highly accessible book *The Tibetan Book of Living and Dying* (New York: HarperOne, 1994).
2. To learn more about universal design for learning principles, see the Center for Applied Special Technology's *UDL guidelines: Version 1.0* (Wakefield, MA: Author, 2009b); available online at http://www.udlcenter.org/aboutudl/udlguidelines.

3. The skill sets in Chapters 2 and 3 are not comprehensive and represent a fundamental set of skills to get you started in your consideration of counseling older adults. For a more comprehensive list and description of skills, consider Ivey, Ivey, and Zalaquett's exceptional *Intentional Interviewing and Counseling* (Belmont, CA: Brooks/Cole, 2009), McHenry and McHenry's *What Therapists Say and Why They Say It* (Boston: Allyn & Bacon, 2007), and Erford, Eaves, Bryant, and Young's *35 Techniques Every Counselor Should Know* (Upper Saddle River, NJ: Pearson, 2010).

NOTES

1. Consideration of universal design for access in counseling is based on universal design for learning (UDL) principles. UDL principles essentially are those that are used to ensure equal access to learning for all people, regardless of ability or disability status.
2. This too is culture specific.
3. While we are on the topic of seating, think in terms of your older clients' needs. Some older clients will need seating that is easy to get in and out of.
4. This may also include activities of daily living (ADLs) and/or instrumental activities of daily living (IADLs).
5. We will discuss the therapeutic alliance and working relationship more fully in Chapter 5.
6. See Edward Teyber's *Interpersonal Process in Psychotherapy: An Integrative Model* (Belmont, CA: Brooks/Cole, 2005) for an excellent elucidation of using the relationship for therapeutic gain.
7. For an exceptional example of role-play within the context of counseling, see John Krumboltz's work in Jon Carlson and Diane Kjos's video *Cognitive-Behavioral Therapy With Dr. John Krumboltz: Psychotherapy With the Experts* (Upper Saddle River, NJ: Pearson (Merrill), 2000).
8. This is not a script. You will use your own words to convey similar sentiments.

CHAPTER 4

Psychodynamic and Existential Foundations in Counseling Older Adults

First tell yourself what you would be, then do what you need to do.

—Epictetus (55 C.E.–135 C.E.)

In this world nothing can be said to be certain, except death and taxes.

—Benjamin Franklin (1706–1790)

In this chapter you will review basic Freudian psychoanalytic concepts and explore three major intellectual streams of psychodynamic theory—ego psychology, object relations, and self psychology. You also will be introduced to existential theory. You will learn about the application of these theories to aging. You will learn about existential anxiety, a particular manifestation of this—death anxiety—and defenses that individuals, including older clients, use to protect themselves.

EGO PSYCHOLOGY, OBJECT RELATIONS, AND SELF PSYCHOLOGY

Mention psychotherapy to anyone and the first name that likely enters his or her mind is Sigmund Freud. And rightfully so. Dr. Freud was the prime mover behind psychoanalysis, the foundation of much of counseling and therapy. The field of psychodynamic therapy has evolved considerably over the past many years, yet to say that Freud's contributions remain significant is a gross understatement. One of the lasting strengths of Freudian therapy is its focus on *depth* in understanding humans and on revealing the unconscious forces and meanings that influence our thoughts, feelings, and behaviors (see Arden, 2007). Later life for many is a time of reflecting on *meaning*—what one's life has meant and what life means generally. Making conscious that which formerly was unconscious might allow a client to make great strides in meaning-making and add to the depth of understanding he or she has about his or her life.

Freud, unfortunately, had an ageist bias. Intriguingly, in his middle age Freud composed an essay, "On Psychotherapy," in which he indicated that older people would not benefit from treatment (Hepple, 2004). Freud wrote, "Near or above the age of fifty, the elasticity of mental processes on which treatment depends is, as a rule, lacking: old people are no longer educable" (1905, cited in Arden, 2007, p. 324). This bias carried down through the years and influenced not only orthodox psychoanalysis but counseling and therapy more generally.

Recently psychodynamic therapists, as well as other mental health providers, have come to appreciate that later life continues to be a time of growth and development and that older adults indeed can and do benefit from counseling (see Biggs, 1998; Claudel, 2004; King, 1974). King (1974) reported success in conducting psychoanalysis with older adults. She believed challenges in later life resulted from those conflicts in earlier life that had not been worked through (1974, 1980, cited in Biggs, 1998). Common issues she saw in older adults included decreased sexual energy and inability to have children, replacement at work by younger adults, fear of retirement, loss of one's own parents, aging and illness, and the increased possibility of one's own death (King, 1974).

Each of these issues has psychodynamic implications (King, 1974). King believed that decreased sexual energies may result in feelings of loss of control over others, because of the inability to control others through one's sexuality. Replacement in work roles by younger people may result in a sort of narcissistic injury to the self that identifies its value in terms of work; fear of retirement, too, may result in narcissistic injury due to heavy investment of self in the role of work. Loss of parents may be particularly hard on those older adults who have not individuated. Aging and illness may result in becoming dependent on others, including others for whom one may have had contempt or disdain. An increased possibility of death may be particularly difficult for those who have been in denial of their own death.

Why do older adults benefit from psychoanalysis? King (1974, 1980, cited in Biggs, 1998) believed there were two reasons. First, older clients are more mature, which results in a stronger working relationship with the therapist. Second, older clients are less influenced by sexual and aggressive impulses, which she believed allows them to be more flexible in their use of defense mechanisms and to have a greater and more conscious ability to try out new ways of being.

King was not alone in believing in the benefit of psychoanalysis with older adults. Claudel (2004) stated that older adults could benefit from psychoanalysis if that therapy was sensitive to the three areas of mourning common in later life: mourning of the loss of objects, loss of function, and loss of self. Though restricted to issues of loss, Claudel (2004) acknowledged that older adults could make good use of therapy, could change, and could adapt.

Biggs (1998) valued a psychodynamic perspective on working with older adults by way of two processes. Like King (1974, 1980, cited in Biggs, 1998), Biggs believed that the roots of adult development reside in the experiences of childhood; Biggs (1998), too, valued understanding intergenerational transference phenomena.[1]

Unlike Freud, then, who was pessimistic about psychoanalysis with older adults, contemporary clinicians are optimistic that older clients can benefit from counseling because of clients' maturity and flexibility. They believe that older clients can benefit from counseling if the counseling focuses on issues of mourning and loss (broadly defined), recognizes childhood antecedents of late life development, and works with transference phenomena.

Before you read any further, reflect on your beliefs about older adults and change. Do you believe that older adults can benefit from counseling because they *can* change, or do you believe that older adults cannot benefit from counseling because they are set in their ways? Your answer to this question will have marked implications for your work in counseling.

Basic Freudian Concepts. There are fundamental concepts of Freud that even today command a counselor's attention. Freud conceptualized the mind as comprising three regions, which he termed the **unconscious,** the **preconscious,** and the **conscious** (Mitchell & Black, 1995). In the unconscious resides those thoughts and feelings that are objectionable or that a client experiences as conflictual. The preconscious contains tolerable thoughts and feelings—that is, those that have the potential to become conscious. The conscious comprises any and all thoughts and feelings of which a person is aware. Freud believed that, through the process of **free association,** a person makes conscious that which is not conscious.

He further posited that, through psychoanalysis, a therapist becomes the object of a client's **transference;** that is, a client projects his or her unwanted thoughts and feelings onto the analyst. These nonconscious thoughts and feelings are based in the client's infancy and childhood

experiences. With transference being the core encounter in psychoanalysis, Freud came to believe that the best therapist was one who would
maintain a *tabula rasa* stance (see Kahn, 1997). Just as a motion picture
is best seen on a blank screen, so too, Freud believed, are a client's nonconscious thoughts and feelings brought to light in their transference
onto a blank therapist.

Freud also, being the Darwinian that he was, focused to a large
extent on the concept of instinctual processes—**drives**—that animate
a person's psyche. He proposed two drives—the sexual drive and the
aggressive drive—and believed that both of these drives influence each
one of us (Mitchell & Black, 1995).

Freud later believed that humans could not fully be understood strictly
in terms of the unconscious, preconscious, and conscious or strictly in
terms of drives, so he extended his theory to include a tripartite mental
structure composed of the id, ego, and superego that function something
like three members of a family. At one extreme is the **id**, the most primitive component, something of a wild child filled with "raw, unstructured,
impulsive energies"; at the other extreme is the **superego**, a parentlike
structure that functions as the font of morality and self-restraint (or rather
constraint); between them resides the **ego**, the mediator, that keeps a check
on the energies of the id while also trying to satisfy some of the demands
of the superego (Mitchell & Black, 1995, p. 20). Though presenting a tri-
une psyche, Freud clearly showed greatest interest in the workings of the
id, where he believed primitive sexual and aggressive urges reside.

One way in which you can apply Freud's concepts to your work
with older adults is to ask yourself, when listening to your client's story,
whether your client's statements are primitive and childlike ("It isn't fair
that I have cancer"), parentlike ("I must show self-restraint and not let
my children know how I feel"), or something in between ("I have cancer,
but I am committed to dealing with it openly"). The first is a statement
typical of the id, the second of the superego, and the third of the ego.

Ego Psychology

Ego psychology, though sensitive to Freud's drive theory, instead elevates
the role of the ego in human functioning. Ego psychology states that the
id, ego, and superego are indeed constantly challenging one another.
Unlike Freud's focus on the workings of the id, however, ego psychology focuses on the functioning of the ego, specifically on how the ego
manages the id by allowing some of the id's instinctual desires to be
gratified (Magnavita, 2008). Whereas Freud reduced everything to the
functioning of the id's aggressive and sexual longings, ego psychology

emphasizes the idea that the ego can neutralize the aggressive and sexual nature of the drives (Mitchell & Black, 1995).

This occurs through the use of defense mechanisms. **Anna Freud** described a number of defense mechanisms and presented detailed case studies of the defenses. In her book *The Ego and the Mechanisms of Defense*, Anna Freud discussed how the ego utilizes defense mechanisms in its attempts to avert unpleasant feelings and thoughts and to contain the id's push for gratification (Freud, 1936).

One other major change began to take place. Therapists began to understand analysis not so much in terms of helping a client merely *understand* the workings of the id but instead as a place for a client to *work through* and refashion early developmental experiences (Mitchell & Black, 1995). In this way, a client could learn ways to strengthen his or her ego functioning (see Sue & Sue, 2008). This represented a major shift in the field of analysis. Understanding was not the sole purpose of analysis; rather change through experience with the therapist was the road to growth.

Object Relations

Freud envisioned human development as one where the primitive, animalistic id becomes managed by the civilizing ego, which also satisfies the needs of the superego, whereas the object relations school views the id as being "wired for human interaction" from the start (Mitchell & Black, 1995, p. 113). According to **object relations,** infants do not need to be socialized to become human—infants begin their lives fully human. Furthermore, infants are designed to have "harmonious interaction and nontraumatic development" with others but are frustrated by less than optimal parenting (Mitchell & Black, 1995, p. 114). This postmodern view, in other words, conceptualizes the self as relational (Magnavita, 2008).

Freud noted the phenomenon of **repetition compulsion** in which a client repeatedly engages in maladaptive thoughts, feelings, and behaviors. Kahn (1997) described the repetition compulsion as the "need to create for ourselves repeated replays of situations and relationships that were particularly difficult or troubling in our early years" (p. 25). Furthermore, Kahn (1997) noted that the repetition compulsion could be an expression not only of how early parent–child relationships were but of how these relationships could have been. In other words, sometimes the client will replay in therapy the actual script of his or her early relationship with a parental figure, and at other times the client will play out in therapy a script of how he or she would have liked that relationship to have been.

Object relations understands the repetition compulsion as a libidinal drive trying to cleave to unattainable objects. Objects, as referred to here, are not just things but also people and even oneself. Even though pleasure can be a wonderful way to relate to others, for those who have been abused as children, pain too can be a way to relate (see discussion of Fairbain in Mitchell & Black, 1995). In other words, children who are raised in a healthy, loving environment grow into adults who seek connection through pleasure (broadly defined); those who are raised in an unhealthy, abusive environment seek connection through pain.

Children, however, do not need to be raised in a perfect household. Winnicott promoted the idea of good-enough mothering (Mitchell & Black, 1995). A good-enough mother is one who generally sees to the child's needs but is able to "recede when she is not needed" so that the child learns that he or she can function socially, independent of the parent (Mitchell & Black, 1995, p. 128). We will broaden the term "good-enough mothering" to include any parental figure and call it **good-enough parenting**.

Adults repeat the relationship patterns they learn in childhood (Mitchell & Black, 1995; Sue & Sue, 2008). If patterns of relationships are learned, then they can be unlearned, and new patterns can be learned to replace them. This is the fundamental principle underlying object relations therapy. An adult who in childhood did not receive good-enough parenting needs to unlearn those maladaptive patterns of being and replace them with more adaptive patterns. And this can occur through a good-enough parenting experience in therapy. In this case, the counselor becomes the good-enough parent to his or her older client, providing the client with the experiences missed in childhood. Through living a new relationship with the counselor—a relationship that was lacking in the client's childhood—the client learns a new, healthy, adaptive way of relating to others (see Kahn, 1997). Older adults who live this new relationship can learn healthier ways of relating to people in their day-to-day lives.

Self Psychology

Self psychology is an evolving theory of psychosocial development, health, and pathology (Fosshage, 1998). Recall that Freud believed human character develops through the struggle between the animalistic id and the civilizing ego that seeks to satisfy the superego (Mitchell & Black, 1995). **Heinz Kohut**, the driving force behind self psychology, focused his attention on what he believed was a widespread sense of feeling alone and alienated in the world (Mitchell & Black, 1995). According to Kohut, it was not that human troubles were the result of guilt over the forbidden wishes of the id but because humans moved through life without *meaning* (Mitchell & Black, 1995).[2] Kohut believed that children are designed to experience a social, communal life that allows them to feel connected to others (Mitchell & Black, 1995).

Freud saw the libidinal urges initially as being directed toward the self and subsequently toward external objects (namely, parents who become the child's "love objects") (Mitchell & Black, 1995, p. 150). Freud thought that the more self-involved was the child, the less *other-involved* he or she would be. Kohut believed that loving oneself, contrary to lessening the ability to love others, actually contributes to this ability. As you might expect, Kohut focused a great deal on trying to understand his clients from their points of view; he called this "empathic immersion" and "vicarious introspection" (Baker & Baker, 1987; Mitchell & Black, 1995, p. 157).

Through his empathy-focused work with clients, Kohut came to believe that problems are the result of a dysfunctional sense of self. He believed that there was a central developmental task that defines all humans: "the consolidation and maintenance of a positive cohesive sense of self" (Fosshage, 1998, p. 5). He believed issues regarding the sense of self present themselves throughout the life span (Fosshage, 1998). He further believed that this sense of self is embedded in a "striving for intergenerational continuity" (Fosshage, 1998, p. 7). In other words, older adults seek connection on some level with those who come after them, and they want subsequent generations to be successful.

Kohut believed that healthy development results from the experience of three fundamental types of relationships or needs: mirroring, idealized parental imago, and twinship (Baker & Baker, 1987; Fosshage, 1998) (see Table 4.1). **Mirroring** relationships are those in which the self is met with delight and joy by another (namely, a parent or parental figure). Kahn (1997) described mirroring as the experience of a parent's valuing of the child as "special, wonderful, and welcome" (p. 91). Mirroring creates "a sense of self-worth and value" (Baker & Baker, 1987, p. 3).

TABLE 4.1   Kohut's Three Fundamental Relationships

Need	Description
Mirroring	Child experiences parental figure's expression of delight and joy in the child.
Idealized parental imago	Child experiences parental figure as a calm, powerful protector.
Twinship	Child experiences a sense of belonging or similarity to parental figure.

Note: Baker and Baker (1987), Fosshage (1998), Kahn (1997).

Idealized parental imago[3] relationships are those in which the self perceives another (typically a parent or parental figure) as someone who is a calm but powerful protector of the child's self. **Idealizing allows children to experience "help, protection, and comfort"** (Baker & Baker, 1987, p. 4) and, in appropriate doses, allows them to internalize these experiences so that they can—across their life spans—provide help, protection, and consolation to themselves.

Twinship relationships are those where a child has a sense of belonging—a feeling of similarity—to another (again, typically a parent or parental figure). Baker and Baker (1987) provided the example of a young boy beside his father "shaving" with a bladeless razor while his father also shaves. The boy experiences the feeling of being like his father. Twinship needs that are experienced in childhood result in the ability to feel close to and connected to others in adulthood (Baker & Baker, 1987).

Each of these types of experiences—mirroring, idealized parental imago, and twinship—contribute to a child's (and, eventually, to an older adult's) healthy narcissism—a sense of self as special, safe, and connected to others (Mitchell & Black, 1995). Kohut proposed that as a child experiences the normal disappointments found in day-to-day living (that, for example, the calm, powerful, idealized parent from time to time loses his or her temper), the child acquires the ability to self-soothe and subsequently develops a more realistic sense of self (Mitchell & Black, 1995). In other words, experiencing mirroring, an idealized parental imago, and twinship result in healthy development (Kahn, 1997).

For Kohut, *insight* into the needs one lacked in childhood was not enough to engender change; rather a client needed new interpersonal experiences for change to take place (see Baker & Baker, 1987; Kahn, 1997). Kohut applied to transference phenomena his understanding of the three types of relationships discussed above, resulting in the concepts of mirroring transference, idealized parental imago transference, and twinship transference. Mirroring transference occurs when the client perceives the therapist to be nurturing to the extent that he or she "can begin to feel more seen, more real, and more internally substantial" (Mitchell & Black, 1995, p. 161). Idealized parental imago transference is the phenomenon of the client perceiving the therapist to be powerful and perfect and "feels himself to be increasingly strong and important by virtue of his connection to this powerful and important other" (Mitchell & Black, 1995, p. 161). Twinship transference describes the phenomenon of the client perceiving the therapist as *like* the client in some *important* way(s)—for example, "feeling a like-gendered analyst shares a sensibility about being male or female" (Mitchell & Black, 1995, p. 161).

Kohut believed that, over time, clients who experienced mirroring, idealized parental imago, and twinship transferences would "develop a more reliable sense of vitality or well-being" (Mitchell & Black, 1995, p. 161). For this reason, Kohut supported a client's transference experiences of the therapist, *in loco parentis* as it were, and, in doing so, expected that the client would experience the sense of specialness, safety, and connection to a like other that he or she otherwise lacked.

Self Psychology and Late Life: The Case of Alzheimer's Disease. Self psychology can be applied to issues of late life. As an example, consider Alzheimer's disease (AD) from a self psychology perspective. Lazarus, Cohler, and Lesser (1996) explored the experience of the dissolution of the self in community-dwelling elders with AD. They found lower levels of self-esteem, a tendency to idealize the interviewer, and a sense of fragmentation in those with AD. They offered intriguing possibilities in using self psychology to support healthier defenses in older adults with AD. They suggested that clinicians communicate empathy to those with AD through having an understanding attitude toward the "frustration and feelings of loss related to cognitive decline" (Lazarus et al., 1996, p. 256), a sort of empathic immersion or vicarious introspection. They supported the inclination of a person with AD to talk about the past as a way to decrease the likelihood of depression as well as a way to demonstrate that his or her cognitive functioning remains intact for some things. Lazarus et al. (1996) recognized value in the experience of hallucinations of loved ones that occur to some people with AD and suggested that hallucinations may be adaptive in that—through representing a desired connection with an empathic parental figure—they reduce the sense of fragmentation and loneliness the person with AD has. In fact, Lazarus et al. (1996) recommended neither denying nor challenging the hallucinatory experiences of the person with AD but instead reflecting the positive feelings experienced by the hallucinating person back to that person and then encouraging him or her to focus on relationships with staff and living loved ones. Lazarus et al. (1996), too, noted the importance of communicating to staff the life history of the person with AD as a way to increase the likelihood of staff's understanding and empathic interactions with the patient and recommended that elders' families share with staff their loved ones' life stories through word or perhaps video. By using one or more of these interventions, a counselor might help bolster the sense of self of a person with AD.

When you work with a person with AD or other dementia from the perspective of self psychology, consider that you will observe lower self-esteem in the client, idealization of the counselor, and fragmentation. Your task will be threefold: to (a) support AD clients in talking about their past, (b) recognize the value of hallucinatory experiences of loved ones and reflect back to the client the positive feelings such experiences engender, and (c) encourage clients to engage with staff and current family members.

EXISTENTIAL ANXIETY, DEATH ANXIETY, AND DEFENSE MECHANISMS

In the 20th century, existentialism developed as a philosophical system focused on the human condition. It evolved from the work of Martin Heidegger, Karl Jaspers, and others, and it entered the vernacular by way of the works of Jean-Paul Sartre, Albert Camus, and others. Sartre coined the phrase "existence precedes essence" to indicate that there is no objectively definable quality of being human. In other words, one is what one makes oneself (see Crowell, 2004). In existentialism, one's *humanness* is the result of neither biology nor environment nor culture. There is no objective *meaning*; rather each of us makes meaning.

Existential Anxiety

What does "existence precedes essence" have to do with anxiety? From an existential perspective, the fact that one has the freedom to *be* whatever one chooses to be results in anxiety. Just as a fear makes concrete our helplessness, "in anxiety, as in fear, [one grasps oneself] as threatened or as vulnerable; but unlike fear, anxiety has no direct object" (Crowell, 2004). **Existential anxiety**, then, forces a person to abandon the distraction found through one's "roles or projects" (Crowell, 2004). In other words, roles and projects provide us with and *prop up* a sense of self. For North Americans, roles and projects most often revolve around work. Think of how often you have asked people you have just met, "What do you do for a living?" or, if they are retired, "What did you do for a living?" They answer, "I am a therapist" or "I am a carpenter" or "I was an interior decorator." Your asking the question results in the respondent identifying his or her *self* by his or her work. In other cultures, the salient question may be "What book are you reading?" or "What clan do you belong to?" No matter the particulars of the question, you likely will not hear a person respond simply, "I exist."

Existential anxiety is an anxiety that says in essence you are not your job, you are not your family, you are not whatever is your role or project. Someone experiencing existential anxiety " 'sees through' the phoniness of those who, unaware of what the breakdown of anxiety portends, live their lives complacently identifying with their roles as though these roles thoroughly defined them" (Crowell, 2004).

Furthermore, if there is no essential self, then what does one make of death? Existentialism posits that existential anxiety is at the root of **death anxiety**. Without an essential self, there is no continuation of the self beyond death. Death becomes the ultimate annihilation—annihilation of the self.

Crowell noted that because we construct our identity through our roles and projects, when these roles and projects subside, so does our sense of self, our sense of being (Crowell, 2004). As he stated, "In a manner of speaking I am thus brought face-to-face with my own finitude, my 'death' as the possibility in which I am no longer able to be anything" (Crowell, 2004). This understanding of the mortality of the self can prompt us to finally comprehend that we create our identity through the choices of roles and projects we make. In other words, we—each one of us—are responsible for the choices we make (Crowell, 2004).

We can define existential grief, then, as the sadness that is the result of knowing that there is no essential self and the knowledge (whether conscious or not) that mortality spells absolute annihilation. Furthermore, existential grief may manifest itself in one or more ways. Caro (2007) identified six transpersonal themes of existential grief. These include the realms of the body, emotions, the mind, spirituality, the community, and creativity. The themes comprise the following:

1. feelings of chest and throat constriction and feelings of physical dissociation or fragmentation (body);
2. despair, loneliness, emotional pain, sadness, anger, fear, peace, joy, and fearlessness (emotions);
3. thoughts of meaninglessness and questions of why and how, longing, hiding, justice, and acceptance (mind);
4. spiritual questioning, faith or humanistic independence, authenticity, and connection to earth, animals, and spirit (spirituality);
5. separation from others, existential aloneness, isolation, creation of community, friendship, and parent–child connection (community); and
6. loss or freeing of creative expression (creativity).

Her conceptualization of existential grief was broad and suggested that different people experience existential grief in distinctive ways, emphasizing one or more domains over the others or, within domains, emphasizing negative, positive, or a combination of negative and positive qualities. The next time you are counseling an older client, listen for themes related to the body, emotions, the mind, spirituality, the community, or creativity and listen, too, for negative, positive, or a combination of negative and positive qualities in the themes.

Meaning and Placement in Long-Term Care. Flinders (2003) wrote of the struggles of later life in terms of *meaning*, specifically the "forces of opposing meanings" (p. 258). By this she suggested the dialectic that exists in Western culture between the "view toward living" and the "view toward death" (Flinders, 2003, p. 258). She posited that the challenges that exist in later life are in large part due to the disconnect between a culture that places great value on youth and the ultimate reality of decline leading to death that is the inevitability of late life. She discussed how conflict plays out when an older adult is placed in nursing care and how families manage visitation. Specifically, she noted distress that family members might feel upon placement of a loved one and how they may not have a solid sense of the root of their upset.

Following Halpert (1991, cited in Flinders, 2003), Flinders placed the root of this distress in fears of "abandonment and murder" as well as an existential anxiety at seeing one's own future in the situation of a loved one in terminal decline (pp. 258–259). Under these circumstances, part of the work of the counselor is to help family members gain insight into the foundations of their distress as well as to help them work through their fears. Flinders (2003) posited that working with family members subsequently can help elders adjust to life in a nursing facility by helping family members clarify the *meaning* that surrounds the frequency of their visitation and adjust their visiting schedule so that it contributes to the adjustment of the elder to nursing home life. When you work with families who have placed a loved one in nursing care, it could be beneficial to explore with them the roots of their distress—namely, do they feel that they are abandoning their loved one or in some way symbolically *murdering* the loved one? Do they see their own mortality reflected in the mortality of their loved one? Perhaps if a client's family members could be more conscious of and honest with themselves around these issues, they may be able to adapt their visits to maximally contribute to their loved one's becoming accommodated to living in nursing care.

Flinders (2003) discussed issues that may arise in a counselor who works with older adults. Among these are the unconscious use of deficits models of aging (instilling in the counselor an expectation for no change) (Hinze, 1987, cited in Flinders, 2003), narcissistic injury to the clinician's self through seeing oneself reflected in an elder in decline (Zinberg, n.d., cited in Flinders, 2003), and the perception of symptoms in elders as the result of cognitive decline rather than issues that can be worked through (Sandler, 1984, cited in Flinders, 2003).

Each of these issues represents a countertransference based on the counselor's background, lived experience, training, philosophy, and theory of aging.

Flinders (2003) observed that old age can be a time of life filled with *meaning*. She noted that conflicts may arise after a loved one's death regarding the ambivalence one feels toward the loved one. This ambivalence is the result of a struggle between the positive feelings one may have about the loving qualities of the deceased elder and the negative feelings about the painful qualities of the deceased elder. Resolving these conflicting feelings may aid the grieving process.

Finally, Flinders (2003) discussed the conflicts that arise in placement in nursing care and related it to "fear of disloyalty and loss of love" (p. 260). By broadening one's view, she believed that a loved one in nursing can see him- or herself as part of "the larger scheme of humankind" (p. 260) and continue to live a meaningful life. This is akin to developing what Tornstam identified as gerotranscendence.

Death Anxiety

Carl Jung "never met a patient over forty whose problems did not root back to fear of approaching death" (Smith, 1991, p. 333). Even though Jung was not an existentialist, for him death was a major motivating factor in human life. But what is death anxiety? It is a multidimensional construct, comprising "lack of fear of death," "experience in death and dying," and "awareness of the ever present potential of death" (Stout, Minton, & Spikla, 1976, cited in Pollak, 1979–1980, pp. 98–99). In their study, Stout et al. identified six factors of death and dying. Two of the factors are negative: (a) death perceived as "pain, loneliness, and failure" and (b) "punishment for wrongdoing and the forsaking of dependents, with accompanying guilt feelings." Three are more or less neutral: (c) "the unknown, the mysterious, the ambiguous"; (d) "a natural end to existence"; and (e) "indifferen[ce]." And one is positive: (f) "courage and an afterlife of reward" (1976, cited in Pollak, 1979–1980, pp. 98–99). This suggests that death anxiety may be conceptualized along a continuum; not all clients will experience or express the same degree or the same type of death anxiety.

Fortner and Neimeyer (1999) reviewed, summarized, and evaluated research on death anxiety and older adults. Their principle findings revolved around death anxiety and ego integrity, physical problems, psychological problems, and to a lesser extent institutionalization. They also reported more subtle findings regarding death anxiety and age, gender, and religiosity.

Recall Erikson's (1982) late-life stage of ego integrity versus despair. Ego integrity is the sense that one has achieved and can be satisfied with (or at least accept) one's history, whereas despair is a sense that one's efforts were not enough, and one no longer has the time needed to finish unfinished business (Wagner & Lorion, 1984). Fortner and Neimeyer (1999) found that the less *ego integrity* older people had, the higher their death anxiety. In other words, older adults who reported less life satisfaction or experienced a lesser feeling of purpose in life were more likely to report more death anxiety. Second, older adults with more *physical problems* reported higher death anxiety than did those with fewer physical problems. Third, those with more *psychological problems* reported higher death anxiety than did those with fewer psychological problems. Fourth, elders who were *institutionalized* (i.e., in nursing care) tended to report higher levels of death anxiety than did those who live in the community or in less restrictive environments, though this finding was not unequivocal (Fortner & Neimeyer, 1999). In terms of counseling, this means that you may be called on more frequently to address death anxiety when your client presents with lower levels of ego integrity, has more physical or psychological problems, or resides in an institution.

There is no straight, linear relationship between death anxiety and age; rather, death anxiety decreases from middle age to old age then flattens (Fortner & Neimeyer, 1999). In other words, older adults, in general, have lower levels of death anxiety than do middle-aged adults. However, once we reach our later years, death anxiety does not decrease even more or, interestingly, begin to increase again. Fortner and Neimeyer (1999) reported no relationship between death anxiety and gender: Neither males nor females are more likely than the other to report experiencing death anxiety in late life. In terms of death anxiety and religiosity, older adults who report having religious beliefs also report less death anxiety, though interestingly there is no correlation between religious behaviors (e.g., attending services) and death anxiety (Fortner & Neimeyer, 1999). Although one cannot change an older adult's age, one may explore with an older client his or her religious beliefs as an intervention that potentially could mediate death anxiety.

Two of the most salient features of death are its inevitability and the possibility of its permanence; other features are death's unpredictability, our inability to control it, and its uncertainty (Pyszczynski, Greenberg, Solomon, & Maxfield, 2006). One relatively common factor in negative perspectives on death is what has been called "fear of dying of self," "fear of ceasing to be," or "fear of extinction, annihilation, obliteration, or ceasing to be" (Choron, 1964, Collett & Lester, 1969, Kastenbaum & Aisenberg, 1972, all cited in Pollak, 1979–1980, p. 98), a factor that clearly has its roots in existentialism. Although existentialism no longer

has the intellectual cachet that it once had, its legacy has been invigo-
rated by a relatively novel and promising line of thought and research,
terror management theory (TMT).

Terror management theory posits that "thoughts of death affect
human attitudes and behaviors that bear no obvious or logical relationship to the problem of death" (Pyszczynski et al., 2006, p. 328). The *terror* in TMT is "existential terror" (Pyszczynski et al., 2006), an intensity
of feelings of existential anxiety, of death anxiety. Existential terror can
be managed in two ways: by upholding a particular cultural worldview
or by propping up self-esteem (through fulfilling the demands of the particular cultural worldview to which one subscribes). Rather than speaking of a continuum of death anxiety, Pyszczynski et al. (2006) speak
in terms of *mortality salience*, which comprises reminders of death.
Mortality salience may be very subtle or quite tangible.

Through research, Pyszczynski et al. (2006) and others have found
that increasing self-esteem reduces the intensity of anxiety felt when one
is threatened. That is, those with higher self-esteem feel less anxiety
when faced with a threatening situation. Furthermore, subtle mortality
salience makes one more likely to increase attempts to boost one's self-
esteem, as well as to react positively to people with similar worldviews
and negatively to people with conflicting worldviews. When self-esteem
is boosted, or when one's worldview is shared by others, an individual
no longer has a strong a need to increase self-esteem or defend his or her
worldview in response to mortality salience. When a person's self-esteem
or worldview is threatened, that person is more likely to have greater
access to thoughts of death, whereas increases in self-esteem or validation of one's worldview reduces access to thoughts of death. Finally, if
one believes in a life after death, mortality salience has no effect on the
strivings for self-esteem or on the need to defend one's worldview against
other, conflicting worldviews (Pyszczynski et al., 2006).

People respond to thoughts of death by proximal or distal defenses
(Pyszczynski et al., 2006). Proximal defenses are those that "push such
thoughts out of consciousness or push the problem of death into the
distant future" (Pyszczynski et al., 2006, p. 329). Distal defenses are
more indirect and comprise strategies that include holding fast to one's
cultural worldview and endeavoring to increase self-esteem and develop
close relationships with others (Pyszczynski et al., 2006). In sum, people
defend against death anxiety through distancing, cultural worldviews,
and self-esteem—each of which reduces anxiety caused by thinking
about death (Pyszczynski et al., 2006).

Cultural worldviews more often than not contain belief in the afterlife
or the continued existence of a *self* after death (Pyszczynski et al., 2006).
Consider, for example, the Christian concept of the soul or the Hindu

concept of Atman. These cultural worldviews also contain precepts that, when followed, result in an increase in self-esteem. TMT might predict, for example, that humanists who choose not to kill because they believe in the value of human life increase their self-esteem because they are fulfilling part of the cultural worldview (in this example, humanism) to which they subscribe.

Threats to meaning in life (i.e., meaning that is derived from one's cultural worldview) result in compensation or the use of **defense mechanisms** (Pyszczynski et al., 2006). Compensation is an attempt to find ways to increase self-esteem and/or cling more strongly to one's worldview. Defense mechanisms are thoughts, feelings, or behaviors used to avoid painful thoughts and feelings. Compensation and defense mechanisms both represent attempts to manage existential terror by shielding oneself against thoughts of death or by propping up self-esteem or one's cultural worldview.

Suppression is the most common defense mechanism in response to thoughts of death (Pyszczynski et al., 2006). When people are reminded of their mortality, they most often respond by suppression, but they may respond in other ways as well: clinging more intensely to their cultural worldview, distancing themselves from reminders of mortality, and trying to increase their self-esteem (Pyszczynski et al., 2006). Fear of death is unique in that there is nothing any human can do to evade death; that is, we can safely predict (and with great accuracy) that each of us, sooner or later, will die (Pyszczynski et al., 2006). We may not know how we will die, or when we will die, but we *will* die.

Awareness of death results in anxiety, and this anxiety interferes with the day-to-day tasks that are necessary to maintain one's existence; hence, utilizing terror management strategies can be adaptive (Pyszczynski et al., 2006). For better or worse, as humans we are aware of our mortality, so it is sensible that we develop strategies to manage this awareness. As such, terror management may be a means for growth and positive change (see Cozzolino, 2007, and Cozzolino et al., 2004, both cited in Pyszczynski et al., 2006).

TMT has implications for older adults (Pyszczynski et al., 2006). For example, it has been found that elders closer to death have less defensive and more flexible coping styles. Younger adults, when faced with mortality salience (whether subtle or obvious), respond with more harshness toward the ethical wrongdoings of others. When older adults experience explicit mortality salience, the harshness of their judgments of others, however, is not affected; when experiencing subtle mortality salience, older adults are more *lenient*.

This increased flexibility and lenience is hypothesized to be the result of three factors (Pyszczynski et al., 2006). First, older adults are closer to death, and they are more frequently reminded of it (e.g., through the loss to death of friendships or family members). Second, that which brought older adults their self-esteem earlier in life no longer has the same power (e.g., gainful employment). Third, older adults, at least in North America, are constrained by a cultural worldview that values youth; the fact that older adults no longer possess youth puts them in conflict with this worldview. According to Pyszczynski et al. (2006), older adults who constructively age are those who engage in "psychological reorganization that leads to a general improvement in psychological functioning and well-being" (p. 351).

Pollak (1979–1980) found, similar to Pyszczynski's findings, that fear of death did not increase as a person got older and closer to death. His review of studies of death anxiety revealed that higher levels of death anxiety are found in people with lower senses of "effectiveness, mastery, and power"; conversely, lower levels of death anxiety are found in people with higher levels of self-esteem as well as feelings of "meaning and purpose" (Pollak, 1979–1980, p. 115). Death anxiety is greater, too, in people with higher general levels of anxiety; that is, those people who suffer from generalized anxiety are also likely to experience death anxiety; in fact, people who suffer from psychological problems more generally also suffer from death anxiety. Furthermore, those who are conscious of their death anxiety tend to use the defenses of denial or rationalization; those for whom death anxiety is unconscious tend to experience attitudes of "ambivalence, revulsion, and dread" toward death (Pollak, 1979–1980, p. 115). This suggests that counseling interventions designed to strengthen self-esteem and reduce psychological problems—specifically, generalized anxiety—will result in a lessening of death anxiety.

Internal and External Resources for Dealing With Death Anxiety. Sears (2007) believed that death anxiety can be worked through *internally* in the integration of wisdom from Eastern philosophical traditions within an existential therapeutic approach. He noted that North Americans are ill prepared for death and hence avoid cognitions about it. Because of this lack of preparation, when death comes it is met with difficulty. Sears posited that by reflecting on death from an Eastern perspective, clients can experience a healthier grieving process. Sears (2007) noted that Buddhists have a liberatory approach to preparing for death, whether one's own or that of a loved one. The approach he discussed comprises four considerations or contemplations (see Table 4.2). The first is the *universality of death*, the fact that absolutely every living being dies. The second is the *inevitability of death*, the fact that no one escapes the reality of death. The third is the *unknown time of one's death*, the fact that one does not know when death will occur. The

TABLE 4.2   Four Contemplations on Death

Contemplation	Description
Universality	Every living being dies.
Inevitability	There is no escape from death.
Time	Time of death is unknown.
Manner	Manner of death is unknown.

Note: Sears, R. W., *Contemplation of Death in Existential Psychotherapy and Eastern Wisdom Traditions*, paper presented at the 115th annual convention of the American Psychological Association, 2007.

fourth is the *unknown manner of death*, the fact that one does not know how one will die. Sears believed that although contemplating on these four considerations may not remove the pain of death, it can help clients experience a less encumbered grieving process. When working with some terminal or bereft clients, consider whether exploring these facets of death would be helpful in their acceptance of the reality of death.

Conversely, an *external* resource—the development of close, loving relationships—buffers an individual against death anxiety (Mikulincer, Florian, & Hirschberger, 2007). Why? First, the denial of one's mortality is a major stimulus for developing and maintaining close relationships (Mikulincer et al., 2007). Second, maintaining close relationships shields one from death anxiety, whereas losing a close relationship increases the salience of death anxiety (Mikulincer et al., 2007). Third, attachment security tempers one's dependence on close relationships to manage death anxiety; that is, the more securely attached one is in one's relationships, the less intensely one needs to rely on relationships to manage death anxiety (Mikulincer et al., 2007). Fourth, close relationships, in their role as buffers against death anxiety, interact with other cultural phenomena and worldviews that shield one from the terror of death. In addition to helping a client internally process thoughts and feelings regarding death, you also might encourage clients to develop, maintain, or strengthen social relationships—whether friendship, familial, or romantic—as a way to manage death anxiety.

Defense Mechanisms

Because clients utilize defense mechanisms to defend against existential and death anxieties and other challenges in life, we will turn our discussion to these phenomena. In this section, we will define defense mechanisms more generally and address the major, specific defense mechanisms. Defense mechanisms are strategies used by people to manage anxiety arising from unwanted or unmanageable feelings. In psychodynamic terms, defense mechanisms are processes used in the service of the ego to manage anxiety arising from conflict between the superego and the id.

Defense mechanisms as a class are not bad. Some defense mechanisms are adaptive and healthy, whereas others are maladaptive and unhealthy. When you are working with an older client, one of the things you can do is try to identify which defense mechanisms your client uses and whether those mechanisms are healthy or unhealthy. Furthermore, you can help a client move away from using unhealthy mechanisms by replacing them with healthy mechanisms.

George Vaillant (1985), a psychiatrist at Dartmouth Medical School, organized defense mechanisms into a hierarchy comprising four levels: psychotic, immature, neurotic, and mature (see Table 4.3 and Table 4.4). *Psychotic defenses* are the most severe of the defenses, whereas *immature defenses*, though less severe, are still maladaptive. *Neurotic defenses* comprise a third class, whereas *mature defenses* are the most adaptive of the defenses. Bowins (2004) suggested that the more adaptive and healthy defense mechanisms are more common and serve individuals better than those that are more severe and dysfunctional (and less common).

Some of the more common, empirically recognized unhealthy defense mechanisms include depression, denial, projection, fantasy,

TABLE 4.3   Vaillant's Four Levels of Mechanisms of Defense

Psychotic	Immature	Neurotic	Mature
Delusional thinking	Acting out	Controlling	Altruism
Denial of external reality	Blocking	Displacement	Anticipation
Distortion	Dissociation	Externalization	Asceticism
	Hypochondriasis	Inhibition	Humor
	Introjection	Intellectualization	Sublimation
	Passive-aggression	Rationalization	Suppression
	Projection	Reaction formation	
	Regression	Repression	
	Schizoid fantasy	Sexualization	
		Somatization	

Note: Vaillant, G. E., "An Empirically Derived Hierarchy of Adaptive Mechanisms and Its Usefulness as a Potential Diagnostic Axis," *Acta Psychiatrica Scandinavica Supplementum*, 71(319), 171–180, 1985.

TABLE 4.4   Defense Mechanisms and Definitions

Mechanism	Definition
Acting out	Engaging in a negative behavior in place of allowing oneself to acknowledge feelings
Altruism	Care or benefit of another without concern for self
Anticipation	Responding to the environment through emotions felt prior to rather than subsequent to consequences
Asceticism	Exercise of denial or self-discipline
Blocking	Unanticipated disruption in the flow of one's thoughts
Controlling	The belief that one has control over all areas of one's life
Delusional thinking	Grossly inaccurate perception of reality, often in the psychotic range and persecutory
Denial of external reality	Refusal to acknowledge external realities
Displacement	Expressing feelings toward a person (or other being, such as a pet) that are too uncomfortable to be expressed toward the actual object
Dissociation	Loss of sense of self, often associated with a loss of sense of time
Distortion	Misinterpretation of a situation
Externalization	Attributing one's behaviors to external phenomena
Humor	Finding examples of humor, playfulness, irony, or the comical in oneself, others, or the environment
Hypochondriasis	Chronic belief that one is physically ill or suffering from one or more illnesses
Inhibition	Excessive restriction of one's range of affect or behaviors
Intellectualization	Focus on reason and logic to the exclusion of feelings
Introjection	Assuming the feelings or thoughts of another
Passive-aggression	Acting aggressively toward another or the environment, not actively, but by the absence of prosocial behavior
Projection	Shifting one's own repressed thoughts and feelings onto another person or being
Rationalization	Justification of one's thoughts, feelings, or behaviors through reason, even if implausible
Reaction formation	Expressing the opposite (typically negative) feelings and behaviors to one's actual, though repressed, feelings

TABLE 4.4 (*Continued*)   Defense Mechanisms and Definitions

Mechanism	Definition
Regression	Movement in thought, feeling, or behavior to one experienced at an earlier, less mature stage of life
Repression	Unconscious holding back of unpalatable thoughts or feelings
Schizoid fantasy	Withdrawing into fantasy to avoid interpersonal interactions
Sexualization	Assuming carnality in or imposing carnality on a person or situation
Somatization	Somatic (i.e., bodily) complaint
Sublimation	Engaging in socially desirable acts or actions in place of unmanageable feelings
Suppression	Conscious holding back of unpalatable thoughts or feelings

Note: The list of mechanisms of defense is from Vaillant (1985). The definitions are my own.

identification, and intellectualization (Luborsky & Barrett, 2006). *Depression* as a defense is a response to unpleasant thoughts and feelings by shutting down, giving up, and having a general passivity. *Denial* is a phenomenon whereby a person rejects an objective reality. For example, a person who is the survivor of the traumatic death of a loved one may deny that loved one's death.[4] *Projection* is the *placing onto another* those thoughts and feelings that one finds distressing. For example, a client who is hostile toward others may project and believe that others are hostile toward him or her. *Fantasy* is thought that is not associated with reality. One may, for example, fantasize that one is rich and engage in "rich people" behaviors even though one is spending oneself into insurmountable debt. *Identification* is the nonconscious modeling of one's behaviors on those of another person or group of people. For example, an older client may begin to dress more and more like her beloved counselor. *Intellectualization* is emotionally detached mentation that allows a person to avoid unpleasant thoughts, feelings, or behaviors. For example, an older client who was abused as a child may talk about the abuse in an emotionally detached way.

Adaptive defense mechanisms include humor, anticipation, suppression, altruism, and sublimation. *Humor* is the ability to use laughter or jokes to deal with a difficult situation or the capacity to see the lighter side of a difficult situation. It is the healthy expression of thoughts or behaviors that result in a general sense of lightness and feeling good. It is expressed through making a funny statement, telling a joke or funny story, or engaging in a nonharmful behavior that is funny or laughable. Healthy humor is not denigrating, hostile, or off-putting of others or oneself. *Anticipation* refers to the sense of looking forward to something (e.g., a vacation, trip, date, or some other future action). *Suppression* is the conscious and deliberate choice to ignore *for a period of time* a distressing thought, feeling, or behavior, such as worrying about some of the details of one's upcoming hospitalization and surgery. It is the conscious act of temporarily putting a difficult issue to the side until a time when one can more effectively address it. The key to suppression is that it is a conscious decision, unlike repression, which is an unconscious activity. *Altruism* is the channeling of energies into doing good acts, such as teaching someone how to do something, volunteering with a charitable organization, or engaging in some other activity that benefits another. *Sublimation* involves the channeling of unpleasant sexual or aggressive urges into socially acceptable activities. It is the utilization of one's energies in alternative, constructive activities. An example is the person who works out his or her hostility through physical culture, such as playing tennis or some other sport. You will oftentimes hear such people say that they got out some of their negative feelings after playing a sport.

Segal, Coolidge, and Mizuno (2007) categorized each of the 26 defense mechanisms into one of five categories, including maladaptive and adaptive. Maladaptive defense mechanisms included acting out, inhibition, passive-aggression, projection, regression, and withdrawal. Adaptive defenses comprised humor, sublimation, and suppression.

For this discussion let us define the maladaptive defenses of acting out, inhibition, passive-aggression, regression, and withdrawal.[5] *Acting out* typically involves impulsively engaging in an antisocial activity. *Inhibition* is the constriction of behaviors; it is restraint or holding back, an inability to act spontaneously. *Passive-aggression* in some ways is the opposite of acting out, for it entails withholding a behavior as an act of hostility. *Regression* means acting in a childish or childlike way. It is acting in a way that is a reversion to an earlier time in life. *Withdrawal* means the removing of oneself from cues that cause pain and distress. An example would be refusing to go out with married friends after the loss of a spouse because their marriage is a reminder of the fact that one is now alone.

Segal et al. (2007) found no differences based on age for adaptive defense mechanisms. That is, older adults were just as likely as younger adults to utilize adaptive defenses. Conversely, younger adults were more likely than older adults to use the maladaptive defenses of acting out, passive-aggression, and regression. Segal et al.'s (2007) good news is that their study suggests that the use of adaptive defenses—humor, sublimation, and suppression—tends not to change over the course of one's life, whereas maladaptive defenses—notably acting out, passive-aggression, and regression—tend to be utilized less frequently as one ages. This suggests that once someone acquires an adaptive defense mechanism, he or she tends to keep that mechanism, even into old age (Segal et al., 2007). Perhaps those clients who utilize unhealthy defense mechanisms may be particularly amenable to change, especially in old age. This argues for working with older clients to replace maladaptive defenses with adaptive defenses.

We have explored separately psychodynamic theory and existential theory, death anxiety, and defense mechanisms. Psychodynamic and existential theory can be integrated in considering mechanisms of defense and death anxiety (Firestone, 1993). In his article "Individual Defenses Against Death Anxiety," Firestone (1993) described specific mechanisms that can come into play to defend against death anxiety. Congruent with psychodynamic conceptualizations, he believed that trauma early in life results in the development of defense mechanisms. Specifically, he noted that North American children grow up in families where spouses defend against their own death anxiety by withdrawing from authentic relationships with each other and maintain a relationship lacking in "intimacy and closeness" (Firestone, 1993, pp. 502–503). Furthermore, these families exist within the dominant culture, which itself is rich in the denial of death. Children, in response to being frustrated and emotionally deprived, respond through the defense mechanism of *fantasy*; namely, they fantasize "connection with the mother" (Firestone, 1993, p. 503). When the child learns of death, the child's now flawed belief in his or her omnipotence is annihilated, and he or she *withdraws* his or her authentic feelings for others and replaces them with the *fantasy* of connection and self-parenting.

To not feel overwhelmed by the reality of one's ultimate death, an individual will use defense mechanisms, notably those of denial and displacement (Firestone, 1993), broadly defined. An individual may deny that death will occur or may displace the fear of death onto some other issue. *Displacement* means focusing an object of concern onto something else. In this case, it may mean that instead of experiencing anxiety at the thought of death, one experiences fear, for example, that one will "fail" at retirement or in one's relationship with one's spouse.

Firestone proposed a set of six defenses specifically utilized to defend against death anxiety; these are what he called "self-nourishing habits," "preoccupation with pseudoproblems," "vanity–specialness," "addictive couple bonds," "gene survival," and "progressive self-denial" (Firestone, 1993, pp. 506–512). *Self-nourishing habits*, as a defense, is the repression of feelings and the withdrawal of close emotional ties to family through the use of drugs and other means. *Preoccupation with pseudoproblems* is a specific manifestation of the mechanism of displacement, where an individual, instead of squarely acknowledging his or her fear of death, develops "agoraphobia, cardiac-arrest phobia, animal phobias, and most particularly ... claustrophobia" (Firestone, 1993, p. 508). *Vanity–specialness* is a defense of fantasy. The fantasy is of a grandiose self—a sense that one is in some way special, perhaps even very special. This defense typically masks feelings of inadequacy. Taken to its extreme, it can manifest in the belief that death happens only to other people. *Addictive couple bonds* refers to a defense in which members of a couple appear to desire closeness and intimacy, yet in reality they reject it. They replace authentic closeness and intimacy with a fantasy of escaping "death through merging with another person," the loved one (Firestone, 1993, p. 509). *Gene survival* refers to the defense phenomenon of the belief that children belong to their parents. It is a fantasy of escaping death through parent–child merger. Finally, *progressive self-denial* is an acting-out defense by what Firestone called "committing small suicides on a daily basis ... in an attempt to accommodate to death anxiety" (Firestone, 1993, p. 511). That is, instead of being cognizant of death, a person, in some small way, acts out a representation of his or her death. As defenses are loosened, death anxiety increases, but increases in self-actualization and individuation reduce death anxiety (Firestone, 1993).

Role of the Counselor

How do you apply your insights, knowledge, and wisdom as they relate to death anxiety to work with older adults? Wass and Meyers (1982) provided some very practical suggestions. First, they recommended that counselors be self-aware of their own attitudes, thoughts, feelings, and behaviors regarding aging, death, and grief. What are the thoughts we tell ourselves about aging and death, both that of others and our own? To what extent do we experience dread or anxiety around aging or death? What behaviors follow from our thoughts and feelings? How honest are we with ourselves?

Second, Wass and Meyers (1982) indicated that counselors should take on two roles regarding death. One role is that of providing comfort and help. They recommended death education—whether formal or informal, whether through books and articles or other counselors and caregivers—to help us improve our ability to provide the comfort and help needed around death. Death education might help not only our professional development but also our personal development, for the other role that a counselor plays is that of *griever* him- or herself when a client dies (Wass & Meyers, 1982).[6] Healthy grieving is more likely to occur when one has worked through one's own thoughts and feelings about death. In the words of the ancient Greeks, "Know thyself." Healthy grieving might also be more likely when a counselor attends the memorial service for a client who has died, utilizes professional helpers to work through the grief, or relies on a social network for support.

When dealing with death anxiety, counselors must utilize their entire range of listening skills and communication interventions (Wass & Meyers, 1982). As counselors we must pay special attention to the nonverbal (and typically less conscious) cues given to clients that indicate our true attitudes and feelings toward death (Wass & Meyers, 1982).

Finally, Wass and Meyers (1982) indicated the importance of counselor flexibility and ability to customize counseling interventions to meet the specific and contextual needs of a client. They recommended the therapeutic use of life review and reminiscence to help dying persons work through conflicts and become less fearful of death (Wass & Meyers, 1982).

CHAPTER SUMMARY

In this chapter, we reviewed basic Freudian concepts and then explored three neo-Freudian traditions—ego psychology, object relations, and self psychology. We addressed existential theory, especially in terms of death anxiety, and its correlate in terror management theory. We identified major types of defense mechanisms and addressed how some of them may be adaptive, whereas others may be maladaptive. We drew links between psychodynamic and existential theory, death anxiety, and defense mechanisms. Finally, we addressed some ways in which counselors can utilize this information when working with older clients. In Chapter 5, we will address practical issues in dealing with transference and countertransference and other phenomena that arise within the context of counseling older adults.

CASE STUDY

Erik is a 62-year-old man who comes to you with complaints of restlessness and increasing difficulties in leaving the house. He describes himself as "driven" and "a bit of a workaholic" and also states that he is increasingly irritated by his coworkers, most of whom are younger than he. Erik immigrated to the United States from Germany when he was 25 to attend graduate school. He remained in the United States after graduation, found gainful employment as an electrical engineer, and became a citizen. He married and had two children, now in their 30s. He has worked since age 27 and has had a very comfortable life, but he keeps asking himself, "Is this all there is? I've worked hard, I've married, I've seen my children through school, but I feel like 'so what?' My boss doesn't appreciate my work. My kids are lazy. My wife and I used to be close; at least, I think we used to be." He describes a childhood in which his father was rather distant and, in Erik's words, "a stranger, someone who never talked about his own childhood or his own parents." According to Erik, his mother was the only "true parent" he had, though she was never satisfied with Erik's accomplishments, whether in school, work, or his personal life. You notice that as Erik has been delving deeper into his concerns, he has been coming to his counseling sessions later and later. You are considering whether to bring his tardiness to his attention.

Questions

1. Is Erik using any defense mechanisms? If so, which one(s)? Are they adaptive? Maladaptive?
2. Do his defenses need to be addressed? If so, as his counselor, what would you do?
3. Describe Erik in terms of good-enough parenting. Feel free to speculate.
4. Discuss the case of Erik from a self psychology perspective. How, if at all, might twinship, idealized parental imago, or mirroring needs have or have not been met?
5. Identify any existential concerns present in the case of Erik.
6. Discuss the case of Erik from the perspective of terror management theory.

CHAPTER QUESTIONS

1. What do you make of Freud's criticism of analysis for people middle-aged and older, especially given that Freud was himself middle-aged when he made that statement?
2. What is the main difference between orthodox psychoanalysis and ego psychology?
3. Describe the central tenet of object relations.
4. From an object relations perspective, do you project onto current relationships the patterns of social interaction you learned in childhood? If so, give an example.

5. Define mirroring, idealized parental imago, and twinship needs, and give an example of each.
6. What are the four levels of mechanisms of defense? What is the most "healthy" level? What is the least "healthy" level?
7. Define defense mechanisms. Define three healthy and three unhealthy defense mechanisms, and give an example of each.
8. Give an example of the sublimation of the sexual urge.
9. Can one identify one's own mechanisms of defense? Why or why not? Can you identify which mechanisms of defense *you* typically use?
10. What might be the mortality implications for a family visiting a loved one in nursing care too frequently or not frequently enough?
11. What does "existence precedes essence" mean?
12. How can a person reduce existential terror?
13. Identify Firestone's six defenses against death anxiety, and give an example of each.

GLOSSARY

Anna Freud: Sigmund Freud's daughter, focused on identifying the influence of defense mechanisms on human experience.

Conscious: includes any and all thoughts of which one is aware.

Death anxiety: is the (usually) unconscious fear of cessation of being.

Defense mechanism: is a thought, feeling, or behavior that is used to avoid the distress of sexual or aggressive drives.

Drives: are impulses to act; according to orthodox psychoanalysis there are two drives—the sexual drive and the aggressive drive.

Ego: functions as the mediator of the psyche, taming the id's impulses to satisfy the superego's need for restraint.

Ego psychology: focuses on the mediating function of the ego, rather than on the impulses of the id (the traditional focus of psychoanalysis).

Existential anxiety: is the fear that life ultimately is meaningless and/or the fear of cessation of being (death).

Free association: is the psychoanalytic technique of speaking whatever comes into one's mind, in the belief that this will uncover unconscious processes.

Good-enough parenting: is the idea that children do not need to be raised by perfect parents; rather, they need to be raised by parents who generally provide for the child but move into the background from time to time, which allows children gradually to learn to function socially on their own.

Heinz Kohut: was the moving force behind self psychology, an offshoot of psychoanalytic theory that focuses on the potentially corrective value of the client–therapist relationship.

Id: is the wild child of the psyche, containing the sexual and aggressive impulses.

Idealizing: is the experience of a parental figure as a calm and powerful protector.

Mirroring: is the experience of being valued and having a parental figure take delight and joy in the child.

Object relations: is a branch of psychodynamic therapy that focuses on the self as it relates to objects (i.e., other people).

Preconscious: comprises mentations that are not presently, but can become, conscious.

Repetition compulsion: is the impulse to engage in painful ways of relating to others as a repetition of the ways of relating learned in childhood.

Self psychology: is a branch of psychodynamic therapy that focuses on meaning and social relationships in the development and maintenance of psychological well-being.

Superego: is the parental arm of the psyche, the font of morality and self-restraint.

Terror management theory: is a school of thought that posits that humans respond to death anxiety either by adhering to their cultural worldview and/or by working to increase their self-esteem.

Transference: is a phenomenon noted by Freud in which a client projects onto a therapist unwanted thought and feelings.

Twinship: is the experience of oneself as being like the parental figure, hence, as belonging.

Unconscious: is composed of those mentations that are too fearful or distressing to be allowed into conscious thought.

FURTHER INFORMATION

1. An exceptional source for learning about psychodynamic approaches to counseling is Mitchell and Black's *Freud and Beyond* (New York: Basic Books, 1995).
2. A highly readable integration of self psychology and object relations with humanistic psychology is Kahn's *Between Therapist and Client* (New York: Freeman, 1997).

3. The best resource for considering meaning in counseling continues to be Yalom's moving and beautifully written classic *Existential Psychotherapy* (New York: Basic Books, 1980).
4. Yalom also has an engaging book that explores death anxiety and its manifestations: *Staring at the Sun: Overcoming the Terror of Death* (San Francisco: Jossey-Bass, 2008).
5. A historical look at perspectives toward death in Western culture is found in Aries's *Western Attitudes Toward Death* (Baltimore: Johns Hopkins University Press, 1974).
6. Terror management theory derives from Becker's seminal work *The Denial of Death* (New York: Free Press, 1997), a classic in the field of death studies.

NOTES

1. In counseling older adults, transference phenomena will occur in the context of an older client projecting oftentimes onto a younger counselor (see Knight, 2004). We will discuss transference (and its counterpart countertransference) more fully in Chapter 5.
2. On this dimension, self psychology shares a commonality with existential psychology.
3. *Imago* is just a fancy word for image or figure. To make it more accessible, we should call Kohut's concept the "idealized parent figure." Unlike Kohut, we should strive to eschew obfuscation.
4. There is a particularly poignant example of denial in an episode of HBO's *Six Feet Under* (Ball, 2004) in which the grieving son, Nate, follows a dog to a psychic who tells him that his deceased wife, Lisa, is really alive. Nate, an otherwise rational character, spends the episode in denial of her death.
5. The maladaptive defense mechanism of projection and the three adaptive defenses of humor, sublimation, and suppression have been defined above.
6. To this latter role let us add *empathic griever* when working with a client who is experiencing loss through death of a loved one.

CHAPTER 5

Transference and Other Counseling Processes With Older Adults

We do not see things as they are, rather we see them as we are.

—The Talmud

I was raised to believe that how I saw myself was more important than how other people saw me.

—Anwar Sadat

CHAPTER OVERVIEW

In this chapter we will explore in more depth elements of the process of counseling, drawing on understandings rooted in psychodynamic theory. We will explore the phenomena of transference and countertransference, especially as they relate to younger counselors working with older clients, and will look closely at Bob Knight's analysis of the forms that transference and countertransference take when working with older adults. We will discuss how to work with transference and countertransference to the benefit of our clients. We also will address the therapeutic alliance, resistance, working through, and termination.

Have you ever been involved in a minor fender bender, where two cars barely bump one another? And even though there is no damage to the other person's car—not even a scratch—he begins shouting that you are a terrible person, you should not be allowed to drive, and so on. You think to yourself, "What's up with this? This person doesn't even know

me. If he did, he would know I'm not at all like what he assumes I am."
If you have had this kind of experience, you have been on the receiving
end of a phenomenon akin to transference.

Have you ever met someone and immediately—in that moment—*fell
in love* (or so you thought)? Did you assume that the other person had
characteristics you desired in a mate even though you did not know the
person? As you got to know the person more, did you have the experience of seeing more and more of his or her true self rather than the idealized characteristics you placed on him or her? If so, you have had an
experience akin to countertransference.

Transference and countertransference are two sides of the same coin.
They both refer to unconscious *material*—repetitive relational patterns,
templates, or recurrent themes (Teyber, 2006). Transference refers to the
templates that clients bring into the counseling room and through which
they see the counselor and counseling relationship. **Countertransference**
refers to the templates counselors bring into the consulting room and
through which they see the client and the counseling relationship. Kahn
(1997) called these the "two hidden dramas" that are present—one in
the unconscious of the client and the other in the unconscious of the
counselor (p. 127). In other words, in addition to the manifest (i.e., evident, conscious, rational) process in counseling, there also is a latent
(i.e., hidden, unconscious, nonrational) process in counseling—transference and countertransference.

Transference occurs when clients unconsciously project onto a counselor a relationship template that has its origins in an earlier client familial relationship. Typically, when a counselor and client work together,
the type of transference is related to the client's relationship with his or
her parent or significant guardian figure. Countertransference is similar to transference, the difference being that countertransference is the
unconscious projection made by the counselor onto the client. In either
case—transference or countertransference—the parties involved do not
see each other as they are; instead they see each other through the dis-
torted filter of their earlier life experience.

Oftentimes counselors are older than their middle-aged or younger
clients, and so it is easier for clients to experience parental transference toward their counselor. Transference phenomena may be unique
when working with older adults, however, in that it is an older client
who oftentimes works with a younger counselor. Hence, the older client
projects onto a younger counselor (see Knight, 2004). Between an older
client and a younger counselor, transference can be the typical phenomenon, where the client perceives the counselor as a parental figure, or
it can be reversed. Hildebrand (1986, cited in Biggs, 1998) coined the
term **inverted transference** to describe the phenomenon of an older client

responding to a younger clinician as a *child figure* (i.e., a son or daughter figure) rather than as a parent figure.

TRANSFERENCE

Transference comprises the recurrent relational patterns, repetitive themes, or templates that a client brings into the consultation room and through which the client sees and experiences the counselor, the counseling relationship, and the world. It can be conceptualized as client placement of an old template onto a new person (the counselor) in the unconscious hope of experiencing again a person from the client's past (see Roth, 1990). It is experiencing the counselor as if he or she were a parental or other significant figure from the client's childhood (see Gabbard, 1990).

Transference is one side of the transference–countertransference coin. It is one partner in the two-partner dance played by the client–counselor dyad. Below we will look at transference from several perspectives, including that of Freud and his concepts of templates and repetition compulsion; John Bowlby's and Mary Ainsworth's concept of attachment styles; Karen Horney's three interpersonal interaction styles; and Heinz Kohut's mirroring, idealized parental imago, and twinship transference. We will conclude with a review of Bob Knight's thoughtful and nuanced understanding of the particular manifestations of transference when working with older adults.

Freud's Templates and Repetition Compulsion

Transference is the lens through which the client perceives the counselor. Historically, transference was conceptualized as comprising two components that have their roots in Freudian theory: templates and the repetition compulsion (Kahn, 1997).[1] *Templates* refer to the blueprints or patterns we establish early on in life that guide us in our interactions with others later in life (Kahn, 1997). For example, if a client had trusting relationships with his or her parent as a child, he or she likely would assume that the new relationships he or she develops later with significant others, *including those in late life*, will be trustworthy. This could carry over into counseling by a client interacting with the counselor in ways that assume the counselor is trustworthy, even if this template is a distortion. Transference, in fact, can be conceptualized as "distorting reality either by demonizing or deifying" another person (Araoz, 2006, p. 81). Transference is based not on the counselor who is its object but on experiences learned by the client with an early parental figure.

The *repetition compulsion* is the urge or impulse to replicate later in life, including in late life, troubling relationship patterns from the past; it is the need to recreate "situations that had a bad ending" (Kahn, 1997, p. 25). If a client chronically was ignored by his mother in childhood, when he grows up, he likely will develop relationships marked by being ignored by the significant other. This could carry over into counseling. The client may interact with the counselor in ways that result in the likelihood that the counselor will ignore him. Of course, all of this would occur unconsciously by the client (and it is hoped would be recognized and worked with by the counselor).

Anna Freud (1966) referred to transference as "impulses experienced by the patient in his relation with the analyst which are not newly created by the objective analytic situation but have their source in early ... object relations and are now merely received under the influence of the repetition compulsion" (p. 18). Similarly, Michael Kahn (1997) defined transference as the experience in which "the client transfers onto the therapist the old patterns and repetitions" or in which the client projects onto the therapeutic endeavor how he or she wishes an earlier relationship had been (p. 27).

Transference is a pervasive phenomenon that plays out in every one of us in our day-to-day lives (see Araoz, 2006; Kahn, 1997). Transference is the relationship pattern forged in one's early relationship with a significant parental figure that becomes de facto the way of interacting with significant others later in life. Relationships throughout one's life—including those in late life—develop as variations on a theme learned in early life (Kahn, 1997). As an explanation of circumstances that create patterns early in life, John Bowlby and Mary Ainsworth developed a theory of attachment styles.

John Bowlby's and Mary Ainsworth's Attachment Styles

John Bowlby, an English psychiatrist and psychoanalyst, and **Mary Ainsworth,** an American developmental psychologist, developed and refined a theory of attachment to describe infant experiences (Ainsworth, 1969, 1971; Ainsworth, Blehar, Waters, & Wall, 1978; Bowlby, 1988). In their view, an individual develops one of three attachment styles in infancy. The attachment styles are related to the type of interactions a child has with his or her *mother* in infancy (Mitchell & Black, 1995), though in our discussion we will broaden this to include the attachment styles a child would have with his or her significant parental figure or guardian. Bowlby believed that the fundamental *anxiety* present in life is separation anxiety, with *anger* being a reaction to separation, and

TABLE 5.1   Bowlby's and Ainsworth's Attachment Styles

Type	Qualities
Secure	Can be separated from guardian without tremendous distress; wants to be comforted by guardian when afraid; is happy when he or she is reunited with guardian; can interact with strangers but prefers the company of guardian; can explore the environment using the guardian as a secure base
Anxious resistant	Distrustful of strangers; extreme distress when separated from guardian; clingy; fearful of abandonment; unable to be comforted by reunion with guardian
Anxious avoidant	Little interest in guardian; does not seek guardian for comfort; no preference for guardian over stranger

Note: Ainsworth (1969, 1971), Bowlby (1988).

detachment from the need for attachment to the mother being the primary defense (Mitchell & Black, 1995).

Although there are many subsequent relationships (including changed relationships with guardians or parental figures, spouses, other family, or friends) that result in shifts in a learned attachment style, quite possibly the style acquired in infancy will carry through to childhood, adolescence, adulthood, and even into later life. Bowlby's and Ainsworth's three styles are secure attachment, anxious resistant attachment, and anxious avoidant attachment (see Table 5.1).

Secure Attachment. **Secure attachment** is marked by several qualities. First, the infant shows an appropriate level of distress (neither detached nor overly clingy) when separated from his or her guardian. He or she seeks comfort from the guardian if he or she becomes afraid. He or she expresses joy or delight when reunited with the guardian. Furthermore, he or she interacts comfortably with strangers but prefers the company of his or her guardian. If a child experiences secure attachment in infancy, when he or she grows up, he or she will be able to develop secure attachments in adulthood and late life. An older client who has experienced secure attachment may present to the counselor as an individual who is trusting of others, shows appropriate levels of self-esteem (neither overestimating nor undervaluing his or her worth), is able to communicate feelings, and can interact comfortably in social settings. These qualities clearly are highly desirable in a client as they may facilitate therapeutic outcomes.

Anxious Resistant Attachment. Anxious resistant attachment is evident in an infant's distrust of strangers, extreme distress when separated from the guardian, fear of exploration of the environment, fear of abandonment by the guardian, and an inability to find comfort in being reunited with the guardian. He or she is not sure that his or her guardian will be available if needed (Bowlby, 1988). If an infant experiences anxious resistant attachment, he or she may continue to develop ambivalent, insecure attachments in adulthood and late life. An older client whose attachment style has been anxious resistant may present in counseling as a client who is more generally distrustful of others, fears abandonment by others, and has a very difficult time responding to termination.

Anxious Avoidant Attachment. Anxious avoidant attachment is evident in the infant's shunning of or lack of interest in the guardian. In this case, the infant does not seek out the guardian for comforting and has no preference for the guardian over a stranger. He or she "expects to be rebuffed" by the guardian (Bowlby, 1988, p. 124). If a child experiences anxious avoidant attachment in infancy, he or she may develop avoidant, insecure attachments in adulthood and late life. A older client whose attachment style has been anxious avoidant may present in counseling—if he or she even enters counseling—as being disinterested and detached, expressing self-sufficiency, and having low expectations.

One of these types of attachment—secure, anxious avoidant, and anxious resistant—will predominate in your style of being as well as in that of your older clients. When you look honestly at yourself, are you more of a secure, anxious avoidant, or anxious resistant counselor? You may ask yourself this question about each of your older clients, too. The themes carried forward from infancy may present themselves in the stories the client tells about him- or herself, about others, and even about the counseling relationship. Next, we will explore the interpersonal interaction types identified by Karen Horney and whether they bear any resemblance to Bowlby's and Ainsworth's attachment patterns.

Karen Horney's Three Interpersonal Interaction Types

Karen Horney (1945/1992), a distinguished psychiatrist and psychoanalyst, conceptualized clients as roughly falling into one of three patterns: moving toward people, moving against people, or moving away from people—corresponding to compliance, aggression, or detachment (see Table 5.2). *Moving toward* people are individuals who deal with their anxieties by moving toward others, that is, by seeking affection and approval. In other words, they need to be liked by others. Moving toward people are looking for a significant *other* who will be their savior and protector—someone who will approve of them, love them, and care for them. Moving toward people are compliant, placaters, individuals who lose themselves for their idealized other. They tend not to criticize or

TABLE 5.2   Horney's Three Neurotic Types

Type	Qualities
Moving toward	Compliant; needs to be loved, cared for, rescued; looks to others for self-worth; dependent; self-effacing; represses aggression
Moving against	Aggressive; controlling; exploitative; rejects the warm feelings of others; needs to fight, to be superior; represses warm feelings
Moving away from	Detached; estranged from others and self; nonparticipatory; needs to feel autonomous; needs privacy and independence; feels superior toward others; suppresses feelings

Note: Horney, K., *Our Inner Conflicts: A Constructive Theory of Neurosis,* Norton, New York, 1945/1992.

make demands on others. Moving toward people tend to denigrate themselves, take blame, and believe that others are superior to them. They look to others for their senses of self-worth. In other words, they look to how other people see them, not how they see themselves, to evaluate their self-worth. Horney noted that this type carries a set of values: love, self-sacrifice, generosity, and so forth. This type also tends to have repressed aggressive impulses. The moving toward pattern or template allows individuals to deal with their anxieties by presenting themselves with a facade of wholeness and connectedness. The moving toward dominant theme is "If only [I] can find a person who loves [me], *everything* will be all right" (Horney, 1945/1992, p. 59). Moving toward people see the world and the counselor through this *need for love and approval* lens.

In contrast to moving toward people are *moving against* people. Moving against people are those who deal with their anxieties by aggressing toward others. These people tend to think that it is others who are aggressive, to have a need to control others, to feel strong, to use and exploit others, to not feel or demonstrate feelings of warmth and love, to show disregard for the feelings of others, to fight, to reject the warmth or love of others, and to be recognized and honored. The moving against person's motto is "Might makes right" (Horney, 1945/1992, p. 69).

Finally, *moving away from* people are those who deal with their anxieties through detachment from others. The moving away from people are estranged from others, estranged from themselves, lifeless, observers of but not participants in life, and emotionally isolated—neither solicitous nor volatile. They have a strong desire for autonomy and self-reliance, privacy, and independence. Moving away from people dislike being obligated toward others, minimize their own needs in order to make independence *easier,* reject convention, and are compelled to feel superior to others. They want to be recognized as extraordinary, without demonstrating such; they need to feel unique or special—better than others. They are inclined to suppress emotions and to focus more on reasoning or intellectual endeavor, becoming something akin to a human computer. They are intensely defensive when it comes to their detached stance toward life. The moving away from person's mantra might be "Do not touch me," a message implying both superiority to and detachment from others.

Just as you can consider a client's transference as being influenced by his or her secure, anxious resistant, or anxious avoidant attachment style from infancy, so too can you consider a client's transference as being marked by either moving toward, moving against, or moving away from interpersonal types.

Consider, too, that Horney's moving toward type roughly corresponds with Bowlby's and Ainsworth's anxious resistant attachment style. The moving away from type is similar to the anxious avoidant attachment style. Although the moving against type does not have a clear corollary with a particular attachment style, we might consider that it results from acquiring an insecure rather than secure attachment style. Together, Bowlby's and Ainsworth's three attachment styles as well as Horney's three interpersonal types represent two perspectives on understanding transference. Heinz Kohut offers yet a third, though related, conceptualization.

Heinz Kohut and Mirroring, Idealizing, and Twinship Transferences

In Chapter 4, we discussed Heinz Kohut's conceptualization of mirroring, the idealized parental imago, and twinship experiences in childhood. Kohut understood transference to comprise mirroring, an idealized parental imago, and/or twinship. *Mirroring transference* occurs when clients perceive the analyst (or, in our case, the counselor) to be nurturing to the extent that the clients "can begin to feel more seen, more real, and more internally substantial" (Mitchell & Black, 1995, p. 161; see also Gabbard, 1990). That is, although the clients know that they are separate from the counselor, they believe that the counselor has importance only from the perspective of having the potential to meet their needs (see St. Clair, 1986). *Idealized parental imago transference* is the phenomenon of clients perceiving the therapist to be powerful and perfect and "feel[ing themselves] to be increasingly strong and important by virtue of [their] connection to this powerful and important other" (Mitchell & Black, 1995, p. 161; see also St. Clair, 1986; see also Gabbard, 1990). *Twinship transference* describes the phenomenon of clients perceiving the therapist as like themselves in some important way(s)—for example, "feeling a like-gendered analyst shares a sensibility about being male or female" (Mitchell & Black, 1995, p. 161). In other words, a client presupposes that the counselor is like him- or herself (St. Clair, 1986).

Kohut believed that, over time, clients who experience mirroring, an idealized parental imago, and twinship transferences will acquire a certain liveliness, a *joie de vivre* (Mitchell & Black, 1995, p. 161). Kohut therefore advocated for clients who experience the therapist as a parental figure. He believed that if clients have this experience, they will experience the sense of being unique, safe, and like others.

Kohut, however, was a subjectivist, not an objectivist; a relativist, not a positivist; and collaborative, not authoritarian (Fosshage, 1998). Because of this, he proposed that therapists utilize empathy when working with clients. This was in contrast to the cool, distant demeanor of classical Freudian analysts. By utilizing empathy, Kohut meant that therapists should try "to listen and understand from within the vantage point of the [client]" (Fosshage, 1998, p. 3).

For Kohut, being a therapist was not about being the *tabula rasa*; rather it was about being an empathic *other* seeking to understand his or her client's subjective reality, especially as it relates to the lack of development in mirroring, the idealized parental imago, and twinship (Mitchell & Black, 1995). This is a subtle point that deserves thoughtful consideration.

Through what Kohut called *transmuting internalization*,[2] a client can—over time and with the experience of letdowns in the therapist from time to time—*internalize* the experiences of mirroring, idealizing, and twinship and thus be back on the path to "vitality, meaning, and creativity" (Mitchell & Black, 1995, p. 169). In fact, it is through this resolution of deficits in mirroring, idealizing, and twinship that a client develops a healthy self (Magnavita, 2008). This can be as true for older adults as it is for younger adults. For Kohut, *insight* into the needs one lacked in childhood was not enough to engender change; rather, clients need new interpersonal experiences for change to take place (see Baker & Baker, 1987; see also Kahn, 1997).

Our discussion up to this point has been general enough that it could be applicable to individuals in early adulthood, middle age, and later life. But is there anything unique to transference and countertransference when they occur within a therapeutic relationship with an older client? With no doubt, I would venture that Bob Knight would say, "Yes."

Bob Knight's Transference Templates With Older Adults

Bob Knight (2004), a most distinguished professor of gerontology and psychology at the University of Southern California, has written

TABLE 5.3   Older Client–Younger Counselor Transference and
Countertransference

Phenomenon	Expression
Transference	Child, grandchild, parent, spouse at a younger age, authority figure, erotic
Countertransference	Parent, grandparent, aging, dependency, and death anxiety

Note: Knight, B. G., *Psychotherapy With Older Adults* (3rd ed.), Sage, Thousand
   Oaks, CA, 2004.

extensively about transference and countertransference in work with
older adults (see Table 5.3). He identified specific ways in which transference and countertransference manifest when working with this population. An older client, for example, may on some level relate to the
counselor as if he or she were the client's child, grandchild, parent, or
spouse at a younger age or an authority figure, or he or she may experience erotic transference (Knight, 2004). Conversely, a therapist may
relate to an older client as if the client were a parent or a grandparent
or may experience countertransference related to aging, dependency,
and death anxieties (Knight, 2004). In our discussion, we will review
Knight's (2004) analysis of transference and countertransference with
older adults.

   Child Transference. A child transference occurs when an older client
relates to the counselor as if he or she were the client's child. This does
not mean that the client perceives the counselor as someone who is an
infant, in middle childhood, or in adolescence. After all, the older client's children may be middle-aged adults or in some cases older adults
themselves. If you are a middle-aged or an older adult and so is your client's child, there is a possibility of child transference. The details of the
transference may differ depending on the particular older client and on
the issues that he or she is working through with his or her children.

   Knight (2004) suggested that a common concern in child transference
revolves around whether the child will be available to care for the older
parent when the parent needs care. In counseling, this may manifest in a
concern about whether the *counselor* will be there for the client when the
client needs care. This issue essentially is about dependence on another in
late life, namely, parent dependence on a child or child figure.

   Grandchild Transference. An older client may perceive the counselor as a grandchild figure. This may occur especially when the counselor is roughly the same age as the client's grandchildren. Knight
(2004) noted that oftentimes a grandparent has an idealized image of
his or her grandchild, open communication, and candidness in talking

about the *parent's* generation (i.e., the grandparent's sons or daughters, who are the children's fathers or mothers). The grandchild transference, then, may be marked by some idealizing of the counselor, open communication with the counselor, and comfort in talking about the older client's children with the counselor. However, if there are negative feelings, thoughts, and behaviors toward the grandchild, these too may be brought into the counseling sessions and experienced by the client and counselor (Knight, 2004).

Parental Transference. When we think of transference, most commonly we think of a parent figure transference—that is, one in which the client brings into counseling elements of his or her relationship with a parent. Knight (2004) suggested that this is more common when the client is ill, disabled, or in some other ways more dependent on others or when the older client has had a challenging relationship with his or her parent that has continued to be unresolved. Also true of grandchild transference is that a counselor may use parent transference to support the client in resolving whatever problems are present, just as a good parent will support his or her children in resolving their problems. Also as in grandchild transference, older clients' unresolved difficulties with parent figures may be transferred onto the counselor and may require patience, skill, and sensitivity on the part of the counselor to help the client in the process of working through.

Spouse at a Younger Age Transference. Yet another type of transference occurs when an older client perceives the counselor as if he or she were the spouse or partner at the time roughly of the age of the counselor or at a particularly difficult and unresolved time with the spouse (Knight, 2004). For example, if you were a 45-year-old woman counseling a 75-year-old heterosexual married man, that older client might interact with you in ways similar to the ways he interacted with his wife when she was 45 years old. If you were a counselor working with a client who had unresolved negative feelings toward his or her spouse or partner (e.g., related to an affair your client's spouse or partner had a number of years ago), your older client might bring these negative feelings into the counseling session and express them toward you. Both of these are examples of transference toward the counselor as a spouse or partner when the partner was younger.

Authority Figure Transference. An older adult client may experience his or her counselor as an authority figure—someone who makes the decisions, provides the answers, and intervenes with others (Knight, 2004). Your task as counselor under these circumstances is to support your clients in making decisions for themselves, to provide their own answers to the challenges in their lives, and to act on their own behalf when engaging with others.

Erotic Transference. Erotic transference is a common transference in counseling and may occur between most any client and counselor. It is manifest through belief that one is falling in love with the counselor or has romantic or sexual feelings toward the counselor. Knight (2004) noted that erotic transference rarely is discussed in relation to older adults because of social norms that desexualize older adults. Because of this, it may be relatively easy for a counselor to fail to identify, to deny, or to dismiss erotic transference if and when it appears in the counseling relationship with an older client.

COUNTERTRANSFERENCE

Recall from above that countertransference refers to the recurrent relational patterns, repetitive themes, or templates that a counselor brings into the consultation room and through which the counselor sees and experiences the client and the world. It is the second side of the transference–countertransference coin. It is the second partner in the two-partner dance played by the client–counselor dyad. Just as a client's view of counseling is a "series of events organized ... according to his or her unconscious templates and repetitions" (Kahn, 1997), so too is the view of the counselor. Because of this, it is important for the counselor to be aware of his or her part in the counseling relationship and to continually be critical (as in *critique*) of his or her subjective view of the counseling relationship (see Kahn, 1997). Today, the definition of countertransference has expanded and includes any and all responses the counselor has to a client (Kahn, 1997).

Kahn's Four Types of Countertransference

Kahn (1997) wrote about four possible types of countertransference responses: responses that are realistic, responses to transference, responses to material that the counselor finds personally troubling, and responses that are characteristic of the counselor (see Table 5.4).

Responses that are realistic are those that most anyone would make toward a particular client (Kahn, 1997). A number of years ago, I worked with an older man who was particularly brusque; I felt a certain sense of dread when the day and hour came for our sessions. I think most anyone would have felt much the same way around him.

Responses to transference are those that are made in response to the client's transferential themes, templates, or relational sequences (see Kahn, 1997). Roth (1990) called this *empathic countertransference.*

TABLE 5.4   Sources of Countertransference

Countertransference Sources	Definition
That are realistic	Response to the client is similar to response most anyone would make to this type of client.
That are to transference	Response is made in reply to the client's transferential themes, templates, or relational sequences.
That are to material the counselor finds personally troubling	Response is made that is the result of unresolved issues the counselor has related to the material brought up by the client.
That are characteristic of the counselor	Response is a typical response made by the counselor, no matter the situation, the person, and so forth.

Note: Kahn, M., *Between Therapist and Client: The New Relationship* (Rev. ed.), Freeman, New York, 1997.

An older client, for example, may continually inquire as to whether his or her counselor will be available for sessions and whether and when the counselor will be taking vacations or holidays. The client does this because his or her template includes the worry that people will not be there for him or her when he or she needs them. The counselor responds by reassuring and feeling a sense of self-importance and being needed. That is a response to the transference.

Responses to material the counselor finds personally troubling are those made that say more about the counselor's issues than they do about the client's issues (see Kahn, 1997). They are responses made as a result of unresolved issues the counselor has in relation to the material brought up by the client. A 70-year-old client, for example, comes to a counselor wanting to discuss his mortality. The counselor, in her 30s, lost her father at an early age and has many unresolved feelings related to loss and death, so whenever the client began to speak about mortality, the counselor changes the subject.

Responses that are characteristic of the counselor are those responses that the counselor *as a person* typically makes (Kahn, 1997). Roth (1990) called this *characterological countertransference*. If a counselor has a strong need to be liked, he or she may respond to the client in ways that he or she feels will increase the likelihood that the client will like him or her. This may include such behaviors as complimenting the client, not confronting the client even when it is therapeutically appropriate to do so, and so forth.

Knight's Countertransference Templates With Older Adults

Specific countertransference relationship templates or themes include parental and grandparental relationships and responses related to the themes of aging, dependency, and death (Knight, 2004).

Parental Countertransference. If a client is older than the counselor, especially a generation older, the counselor may experience parent countertransference in which the counselor relates to the client in ways that he or she related to a significant parental figure from his or her childhood. Possible countertransference dynamics could include an overcommitment to change, irrational anger toward the client, hurt if the client questions the counselor's expertise, or most any other ways that may mark the relationship between child and parent (Knight, 2004). Furthermore, Knight (2004) indicated that one should consider parent countertransference if one experiences any of the following: a belief that therapy would not be beneficial to the client in spite of evidence to the contrary; a belief that the client has dementia in spite of evidence to the contrary; a desire for the client to receive medical rather than psychological treatment in spite of evidence to the contrary; feelings of boredom, fatigue, or helplessness when with the client; or intense emotions atypical of the counselor. The essential experience of parent countertransference is one in which the counselor has not worked through a particular issue related to his or her aging parent, including illness, decline, and/or death; the essential experience to avoid is letting personal issues interfere with the client's course of counseling (Knight, 2004).

Grandparental Countertransference. Grandparent countertransference refers to relating to the client in ways similar to how the counselor relates (or related) to his or her grandfather or grandmother. This relationship may be marked by warm feelings toward the client (as one had toward one's grandparents) and a need to protect the older client from a problematic middle generation (Knight, 2004). Although on the surface this warmth and protectiveness may seem benign, in fact it could be problematic if it leads to counselor denial of the client's real problems or nontherapeutic interactions with the client's adult children (Knight, 2004).

Aging, Dependency, and Death Anxiety Countertransference. We discussed existential concerns in Chapter 4. Knight (2004) also recognized concerns ultimately related to death and dying when he discussed countertransference issues around aging, dependency, and death.

Knight (2004) suggested that counselors who work with older adults are forced to confront and address issues that tend to remain hidden in our society—issues of aging, dependence on others, and ultimately death. He believed that counselors who work with older adults can develop an appreciation for the fact that each life has its limits and ends in death—a fact that many people do not address earlier in life, may avoid, or may be dealing with in their own personal life. He noted that those who work with older adults de facto are going to come into contact with those who are ill, dependent, and dying. Those who work with older adults are going to experience deaths of clients. To remain effective, as well as to maintain their humanity and well-being, counselors need to find ways to memorialize, grieve, and recognize their work. Experientially they are going to know aging, dependency, and death in a way that may be well beyond the comprehension of their peers (Knight, 2004).

WORKING THROUGH

How does one work with transference and countertransference? How does a counselor use the transference and countertransference for therapeutic gain? In terms of transference, a counselor must recognize or identify it, explore the roots of it, and interpret it (Knight, 2004). **Working through** the transference also means the older client incorporates the interpretation into his or her being, such that he or she can abandon his or her maladaptive templates and repetition compulsions (Kahn, 1997) and can *act* toward others in a more authentic way rather than *react* based on patterns learned early in life. Working through means collaboration between an older client and counselor, allowing the client an opportunity to try new ways of responding to situations that otherwise would trigger maladaptive relational patterns (see Teyber, 2006), to take stock of these new responses, to learn from mistakes, and to move forward. These situations can occur within the context of the counseling relationship. If an older client can successfully practice new behaviors within the context of counseling, he or she can then apply them in his or her life outside of the consulting room.

For Freud and those who have come after him, therapy was an ideal venue in which to work through the transference because templates and repetition compulsions—just as they manifest in a client's day-to-day life—also manifest in the client's relationship with the therapist (Kahn, 1997). Just as an older client's current relationships are seen and experienced through the lens of early life relationships with significant others, so too is his or her relationship with a counselor experienced through this lens.

Although Freud believed that recognizing the transference was an essential mechanism of change, the psychoanalyst Merton Gill believed that this was not enough to effect change and suggested that a client needed to have a new experience in therapy (Kahn, 1997). Specifically, the client needed to experience the old template with the therapist, convey to the therapist those feelings stimulated by the old template, and

TABLE 5.5   Obstructive Countertransference

Focus	Description
Counselor blindness	Blindness toward client's true issue or focus on counselor's personal issues
Counselor working through	Counselor uses relationship to work through his or her personal issues
Unconscious influence	Counselor unconsciously gives client queues regarding what thoughts, feelings, and behaviors are acceptable within the context of counseling
Wrong focus	Counselor focuses on his or her issues rather than client's needs
Role compliance	Counselor takes on role given to him or her by client

Note: Racker (1968, cited in Kahn, 1997, pp. 131–142).

have the therapist nondefensively discuss these feelings with the client, the result being that the client learned how old templates were created from early life relationships (Kahn, 1997).

In terms of countertransference, a counselor must recognize it and use it as a foundation for empathy toward the client. If this is not done, the countertransference can interfere with the counseling process. This "obstructive countertransference" (as opposed to "useful countertransference") could manifest in one of five ways (Racker, 1968, cited in Kahn, 1997, pp. 131–142) (see Table 5.5).

First, countertransference could blind a counselor to those issues that are most relevant to the client, or it could press the counselor to focus on his or her own issues rather than those of the client (Kahn, 1997). For example, if an older client comes to counseling to work through a discrete problem in her relationship with her spouse—say, for example, boredom after 30 years of marriage—but this is not a problem relevant to the counselor, the counselor unconsciously may ignore this problem and look for some other issue on which to work.

Second, countertransference could result in the counselor using the client to work through his or her own issues (Kahn, 1997). If a counselor, for example, is working with an older adult and the counselor has unresolved issues related to his or her emotional abuse by a parent, and the counselor experiences a parent countertransference, he or she may unconsciously try to replicate the dynamic present in childhood and try to work through *that* relationship instead of working on the actual client's real-life issue.

Third, countertransference could result in the counselor unconsciously emitting verbal or behavioral signals related to the counselor's (and not the older client's) issues that induce the client to respond in a certain way (Kahn, 1997). A counselor who is uncomfortable with older adults' sexuality, for example, may look away from a client or not respond when the client begins to speak about sexual issues; this unconscious communication could result in the older client not discussing sexual issues or the client ending counseling and looking for another counselor.

Fourth, countertransference could result in responding to the client in ways that focus on the counselor's issues and not the client's needs (Kahn, 1997). A counselor who has issues with intimacy may be formal and cool when interacting with his or her client in order to maintain a sense of distance, even if what the client needs is a warm relationship with his or her counselor.

Finally, countertransference could result in the counselor taking on the role, template, or relationship that the older client transmits to him or her (Kahn, 1997). If an older client with strong dependency needs, for example, unconsciously continues to press the counselor to act as an *authority figure*, the counselor may indeed unconsciously take on this role to a greater extent than he or she would otherwise and to the detriment of his or her client.

Kahn (1997) noted that countertransference referred to all feelings toward the client and deduced therefore that empathy, being a *feeling*, was rooted in countertransference, specifically in countertransference that was a result of transference. Kahn (1997) believed, too, that this empathy could be therapeutic if the clinician was able to maintain " 'optimal distance' from the feeling" (p. 139). By *optimal distance* Kahn meant that the empathy could be felt without overwhelming the clinician. A clinician who effectively uses countertransference is one who is aware of his or her feelings toward a client, is aware of his or her limitations in terms of awareness, seeks consultation when indicated, and is open to the reality that one's view of one's client is subjective (see Kahn, 1997). Countertransference is something not to be repressed or suppressed; it is something to be embraced as a font of understanding and compassion and used in the service of the client.

THE THERAPEUTIC ALLIANCE AND RESISTANCE

Therapeutic Alliance

The **therapeutic alliance** refers to the quality of the relationship between the counselor and the client necessary for therapeutic progress to be made. Sometimes you will hear this being described as the working alliance, the therapeutic relationship, or the working relationship. A strong therapeutic alliance early in treatment increases the likelihood of a positive outcome (see Gabbard, 1990). The therapeutic alliance is a collaborative relationship built on good rapport between counselor and client. Therapeutic success cannot be imposed on clients. Rather, clients need to engage in a collaboration with the counselor in effecting change in their lives.

The therapeutic alliance can be developed and strengthened through thoughtful use of the Rogerian skills of empathy, genuineness, and unconditional positive regard (Rogers, 1961/1995). *Empathy* means seeing and feeling the world as clients see and feel it; it means experiencing clients' joys and disappointments as *they* experience them. *Genuineness* means the counselor engages with the client as his or her own true self, not putting on a facade, not pretending to be someone the counselor is not. *Unconditional positive regard* means that the counselor accepts the client as he or she is—not demanding constraints on client thoughts, feelings, or behaviors. Unconditional truly means *unconditional*—without condition.

Teyber (2006) believed that empathy is the foundation of the therapeutic alliance. He believed that a client will feel understood if the counselor reflects back to the client essential feelings or key issues and identifies a common theme or pattern present in the client's stories. Through doing this, Teyber believed that the client will experience feeling understood and validated, an experience the client may not have had in his or her family of origin. In fact, Teyber posited that this familial invalidation of the client's experience contributes to client feelings of disempowerment and a lack of self-awareness of feelings, values, and wants. Understanding, then, is demonstrated through expressing the core meaning of the client's stories (Teyber, 2006).

Resistance

Resistance goes hand in hand with the therapeutic alliance. Resistance can be conceptualized as the attempt to thwart the counseling process, the counselor, or the counseling relationship. It is an attempt by the client "to preserve the status quo" (Gabbard, 1990, p. 12). Driven by the desire to avoid shame, guilt, anxiety, or ambivalence, resistance is a normative phenomenon (see Gabbard, 1990; Teyber, 2006). Some very common manifestations of resistance are coming late to sessions, forgetting therapeutic advice, being silent, emphasizing irrelevant or inconsequential material in counseling, and forgetting to pay the bill (Gabbard, 1990).

To address resistance, a counselor needs to acknowledge any real constraints that the client has, as well as offer the possibility that there may be underlying issues (see Teyber, 2006). For example, I once worked with a client who had mobility issues related to a chronic disability. He routinely came to sessions late and also routinely apologized for how long it would take him to get to my office because he could not walk fast enough to catch the bus. To successfully address this issue, I wanted to acknowledge that indeed he did have mobility issues (that much was clear) *and* that I was wondering if something more might be going on (after all, I knew enough about his life to know that he could have left his house earlier to make it to the bus stop on time to catch the bus). If I just expressed the first half of the equation—namely, being empathic— I would have been denying the possibility of further exploration. If I just expressed the second half—that maybe something more was going on—I might have come across to my client as disbelieving and lacking in understanding and empathy.

Considered from the perspective of transference, resistance makes perfect sense. Consider a client who has a template learned early in life and continually engages in a repetition compulsion. A counselor seeks to challenge the template and repetition compulsion by recognizing, identifying, and wanting to talk about them. The client, fearful of burdening the counselor, wants to avoid dealing with the template or repetition compulsion (see Kahn, 1997). This is resistance.

TERMINATION

Termination—that is, ending counseling—is an issue of great importance. Just as all counseling relationships and endeavors have a beginning, they have an end. The big question is not *if* counseling will end, but *when* it should end (see Roth, 1990).

Endings can be *natural* (Teyber, 2006). That is, they can occur at the point when the work of counseling has been completed. Conversely, endings can be *unnatural* (Teyber, 2006). An economic, educational, or social constraint may affect the length of counseling—for example, an older client may be allowed only a set number of sessions by an agency or a counselor-in-training is moving on in his or her training. Whether the ending is natural or unnatural, it is essential that both the counselor and the client accept that the relationship will end, indeed that it must end (Teyber, 2006).

It can be helpful to the client if the counselor can *count down* the number of sessions until the termination, allow the client to safely express his or her feelings, remain nondefensive in the face of transferences that resurface, and manage the countertransference around termination and endings (Teyber, 2006). It may be most helpful for the client if termination includes a review of the course of counseling and the progress the client has made, a prediction that the client will face situations that may trigger his or her "dysfunctional pattern," and practice in how to respond to the triggers (Teyber, 2006, p. 397). A good therapeutic termination will end with a warm and supportive good-bye.

Knight (2004) wrote about termination when younger therapists work with older adult clients. He noted that oftentimes the therapist (or counselor) has a greater emotional difficulty with termination than does the client because the client has had a lifetime of experience with endings. For the counselor, this difficulty is related to countertransference and the particular ways in which the therapist experiences his or her older adult clients. Knight (2004) suggested that therapists may feel more ineffective or incapable when working with older adults, and this feeling may be highlighted by termination. The reality is that older adults oftentimes have problems that cannot be *solved* or issues that cannot be *fixed*, such as chronic or terminal illness, mobility problems, vision or hearing disability, low fixed incomes, or other troubles (Knight, 2004), and this reality is distressing to the counselor.

CHAPTER SUMMARY

In this chapter, we explored transference and countertransference in work with older adults. We considered Freud's concepts of templates and the repetition compulsion; Bowlby's and Ainsworth's attachment styles; Horney's three interpersonal interaction types; Kohut's concepts of mirroring, idealized parental imago, and twinship transference; and Knight's explication of transference templates in work with older adults. We identified Kahn's four types of countertransference and Knight's countertransference templates in work with older adults. Finally, we discussed working through, the therapeutic alliance, resistance, and termination. With a foundation in psychodynamic and existential theories (Chapter 4) and a stronger understanding of fundamental processes that occur in counseling (Chapter 5), we will explore in Chapter 6 a number of theories of counseling that have particular relevance to work with older adults.

CASE STUDY

Mrs. Alise is a 75-year-old European American woman. She arrives at the office for a 10:00 a.m. appointment. She comes into the session complaining about how difficult it was to find the office, how staff are unfriendly, and how she needed to leave by 10:30 at the latest. She also complains of increasing difficulties with mobility and increasingly poor eyesight. She is on a fixed income and has concerns about how she will pay for counseling. The counselor, a 28-year-old gerontological counseling student, leans forward, empathizes, and says, "It sometimes *is* hard to find the office, and I imagine this is especially so if getting around is not easy. In terms of payment, if that is difficult, we do have a sliding scale. Before we go much further, though, I want to let you know that I am a counseling student, and I work under the direction of a supervisor." These comments are met with rejection by Mrs. Alise, who says, "It's a dog-eat-dog world out there. Don't pity me. I don't want your pity. I don't need your pity." Furthermore, she shakes her head and says, "How old *are* you? What can somebody your age offer me? And on top of it, you're a student! Hmm. I don't know if this is going to work for me." The student counselor shrinks back and thinks, "I *am* too young, and what do *I* know about counseling, especially counseling older adults? Maybe she *would be* better off seeing someone older and more experienced."

Questions

1. Identify the transference phenomenon in this case study.
2. Identify the countertransference phenomenon.
3. Which of Horney's three *types* most closely fits Mrs. Alise?
4. Which of Bowlby's and Ainsworth's three attachment styles most closely fits Mrs. Alise?
5. How would you characterize the quality of the therapeutic alliance?
6. Explain what *working through* might look like in this circumstance.
7. What issues might arise regarding termination?

CHAPTER QUESTIONS

1. Define transference and countertransference. Which is likely to impact counseling?
2. Name and describe the three styles of attachment. What is their relevance for work with older adults?
3. What are the four types of countertransference identified by Kahn? Define each, and give an example.

4. What are some common transference phenomena in work with older adults that have been identified by Bob Knight? In other words, what are some relationships that an older adult client might project onto a counselor?

5. What are some common countertransference phenomena in work with older adults that have been identified by Bob Knight? In other words, what are some relationships that a counselor might project onto a client?

6. Define obstructive countertransference, and give an example.

7. How do transference and countertransference in work with older adults differ from those in work with a younger population?

8. Discuss how parent transference may manifest in work with older adults.

9. Discuss how parent countertransference may manifest in work with older adults.

10. What steps could a counselor take to identify his or her countertransference?

11. Define the concept of a therapeutic alliance. How would you go about developing a therapeutic alliance with an older adult client? What factors come into play?

12. What is meant by working through?

13. Define resistance. How might your older adult clients demonstrate resistance? How might you use resistance therapeutically?

14. Do you agree or disagree with the statement, "There is no resistance; there is only the counselor who has not yet figured out how to work with his or her client"?

GLOSSARY

Countertransference: is the projection onto a client a relationship template that has its origins in an early life relationship.

Inverted transference: is the phenomenon of an older adult client responding to a younger adult clinician as a *child figure* (i.e., a son or daughter figure) rather than as a parent figure.

John Bowlby and Mary Ainsworth: were the two figures predominantly responsible for the concept of attachment styles in early childhood.

Karen Horney: was noted for her theory of three styles of being: moving toward, moving against, and moving away from.

Resistance: is the phenomenon in which a client resists or avoids the therapeutic work of counseling.

Secure attachment: is marked by a relationship with the parental figure that allows for safe exploration of the environment.

Termination: is the final phase of the course of counseling, when counseling ends.

Therapeutic alliance: is the working relationship between the counselor and the client.

Transference: is the projection onto a counselor a relationship template that has its origins in an early life relationship.

Working through: is the process in which transference is identified and explored and in which the client is provided with a new, therapeutic experience.

FURTHER INFORMATION

1. For a deeper understanding of transference and countertransference in work with older adults, a must-read is Bob Knight's *Psychotherapy With Older Adults* (Thousand Oaks, CA: Sage, 2004).

NOTES

1. Today, the concept of transference is broader than in Freud's day and includes all of a client's thoughts, feelings, and behaviors toward the counselor (see Teyber, 2006).
2. Here we go again. For Kohut, *transmuting* refers to transferring, and *internalization* refers to incorporating something into one's sense of self. Hence, a *transmuting internalization* is a transferring of an external experience (e.g., my experiencing a calm, powerful parental figure) to an internal experience (me experiencing myself as calm and powerful).

CHAPTER 6

Approaches to Counseling Older Adults

The unexamined life is not worth living.

—Socrates (469–399 BCE)

We tell ourselves stories in order to live.

—Joan Didion (2006)

CHAPTER OVERVIEW

In this chapter we will consider specific approaches to counseling that are oftentimes used in work with older adults. These include individual and group interventions. We will briefly review psychodynamic approaches and interpersonal therapy, and we will address in-depth cognitive behavioral approaches and reminiscence, including structured life review and guided autobiography.

Counselors attend to and adapt their approaches to working with a client based on the client's developmental changes in later life, the particular cohort to which the client belongs, and the social context in which the client lives (Knight & Satre, 1999). Knight's (1996, cited in Knight & Satre, 1999) contextual, cohort-based, maturity-specific change model of later life suggests that older adults are more mature than younger people in many ways and also face particular challenges that are relatively unique in later life. Examples are dealing with the death of loved ones or with multiple chronic medical conditions. Furthermore, older adults belong to a particular cohort with a collection of experiences, memories, and norms that differ from those of the present. As such, we will address issues of maturation, cohort, and social context.

Maturation issues present in later life of particular relevance to the counselor revolve around cognitive changes, including cognitive slowing, differences in intelligence factors, changes in learning and memory, and changes in personality and emotions (Knight & Satre, 1999). The speed of response of adults slows as one ages; it may be that older adults' brains process abstract material faster but in doing so slow reaction times (see Salthouse, 1985, cited in Knight & Satre, 1999). Differences in intelligence factors refer to differences specifically in **fluid intelligence** versus **crystallized intelligence.** Fluid intelligence decreases with age; crystallized intelligence changes only after age 70 and may be the result of dementia or other illness (see Labouvie-Vief, 1985, and Schaie, 1996, both cited in Knight & Satre, 1999). Older adults may have a larger cache of knowledge (based on their extensive life experiences), whereas the young may depend on higher levels of energy and speed to compensate for their smaller reservoirs of knowledge (Rybash, Hoyer, & Roodin, 1986, cited in Knight & Satre, 1999). Learning and memory in later life suggest that older adults' **working memory** (the part of memory through which data must be processed to be stored in long-term memory) decreases in later life (Light, 1990, Salthouse, 1991, both cited in Knight & Satre, 1999). This decrease in working memory suggests that counselors should decrease the speed and complexity of language used in clinical activities with older adults and encourage the use of mnemonic aids as compensatory tools (Knight & Satre, 1999) to ensure that clinical material is meaningful and relevant and that the older adult client remains motivated (see Botwinick et al., 1984, cited in Knight & Satre, 1999). Research on personality in later life suggests that although older adults do not have radically different personalities than they did in earlier adulthood, they believe that they have changed in positive ways (Bengtson, Reedy, & Gordon, 1985, cited in Knight & Satre, 1999). Research on emotions in later life suggests that older adults experience more complex (i.e., nuanced) and less extreme emotions (Shulz, 1982, cited in Knight & Satre, 1999) as well as focus on more emotionally close relations (Carstensen, 1992, cited in Knight & Satre, 1999). Counselors should anticipate more complex and subtle emotions when working with clients in later life (Knight & Satre, 1999).

In sum and overall, maturational changes in late life suggest stability in personality, more nuanced emotions, focus on emotionally close relationships, and stability in crystallized intelligence (Knight & Satre, 1999). As a counselor, you can expect that an older client's personality will be similar to what it was when he or she was younger. You should not expect extremes of emotion but you should be sensitive to more nuanced emotions. You should explore with your older clients their emotionally close relations—these especially may be a resource for your clients. Finally, you may find a slowing of older clients' fluid intelligence, even though their store of crystallized intelligence remains relatively stable.

Cohort distinctions revolve around differences between older adults and younger adults, often attributed to aging, but in reality attributable to the particular sociocultural-historical milieu in which the older adult exists (Knight & Satre, 1999). As Knight and Satre (1999) wrote,

> Cohort differences are explained by membership in a birth-year-defined group that is socialized into certain abilities, beliefs, attitudes, and personality dimensions that will stay stable as it ages and that distinguishes that cohort from those born earlier and later. (p. 193)

Examples of commonly recognized older adult cohorts in the United States are those associated with World War II, the Great Depression, the cold war, the Vietnam War, and the Summer of Love. Common differences between cohorts include later born cohorts having more years of school, later born cohorts being stronger in ability to reason and in spatial orientation, later born cohorts' increasing levels of extroversion, and earlier born cohorts' stronger arithmetic and verbal abilities (see Schaie, 1995, 1996, cited in Knight & Satre, 1999). Some cohort beliefs can interfere with older adults' seeking counseling services—namely, the beliefs that older adults are less valued than other segments of the population, that psychological problems are a sign of personal or spiritual weakness, or that it is more important to take care of others than of oneself (R. S. Haight, 2005).

Finally, the **social context** of older adults refers to the milieu in which they exist today, including the environments in which they live and socialize (e.g., assisted living or nursing care, gated communities for adults age 55 and older, or older adult community centers) and the rules under which they live (e.g., those related to Medicare, conservatorship, or elder abuse laws) (see Knight & Satre, 1999). A counselor must understand what are the expected norms, what is the client's actual experience, and what are the differences between expectations and reality (Knight & Satre, 1999). It is essential that counselors who work with older adults become informed about the social systems in which their older adult clients function (Knight & Satre, 1999).

One specific issue to keep in mind regarding counseling older adults is the fact that many older adults are referred to counseling by a loved one or physician; because of this, it is important for you to explore with older adult clients their understanding of why they are seeing a counselor and their expectations and motivations (see Abeles et al., 1998). The current cohort of older adults may be less receptive to counseling and may identify counseling as stigmatizing, so it is important for counselors to address this issue directly (Abeles et al., 1998). Likewise, given many older adults' lack of familiarity or experience with counseling, a counselor may wish to provide information to the client about how counseling functions, how it is structured, and its rationale (see Abeles et al., 1998). Many older adults suffer with various sensory impairments (e.g., hearing, visual, or mobility impairments), so counselors should be active in compensating for the particular impairment(s) of the client (see Abeles et al., 1998). Furthermore, counseling older adults may best be conceptualized as a part of the older adults' biopsychosocial system, so coordinating one's treatment with that of physicians and other health care professionals is important; clinical presentations seen in counseling may be the result of medical problems (Abeles et al., 1998). Finally, as a counselor, it is important to be self-aware of one's negative perceptions of aging and of older adults (see Abeles et al., 1998), as negative perceptions will adversely affect one's ability to successfully counsel.

Several specific approaches to counseling and therapy have been applied to work with older adults: group or individual counseling, cognitive behavioral, brief psychodynamic and interpersonal approaches, couple and family counseling, psychoeducation, and approaches that specifically use cognitive training, behavior modification, or changes in the client's environment (Abeles et al., 1998). Some approaches, such as cognitive behavioral therapy, have been adapted to work with older adults; others, such as life review, have been developed specifically for older people.

In this chapter, we will review some of the specific interventions that are used with older adults, including psychodynamic and analytic therapies, interpersonal therapy, cognitive behavioral therapy, and two approaches to reminiscence: structured life review and guided autobiography. Family counseling will be discussed in Chapter 13.

As you learned in Chapter 4, negative biases in the application of therapies with older adults have been present at least since the time of Freud, who thought old people were ineducable. In large part, Freud's bias provided a foundation for bias in the development and research of counseling and therapy approaches, which historically had been developed primarily for young to middle-aged adults or for children (see Hepple, 2004). Contributing today to a bias against counseling and therapy approaches for older adults is the move toward biological psychology and psychiatry (Hepple, 2004), with its philosophies of reductionism and materialism. In spite of these biases, a number of therapeutic approaches have been successfully applied to work with older adults.

PSYCHODYNAMIC APPROACHES

Psychodynamic Therapy. Psychodynamic approaches to work with older adults emphasize gaining insight into previously nonconscious processes that influence one's day-to-day life. By working through these issues, clients gain insight that results in their freedom from that which was previously constrained. Issues often revolve around childhood and limitations of one's caregiver. In terms of work with older adults, counselors may ignore "infantile needs" of an older client because they have not worked through their own anxieties of dependency in late life, ignore or ridicule erotic transference because of discomfort over the idea of sexual older adults, or experience countertransference of "ideali[z]ed care fantasies" due to anxieties about their own older family members (see Hepple, 2004, p. 373).

Group Psychodynamic Therapy. Group psychodynamic therapy shares the same focus as that of individual psychodynamic counseling, namely, the exploration of interior experience and of relations with others. The central tasks performed in a psychodynamic counseling group are the identification and examination of group members' relationships with one another and with the group leader(s), patterns of interaction that characterize the group, and group members' interior experiences (see R. S. Haight, 2005). The objective of this examination is to help group members develop insight into the foundations of their way of being in the world and how it affects themselves and their relations with other people (R. S. Haight, 2005). A large part of the group psychodynamic counseling experience is the identification and examination of transference in the here-and-now interactions between group members and between members and the leader(s) (R. S. Haight, 2005). Because older adults may be less inclined to communicate negative transference vocally, it is important for the group leader(s) to attend to the nonverbal behaviors expressed by group members for cues to their feelings (R. S. Haight, 2005). Subsequent to attending, a counselor may ask group members "what it was like" to observe specific behaviors or to hear other group members' thoughts or see their feelings (R. S. Haight, 2005, p. 235).

It is important to attend to issues of leadership, group norms, and each individual's role when facilitating psychodynamic counseling groups (R. S. Haight, 2005). Leadership requires the counselor or facilitator to structure and develop the group so that there are clear boundaries; this is most readily accomplished by screening and limiting membership on one or more factors, developing group rules, and maintaining healthy boundaries (R. S. Haight, 2005). Solid leadership may be required in

the groups for older adults to address and work through issues related
to cohort norms (e.g., "politeness and civility, discretion and decorum"),
to teach group members how to express feelings through modeling, and
to address issues of tardiness and absence, which requires considerable
sensitivity to the real medical and social constraints that exist in late life
that contribute to such (R. S. Haight, 2005, p. 237). Furthermore, group
leaders may need to address those feelings that lie under a group member's acting out—for example, a sense of isolation (R. S. Haight, 2005)
or of unworthiness.

Group norms refer to the values and the culture that develop in a
particular group. Group norms that may be important in groups with
older adults include repeating statements or comments (to provide
accommodation for those with hearing impairment), using cohort-
normative words and metaphors, or encouraging members to socialize
with one another outside of and in addition to the group (R. S. Haight,
2005).

In any psychodynamic group, individual members will adopt roles
that are familiar to them or that serve some function in the group (R.
S. Haight, 2005). Some group members may take on the role of host
or hostess, devil's advocate, caretaker, comedian, or socializer (R. S.
Haight, 2005). A skilled counselor or facilitator will recognize and help
group members identify these roles, ask what functions they serve in
the group and outside of the group, and assess the adaptiveness of their
impact (R. S. Haight, 2005).

Cognitive Analytic Therapy. **Cognitive analytic therapy** integrates
object relations therapy with cognitive therapy (Hepple, 2004). It focuses
on "shared meaning in the context of the client's life story and recognizes the importance of the dialogue" (Hepple, 2004, p. 372). In essence,
cognitive analytic therapy addresses trauma from earlier times in the
production of current pathology by placing all in the context of a person's life story (Hepple, 2004).

INTERPERSONAL THERAPY

Interpersonal therapy is an approach that focuses on perturbed interpersonal relationships by addressing four factors: "role transition, role dispute, abnormal grief, and interpersonal deficit" (Hepple, 2004, p. 374).
The objectives of interpersonal therapy are to help a client develop adaptive relationships by tweaking or in some cases significantly changing
one's roles, express feelings, and develop stronger communication abilities (Hepple, 2004). In doing so, a client should experience improved
functioning and reduced symptoms (Hepple, 2004).

COGNITIVE BEHAVIORAL THERAPY

Cognitive behavioral therapy (CBT) is one of the most common forms of therapy, both with the general population and with older adults. Cognitive behavioral therapy is a two-pronged approach that seeks to identify and challenge maladaptive thoughts and behaviors and to replace them with more adaptive thoughts and behaviors. Negative thoughts are challenged by helping a client evaluate the accuracy of a thought, identify errors in thinking, consider how one's negative thoughts have an impact on one's well-being, and develop alternative perspectives (Hepple, 2004). Behaviorally, a client may be taught a number of techniques to monitor and decrease maladaptive behaviors while increasing adaptive behaviors through reinforcement.

One example of a behavioral intervention is the use of the California Older Persons' Pleasant Events Schedule (COPPES) in the treatment of depression in later life (Gallagher-Thompson, Thompson, & Rider, n.d.). Using the COPPES, an older client rates the frequency and pleasantness of a number of potentially pleasant events. The list is then used to identify activities that an older client finds pleasant, as an aid in designing interventions to increase the frequency of pleasant events, and as a way to monitor this increased frequency. Examples of pleasant events are "Being with friends," "Listening to music," or "Shopping" (Gallagher-Thompson et al., n.d., pp. 2–3).

Cognitive behavioral therapy can be readily applied to older adults and may be particularly efficacious because of its focus on the present, its skill enhancement and practicality, the fact that it is highly structured, the emphasis on self-monitoring, its psychoeducational orientation, and the fact that it is goal oriented (Morris & Morris, 1991, cited in Laidlaw, Thompson, Dick-Siskin, & Gallagher-Thompson, 2003). It has been found to be effective in treating depression, anxiety, and dementia-related problematic behaviors in older adults (Hepple, 2004), as well as chronic illness, disability, alcoholism, and insomnia (Laidlaw et al., 2003).

However, CBT may need to be adapted for older adults who exhibit cognitive or sensory impairments (Kraus, Kunik, & Stanley, 2007). Specific adaptations include vocal and verbal repetition of concepts, using educational-level-appropriate wording, chunking CBT concepts, or presenting CBT concepts more slowly (Kraus et al., 2007). Specific CBT techniques that can be used with older adults include (a) retraining their breathing (when appropriate), in which clients who exhibit anxiety are taught to mindfully slow their breathing and in doing so become more relaxed; (b) challenging maladaptive thoughts, in which clients are taught to identify maladaptive thoughts, challenge them, and replace them with adaptive thoughts; and (c) learning to decrease unhealthy behaviors and increase pleasant behaviors (Kraus et al., 2007).

Cognitive behavioral treatment approaches may need to be adapted to meet the needs of older adults based on the impact of developmental changes in later life, the older adult's particular cohort, and the social context in which older adults function. Developmental changes in *speed of processing* suggest that counselors should slow down their vocal interactions with older clients, check to see that the older client is remembering information discussed in the session, use simpler sentences and phrases when speaking, and repeat and summarize new material (and ask the older client to do the same) (Knight & Satre, 1999). Changes in *intelligence* (e.g., the ascendancy in later life of crystallized intelligence over fluid intelligence) suggest that counselors help clients identify the strengths and skills that they already have (including skills that the counselor may lack), reduce reliance on client inferential reasoning and problem-solving ability, and increase the level of leading "the older client to conclusions" (Knight & Satre, 1999, p. 191). *Emotionality* changes suggest that older clients' experience of emotions is more nuanced and complex and may include coexperience of discrepant emotions (e.g., happiness and sadness); the CBT counselor then might encourage clients to focus on the positive emotions in addition to the negative (Knight & Satre, 1999). Finally, older adults' *scripts* and *schemas* may be more transparent and easier to identify "across multiple situations and multiple relationship interactions," allowing both the counselor and the older client to identify and alter maladaptive scripts, schemas, and themes (Knight & Satre, 1999, p. 192).

Cohort differences in later life require the counselor to attend to the "folkways of members of earlier born cohorts" (Knight & Satre, 1999, p. 193). This means understanding the older adult's *weltanschauung* (i.e., worldview) and what life was like for an older adult of that cohort during his or her childhood, adolescence, and early, mid-, and later life (Knight & Satre, 1999). For a counselor of older adults, understanding cohort differences means becoming multiculturally competent; in this context the culture is the cohort. For many current cohorts of older adults, cognitive behavioral therapy, like other therapies, is a relatively foreign concept. Compensation for this may require the counselor to explain the particulars of CBT, the rationale for it, and the particulars of the approach, including the active role of the client and the necessity of completing homework assignments (Knight & Satre, 1999). On the part of the counselor, it may require changing the wording of assessment instruments, assignments, and so forth and attending to the cohort on which assessments are normed (Knight & Satre, 1999).

To be most effective, counselors also need to understand the social context in which older adults live (Knight & Satre, 1999). For the CBT counselor, this will require understanding the environmental sources of reinforcement for maladaptive thoughts, feelings, and behaviors (Knight & Satre, 1999). Changes in the older adult client's thoughts, feelings, or behaviors may require changes in his or her environment.

Group cognitive behavioral therapy shares in common with other cognitive behavioral approaches the objective of producing change in one's life through changing one's thoughts and behaviors. Unlike a hierarchical structure found in many psychodynamic approaches, group CBT tends to be collaborative (R. S. Haight, 2005). Ironically, this use of collaboration may be an initial stumbling block for older adults, who may classify counseling as a specialty within the medical industry, an industry that tends toward the hierarchical. It can be valuable to present group CBT to older adults as akin to "taking a class" (R. S. Haight, 2005, p. 241).

In CBT groups, participants should anticipate receiving feedback from other group members as well as the facilitator(s), engaging in homework assignments, experiencing results, and identifying positive changes (R. S. Haight, 2005). Each group member will identify his or her maladaptive thoughts and behaviors and do homework between group sessions to learn to replace maladaptive thoughts and behaviors with more adaptive ones (R. S. Haight, 2005). Not only will the counselor or facilitator teach group members how to change thoughts and behaviors, he or she oftentimes will provide psychoeducational interventions consisting of information about the aging process, the connection between physical illness and depression, how to recognize anxiety, how substance abuse is used as self-medication, or caregiving issues (R. S. Haight, 2005).

CBT groups for older adults are more likely to be successful if the facilitator is flexible, slows down the pace of the group (Gallagher-Thompson & Thompson, 1996, cited in R. S. Haight, 2005), reviews and repeats specific concepts and specific techniques (Thompson et al., 2000, cited in R. S. Haight, 2005), explains how specific techniques produce results, and expects progress in the form of successive approximations (R. S. Haight, 2005).

REMINISCENCE, LIFE REVIEW, AND GUIDED AUTOBIOGRAPHY

In this section, we will define **reminiscence** broadly as well as specifically and look at some of the ways in which reminiscence is used. In addition to the particulars specific to reminiscence, we will look at two other major approaches to therapeutic remembering: structured life review and guided autobiography. In brief, reminiscence is a less structured intervention in which older adults are "stimulated to recall memories and share them with each other," whereas life review is a more highly structured experience in which older adults are encouraged in "re-evaluation, resolving conflicts or assessing adaptive coping-responses" in their lives (Bohlmeijer, Smit, & Cuijpers, 2003, p. 1089). Guided autobiography is yet another type of reminiscence, focusing on exploring the meaning of one's life. A focus on the past and on the use of memory, then, is a hallmark of reminiscence, life review (Burnside & Haight, 1992), and guided autobiography.

Both reminiscence and life review benefit from being "non-stigmati[z]ing, easy to use and easily administered" (Bohlmeijer et al., 2003, p. 1088), and each has been used to support cognitive functioning in those suffering from dementia and to improve life satisfaction and quality of life (Bohlmeijer et al., 2003). There is some evidence that reminiscence is effective at improving self-esteem among nursing home residents (Chao et al., 2006).

Reminiscence and life review also have been used to treat depression in late life, and—though not unequivocal—they may be as effective as pharmacotherapy or psychotherapy, especially with those older adults suffering from more severe depressive symptoms. They have been effective, it seems, in community-dwelling older adults (Bohlmeijer et al., 2003), even if the effects on depression among older adults is unclear (Chao et al., 2006; Hsieh & Wang, 2003). Lack of unequivocal evidence for the effectiveness of reminiscence with older adults likely is the result of varied goals, types of reminiscence, dependent measures, assessment instruments used, populations, and small sample sizes (Lin, Dai, & Hwang, 2003).

Reminiscence

Reminiscence is "the process of recalling past events and experiences" (Coleman, 2005, p. 301) or the "process of recalling long-forgotten experiences [and] events which are memorable" (Burnside & Haight, 1992, p. 856). Reminiscence requires verbal exchange with at least one other person, the revealing of personal historical memories, and not the telling of recent or current experiences (Burnside & Haight, 1992). Reminiscence typically is used to "provide a basis for other groups," "increase interactions with peers," "focus conversations," and "find commonalities" (Burnside & Haight, 1992, p. 857). Before reminiscence can begin, an older client must demonstrate the ability to attend, to communicate verbally, to be able to respond to others' reminiscence, and to recall personal historical experiences (Burnside & Haight, 1992).

Reminiscence can be conceptualized as a five-stage framework, comprising antecedents, assessments, purpose-setting, treatment modality, and outcomes (Lin et al., 2003). The antecedent stage is present when there are life events that may trigger an interest in reminiscence or the suggestion of reminiscence as a therapeutic intervention; antecedents include such experiences as "aging, stress, relocation" and "transition" (Lin et al., 2003, p. 299). The assessment stage is that in which a counseling or other allied health care professional administers "psychometric ... self-report ... [and] observational instruments" (Lin et al., 2003, p. 299). The purpose-setting stage is that in which the purposes for the reminiscence intervention are identified. In the treatment modality stage, the counselor and client may decide between traditional reminiscence, life review, guided autobiography, or other reminiscence approaches. Finally, the outcomes stage is that in which one measures the short-term (e.g., "decreased isolation, increased self-esteem, [and] increased socialization"), long-term (e.g., "adaptation, increased life satisfaction, [and] increased quality of life"), and integrity-focused (e.g., "increased well-being [or] decreased depression") goals (Lin et al., 2003, p. 299).

The foundations of reminiscence lie in Erikson's understanding of the final stage of development (integrity versus despair) and Robert Butler's concept of life review (Coleman, 2005). By integrity, Erikson meant the acceptance of the life one has lived, understanding that one's life had to be the way it was (Erikson, 1963, cited in Coleman, 2005). By life review, Butler meant the process people go through as they approach the end of life, resolving and reconciling their difficult memories (Butler, 1963, cited in Coleman, 2005).

Reminiscence can have many different functions: identity maintenance, life review, disengagement, re-engagement, rumination, obsession, and avoidance (Coleman, 2005) (see Table 6.1). *Identity maintenance* reminiscence refers to the use of memories and remembering to shore up one's sense of self, to maintain one's identity (Coleman, 2005). Think of the stories you tell others and yourself about who you are; what your values are; how you think, act, and feel; and how you respond to situations. In the telling of the stories, you may be strengthening your sense of self. This is reminiscing for the purpose of no change, for the purpose of maintaining the status quo.

In contrast, *life review* reminiscence has as its objective the idea that one can change and grow through remembering, evaluating, and coming to a resolution about one's life and activities (Coleman, 2005). Life review reminiscing has been shown to be associated with greater well-being among those who had negative attributions about their past (Coleman, 1974, cited in Coleman, 2005).

TABLE 6.1   Functions of Reminiscence

Function	Description
Identity maintenance	To maintain one's identity and sense of self
Life review	To grow through remembering
Disengagement	To recall the past in order to withdraw from daily life
Re-engagement	To recall the past in order to refocus energies on the present
Rumination	To recall events that resulted in feelings of guilt and remorse
Obsession	To repeatedly recall painful memories, without resolution
Avoidance	To not recall painful memories in an attempt to avoid working through

Note: Coleman, P. G., "Reminiscence: Developmental, Social and Clinical Perspectives," in *The Cambridge Handbook of Age and Ageing*, Cambridge University Press, Cambridge, UK, 2005.

Disengagement reminiscing suggests that older adults recall memories as a way of withdrawing from day-to-day life, shutting down as one approaches the end of life (Coleman, 2005). It is in contrast to *re-engagement* reminiscence, a recalling of the past not to withdraw but to refocus one's energies on engaging with one's environment at a more global, holistic, spiritual, and cultural level (Coleman, 2005).

Some types of reminiscence actually may be harmful. *Ruminative* reminiscence, with its focus on guilt and regret, has been found to be associated with extended grief in response to loss (Coleman, 1986, cited in Coleman, 2005). *Obsessive* reminiscence is that in which older adults end up in a recursive loop of recalling painful memories, without ever resolving or reconciling (Wong & Watt, 1991, cited in Coleman, 2005). *Avoidance* of reminiscing about painful life events, too, may be maladaptive; those who avoid are not likely to achieve a state of mastery over those memories, resulting in unresolved issues that can last throughout their lives (see Hunt & Robbins, 2001, cited in Coleman, 2005).

Webster's Reminiscence Functions Scale characterizes reminiscence by its various potential functions: boredom reduction, bitterness revival, conversation, death preparation, identity, intimacy maintenance, problem solving, and teaching/informing (Webster & Gould, 2007). *Bitterness revival*, for example, is the recollection of unpleasant memories in order to maintain negative cognitions and feelings about other people (Webster, 2001, cited in Coleman, 2005). *Boredom reduction* refers to engaging in reminiscence in order to do something in an otherwise dull environment (Gibson & Burnside, 2005).

Interestingly, older adults do not reminisce more than younger adults, though their reminiscences do serve different functions (de Vries & Watt, 1996; Webster & Gould, 2007). Whereas younger people use reminiscence to reduce boredom, to develop identity, to problem solve, and to revive bitterness, older people tend to use reminiscence to maintain intimacy, to teach or inform (a generative activity), and to prepare for death (Webster & Gould, 2007). In other words, younger adults tend to reminisce for *self* functions, whereas older adults tend to reminisce for *social* functions (Webster & Gould, 2007). This may be because of changes in life goals across the life span, with identity consolidation (interior life-oriented) occurring earlier in life and generativity (externally oriented) later in life (Webster & Gould, 2007).

When asked about vivid life memories, younger adults tend to describe very intimate memories, whereas older adults tend to describe memories with low levels of intimacy. Furthermore, when reminiscing, older people are less likely than younger people to identify memories that have negative valences (Webster & Gould, 2007). Older adults, too, are more likely to describe reminiscences that are a "series of events that summarize a life" (Webster & Gould, 2007, p. 156), whereas younger adults describe reminiscences that comprise a single event plus its long-term consequences (Webster & Gould, 2007). One possible explanation for the fact that older adults are less likely than younger adults to reminisce traumatic or negative events may be that older adults have in some sense worked through the negative events in their lives, so much so that those events are no longer seen as important, or their negative valence is no longer so strong (Webster & Gould, 2007). One possible explanation for the fact that older adults are more likely to offer life reviews rather than merely reminiscence of a particular event may be that older adults have consolidated their life experiences into a more coherent whole—"some form of existential lesson"—that they may pass on to younger generations (Webster & Gould, 2007, p. 164).

Analyzed by themes, old-old adults are more likely to have memories that are life reviews whereas younger adults are more likely to report memories that are traumatic (Webster & Gould, 2007). No matter the age group (younger, middle-aged, or older), people are more likely to report the **reminiscence bump:** recalling vivid memories of events from their late adolescence or early adulthood (Webster & Gould, 2007).

There is some evidence that suggests that those who reminisce more tend to have more negative vivid memories and tend to rate those memories as impacting their lives more (Webster & Gould, 2007). Those whose reminiscences were life reviews rather than trauma were more likely to reminisce for reasons of death preparation or to teach or inform and were less likely to reminisce for the reason of bitterness revival (Webster & Gould, 2007).

The fact that older adults' reminiscences tend to be less negative and less likely produced for the reason of bitterness survival may suggest that as an older client nears the end of life, he or she is more likely to focus on those relationships with others that strengthen positive emotions (see discussion of Carstensen, 1995, Charles, Mather, & Carstensen, 2003, and others, cited in Webster & Gould, 2007), or that an older client is more competent at emotion regulation and is more inclined to regulate in favor of positive emotions (see Alea, Diehl, & Bluck, 2004, cited in Webster & Gould, 2007).

Group Work in Reminiscence. One advantage of reminiscence work is that it can be conducted individually or in groups. Reminiscence groups can be used to empower older adults by encouraging group members to experience control—by supporting them in making an active decision to attend and participate in the group, by making them accountable for recalling stories of their lives, and by acknowledging them as the true experts on their lives (Gibson & Burnside, 2005). The function of the group counselor or facilitator is twofold: encouraging each member to tell the stories of his or her life and encouraging the group to listen to and really hear the storyteller (Gibson & Burnside, 2005).

Gibson and Burnside (2005) recommended a structure for reminiscence groups that comprises 10 to 12 group members and about 8 to 12 weekly meetings of about 2 hours each. Reminiscence groups have a relatively open approach to themes, looking to group members themselves to generate themes. Themes can be organized chronologically (e.g., childhood through adulthood through old age), or a group may choose to focus on one time of life (e.g., early adulthood) and explore various themes associated with that time (e.g., finishing one's education, one's early work life, or marriage and relationships) (Gibson & Burnside, 2005). Ideally, reminiscence groups will explore more general, safer, and happier themes earlier in the group and explore more intimate and sadder themes that may call for more reflection and evaluation later in the group, after the group has become more cohesive and trusting (Capuzzi & Gross, 1998, cited in Gibson & Burnside, 2005).

A valuable technique for some reminiscence groups is the use of **props** or **triggers**—sensory experiences or objects that elicit memories (Gibson & Burnside, 2005). Triggers can be as simple as music from a particular era (e.g., the Great Depression or the Korean War) that evokes a sense of place, time, or person; other triggers include tastes and smells that prompt recall of a particular place, time, or person (Gibson & Burnside, 2005). The sensory experiences that would be most evocative for a group depend on the cohort of that group and the particular experiences of the group members. Objects, too, can be evocative; these may include such things as newspaper headlines, photographs, or handmade objects. Participants in the group can be encouraged to share objects, music, food, or other items that are particularly meaningful to them.

Reminiscence groups can be useful for people suffering from mild and moderate dementia (Gibson & Burnside, 2005). It has been noted that "reminiscence can assist communication, personal relationships, and provide a sense of achievement, pleasure, and camaraderie" (Gibson & Burnside, 2005, pp. 184–185). Adaptations to maximize the benefits of the group for participants with dementia include reducing the group size to two to four members; placing more emphasis on nonverbal communication; screening for aggressiveness, depression, hostility, and perseveration of memories; adapting the length and frequency of the meetings (e.g., perhaps shorter, more frequent meetings); using structure and ritual to promote a sense of safety; and attending to the emotional content and not the veracity of memories (Gibson & Burnside, 2005).

Life Review

Life review, one of the major types of reminiscing, is a structured procedure for recalling and making sense of memories. Coleman (2005) indicated that life review "implies a search for meaning through reflection on one's life's experience" (p. 305), whereas Burnside and Haight (1992) defined life review as the "retrospective survey of existence, a critical study of a life, or a second look at one's life" (p. 856). Life review requires an evaluative component; recall of the full span of one's life (early childhood through late life); a willing listener; a willing reviewer; use of memory and recall; addressing the full range of emotional content, typically 4 to 6 weeks to conduct the review; and attention to the self (Burnside & Haight, 1992). Before life review takes place, participants must be old enough to have enough of a life to conduct a review, have the ability to recall memories, and have the ability to communicate (Burnside & Haight, 1992). Typical uses of life review include recall and examination, evaluation of one's past life, preparation for the future, and examination of one's conscience (Burnside & Haight, 1992).

Research on life review has shown that it is associated with "creativity, spirituality, and generativity," as well as "openness to experience, personal growth, and ... identity exploration and problem solving" (Coleman, 2005, p. 305). Although not correlated with self-reported life satisfaction, life review may be particularly helpful to those who have had particularly complicated lives (Coleman, 1986, Parker, 1995, Wink & Schiff, 2002, each cited in Coleman, 2005).

Structured **life review**, based on Erikson's eight-stage life span developmental model (see Chapter 1), is a specific technique for guiding older adults through the memories of their lives (B. K. Haight & Haight, 2007). It is conducted over six to eight 1-hour sessions and is organized developmentally, with an introductory first session, an integrative final session, and the middle sessions that include guided reminiscences of early childhood, childhood, young adolescence, adolescence, young adulthood, and older adulthood (B. K. Haight & Haight, 2007). Each session is used to address one or more of Erikson's stages:

1. trust versus mistrust
2. autonomy versus shame and doubt
3. initiative versus guilt
4. industry versus inferiority
5. identity versus role confusion
6. intimacy versus isolation
7. generativity versus stagnation
8. integrity versus despair

In the structured life review, questions related to an Eriksonian stage are posed to the client and serve as prompts.[1] The client then will reminisce and, in doing so, "reframe and reconcile the memory of a stage" that had not been successfully worked through before (B. K. Haight & Haight, 2007, p. 11). Through reconciling stages, the older client will move toward fulfilling the work of the final stage, integrity, that is, accepting the life that he or she has lived.

The objective, then, of structured life review is to help a client move toward integrity, as defined by Erikson (B. K. Haight & Haight, 2007). Recall that Erikson's theory is epigenetic: successful resolution of later stages is dependent on successful resolution of prior stages. In structured life review, a client can be moved to work through those stages—stage by stage, session by session—that had not been successfully worked through in the past. By doing this, the client is more likely to achieve a state of integrity. Other structured life review reported benefits include a decrease in feelings of depression, higher levels of life satisfaction, greater social connection with friends and family, self-acceptance, bonding, catharsis, improved relationships, and peace (B. K. Haight & Haight, 2007).

Structured life review has four features that distinguish it from other approaches to reminiscence: structure, duration, individuality, and evaluation (Haight & Dias, 1992, cited in B. K. Haight & Haight, 2007). First, structured life review is unique in its use of Erikson's life span developmental stages to *structure* the interviews (B. K. Haight &

Haight, 2007). A key benefit of using this structure is that it provides a scaffold to both the interviewer and the client in addressing major issues from each of life's stages; that is, from birth through early and late childhood, adolescence, and early, middle, and late adulthood. This structure is in contrast to many other forms of reminiscence that are more unstructured, free-form, and fluid. Although structured life review comes with a standard set of prompting questions to help the client think and remember, these questions are not intended to be rigidly applied to any given client; and, in fact, structured life review supports both interviewer and client deviation from the standard questions when those deviations are therapeutic and serve to move forward the structured life review (B. K. Haight & Haight, 2007).

Second, structured life review is unique, too, in its *duration*: six to eight 1-hour sessions typically conducted over a period of 8 weeks (B. K. Haight & Haight, 2007). Research has demonstrated that clients need at least 6 weeks of sessions to develop a trusting relationship with an interviewer and to review their lives (B. K. Haight & Haight, 2007). Reminiscence approaches that are conducted in fewer than 6 weeks are less likely to demonstrate the same degree of effectiveness. B. K. Haight and Haight (2007) discovered that clients were not likely to more fully open up to the interviewer until session four; furthermore, it appeared that by session four clients either became committed to the structured life review or quit.

Third, unlike group forms of reminiscence (see, e.g., guided autobiography below), structured life review is conducted *individually*, that is, one-on-one: one counselor or interviewer and one client. It is argued that this has the benefit of ensuring confidentiality and privacy and contributes to a sense of safety, which allows the client to be more trusting and more honest in the process (B. K. Haight & Haight, 2007).[2] Confidentiality and safety are particularly important when clients bring up unresolved conflicts or lifelong secrets that may have never been shared with anyone else (B. K. Haight & Haight, 2007).

Fourth, structured life review is distinguished from other approaches by the value it places on *evaluation* of the life events recalled by the client (B. K. Haight & Haight, 2007). Evaluation helps in the process of "understanding why the past life was lived the way it was" (B. K. Haight & Haight, 2007, p. 27). This understanding ultimately can lead the client to integrity. Unlike merely remembering facts (e.g., the make and model of one's first car), structured life review encourages clients to identify associated feelings and meaning. This evaluation and not mere recall of past events is the most significant distinguishing and defining feature of structured life review and is truly the feature around which this approach is structured and conducted.

Additional features that differentiate structured life review from other approaches include its emphasis on hard work, focus on the self, repetition of memories, locus of power and control, support for supervision, insistence on confidentiality, use of audio recording, and discouragement of life review with relatives (B. K. Haight & Haight, 2007). Unlike reminiscence, which can comprise only pleasant memories, structured life review asks clients also to address what may be painful memories, for working through painful memories may be necessary to reconcile the task at a particular Eriksonian stage. In reminiscence, too, one can recall the facts of the past without describing any self-involvement (e.g., "It was rare to have sugar and butter during the Depression."). In structured life review, clients may be asked for their thoughts or feelings about a memory to help them describe their self-involvement in their memories (e.g., "I was a kid during the Depression, and it used to make me sad that we couldn't have any cakes or cookies. In fact, I resented that."). In structured life review, unlike some other approaches, clients are encouraged to repeat memories as part of the working-through process. In fact, sometimes it is only through repeated exposure to painful memories that the pain they currently cause can subside. Unlike a conventional therapeutic relationship where the bulk of power and control lies with the counselor, structured life review places power and control in the hands of the client, allowing the client to determine the pace and direction of the experience, even though prompted and guided by the person who is listening. Structured life review encourages listeners to receive supervision, to maintain confidentiality, and to audio record sessions. Finally, B. K. Haight and Haight (2007) pointed out the reasons that structured life review should not be conducted with one's family members. The reasons revolve around one's feeling that one cannot be completely honest in communicating one's stories to a relative (e.g., for fear that the relative would not understand, or does not have the maturity, or would negatively evaluate the person remembering).

Guided Autobiography

Guided autobiography is a structured experience to help older adults explore the meaning of their lives. It is a process by which older adults can promote an understanding that one's "life has mattered, that it has had a purpose or an impact on the world" (Birren & Deutchman, 1991, p. 1). Guided autobiography is not therapy (Birren & Deutchman, 2005), though it may be therapeutic. It does not focus on problems or problem resolution; instead it supports older adults in the remembering of the experiences of their lives (Birren & Deutchman, 2005). Some of the areas in which guided autobiography may be helpful are acceptance of death, coping and adaptation, relief from depression, generativity, integration, interpersonal connection, meaning, reconciliation, role clarification, self-esteem, self-actualizing, spiritual well-being, and general well-being (Birren & Deutchman, 2005).

Guided autobiography has both a group component and an individual component. The function of the group component is to help people understand and make meaning from their past through reading and sharing brief, written essays about their lives and sharing their thoughts about these stories (Birren & Deutchman, 1991). Specifically, group members write two-page essays based on an assigned theme about their lives, read these stories to the group, share their thoughts about the stories, and interact with the group—all under the direction of a group facilitator (Birren & Deutchman, 2005). The stories are written individually in the context of structured themes to help clients organize and make meaning of their memories. Themes are organized sequentially to help clients develop a more comprehensive view of the self through recalling and reflecting on one's memories. That is, participants are asked to write brief essays on assigned themes and then to read their essays and comment on them in the context of the group. Benefits of having participants *write* rather than merely verbally tell their life stories are that writing allows a participant to reflect more deeply on his or her memories, is a stimulus for recollection of even more memories, gives the participant greater control to censor material (i.e., to remove material that is irrelevant or material that may feel unsafe or too personal to reveal to group members), and provides a written document that can be shared with those outside the group (e.g., family members or friends) (Birren & Deutchman, 2005).

Although there is considerable flexibility in terms of potential themes, commonly utilized themes are sequenced as follows: major branching points in one's life, family, career, finances, health, love, sexuality, death, and life aspirations and meaning (Birren & Deutchman, 1991, 2005). Additional themes may be developed for particular ethnic/racial, gender, sexual orientation, religious, or cultural groups or cohorts or for specific groups such as veterans or postwar immigrants. As you can see from this list, less sensitive issues (e.g., career and finances) are addressed before those that are more sensitive (e.g., sexuality).

With the theme of health, participants might be invited to write about their health history, their body image and its changes over the years, or health behaviors they have engaged in, and so on. Participants would respond to sensitizing questions by writing a two-page essay, which subsequently would be shared with the group.[3] Some potential sensitizing questions are as follows (Birren & Deutchman, 2005):

- What is your first memory of illness?
- How old were you?
- What did you learn about yourself from this illness?
- How did family members respond?
- What did you learn about your family from this illness?

Guided autobiography promotes integration, fulfillment, and competence (Birren & Deutchman, 2005). It has been found helpful to older adults across a range of factors: increasing one's sense of personal influence and worth, recalling adaptive strategies that were helpful in the past and could be helpful in the present, achieving rapprochement with one's history, and getting beyond one's resentments and negative feelings from the past. It has been found to increase interest in activities or hobbies in which one was formerly interested, promote creation of friendships with other members of the group, amplify the sense of meaning in one's life, and increase one's ability to approach death with a sense that one's life has made a positive difference in the world (Birren & Deutchman, 1991).

Researchers further have found specific benefits in the areas of death acceptance, cognitive functioning, coping, reduction of depression, ego integrity, fulfillment, orientation to the future, sense of continuity, integration, and connection to other generations. In addition, benefits have occurred in the areas of meaning, memory, mental adaptability, reconciliation with the past, clarification of roles or transition into new roles, self-disclosure, self-esteem, self-understanding, social integration, and spiritual well-being (Birren & Deutchman, 1991).

Guided autobiography is used to help older adults integrate and find fulfillment in the lives that they have led not only by helping them recognize that they have personal agendas and are able to adapt but also by strengthening senses of self (Birren & Deutchman, 1991). Through telling the stories of one's life, an older adult makes more explicit his or her identity—sense of self—and the positive and negative qualities that he or she possesses (Birren & Deutchman, 1991). Specifically, guided autobiography helps participants reconcile the **real self** (how one sees one's self) with the **ideal self** (how one wishes one was) and the **social-image self** (how others perceive one). The greater the congruence between one's real self and ideal self, the higher the level of self-esteem; the greater the congruence between the ideal self and the social-image self, the higher the sense of self-efficacy (Birren & Deutchman, 1991). Conversely, the greater the distance between the real and ideal, the ideal and the social-image, or the social-image and the real, the more distress (Birren & Deutchman, 1991).

Guided autobiography can help participants sustain a sense of continuity—that sense that "despite new circumstances, you are still yourself"

(Birren & Deutchman, 1991, p. 15). It, too, can help participants clarify and have a greater understanding of the role that ethnicity, race, culture (Birren & Deutchman, 1991), gender, sexual orientation, disability status, socioeconomic status, or other qualities have played and continue to play in their development. In a similar vein, through sharing stories, guided autobiography can help participants further understand the role that the perpetuation or change of family roles has played in their lives (Birren & Deutchman, 1991). Finally, guided autobiography may assist participants in maintaining or strengthening cognitive functioning, supporting motivation, adapting to new roles, and accepting the reality of the end of life (Birren & Deutchman, 1991).

Facilitators should recall that guided autobiography is not therapy; hence, one should not probe into emotions beyond those that spontaneously emerge and are easily shared (Birren & Deutchman, 2005). Facilitators can best serve the interests of the individual and the group as a whole by allowing emotions to appear rather than seeking them out (Birren & Deutchman, 2005). Facilitators, too, can set the tone for the group by guiding the goals and norms for the group (Birren & Deutchman, 2005). Common guided autobiography group goals are meeting other group members, sharing the stories of one's life, exploring how one's life story is similar to and different from those stories of others, sharing strategies for living, supporting thorough recall of members' stories, and guaranteeing confidentiality (Birren & Deutchman, 2005). Group norms may be modeled by the facilitator; common norms include cultivating a nonjudgmental attitude toward others' life stories, developing empathy, and offering support (Birren & Deutchman, 2005). Guided autobiography groups typically meet for 10 sessions, which can occur daily, weekly, semimonthly, or on whatever schedule works (Birren & Deutchman, 2005). Meetings generally are for 2 hours, with each individual allocated about 15 minutes or so to read his or her essay and about 5 minutes devoted to group interactions after the essay is read (Birren & Deutchman, 2005).

Whether one utilizes structured life review, guided autobiography, or some other approach to reminiscence, it is clear that *coherence* plays a major role in the development of integrity in the story of one's life. Habermas and Bluck (2000, cited in Coleman, 2005) suggested four components of coherence. **Temporal coherence** is the degree to which memories are related in time to one another and to the context in which they were experienced; **cultural coherence** comprises the normative events of one's life (going to school, developing romantic relationships, having children, and so forth); **causal coherence** and **thematic coherence** concern themselves with the degree to which underlying associations are identified so that one's life is understood as being more than a set of random events and experiences (Coleman, 2005). Both structured life review and guided autobiography suggest that articulating a coherent life story can contribute to personal growth and development, even if one's life has been filled with pain and difficulty or previously had been experienced as arbitrary and disconnected.

CHAPTER SUMMARY

In this chapter, we addressed three broad theoretical orientations to working with older adults: psychodynamic, cognitive behavioral, and reminiscence; we also briefly touched on interpersonal therapy. We discussed individual psychodynamic and group psychodynamic approaches and introduced cognitive analytic therapy, a bridge to cognitive behavioral approaches. Psychodynamic approaches have in common the uncovering of unconscious motives rooted in early childhood experiences that influence how older clients interact with others even in late life. Following identification of patterns learned early in life, a counselor might utilize interpersonal therapy to help a client develop healthier here-and-now relationships by altering roles, expressing formerly unexpressed feelings, and more generally developing communication skills. Cognitive behavioral therapies focus on replacing unhealthy thoughts and behaviors with adaptive thoughts and behaviors. Reminiscence approaches comprise reminiscence, life review, and guided autobiography, each of which focuses on the use of memories of life events to help a client understand the arc of his or her life, make meaning of his or her life, and come to a greater understanding of his or her place in the world. Depending on the particular client and his or her presentation, a counselor may utilize one or a combination of these approaches in treatment. In Chapter 7, we will look at the culture of old age and begin to consider some of the contextual factors related to older clients.

CASE STUDY

Dora is a 68-year-old African American woman who participates in a guided autobiography group as part of a class she is taking. She returned to graduate school the year before to acquire a master's degree in gerontology. Although she is excited about being in such a group, she does not have much in the way of specific expectations.

Dora is the primary caretaker for her life partner, Angie, a 70-year-old European American woman with multiple medical problems, including arthritis, which leaves her dependent on Dora for dressing, bathing, housecleaning, and other common activities. They live in a rent-controlled apartment in a medium-size city on the West Coast of the United States, an apartment in which they have resided for the past 20 years.

At the beginning of the first group meeting, Dora is a little disappointed to see that she is the only African American there, but over the course of the meeting, she begins to feel more comfortable. Over the course of several weeks, Dora looks forward to writing about the various assigned themes: her life events, family of origin, career, health, and sexuality. She shares her stories, listens to others, and participates fully in the group.

One week, the assigned theme is "stress," and Dora for the first time finds it difficult to write about the theme. She begins to feel anxious and worried about sharing with the group. For years she has not been honest with herself about the stresses she feels from the sexism, racism, and heterosexism she experiences on a daily basis, in her both personal and professional lives. She prides herself on managing the most egregious and overt experiences but finds more insidious the effects of microaggression—people looking at her suspiciously, hesitating before addressing her, and ignoring her; employees following her around in department stores; and so forth. As she has gotten older, she believes things have gotten worse, which she attributes to her advancing age. "Life has been hard enough being a Black lesbian," she says, "but now being an old Black lesbian... ." Historically, Dora relied on two approaches to coping with stress: one healthy—her spirituality—and one unhealthy—overeating. She finds frightening the thought of revealing her latter strategy and lifelong battle with weight, but she decides to reveal this to the group.

On top of this, Dora of late had been stressed over her caregiving responsibilities for Angie, which Dora increasingly finds physically and emotionally difficult. Dora understands that she and Angie are solidly middle class—"Too poor to afford long-term care, and too rich for Medicaid." Looking distressed, Dora exclaims, "I really don't know what is going to happen to us."

Questions

1. Is a guided autobiography group a good place for Dora? Would she be better served by a structured life review experience? Would she be better served by some other type of reminiscence experience? Why or why not?
2. If you were the group facilitator, what would be your response to Dora?

3. Is Dora in need of psychotherapy or counseling? Justify your answer.
4. How does your race, gender, or sexual orientation influence your reaction to Dora?

CHAPTER QUESTIONS AND ACTIVITIES

1. What are some of the life span developmental issues you should be sensitive to when considering counseling for an older client? Identify at least three issues and discuss them.
2. What are some of the cohort issues you should be sensitive to when considering counseling for an older client? Identify at least three issues, and discuss them.
3. What are some of the social context issues you should be sensitive to when considering counseling for an older client? Identify at least three issues, and discuss them.
4. Compare and contrast a psychodynamic group for older adults with a cognitive-behavioral group for older adults. What do they have in common? How do they differ?
5. What is reminiscence? Which types of reminiscence are positive, and which are negative?
6. Find out more about Webster's Reminiscence Functions Scale (1993, cited in Coleman, 2005). Define the reminiscence functions of boredom reduction, death preparation, intimacy maintenance, and others. Which of these functions does reminiscence serve for you?
7. Define structured life review and the various stages of the process.
8. Participate in or conduct a structured life review. What is the experience like? How does it differ from your expectations?
9. Select one stage of the structured life review (e.g., adolescence). Describe the Eriksonian task for that stage. Write out three open-ended questions or statements that could be used as prompts for that stage in a structured life review interview. These prompts should be items that at some level address the task for that stage.
10. Identify and describe the four unique characteristics of structured life review that distinguish it from other reminiscence approaches.
11. Describe guided autobiography.
12. Think of and write out three guided autobiography themes in addition to the ones listed above. For each theme, write at least five sensitizing questions.

13. In one paragraph each, describe your ideal self, your social-image self, and your real self. Then compare and contrast your real self with your ideal self, your social-image self with your ideal self, and your social-image self with your real self.
14. Participate in (or lead) a guided autobiography group. Describe what the experience is like.
15. What are the similarities and differences between reminiscence, life review, and guided autobiography? How are they similar? How do they differ?
16. If you engage in reminiscence, would you prefer to do so in a group or individually? Why? What are the benefits and limitations of doing so in a group? Of doing so individually?
17. You have a client who is suffering from clinical depression. In addition to referral for a medication evaluation, your client is interested in group counseling. What type of group would you recommend for your client?
18. What if your client is suffering from bereavement? What type of group would you recommend?

GLOSSARY

Causal coherence and thematic coherence: concern themselves with the degree to which underlying associations are identified so that one's life is understood as being meaningful.

Cognitive analytic therapy: is an integration of cognitive therapy with object relations therapy.

Cognitive behavioral therapy: is an intervention in which clients learn to challenge maladaptive thoughts and behaviors and replace them with adaptive thoughts and behaviors, resulting in the greater likelihood of experiencing positive emotions.

Cohort: is a group of people who share some common experience or history.

Crystallized intelligence: is the ability to use specific knowledge (e.g., facts), to draw on one's life experiences, and to utilize skills one has learned.

Cultural coherence: comprises the normative events of one's life.

Fluid intelligence: is the ability to find patterns (or meaning), infer, and problem solve, independent of the particular knowledge (e.g., facts) one has acquired about the world.

Guided autobiography: is a thematically structured group process to help older adults explore the meaning of their lives.

Ideal self: is how one wishes to be.

Life review: is a type of reminiscence in which the stories one tells are organized in such a way as to contribute to working through and integration.

Maturation: refers to the life span development changes that occur in life, particularly in relation to old age and late life.

Props and triggers: are objects or sensory experiences that elicit memories.

Real self: is how one sees oneself.

Reminiscence: is the remembering and retelling of the stories of one's life.

Reminiscence bump: is the phenomenon in which people—regardless of their age—are more likely to report vivid memories or reminiscences from their late adolescence to early adulthood than from other times in their lives.

Social context: is the current milieu in which one exists.

Social-image self: is how others perceive one to be.

Temporal coherence: is the degree to which memories are related in time to one another and to the context in which they were experienced.

Working memory: is that portion of memory that is used for data to be moved to and retained in long-term memory.

FURTHER INFORMATION

1. By far, the most insightful text on psychotherapy with older adults is Bob Knight's aptly titled *Psychotherapy With Older Adults* (Thousand Oaks, CA: Sage, 2004). It is not to be missed, and you cannot consider yourself a learned gerontological counselor without being familiar with this beautifully written book.

2. A thorough and practical overview of cognitive behavioral therapy with older adults is Laidlaw, Thompson, Dick-Siskin, and Gallagher-Thompson's *Cognitive Behavior Therapy With Older People* (New York: Wiley, 2003).

3. An excellent overview of reminiscence is found in Peter Coleman's chapter "Reminiscence: Developmental, Social and Clinical Perspectives" in Malcolm Johnson's *The Cambridge Handbook of Age and Ageing* (Cambridge, UK: Cambridge University Press, 2005).

4. A good source for more information about structured life review is Barbara Haight and Barret Haight's *The Handbook of Structured Life Review* (Baltimore: Health Professions Press, 2007).

5. If you are interested in narrative approaches to work with older adults—especially guided autobiography—a must-read is James Birren and Donna Deutchman's *Guiding Autobiography Groups for Older Adults* (Baltimore: Johns Hopkins, 1991).

6. A breadth and depth of information on group work with older adults is found in Barbara Haight and Faith Gibson's *Burnside's Working With Older Adults: Group Process and Techniques* (4th ed.) (Boston: Jones & Bartlett, 2005).

NOTES

1. See B. K. Haight and Haight (2007) for a list of structured life review questions that can be used in each of the sessions.

2. It can be argued, though, that group experiences are valuable for the "support and camaraderie" that are so often a part of good group experiences (Coleman, 2005, p. 305).

3. See Birren and Deutchman (1991) for sets of sensitizing questions.

CHAPTER 7

The Culture and Context of Old Age

We all live with the intention of being happy; our lives are all different and yet the same.

—Anne Frank (1929–1945)

Moral excellence is the result of habit. We are made just by performing just acts, temperate by performing temperate acts, brave by performing brave acts.

—Aristotle (384–322 BCE)

CHAPTER OVERVIEW

In this chapter, we will begin to look at the culture of old age. We will consider older adults as a unique cultural group, with particular ways of being, specific shared histories, distinct needs, and discrete strengths. We will consider issues of spirituality, diversity, and social justice. We will explore the differences between spirituality and religion, address issues of cultural diversities in elders, and touch on some of the social justice issues—economics and social class—as they relate to later life.

SPIRITUALITY AND RELIGION

Religion in the United States

A recent national survey suggested that about 81% of people in the United States identified themselves with a religion: 77% Christian and about 4% non-Christian (see Kosmin, Mayer, & Keysar, 2005). Fourteen percent identified as nonreligious (including atheists, agnostics, humanists, secular, and those who stated they were nonreligious), and about 5% decline to answer the question (Kosmin et al., 2005). Adults age 65 and older were more likely to identify as religious or somewhat religious than those under age 65 (Kosmin et al., 2005).

Strikingly, about 40% of the survey respondents who identified with a religion did not belong to a religious community or organization such as a church, temple, or congregation (Kosmin et al., 2005), suggesting that a large percentage of people more fittingly might be considered spiritual rather than religious. But what is the difference between being spiritual and being religious?

Spirituality and Religion

Although some identify *spirituality* and *religion* as reciprocal terms, others clearly distinguish between the two. Religion has been called "the outward expression of an inner spirituality" (Cheraghi, Payne, & Salsali, 2005, p. 473). In fact, spirituality and religion can be differentiated by level of experience—spirituality being a more personal, individual-level experience and religion a more social-level experience (Miller & Thoresen, 2003, cited in Hall, Dixon, & Mauzey, 2004).

Spirituality may be defined as "an internal set of values—a sense of meaning, inner wholeness, and connection with others" (Walsh, 1998, p. 72), devotion to a transcendent power (Worthington, Kurusu, McCullough, & Sandage, 1996), or connection with an entity beyond oneself and marked by compassion and a desire to provide for the welfare of other people (O'Hanlon, 2006).

Religions may be defined as "organized belief systems that include shared and institutionalized moral values, beliefs about God, and involvement in religious community" (Walsh, 1998, p. 72) and a religious person as "one who holds religious beliefs and values religion to some degree" (Worthington et al., 1996, p. 449) or who has distinct beliefs and practices (O'Hanlon, 2006).

There are differences between people who define themselves as religious and those who define themselves as spiritual. In one study, participants defined **religion** in terms of personal beliefs as well as organizational (church, congregation, or religious institution) beliefs and practices, whereas they defined **spirituality** in personal or experiential terms (Zinnbauer et al., 1997). People who defined themselves as religious tended to be more authoritarian, orthodox, intrinsically religious, more self-righteous, and more likely to attend church and to have had parents who attended religious institutions (Zinnbauer et al., 1997). Those who identified themselves as spiritual were more likely to have had mystical experiences, have an interest in New Age beliefs and practices, have higher incomes, and express being hurt by clergy (Zinnbauer et al., 1997).

If we accept these definitions or variations thereof, we can then apply them to our older clients. Hence, a client may be spiritual but not religious, religious but not spiritual, spiritual *and* religious, or *neither* spiritual nor religious (see Worthington et al., 1996). We can define, then, an older client who is spiritual but not religious as one who looks for meaning in life; seeks unity with other people; desires wholeness yet does not evince this through a religious organization such as a church, temple, or congregation; may not believe in a god or gods; and may express more flexibility in the application of moral values. An older client who is religious but not spiritual may participate in a religious group, may believe in a god or gods, and may hold moral values that are mandated by the religious group but might not be exploring deeper meaning, completeness, or transcendent connection to other people. An older client who is both religious and spiritual will have at least some qualities associated with being religious and spiritual, whereas an older client who is neither spiritual nor religious may not hold any of these characteristics (see Blando, 2006).

Given that older adults report being more religious than younger adults, it is likely that religion or spirituality may be an important factor in an older client's presentation or resolution of an older client's challenges. In working with older clients, then, a counselor should be attentive to both spiritual and religious factors that are present in the client and his or her life and should consider how spirituality or religion can be called on as resources to facilitate client development.

Spiritual Development and Client Development

When considering an older client's spirituality, a counselor may desire to understand at what stage of spiritual development is the client. One theory of spiritual development comprises seven stages ranging from scourge, emerge, purge to diverge, and then to resurge, converge, and finally merge (Sandhu, 2007).[1] At the *scourge* stage, a person shows no interest in spirituality or spiritual matter. The *emerge* stage is marked by an awakening of a spiritual life, often in response to some life trauma. With *purge*, a person rebuffs his or her former rejection of spirituality. *Divergence* is when a person backslides and has thoughts, behaviors, and feelings related to a life of scourge, whereas *resurgence* is the transcendence of the backsliding. The *converge* stage is demonstrated by an integration of thoughts, behaviors, and feelings about spirituality. The *merge* stage is marked by awareness of union with the transcendent. An older client, then, may be at a stage anywhere from scourge to merge. Although for many people, including older clients, merger can include the concept of a god or a higher being, I believe it also can be experienced nontheistically and can be expressed in nonreligious terms.

A study of the life reviews of hundreds of older adults found that older adults expressed much of their spirituality in nonreligious terms and referred to both internal and external qualities (Bianchi, 2005). Older adults expressed their spirituality *internally* by developing self-esteem, utilizing memories, employing humor and gratitude, and addressing death and mortality (Bianchi, 2005). They spoke about acquiring self-esteem over the course of life and leading life with less bitterness, resentment, and fear and with more confidence—qualities that Bianchi (2005) posited are present in Buddhist enlightenment and the Christian ideal of leading a simple life. Older adults engaged in "harvesting of memories"; by this is meant reminiscing not simply for the sake of reminiscing but instead for the sake of "the present and future" (Bianchi, 2005, p. 322).

Humor and gratitude also are present in the stories of the old, who use these qualities as a means of getting unstuck from bitterness and resentment and opening to gratitude, gratefulness, and thanks (qualities, according to Bianchi, that are present in Jewish and Christian worship) (Bianchi, 2005). Older adults express a "commitment to learning" in all its forms (study, reading, discussion, taking classes, travel-learning); this commitment, for example, is a foundation of Judaism, which places a high value on study of the Torah (Bianchi, 2005) and is found also in Islam, Buddhism, and other faith traditions. Older adults, too, face death by rehearsing "small deaths" (e.g., chronic illness or diminished physical abilities) from which they rebound, not necessarily physically but emotionally—learning not to fear death (Bianchi, 2005, p. 324).

Older adults express their spirituality *externally* by developing purpose, being open to new opportunities, cultivating freedom, strengthening social relationships, creating "intentional communities," and working for social justice (Bianchi, 2005, p. 326). They report finding purpose in their lives through active engagement with their environment. Openness to new experiences is adaptive, in that new experiences (e.g., caregiving for an impaired loved one) are a part of life and a part of aging (Bianchi, 2005). They find freedom in late life, too, freedom from past concerns and old psychosocial scripts (Bianchi, 2005). Family and friends play an important part of older adults' lives, allowing them to maintain and strengthen relationships and to mentor (Bianchi, 2005). Finally, older adults oftentimes work for social justice, wanting to be a part of "leaving the world better for future generations" (Bianchi, 2005, p. 327).

Others have found continuity and continued development of the spiritual lives of older adults (Eisenhandler, 2005). Older adults attend religious services; pray (not only to connect with the divine but also to remember those who are part of one's community—family and friends); read religious texts, devotional literature, or books about religious or civil leaders; engage in devotional groups (for prayer, discussion, study, and sharing); and develop an understanding of the fundamental unity of all. Programs and settings that nourish the religio-spiritual dimensions of life may effectively result in continued development and revitalization in late life (Eisenhandler, 2005).

Are there health benefits that accrue to individuals who are religious or spiritual? Maselko and Kubzansky (2006) analyzed the relationship between men's and women's public religious activity, private religious activity, and spiritual experiences and their self-rated health, psychological distress, and happiness. Public religious activity was defined as attending religious services or participating in other activities at a religious organization or institution; private religious activity was defined as praying outside of the religious environment (e.g., at home), reading the Bible, or meditating; and spiritual experiences were defined as feelings of the transcendent or the divine (Maselko & Kubzanksy, 2006). They looked at the data across three major groups of Christian denominations (Catholic, Evangelical Protestant, and Mainline Protestant) but did not include other religious traditions because of the small sample size. Overall, a higher percentage of women than men reported weekly public religious activity, daily private religious activity, and daily spiritual experience. Although both men and women who reported weekly public religious activity were more likely to report better health, less psychological distress, and more happiness, the strength of the relationship between religious activity and health, distress, and happiness was stronger for men. For men, private religious activity was associated with better health and more happiness; for women, it was associated only with more happiness. For neither men nor women was there an association between private religious activity and psychological distress. Finally, for both men and women, daily spiritual experience was associated with greater happiness; in addition, for women only it was associated with better self-ratings of health. These findings suggest that for some people there may be benefits to health and well-being by engaging in public religious activities, perhaps because of their social element, whereas for others spiritual experience may be beneficial to health and well-being, perhaps because of its ability to provide a greater sense of meaning (Maselko & Kubzansky, 2006). When working with older clients, consider whether public or private religious activity or spiritual experiences may be a source of strength and development. Even if so, this does not mean you should press your client to attend church or temple or engage in spiritual activities; rather it does suggest that you explore your client's experiences of religion and spirituality and the meaning it has for him or her.

The Role of the Counselor in Working With Spirituality

To work with clients around issues of spirituality and religion, the Association for Spiritual, Ethical, and Religious Values in Counseling (2006) recommended that counselors have competence in the following:

1. ability to define religion and to define spirituality;
2. understanding of religion and spirituality within a client's and community's cultural context;
3. self-awareness of one's own religious and spiritual beliefs;
4. self-awareness of one's own religious or spiritual development over the life span;
5. openness to discussing religious or spiritual issues within the context of counseling;
6. self-awareness of the limits of one's knowledge about a client's religious or spiritual tradition and ability to refer out to a counselor with expertise, if necessary;
7. ability, in a client's given issue(s), to determine the prominence of religion and spirituality;
8. receptivity to religious or spiritual matters in counseling, to the degree that a client desires; and
9. ability, to the extent a client needs, to use the client's religious or spiritual beliefs, behaviors, or traditions to help that client meet his or her objectives (adapted from Association for Spiritual, Ethical, and Religious Values in Counseling, 2006; see also Blando, 2006).

One of the first things you can do, then, is ask yourself (and answer honestly) the following questions:

- What are my definitions of religion and of spirituality?
- How competent am I in understanding another's religious or spiritual expression within the context of his or her culture?
- What are my own religious and spiritual beliefs?
- How have my religious and spiritual beliefs and behaviors evolved over the course of my life?

- How open am I in counseling to discussing religious or spiritual matters with a client?
- What are the limits of my knowledge about particular religious or spiritual traditions, and how willing would I be to refer a client to a counselor with more competence in a particular tradition?
- Am I able to assess the importance of a client's religious or spiritual beliefs within the context of a particular client issue?
- How receptive am I to discussing or not discussing—depending on the wishes of a client—religious or spiritual matters in counseling?
- What is my level of competence in utilizing a client's religious or spiritual beliefs or behaviors in helping a client meet his or her counseling goals?

There are a number of counseling approaches and theoretical orientations that are utilized with clients and that can be sensitive to spirituality and religion (Blando, 2006). The approaches range from cognitive-behavioral, experiential focusing, and humanistic, to interpersonal, Jungian, and psychoanalytic, to solution-oriented and of course transpersonal/integrative (see Table 7.1). Furthermore, they span both individual counseling and group work (see, e.g., Hopkins, Woods, Kelley, Bently, & Murphey, 1995). Likewise, a range of issues can be addressed through the convergence of religion, spirituality, and counseling (Blando, 2006). Issues include those across the range of counseling domains, including career, college, couple and family, gerontological, mental health, rehabilitation, and school counseling (see Table 7.2)

Older adults tend to have the highest scores on a scale of spirituality (Hattie, Myers, & Sweeney, 2004). Given this, we might anticipate that older clients may be more likely than younger clients to bring issues

TABLE 7.1   Counseling Approaches and Religion and Spirituality Scholarship

Approach	Reference
Cognitive-behavioral	Tan & Johnson, 2005
Experiential focusing	Hinterkopf, 2005
Humanistic	Elkins, 2005
Interpersonal	Miller, 2005
Jungian	Corbett & Stein, 2005
Psychoanalytic	Rizzuto, 2005; Safran, 2003; Shafranske, 2005
Solution oriented	O'Hanlon, 2006
Transpersonal/integrative	Lukoff & Lu, 2005; Mikulas, 2002

TABLE 7.2   Counseling Specialization and Religion and Spirituality Scholarship

Specialization	Reference
Career	Duffy & Blustein, 2005
College	Johnson & Hayes, 2003
Couple and family	Walsh, 1998, 1999; Wolf & Stevens, 2001; Carlson, Kirkpatrick, Hecker, & Killmer, 2002; Doherty, 2003
Gerontological	Weaver, Flannelly, Strock, Krause, & Flannelly, 2005; Hattie, Myers, & Sweeney, 2004; Dalby, 2006; Tornstam, 1994; Levenson, Jennings, Aldwin, & Shiraishi, 2005; Seifert, 2002; Wink & Dillon, 2003; Langer, 2004
Mental health	Hartz, 2005; Mijares & Khalsa, 2005
Rehabilitation	Kilpatrick & McCullough, 1999; Fitchett, Rybarczyk, DeMarco, & Nicholas, 1999; Fallott, 2001; Polcin & Zemore, 2004; Brooks & Matthews, 2000
School	Sink, 2004; Sink & Richmond, 2004; Wolf & Stevens, 2001; Ingersoll & Bauer, 2004

related to spirituality into the consulting room. The spiritual values of older adults include "integrity, humanistic concern, changing relationships with others and concern for younger generations, relationship with a transcendent being or power, self transcendence, and coming to terms with death" (Dalby, 2006, p. 4)—themes that resonate with Erikson's (1963/1987) argument regarding generativity and wisdom in old age and Tornstam's (1994) focus on gerotranscendence, including a lessened fear of death, a greater understanding of the inner life, and a feeling of union with all of creation (see Atchley, 1999, cited in Levenson, Jennings, Aldwin, & Shiraishi, 2005).

Those older adults who are more extraverted, open to experience, agreeable, and conscientious and who practice meditation are more likely to experience a sense of self-transcendence; those who are neurotic or alienated are less likely to experience this sense (Levenson et al., 2005). By self-transcendence, Levenson et al. (2005) meant "a decreasing reliance on externals for definition of the self, increasing interiority and spirituality, and a greater sense of connectedness with past and future generations" (p. 127). If they are correct, then a counselor might consider recommending meditation and encouraging an older adult client to greater extraversion, openness, agreeableness, and conscientiousness as a path to a more internal self-definition, spirituality, and sense of connection to others.

Mehta (1997) framed the relationship between later life and spirituality and religion in existential terms; namely, with advancing age, an individual subjectively connects the various parts of his or her life—thoughts, feelings, behaviors, experiences, histories—in a way that suggests meaningfulness. As one nears death, one searches for meaning, and religion provides one way of organizing one's life into a more meaningful whole. Although spirituality in later life most often is thought of in terms of end-of-life issues, in reality it is a dimension of human experience that older adults can utilize to find meaning in myriad issues, not just the end of one's life (Seifert, 2002).

Religion and spirituality are positively correlated with psychosocial functioning in later life and can be a thread that allows one to develop a more coherent sense of meaning (see Mehta, 1997). Furthermore, religious older adults may be more likely to engage in social activities that reduce feelings of isolation, that increase senses of self-esteem, and that meet needs to be liked and wanted (Mehta, 1997). Positive social relationships, social and community service, and other sociocreative activities are hallmarks of those who identify as religious (Wink & Dillon, 2003). Those who identify as spiritual are more likely to engage in self-development, personal growth, self-creative, and other wisdom and individual-knowledge activities (Wink & Dillon, 2003).

Counseling older adults need not be deficits focused. Rather, one can consider a wellness, strengths-oriented approach focusing on resilience in later life as well as spirituality. Counselors should listen to their older clients' stories, look for resiliency and spirituality in those stories, and then help clients build on their own resilience and spirituality to become even more adaptive and more fully functioning (Langer, 2004). Counselors should ask older clients to identify those spiritual resources that have given them strength, how they have stayed the same or changed over time, and how they have given meaning to life and then assist the clients with coping in later life (Langer, 2004). Counselors, too, should ask older clients about the activities in which they engage that give meaning to their lives, as well as about social relations—family and friends—that are sources of strength and energy (Langer, 2004).

Most discussions of successful aging have included the dimensions of biopsychosocial health and have not included spirituality (Sadler & Biggs, 2006). Historically, successful aging has been defined as either a state of optimal being relatively free of disease and disability, marked by high functioning and active social involvement (Rowe & Kahn, 1997, cited in Sadler & Biggs, 2006), or a time of selection and optimization with compensation (Baltes & Baltes, 1990, cited in Sadler & Biggs, 2006) in which one continually adapts to the challenges of late life. Given that older adults may become more introspective, engage in considerable reflection, move away from the material and toward a more transcendent view of life, and find meaning in suffering (see Wink & Dillon, 2002,

Erikson, 1963, Tornstam, 1997, and Frankl, 1964, all cited in Sadler & Biggs, 2006), it is reasonable to include spirituality in the concept of successful aging (Sadler & Biggs, 2006). As such, five suggestions are offered to professionals:

1. Value the assessment of the spiritual (and existential) needs of elders.
2. Put spirituality in its rightful place as an element of the holistic care of older adults.
3. Recognize the unique expressions of spirituality (including those that are nonreligious) by any given elder.
4. Attend to the spiritual (and existential) dimensions of elders in counseling.
5. Recognize both the similarities and the differences between oneself and one's clients (Sadler & Biggs, 2006).

Spiritual Assessment

To understand the spirituality and religiosity of one's clients, a counselor has to have some understanding of how to assess these qualities. Several researchers and scholars have addressed spiritual assessment. In this section, we will look at the work of Hays, Meador, Branch, and George (2001); Hodge (2003); Ortiz and Langer (2002); and Nelson-Becker, Nakashima, and Canda (2007).

Hays et al. (2001) developed a 23-item spiritual history scale comprising four dimensions: "God helped," "lifetime religious social support," "cost of religiousness," and "family history of religiousness" (see Table 7.3). The "God helped" factor comprises items related to asking God for help or assistance and receiving help from God. "Lifetime religious social support" items related to the degree to which a person is involved in the social life of his or her religious group, church, or congregation. "Cost of religiousness" looks at detriments of religion—times of conflict, stress, or physical suffering due to one's religion. "Family history of religiousness" items have to do with childhood experiences with church, congregation, and religion and the relationship between child and parent regarding spirituality and religion.

Hodge (2003) designed a six-item Intrinsic Spirituality Scale based on Allport and Ross's (1967, cited in Hodge, 2003) measure of intrinsic religion. Hodge (2003) believed that his measure could be used with both theists and nontheists (such as agnostics or atheists), whether or not such clients' beliefs and behaviors occurred within the context of an organized religious or spiritual group. To do this, Hodge (2003) used

TABLE 7.3   Hays et al.'s Spiritual History Dimensions

Dimension	Description
God helped	Asking for and/or receiving help from God
Lifetime religious social support	Social involvement in church, temple, congregation, sangha, or religious group
Cost of religiousness	Conflicts, stressors, or suffering due to religion
Family history of religiousness	Childhood experiences with church, temple, congregation, sangha, or religious group, as well as relationship between child and parent regarding spirituality and religion

Note: Hays, J. C., Meador, K. G., Branch, P. S., and George, L. K., "The Spiritual History Scale in Four Dimensions (SHS-4): Validity and Reliability," *The Gerontologist, 41*(2), 239–249, 2001.

the term *spirituality*, rather than *religion*, in his items and directed those who use the scale to define *spirituality* for themselves.

Ortiz and Langer (2002) offered a spiritual assessment protocol that can be used to broaden any biopsychosocial assessment of an older adult client to include spirituality and religion. They designed the protocol to help connect older adults with the foundations of "power and meaning" as well as their understanding of the transcendent (p. 15). Their protocol—which can be used any time in the counseling process with older adults—comprised a set of open-ended questions to assess a client's spiritual and religious needs and resources, such as "Can you identify a spiritual force that brings you a sense of comfort and belonging?" or "Privately, what rituals or practices do you engage in that are renewing or comforting?" (Ortiz & Langer, 2002).

Similarly, Nelson-Becker et al. (2007) developed a set of "prefatory questions" and a framework for assessing spirituality in older adults composed of 11 domains that provide a thorough overview of an older adult's spirituality (p. 336). The domains comprised spiritual affiliation, belief, behavior, emotional qualities, values, experiences, history, therapeutic change factors, social support, spiritual well-being, and spiritual focus. *Prefatory questions* assess whether clients use the terms *spirituality, religion,* or *faith* and whether these concepts are important to them. *Spiritual affiliation* questions are used to determine what, if any, religious denomination(s) or spiritual group(s) clients identify with, as well as whether they express a religious or spiritual life outside of a group. *Spiritual belief* queries concern clients' thoughts about life after death, their conception of God or gods, and any other spiritual or religious ideas they hold. *Spiritual behavior* questions focus on the religious or spiritual activities engaged in by clients, "such as attending a faith community, praying alone or with others, meditating, reading, or using scripture or spiritual writing" (p. 337). Spirituality's *emotional qualities* are assessed through questions about any emotions experienced in the context of religion or spirituality, as well as the degree of significance of the emotional experience. Inquiry about *values* is an attempt to more fully understand the older adult client's morality, what he or she holds dear, and how these moral principles affect his or her life. *Spiritual experiences* questions differ from spiritual behavior questions in that whereas the latter seek to understand specific spiritual behavior patterns, the former seek to understand the meaning given to experiences that may or may not have arisen out of specific spiritual behaviors. *Spiritual history* is a history-taking of clients' spiritual and religious paths; it is an assessment of their spiritual development stories—where they came from spiritually, where they are now, and how they got to where they are now. An assessment of *therapeutic change* requires a client to consider how his or her spirituality helped him or her cope during a time of change or challenge. *Social support* questions are meant to assess the degree of social support received and are given within the context of a spiritual or religious community or group. *Spiritual well-being* questions revolve around the extent of a client's "happiness and overall life satisfaction related to his/ her spirituality" (p. 343). Questions of *spiritual focus* (or propensity) address the degree to which a client's spiritual and religiosity are intrinsic (internally focused) or extrinsic (externally focused). Nelson-Becker et al. (2007) recommended that clinicians develop facility in working with issues of spirituality in later life and in understanding the unique role that spirituality plays in some older adult clients' lives. Facility with issues of spirituality in later life may begin with familiarity with spiritual assessment protocols and their use with older clients.

MULTICULTURAL GERONTOLOGICAL COUNSELING

To provide culturally competent gerontological counseling, a counselor must demonstrate competence and humility. In Chapter 9, we will explore in detail the concepts of cultural competence and cultural humility and present information about the cultural experiences of different groups of older adults. For the present discussion, we will define *cultural competence* as the acquisition of multicultural awareness, knowledge, and skills (see Sue, Arredondo, & McDavis, 1992). We become more culturally competent by learning about other groups of people and integrating this information into our understanding of and interactions with others. *Cultural humility* differs from cultural competence in that it requires us to look not merely at group differences but also at individual differences, and it requires us to approach each client as an individual who exists within a cultural context.

It is important to attend to cultural issues to reduce the health care inequalities faced by minority elders, including ethnic and racial minorities, as well as lesbian, gay, bisexual, and transgender (LGBT) elders. Lack of knowledge of others results in fewer (and also more irrelevant) questions, stereotyping, collection of poor quality information, and lack of ability to reliably interpret information.

One can look at older African Americans, Asian and Pacific Island Americans, First Nations elders, and LGBT elders on group levels and understand some of the cohort-related issues specific to group membership. One also can look at individual clients and recognize that they exist as individuals within the context of a culture or perhaps within several overlapping cultures. It is this latter approach—that of cultural humility—in which the wise counselor will find his or her greatest effectiveness. To approach cultural humility, it is beneficial to have some level of cultural competence—including an understanding of the cohort experiences of older adults. In the following section, we will very briefly address some common cohort experiences of older First Nations people, African American people, Asian and Pacific Islanders, Latinos and Latinas, and gay men and lesbians.

COHORT EXPERIENCES OF OLDER ADULTS

Each of us belongs to a cohort, based on the generation of which we are a member and the shared histories and experiences of that generation. Most American adults, for example, belong to a cohort that has as common experiences, among others, the dot-com boom and bust, the 9/11 attacks on the World Trade Center, the wars in Afghanistan and Iraq, and the struggle for marriage and other equal rights for lesbian and gay citizens.

Older adults' cohort experiences, while including current or recent past events, are highlighted by different key events (e.g., the Great Depression or World War II, China's cultural revolution, or the end of South Africa's apartheid). Cohort experiences may differ based on demographic characteristics such as gender, race/ethnicity, ability/disability, or sexual orientation. Furthermore, and importantly, historical events may be a part of the shared memories of today's older adults, even if they were not part of the lived experiences of these older adults. As a counselor, you should reflect on some of the common cohort experiences by race/ethnicity and by sexual orientation shared by your older adult clients. Yeo et al. (1999) discussed many of the cohort experiences

TABLE 7.4   Examples of Common Cohort Experiences

Group	Shared Memory or Cohort Experiences
First Nation elders[a]	Wounded Knee; Battle of Little Big Horn; Navajo Long Walk; Trail of Tears; genocide and relocation by European settlers; occupation of Alcatraz; reservation gaming
African American elders[a]	Slavery; racism and discrimination; segregation; Tuskegee Experiment; Jesse Owens and Joe Lewis; civil rights movement; Rodney King; affirmative action; election of President Barack Obama
Chinese American elders[a]	Secret societies (tangs); immigration; World War II; repeal of the Chinese Exclusion Acts; communism; split between educated suburban and uneducated urban communities; "model minority" bias; diversity of immigrants
Japanese American elders[a]	Immigration; initial ineligibility for citizenship/landownership; World War II; U.S. internment camps; Hiroshima and Nagasaki; Hawaii statehood; model minority; increase in intermarriage
Latino and Latina elders[a]	Diversity; geographic proximity to United States; immigration; development of barrios; strengthening of Spanish-language media; bilingual education; presidential candidacy of Bill Richardson; anti-immigrant sentiment
Lesbian and gay elders	Identity development; increasing visibility; ongoing civil rights struggle; removal from DSM; Stonewall riots; right-wing, religious backlash; extension of benefits; HIV/AIDS; increasing social acceptance

[a] Adapted from Yeo et al. (1999); see also On Lok SeniorHealth & Stanford Geriatric Education Center (2004).

of ethnic minority elders, and the On Lok SeniorHealth & Stanford Geriatric Education Center (2004) provided additional online resources for familiarizing yourself with cultures different from your own. Some examples of common cohort experiences are given in Table 7.4.

Summary

In this section, we briefly discussed cultural competence and cultural humility. We also took a brief look at events that may be part of the shared memories or lived experiences of First Nations, Asian American, African American, Latino and Latina, and lesbian and gay older adults. To be an effective counselor of older adults, you will need to demonstrate both cultural competence in terms of knowledge about a cultural group's history, traditions, and so forth and cultural humility in terms of understanding what shared memories and what lived experiences are parts of your particular client's history and outlook on life. For many older adults, social and economic injustice is part of their lived experience.

SOCIAL JUSTICE

An aging population will have a profound impact on society and social policy in terms of work, financial savings and consumption, the structure of families, social networks, housing, transportation, citizenship and participation in public life, and health and other social services (Forest, 2007). Although medical advances, improved education, increased wealth, savings-promoting policies, and postponement of retirement offer "reasons for optimism," many of the old are impoverished, are the objects of discrimination or abuse, are less autonomous, and have limitations in terms of care networks (Forest, 2007, p. 12). In terms of equity and social justice, older adults need access to good health as well as health care, assistance in finding their way through social programs, allowance for community-level and individual-level choices, and community involvement in decision making (Forest, 2007, p. 23).

Levels of wealth and social class have clear associations with healthy aging. Marmot (2007) discussed health inequalities and aging not only within nations but also between nations. In general, richer nations have a higher percentage of older adults as a proportion of their population than do poorer nations. Richer nations tend to have higher incidences of noncommunicable diseases, whereas poorer nations tend to have more communicable diseases and injuries. Overall, though, there tends to be less illness among higher social classes (what Marmot called "professional and managerial classes") than among lower social groups ("routine and manual classes") (Marmot, 2007, Slide 10).

Social justice issues related to aging include access to health care, housing and long-term care issues, and issues related to financial stability in later life. Martin Kohli (2006), in his excellent chapter on social justice and aging, introduced a number of concepts that are helpful in conceptualizing the parameters of social justice for older adults. Kohli argued that class conflict, which historically was a major social justice issue, has been replaced or masked by generational conflict (i.e., conflict between younger adults and older adults) over the distribution of increasingly scarce social and economic resources. He posited that this is the case because older adults, through social security, are the primary recipients of welfare (in its broadest sense) and because the ratio of older adults to younger adults is increasing.

Kohli (2006) conceptualized old age as a *socially constructed* grouping according to age, generation, or cohort membership. He believed the boundaries of old age are flexible and can be changed, for example, by raising the retirement age. Such an increase could bring to society a reduction *in toto* of the cost of providing social security (Kohli, 2006).

Another factor that impacts a discussion of aging and social justice is the fact that, unlike gender (typically) or race/ethnicity, old age does not have a "fixed membership"; rather, people move into the group defined as *old* as they progress in their life course (Kohli, 2006, p. 3). This is in contrast to conceptualizing age as generational. Kohli (2006) defined **generation** as a "position in the lineage" in a family and the group of people who share a common set of historical experiences (p. 3).

Kohli (2006) addressed the issue of attitudes and beliefs about the equitable distribution of resources in society. He argued that issues of aging and the public are issues of social security or welfare. As such, attitudes and beliefs about aging may be the sole factor or one of the factors that impact reforms in social security.

Kohli believed that inequality between older adults and younger adults is not necessarily unjust, given that younger adults will in time become older adults (see Daniels, 1998, cited in Kohli, 2006). He argued that, in general, it is preferable to have equitable treatment over the life course and across all ages. This argument is one of equality, namely, that all people regardless of age should be treated equally. Kohli discussed *sequential reciprocity, generational equity,* and *compassionate ageism.* **Sequential reciprocity** is the idea that as one ages, one will receive the same benefits as those who are currently old. **Generational equity** (or, more appropriately, generational *in*equity) is the concept that older adults receive more social welfare benefits than do younger adults, especially children. **Compassionate ageism** is the belief that older adults need social welfare benefits because they are poorer and the objects of discrimination.

Kohli (2006) indicated that those who support generational equity— that is, those who support the reduction of social welfare benefits to the old in order to free up these resources for the young—should support social changes such as privatizing social security, reducing social security benefits, increasing the age of retirement, rationing medical treatments, and testing for the privilege of driving and even voting. Counterarguments suggest that social welfare benefits do not disproportionately advantage older adults; rather, they make older adults' economic and social resources more in line with those of the general population (Kohli, 2006). In other words, social benefits level the playing field.

Other counterarguments include the fact that older adults utilize different institutions than do younger adults for their economics resources, that society concurrently could choose to spend more public monies on both older adults and younger adults, and that younger adults and older adults have familial connections that allow resources given to one group also to benefit the other group (Kohli, 2006).

There are political and social issues that might adversely affect distribution of resources to older adults, including reductions in birth rates, longer life expectancies, and earlier retirements in much of the rich world (i.e., in developed nations) (Kohli, 2006). Those who support generational equity believe that because of increasing control of political discourse by older adults (because of the increasing population of older adults), social reforms to promote generational equity will be difficult to implement (see, e.g., Binstock, 2000, and Sinn & Uebelmesser, 2002, both cited in Kohli, 2006). The argument here is that as societies age, they become gerontocracies, which in their own self-interest ensures that welfare policies benefit the aged.

There have been a number of surveys of attitudes and beliefs related to social justice and economic attitudes (see Kluegel et al., 1995, Forma & Kangas, 1999, and Hicks, 2001, all cited in Kohli, 2006). In general, survey responses have suggested that people in most countries believe it is the government's responsibility to ensure that older adults have a reasonable standard of living. Furthermore, surveys have suggested that most people do not believe that social welfare programs for older adults should be cut; in fact, many believe they should be expanded.

Europeans have conceptualized social justice in terms of "prevention of poverty" and "a guaranteed minimum pension," as well as the maintenance of the standard of living, "greater equality among the elderly," and the principle of pay-as-you-go (Kohli, 2006, p. 17). European citizens have preferred to increase contributions or taxes or to lower social welfare benefits over raising the retirement age, preferences that suggest an inclination for sequential reciprocity (Kohli, 2006).

As a counselor and a member of society, you are part of the political discourse on social justice and aging. Your beliefs about older adults— whether you believe they are richer or poorer than younger adults, whether you believe they are more or less politically powerful than younger adults, and so forth—influence your work as a counselor, your priorities as a counselor, and what you believe to be your role as a counselor.

If, for example, you believe in sequential reciprocity *and* you believe that older adults are better off economically than younger adults, you may be less likely to act on reforms that improve access to affordable medical care for older adults. Conversely, if you believe in generational equity *and* you believe that older adults are better off economically than younger adults, you might act on reforms that distribute access to affordable medical care equally across the generations—for children, young adults, middle-aged adults, and older adults. Take the time to consider your beliefs about older adults, their standards of living, their access to health care, and other issues and how your beliefs inform your day-to-day work with clients as well as your work as an advocate for social improvements for the population of older adults.

CHAPTER SUMMARY

We began this chapter by exploring the differences between spirituality and religion. We saw that many older adults self-identify as spiritual, suggesting that counselors consider this dimension of their older clients' lives. Next, we considered the concepts of cultural competence and cultural humility. We also briefly reviewed cohort and historical experiences of First Nations elders, African American elders, Chinese and Japanese American elders, Mexican American elders, and gay and lesbian American elders. Finally, we discussed the issue of social justice and aging, focusing on economic justice and its relative manifestation through sequential reciprocity, generational equity, and compassionate ageism. In Chapter 8, we will address in more depth issues of spirituality in later life.

CASE STUDY

Mrs. Smith is an 85-year-old woman who presents as distressed over her increasing difficulties in paying for rent, buying groceries, and paying for her numerous medications. She has been on a fixed income since her husband died many years ago. In 1929, she emigrated with her family from Germany to the United States. She belongs to a very conservative church and believes that her difficulties are given to her by God to make her a stronger person, but she increasingly finds little solace in prayer. Her oldest daughter asked her to move in with her and her family, but Mrs. Smith declined because, she said, "I do not want to give up my house or my kitchen." She further states that she remembers the Great Depression and that she is "not prepared to live through another one of those."

Questions

1. What are your initial clinical considerations with this client?
2. What are the spirituality considerations with this client, and how would you address them?
3. What are the cultural considerations with this client, and how would you address them?
4. What are the social justice considerations with this client, and how would you address them?

CHAPTER QUESTIONS

1. What is your definition of *spirituality*? What is your definition of *religion*? How are your definitions similar to or different from those of the author?
2. What is a counselor's role when faced with issues related to religion, spirituality, and aging? What are the limits of that role?
3. What would you do if you were counseling an older adult client whose spiritual or religious beliefs differed radically from your own?
4. Compare and contrast the terms *old age*, *cohort*, and *generation*.
5. What is your position on generational equity? Explain. What are some counterarguments to your position?
6. Choose a historical event you are not familiar with, and research it. What is its social impact on elders? What is its emotional impact?
7. What are some of the major cohort markers and experiences for American elders whose background is First Nations? Mexican? Lesbian or gay? African American? Chinese? Japanese? What are the commonalities? What are the differences? What else would you add to these cohort experiences?

GLOSSARY

Compassionate ageism: is the belief that older adults need social welfare benefits because they are poorer and the objects of discrimination.
Generation: is marked by a shared set of historical experiences or by one's relative position in one's family.
Generational equity: is the concept that older adults unfairly receive more social welfare benefits than do younger adults, especially

children, and that resources need to be disseminated equitably
between generations.

Religion: is the more external, behavioral, socially recognized relationship with the transcendent.

Sequential reciprocity: is the idea that as one ages, one will receive the
same benefits as those who are currently old.

Spirituality: is the more internal, personal relationship with the
transcendent.

FURTHER INFORMATION

1. Possibly the most moving book about the culture of old age is Mary
   Pipher's *Another Country* (New York: Riverhead, 1999).
2. A must-read is Martin Kohli's chapter "Aging and Justice," in
   Binstock and George's *Handbook of Aging and the Social Sciences*
   (6th ed.) (San Diego, CA: Academic Press, 2006).
3. For an exceptional discussion of the cohort experiences of ethnic
   minority elders, see Gwen Yeo's et al. paper *Cohort Analysis as a Tool
   in Ethnogeriatrics: Historical Profiles of Elders From Eight Ethnic
   Populations in the United States* (Stanford, CA: Stanford Geriatric
   Education Center, Stanford University School of Medicine, 1999).

NOTE

1. I will leave it up to the reader to decide whether it is a blessing or a
   curse that all of these stages rhyme.

CHAPTER 8

Spirituality and Counseling Older Adults

My religion is to live and die without regret.

—Milarepa (circa 1040–circa 1123 CE)

The most beautiful thing we can experience is the mysterious.

—Albert Einstein (1879–1955)

CHAPTER OVERVIEW

In this chapter, we will consider issues related to spirituality, religion, aging, and counseling. Specifically, we will survey the major world religions, spiritual traditions, and philosophical systems, including Hinduism, Buddhism, Christianity, Confucianism, Islam, Judaism, primal religions, Shintoism, Taoism, and humanism. We will discuss each tradition's perspective on aging and death. We also will look at the role of the counselor when facing issues of spirituality or religion when counseling older adults and their families, especially as they relate to illness and mortality.

MAJOR WORLD RELIGIONS, SPIRITUAL TRADITIONS, AND PHILOSOPHICAL SYSTEMS AND AGING

In this section, we will conduct a short overview of some of the major religious traditions—with one caveat. The overview provided is brief and as such will not address the subtleties present in a religious tradition or discuss to any marked degree the variations found within a tradition.[1]

Also, we will take a look at humanism, though not a religion, per se, as a philosophical system that may influence a client's view of him- or herself and aging.

The discussions provided (and offered in no specific order) are meant as overviews—very general introductions and starting points—so that you may acquire a beginning understanding of religio-philosophical traditions different from your own and how these traditions may influence a client's perspective on aging. You may have a different perspective on religion, spirituality, or philosophy than what is presented here—that is fine. The one thing you heartily are encouraged to do is to study the religious, spiritual, and philosophical traditions of your older clients so that you will have a deeper and richer understanding of your clients' worldviews.

Hinduism

Overview. Dating from around 2500 BCE,[2] **Hinduism**, with about 900 million adherents, is the third largest religion in the world (Coward, Sidhu, & Singer, 2000; "Schools: Hinduism," 2008; Whitman, 2007). Hinduism shares some beliefs with Buddhism (e.g., samsara and karma) or beliefs that have been an influence on Buddhism (e.g., Atman has influenced the Buddhist concept of anatman, reincarnation has influenced the Buddhist concept of rebirth). As such, our discussion of Hinduism will expound on these concepts.

Hinduism exists not as a formal entity or a strict set of doctrines but rather as a set of beliefs and practices, with some commonalities and considerable diversity of expression (Firth, 2005). This diversity of expression is based in part on the education, class, and specific religious traditions of a particular individual (Firth, 2005). Overall, though, Hinduism finds expression in rituals and good acts, prayer, and meditation (Firth, 2005).

Common expressions of Hindu religious practice include the path of devotion, the path of ethical action, the path of knowledge, and the path of physical restraint/yoga (Tarakeshwar, Pargament, & Mahoney, 2003). The *path of devotion* is one of prayer and a striving for oneness with the universal reality; the *path of ethical action* is expressed through good acts without being preoccupied with their effects or expecting something in return; the *path of knowledge* is one of study intended to free oneself of ignorance; and the *path of physical restraint/yoga* is one of a disciplined life—which may include veganism or vegetarianism, meditation, yoga practice, or fasting—to control one's mind (Tarakeshwar et al., 2003).

Unlike many cultures influenced by dogmatic religious or spiritual traditions, a relatively high degree of lenience exists in Hindu culture for the coexistence of conflicting beliefs and behaviors without any necessity for synthesis (Saraswathi, 2005). Both the individual and the community members can hold disparate beliefs and engage in seemingly contradictory behaviors as a normative and acceptable way of being. In this way, Hinduism acknowledges itself as dynamic, integrative, and inclusive (Mannan, 1996).

Hinduism does not discriminate religion from culture; religion is culture, and culture is religion (Coward et al., 2000). As such, when dealing with older Hindu clients, you need to consider all religio-cultural aspects of your client including degree of acculturation, education level, socioeconomic status, roots in rural or urban life, and understanding of religion (i.e., whether your client is more fundamental, moderate, or liberal in interpretation of religion) (Coward et al., 2000).

Every Hindu is born into one of four classes: Brahmin (priests), kshatriyas (warriors and rulers), vaishyas (merchants), and sudras (peasants). Each class is further subdivided based on occupation, with particular rules of appropriate behavior, called **dharma** (Firth, 2005). Dharma is pervasive and impacts all of one's behaviors. Like many non-Western traditions, Hinduism is duty based rather than rights based (Coward et al., 2000). That is, in Hindu culture, one's acts arise out of one's duties rather than from one's rights. For example, in Hinduism, there is a duty to engage in behaviors that support health (Coward et al., 2000); traditional Indian (Ayurvedic) medical care—including using herbal treatments, making dietary changes, and engaging in different behaviors and thoughts—is designed to restore balance and support health (Coward et al., 2000). The objective of **Ayurvedic medicine** ultimately is to aid an individual so that he or she may continue to spiritually evolve (Mannan, 1996).

A fundamental belief of Hindu culture is that of the divinity of all of the universe; that is, all things and all beings share in divinity (Mannan, 1996). Furthermore, Hindus believe in the beginning-less and repeated rebirths known as reincarnation (Mannan, 1996). Accordingly, even when the body dies, there is something in that person that does not die but is reborn into another life (Mehta, 1997). Each individual goes through countless cycles of birth, death, and rebirth, purifying the soul and moving toward the objective of **moksha**, which is liberation from this cycle and full realization of union with the divine reality (Coward et al., 2000).

Karma is the universal law that every action has consequences: Present experiences are based on past karma; future experiences are based on present karma (see Desai, 1988; Mehta, 1997). The consequences of one's behaviors in a previous life influence one's experiences in the current life. Coward et al. (2000) described karma as the phenom-enon in which every action or thought in a past life leaves a trace that, upon rebirth, is transferred to the current life and forms an impulse to act or think. Through free will, these impulses are either accepted or rejected, thereby influencing karma in subsequent lives. Mannan (1996) described karma in terms of unfulfilled desires in a previous life that exert a pull on one's being back to material existence through reincarnation. Karma is inescapable and influences all of one's existence (Firth, 2005). One tangible effect of a client's belief in karma may be an increased ease in accepting misfortunes, pains, and suffering associated with aging—a coping skill that may prove useful in late life (Mehta, 1997).

Particularly relevant for the current discussion is the concept of **ashrama**, the four stages of life, introduced in Chapter 1. Recall that the four stages are that of the student, householder, forest dweller, and ascetic ("Ashrama," 2008; Firth, 2005). For each stage of life, there are appropriate and expected ways of behaving—more socially embedded in earlier life and more detached in later life (Saraswathi, 2005). The student stage is a time of connection to elders, and the householder stage is a time of forming a family. The forest dweller and ascetic stages are marked by a turning from the material world and toward the tran-scendent (Saraswathi, 2005). In later life a person may begin to detach him- or herself from family and community duties and become more autonomous in order to fully grasp the reality of Atman (Saraswathi, 2005). It may be that Hindu people progress through three developmen-tal stages: *youth's* dependence on older adults and cultural and social conformity (roughly comparable to the student stage), *early adult-hood's* rebellious initiation of autonomy (roughly comparable to the householder stage), and *later life's* true striving for autonomy (including control over decision making and increased self-responsibility; roughly comparable to the forest dweller and ascetic stages) (Mines, 1988, cited in Saraswathi, 2005).

The key point to consider is that if you are working with an older Hindu client, be aware that there may be some movement toward greater autonomy (in the Hindu sense) and some level, however subtle, of detach-ment from family and community. This is not to say that older Hindu clients deny their families or ignore their communities; rather it suggests that over time the relationship changes between a Hindu client and his or her family and community. Even within this tradition of increasing autonomy with increasing age, there is a strong and most fundamental understanding of the person-in-context or self-in-community, the con-text being family and community (Coward et al., 2000). As such, con-sider that any decisions made by a client are made within the context of family and community.

A substantial proportion of Hindus follow a tradition of devotion to a single God and seek liberation from **samsara** (the continual cycle of birth, death, and rebirth) to find life with the divine (Firth, 2005; Mehta, 1997). Hindus believe in a fundamental reality, called **Atman**, that exists in every being and that "transmigrates from one life to another" (Firth, 2005, p. 682). Atman is the true self and is distinguished from the construed self (Saraswathi, 2005). Conceptually, Atman is comparable—though not equivalent—to the Christian concept of the soul and is contrasted with the physical body (Mannan, 1996). Atman is the nonmaterial self and is distinguished from the material self (Saraswathi, 2005). Although the material self dies, Atman is eternal. When the material self dies, Atman goes to another plane of existence, which can be at either a higher level or a lower level than the previous plane of existence, based on one's karma (Mannan, 1996). Aging may affect the material body—the physical body—but it does not affect Atman (Mehta, 1997). As one evolves spiritually, one is reborn on a higher plane. One goal of Hinduism, then, is the full recognition of the spiritual self and the reduction of the material self (Saraswathi, 2005), so that one may unite with the divine, thus freeing oneself from the otherwise endless cycle of samsara. An older Hindu client may prepare him- or herself for spiritual evolution with the intent of escaping samsara.

Hinduism and Aging. Mannan (1996) reminded us that Hinduism developed in India at a time when—because of war and disease—life was short, and in the holy texts, Hindus were exhorted to pray for good health. As such, old age was seen as a blessing (Mannan, 1996), a perspective that is accepted even to this day.

As we discussed in Chapter 1, Crawford (2003) reviewed three models of aging—social, medical, and success—discussed them from the context of Hinduism and Hindu ethics, and described a Hindu model of aging. The social model of aging promotes positive and counteracts negative images, posits that quality of life is more important than quantity of life, and posits that older adults have value and are useful beings (Crawford, 2003). The medical model of aging conceptualizes aging as a medical disease to be cured (Crawford, 2003). The success model of aging suggests that successful aging comprises three factors: avoiding illness, maintaining mental and physical health, and being socially engaged (Rowe & Kahn, 1998, cited in Crawford, 2003).

Crawford (2003) criticized the social and medical models of aging as incompatible with Hindu ethics. Incompatibilities revolve around the social and medical models' rejection of physical decline as intolerable, the position that aging, physical decline, and death are unacceptable or that life should be extended indefinitely. Crawford (2003) posited that Hindu scriptures are more congruent with the success model's emphasis on minimizing disease and supporting physical and mental functioning. The success model and the Hindu model of aging diverge regarding active involvement with and participation in life. To Rowe and Kahn (1998, cited in Crawford, 2003) aging well meant physical and mental well-being as well as social involvement; to Hinduism aging well also requires the "primacy of the transcendent" that is union with God (p. 185). Crawford (2003) stated that the Hindu model of aging relies on the *principle of ripeness*, which states, "a person is *right* for a particular stage when he is *ripe* for that stage" (p. 186). In this sense, an older person's decisions in life—and especially the decision to die—should be respected, for they represent the convergence of the *right*ness and the *ripe*ness of the decision.

Finally, in the Hindu model of aging, one's value does not rest on one's age, or beauty, or wealth, or friendships but rather on one's "hunger for the transcendent," which allows one to reconcile the reality of one's mortality and lead life rich in old age (Crawford, 2003, p. 187). This, of course, has implications for dying and death.

Hinduism views death not as an end but as a transition to a life hereafter; death provides relief from suffering, an opportunity for auspicious rebirth, or the full realization of union with the divine (Desai, 1988). It is important for deaths to be "good." Firth (2005) stated, "A good death … occurs in old age, at the right astrological time, and in the right place (on the ground at home if it cannot be on the banks of the sacred Ganges)," with all of life's affairs in order: marriages arranged, conflicts resolved, gifts given, and good-byes having been said (p. 683; see also Mannan, 1996). Good deaths are identified by a shining forehead and peaceful appearance, with eyes and mouth somewhat open; bad deaths are those that "are violent, premature, and uncontrolled … in the wrong place and at the wrong time, signified by vomit, faeces, urine, and an unpleasant expression" (Firth, 2005, p. 683). The latter signs are indications of impurity, as the most impure substances are the discharges of one's body (Coward et al., 2000). Near the end of life, it is not uncommon for the dying person to fast, not only for spiritual cleansing but also to further disengage from the present life and to make certain that there are no signs of a bad death (Firth, 2005).

Crawford (2003) recommended a respectful attitude toward the process of dying, an attitude of noninterference of what is a natural process. He recommended helping the dying person be comfortable, "in order to enable the spirit to have its final moments" (Crawford, 2003, p. 192). An agitated or uncomfortable state while dying could result in a less than auspicious rebirth.

Crawford (2003) outlined the Hindu view of dying and death as follows:

- Death is merely the termination of the physical body, while the subtle body continues.
- Death is the opposite of birth, not of life.
- Birth and death are to be recognized as cyclical and not linear events.
- The essential self is immortal.
- Karma allows a person to connect with his or her extended past history (extending into all previous lives), present, and future (extending into all future lives).
- Though the present life is the result of past karma, future life will be the result of karma acquired in this life.
- Accidents and unexpected events in this life are the result of past karma.
- Death is a certainty.
- Only untimely death is profoundly mourned.
- One should value quality of life over length of life.
- A good death is one that happens in the home and over which a person has control.
- Death is a family, not a solitary, event.
- Cremation is performed after death in order to purify and return "bodies to their original form" (pp. 195–196; see also Mannan, 1996).

Coward et al. (2000) suggested five considerations when working with Hindu clients: understand the influence of the concepts of karma and rebirth on the worldview, actions, and decisions of clients; involve family members in decision making, given the understanding that every person exists within the context of his or her family and community; understand the concepts of purity and impurity and respect the modesty of female clients; utilize objective (i.e., nonfamily) interpreters when needed; and understand that your client also may utilize traditional Indian (Ayurvedic) medical treatment.

Buddhism

Overview. **Buddhism** is a religious, philosophical, and ethical system developed by Siddhartha Gautama (the Buddha) approximately 2,500 years ago. It is a major tradition in Asia. In the West, Buddhism is becoming a major influence on counseling and psychotherapy. Buddhism encompasses many traditions—Zen and Tibetan are among the best known in the West. Some of the most renowned Buddhist leaders are

TABLE 8.1   The Four Noble Truths

Truth	Description
Suffering	Life is filled with stress, dissatisfaction, and unhappiness.
Causes of suffering	Stress, dissatisfaction, and unhappiness are caused by desires and cravings.
Cessation of suffering	To transcend stress, dissatisfaction, and unhappiness, abandon desires and cravings.
Eightfold Path	To abandon desires and cravings, follow the Eightfold Path.

teachers such as the Dalai Lama and Thich Nhat Hahn and, in North America, Pema Chodron and Mark Epstein.

Buddhism tends to be relatively nondogmatic, but there are basic concepts that Buddhists share. Among them are the Four Noble Truths; the Eightfold Path; and the truths of rebirth, anatman, karma, samsara, the six realms of existence, and the five aggregates. To a Buddhist, **rebirth** means that the karmic forces in a previous being's life will influence a future life that takes form. **Anatman** is the opposite of Atman; it is the belief that there is no fundamental soul or spirit that exists in sentient beings, and any belief in such is illusory; that is, there is no essential self. *Karma* and *samsara* are referenced in the previous discussion of Hinduism. We briefly will take a look at the Four Noble Truths, which form the foundation of Buddhist thought. I encourage you to read ancillary texts to gain an understanding of the Eightfold Path, the six realms of existence, the five aggregates, and other Buddhist concepts.

The Four Noble Truths lie at the heart of Buddhist thought (see Table 8.1). According to Buddhists, the Buddha, in enlightenment, understood the reality of existence in the following way. First, all of life is filled with stress, dissatisfaction, and unhappiness: Birth is filled with this, as is youth, adulthood, and old age. Second, this stress, dissatisfaction, and unhappiness are caused by desire and craving. One might desire the past to be different than it was; one might desire the future to bring various comforts. One might crave wealth, power, or beauty. Third, to transcend stress, dissatisfaction, and unhappiness, one must abandon desires and cravings. Fourth, the way to abandon desires and cravings is to follow the Eightfold Path—eight aspects of life that can be lived in a way that destroys desires and cravings.

Buddhism and Aging. Buddhism has a rich tradition around aging, dying, and death. Aging can be a time of great spiritual growth. Developmentally, it can be a time of enlightenment, of having the luxury of reflecting on the Four Noble Truths, and—freed from the cares and worries of early life and midlife—of following more mindfully the Eightfold Path.

One of the most fundamental teachings of Buddhism is that death is inevitable and experienced by all (Keown, 2005). Furthermore, a good death is one marked by "mindfulness and mental clarity," allowing one a greater opportunity for auspicious rebirth (Keown, 2005, p. 952). For Buddhists, a given life begins at the moment of conception and ends at the moment of death (Keown, 2005). The moment of death occurs when the body lacks vitality, heat, and sentience (Keown, 2005). If any of these three qualities are still present, a person is not dead. While in this life, Buddhism embraces compassion and respect for life as two fundamental values (Keown, 2005).

Buddhists are exhorted to show respect and compassion for those who are in persistent vegetative states, for they are living beings (even if they are lacking mental awareness); these people should be given food and water and should be the objects of compassionate treatment (Keown, 2005). Euthanasia and physician-assisted suicide are forbidden because they are the destruction of life (Keown, 2005). However, life does not need to be preserved at any cost. Although a person is not to "make death his [or her] aim," neither shall he or she deny the inevitability of death (Keown, 2005, p. 954). Indeed, a person shall seek to live while also realizing that death will come—in the cases of clients near death, very soon—and preparation for death should be continued (Keown, 2005).

Butzenberger and Fedorova (1989) argued that the Buddha embraced in the Four Noble Truths essentially a medical model: beings experience suffering, the cause of suffering is diagnosable, there is a positive prognosis for suffering, and there is a cure for suffering. When working with older Buddhist clients who are ill or perhaps terminally ill, you should be aware that your client's perspective and behaviors may be influenced by his or her understanding of the Four Noble Truths and other Buddhist concepts. For example, an older Buddhist client may more readily than other clients accept the reality of his or her suffering. Or Buddhist families of dying individuals may have requests atypical in North America regarding the handling of the deceased's body. An effective counselor will be sensitive to the cultural traditions and needs of his or her clients.

Christianity

Overview. **Christianity** is a religious tradition comprising a cluster of religious groups. It is a broad term encompassing a number of religious belief systems ranging from Roman Catholic and Eastern Orthodox, to various Protestant churches, to the Mormon Church and other, newer North American denominations. Christianity manifests through a range of experiences, from traditions steeped in mysticism, complexity, and ceremony, to traditions stripped bare to reveal what believers understand to be the essential truths. The majority of Christians believe in a God who is the creator of the universe, the divinity of Jesus, heaven and hell, and the forgiveness of sins.

Huston Smith (1991), in *The World's Religions: Our Great Wisdom Traditions* (a brilliant, spirited presentation of the world's major religious traditions),[3] described Christianity as a religion that believes that Jesus was born, came to experience the spirit of God, and understood as his mission the healing of humanity and the creation of a new social order, namely, the kingdom of God on earth. Jesus engaged in good works, taught the word of God—"God's overwhelming love of humanity"—and glorified God through his love and integrity (p. 326). Most Christians believe that Jesus was crucified, died, and was resurrected and that his followers subsequently were visited by the Holy Spirit. They tend to believe that Jesus is active even today in a real and concrete way. Smith (1991) identified three essential beliefs shared by many Christians: the incarnation, the atonement, and the trinity. Incarnation refers to the belief that God manifested himself in the human form of Jesus.[4] Atonement refers to the belief that, through Jesus, God made amends for humanity's sins through his death and resurrection. The doctrine of the Trinity holds that there is a single God who takes form as father, son (Jesus), and Holy Spirit.

Traditions vary substantially in beliefs and practices and offer "different accounts of how to live and die properly" (Engelhardt & Iltis, 2005, p. 1045). Though Christianity does not speak with one voice, Engelhardt and Iltis (2005) posited that traditional Christianity has one overarching goal—that of salvation through the death and **resurrection** of Jesus and repentance for one's sins, resulting in the enjoyment of everlasting life after death with God in heaven.

Christianity and Aging. Engelhardt and Iltis (2005) proposed five factors that influence a Christian client's attitudes and beliefs: level of commitment to tradition, degree of focus on ceremony, degree of belief in the divine revelation, level of observance, and level of religious coherence (see Table 8.2). Concerning the level of commitment to tradition, some Christians believe that their tradition has expressed since its inception the ultimate truth about life, the universe, and God. As such, it is unchanging and unalterable. Other Christians hold a more dynamic understanding of their tradition in which theologies evolve over time, and theological innovations are not uncommon. Regarding the degree of focus on ceremony, some Christians are very oriented toward liturgy

TABLE 8.2   Factors Influencing Christians' Attitudes and Beliefs

Factor	Range of Attitudes and Beliefs
Tradition	Tradition expresses immutable ultimate truths versus tradition is dynamic and evolving
Ceremony	Focus on liturgy and ceremony versus eschewing of liturgy and ceremony and focus on other communitarian expressions of faith
Divine revelation	Christianity given to humans by God versus Christianity as a human story in which to find comfort
Observance	Observant and committed to expressing religious behaviors versus nonobservant with no consistent commitment
Religious coherence	Families that share common beliefs about tradition, ceremony, divine revelation, and observance versus families that have discrepant beliefs about tradition, ceremony, divine revelation, and observance

Note: Engelhardt, H. T., & Iltis, A. S., "End-of-Life: The Traditional Christian View," *The Lancet, 366,* 1045–1049, 2005.

and ceremonial expressions of their faiths, whereas others eschew liturgy and ceremonial expression in favor of other communitarian expressions or personal approaches to faith. Regarding degree of belief in divine revelation, some Christians posit that Christianity is a religio-philosophical system given to humans by God through Jesus, whereas other Christians identify their Christianity as a "worldview or narrative within which to find comfort and peace" (Engelhardt & Iltis, 2005, p. 1046). Some Christians are observant, attending church or religious community expressions, praying, and engaging in other religious behaviors, as well as living their lives as consistently as they can with their religio-moral beliefs; others are less committed to being observant and may "act without a consistent commitment" (Engelhardt & Iltis, 2005, p. 1046). Finally, Christians may come from religiously and morally coherent families, in which family members share their beliefs about tradition, liturgy, metaphysics, and degree of being or not being observant; other Christian clients may live in families in which there are covert differences or overt conflict over varying beliefs about tradition, liturgy, metaphysics, and degree of being observant.

As counselors, we can look at our Christian clients through the lenses of these five factors and consider how each client's expression of faith influences our work in the consulting room. For example, as counselors we might support those older clients who are more observant in taking solace and comfort in their religious traditions and rituals, while we might take a different approach with those who are less observant. Those clients who come from morally and religiously cohesive families may have fewer family issues related to aging or death and dying than do those clients whose families are not cohesive. For a client in the latter group, part of our work as a counselor might be to explore—and help that client come to some decisions about—how he or she wants his or her remaining life to unfold and how he or she wants to anticipate dying and death.

In any event, Engelhardt and Iltis (2005) suggested that traditional Christians will view the remainder of their lives as well as their preparation for death as a time "to become reconciled with those whom [they have] harmed and to ask God's forgiveness," to engage in "self examination, repentance, and a final crucified submission to the will of God," and to accept "unavoidable suffering as an opportunity for spiritual growth" (Engelhardt & Iltis, 2005, p. 1046). We might expect Christian clients to anticipate reconciliation, forgiveness, and union with God and family in heaven.

Confucianism

Overview. **Confucianism** is a system of thought, behaviors, and ethics that is infused in a follower's life. Confucius lived about 2,500 years ago in China, where he developed a system of thought laid forth in the *Analects.* His philosophy continues to influence Chinese thought and culture.

Confucius interestingly believed that humans are constrained by fate meted out by a "Supreme Being" as well as by nature, yet he also believed that humans have a responsibility for their deeds, especially in their dealings with other people (Riegel, 2006). In other words, he thought that the duration of our life is given to us by fate, but the endeavors that we undertake are within our control (Riegel, 2006).

Ren, a major Confucian concept, refers to compassion for others (Riegel, 2006). Confucius believed that *ren* is most readily practiced in relation to family, especially in relation to parents and to older brothers and sisters. Furthermore, he believed that the best way to cultivate *ren* is through self-control. Learning self-control means learning *li,* the social rules encompassing "respect for superiors," understanding one's place in society, and learning how to resolve the conflicts between personal wants and societal (including family and community) needs (Riegel, 2006). Confucius greatly valued education and believed in the worth of finding a competent teacher—"someone older who is familiar with the ways of the past and the practices of the ancients" (Riegel, 2006).

Confucianism and Aging. We can say that old age, from a Confucian perspective, is a time of life marked by wisdom and honor. Older adults are revered as the holders of knowledge and as teachers. Old age, too, is a time of life marked by a deeper understanding and ability to express *ren* and *li*.

Western approaches to relationships between health care providers (including counselors) and clients are often marked by a client-centered philosophy that values collaboration between the provider and the recipient of services. In the West, the common contemporary view of care recipients is that they are "rational, self-conscious beings capable of valuing their own lives, and who are consequently entitled to the liberty and rights to choose for themselves" (Tsai, 2001, p. 1). In contrast, the Confucian perspective is more complex and inclusive and views a person as *chun-tze* (Tsai, 2001)—an individual who exists within the context of his or her relationship to others. In this perspective, a person is both rational and autonomous, as well as relational and altruistic, and one's "self actualization involves incessant participating in and promoting of the welfare of [one's] fellow persons" (Tsai, 2001, p. 1).

We can consider *chun-tze* from the perspective of the four principles of biomedical ethics. These principles are "respect for autonomy, non-maleficence, beneficence and justice" (Tsai, 1999, p. 1). Respect for autonomy is regard for a client's right and ability to make decisions about health care; nonmaleficence is a commitment to do no harm; beneficence is the duty to help or assist; and justice addresses fairness and equity. Although each of these principles is present in ancient Chinese medical ethics, in the East, greater cultural emphasis may be placed on beneficence than on autonomy (Tsai, 1999).

Health care providers (in the case of our discussion, counselors) should be sensitive to the general cultural differences that exist between a provider and a recipient and should "learn to appreciate each individual's particular beliefs and values through narratives of morality" (Kim, 2005, p. 1). Health care providers should develop "cultural humility" when working with clients by exploring the points of both convergence and divergence of their and each of their clients' values (Kim, 2005).

How are Confucian principles translated into cultural traits, and how might they manifest in a particular individual? Cheng (1990, p. 1) believed that Confucianism produces three traits: "lack of personality," "lack of principled moral thinking," and "lack of assertiveness." Although these traits are expressed in the negative (i.e., lack of some quality), Cheng (1990) actually defined the traits by what is present in them. By lack of personality, Cheng (1990) meant the universal social contract of behavior based on accepted rules of what is proper and improper. This could manifest in older clients by their strict adherence to Confucian rules of propriety, which may differ from Western expectations of what is appropriate social interaction. Lack of principled moral thinking refers to a moral system grounded in the interactions between agents in relationship, a general absence of hypothetical analysis, and recognition of the inherent stratification of relationships (Cheng, 1990). In other words, moral actions are grounded in relationships and not abstractions. In older clients, this latter point, for example, could manifest by a client feeling responsibility toward his or her counselor given the relationship between them. Lack of assertiveness has its foundations in a focus on harmony and responsibility to others rather than to individual wants and rights (Cheng, 1990). A focus on harmony could manifest itself through an older client deferring to the expertise of the counselor or not disagreeing with the counselor.

Ultimately, goodness is the core moral virtue of the Confucian ethic (Guo, 1995). This virtue promotes valuing human life, beneficence in treating the dying and healing those who are wounded, demonstrating care for those who suffer from disease, honesty, careful study of the techniques of medicine, carefulness in one's work life, dignity in self-comfort, politeness and respect for local customs, equality in treatment of patients, and respect for the scholarship of others (Guo, 1995). From a Confucian perspective, then, a counselor should value human life, kindly treat the ill and dying, be honest, know his or her craft and apply it carefully, self-comfort, be polite and respectful of others' traditions, treat clients equally, and thoughtfully consider research and scholarship in the field of counseling.

Islam

Overview. **Islam**, with over 1.3 billion adherents, has the second largest number of followers, making it one of the world's major religious traditions. Most Muslims live in India, Sub-Saharan Africa, Indonesia and Southeast Asia, Arab nations, former Soviet republics, Turkey, Iran, Afghanistan, and China (Ahmed, 1999, Ramadan, 1999, and Rassool, 2000, each cited in Cheraghi, Payne, & Salsali, 2005). Muslims account for about 15 million of Europe's nearly 500 million people and about 8 million of the United States's 300 million (Ramadan, 1999, Sheikh & Gatrad, 2002, each cited in Cheraghi et al., 2005).

In Islam, humans are understood as being created to serve God and to whom God has sent prophets (Sachedina, 2005). To Muslims, Muhammad was the final prophet, who received the message of God in the *Qur'an*, given to him by the Archangel Gabriel (Sachedina, 2005). The five pillars of Islam are the fundamental statements of the Muslim faith, comprising faith, prayer, charity, fasting, and pilgrimage (see Table 8.3) (Sachedina, 2005).

TABLE 8.3   The Five Pillars of Islam

Name	Description
Iman (Faith)	Belief in God and in Muhammad as his prophet
Salah (Prayer)	Prayer five times a day
Zakah (Charity)	Charitable giving
Sawm (Fasting)	Sunrise to sunset fasting during the month of Ramadan
Hajj (Pilgrimage)	Pilgrimage to Mecca, for those able to do so, at least once in one's life

Note: Sachedina, A., "End-of-Life: The Islamic View," *The Lancet, 366,* 774–779, 2005.

In the Islamic tradition, to honor and serve God, one must commit oneself to the Sacred Law, expressed in the *Qur'an,* the Sunnah (the words and deeds of Muhammad), and Ijtihad (deductive logic) (Gatrad & Sheikh, 2000). The fundamental principles of the law are preserving life, protecting freedom of belief, preserving the intellect, safeguarding honor and integrity, and protecting property (Gatrad & Sheikh, 2000). Considerations of aging and attitudes toward the aged should take into account these fundamental principles.

Islam and Aging. With no single spokesperson, Islam retains a rich tradition of argument, discourse, and pluralism (Sachedina, 2005; see also Gatrad & Sheikh, 2000). Islam exists within cultures with diverse histories, but the tradition of Islam itself focuses on the principles of justice and public good (Sachedina, 2005). Any discussion of aging must take into consideration this tradition of pluralism and these two principles. The following discussion, as such, represents one perspective on Islam and aging (there very well may be others) and should be considered only a starting point for you to explore aging within Islamic cultures more broadly.

Older Muslim individuals may organize their day around their times of prayer and may find it difficult to utilize older adult services that conflict with their prayer times (Mehta, 1997). One task of a counselor may be to help the older Muslim or his or her family resolve conflicts between the obligation and desire to pray and the need to receive particular services. Religion may offer older Muslims a wonderful opportunity: Muslims who attended religion classes, talks, and ceremonies have been found to increase their self-esteem and their social interactions (Mehta, 1997).

Aging is the natural prelude to death, and death is the prelude to judgment day (Mehta, 1997). In Islam, life is sacred, and death is universal and occurs only by God's permission (Sachedina, 2005). This perspective allows for two developments. First, it is proper to engage in activities to forestall premature death; second, there are limits to forestalling death (Sachedina, 2005). The welfare of the dying person is not merely his or her own but also that of his or her family and community; hence, decisions made in regard to treatment at the end of life not only should be made by the dying person but also should take into consideration the welfare of the dying person's family and community (Sachedina, 2005).

Although some Muslim scholars suggest that the four principles of biomedical ethics[5]—which inform counseling—have been found in traditional Muslim societies (Aksoy & Elmai, 2002), others suggest that the principle of autonomy is less relevant in determining the course of treatment, as a client's well-being cannot be separated from the social and familial context in which he or she resides (Sachedina, 2005).

For Muslims, humans are tenants and stewards of the body, which was created by God (Sachedina, 2005). As such, we are to do whatever we reasonably can to maintain health and well-being, which we can do at least in part through attention to diet and exercise (Sachednia, 2005). Pain and illness, however, are also components of life (Cheraghi et al., 2005), as is aging, and one must consider that aging is part of God's plan for humanity, a belief that supports acceptance of aging as the will of God and a time for making amends for past sins (Mehta, 1997).

Some suggest that pain, when it occurs, becomes a situation through which God tests our spirituality and reminds us that "ultimately we belong, and will return to, God" (Sachedina, 2005, p. 777; Al Jibaly, 1998, cited in Cheraghi et al., 2005). Pain, too, offers opportunities to demonstrate hope and trust in God's mercy (Sachedina, 2005). Others suggest that pain is punishment meted out for sin and can be an opportunity for the sinner to purify his or her behavior and ask for God's forgiveness (Sachedina, 2005). This discussion is relevant when we consider the myriad pains that can occur in later life as well as the opportunities to do that which is reasonable in maintaining one's health. Working with an older Muslim client, a counselor may want to acquire a deeper understanding of the meaning of pain to that client. In other words, does the client experience pain as a spiritual test, as punishment, or in some other way?

Death should be understood as a transition from this life to the resurrection (Cheraghi et al., 2005). Though one's body dies, one's spirit lives on. Prayer can act as "the salvation in both health and in sickness" (Cheraghi et al., 2005, p. 469). To older Muslims, death, like illness and pain, can be accepted as part of life, with "patience, meditation and prayers" (Cheraghi et al., 2005, p. 469; see also Mehta, 1997). Acceptance of pain or illness or death can have a positive effect as a coping mechanism to deal with difficult personal or life circumstances, but its misunderstanding can have a negative effect in that it may promote an external locus of control and sense of hopelessness or resignation that results in the abandonment of reasonable and acceptable pain reduction, curative, or palliative resources (Mehta, 1997). Counselors should support older practicing Muslims who experience illness or pain or who are nearing end of life and who wish to pray for acceptance of the will of God, for forgiveness, and so forth. Counselors, too, should identify that balance between acceptance as a mechanism of coping with pain, illness, or dying and hopeless resignation to pain, illness, or dying.

Judaism

Overview. **Judaism** developed about 3,500 years ago. According to Smith (1991), it is best understood in its search for meaning in and through God, creation, humanity, history, morality, justice, suffering, and Messianism. God is envisioned as a single, transcendent being filled with love, majesty, and righteousness (Smith, 1991). The universe and all that is in it was created by God, hence it has inherent goodness (Smith, 1991). Humans, too, were created by God, free to direct their own futures (Smith, 1991). Practicing Jews may believe that God interacted (and continues to interact) with His creation throughout history (Smith, 1991). Morality is born out in the Ten Commandments, given by God to Moses and ultimately to the world. Justice, too, is valued and expressed in stories of brave prophets who stood up to powerful leaders and condemned injustice (Smith, 1991). Suffering may be seen as a way for God to teach and also as a vicarious experience that allows others to be spared (Smith, 1991). Messianism has taken various forms, including those of a personal redeemer or a redemptive idea to accomplish Jewish renewal (Smith, 1991).

In general, in Judaism, practice and action are valued over dogma (Smith, 1991), and ritual has a special place, whether it is in praying and lighting the candles on Sabbath, celebrating Passover, or taking part in other special activities. Judaism posits that God revealed His insights because He chose to do so. Judaism promotes responsibility in keeping the Law. In general, Judaism posits that God is just and merciful, that God transcends, that God is omnipresent and omnipotent in all of creation, that God is a being who has always been, and that God is interested in and will judge the deeds of humans ("Judaism," 2008). In addition to a belief in God, Judaism holds the *Torah* as the record of the covenant between God and the Jewish people and Israel as the homeland of the Jewish people. Smith (1991) noted the tremendous diversity within Judaism regarding faith and observance and the tremendous place that culture and the nationhood have in the Jewish psyche.

Judaism and Aging. There are at least three fundamental Jewish beliefs relevant to aging and end of life: "the body belongs to God; human beings have both the permission and the obligation to heal; and, ultimately, human beings are mortal" (Dorff, 2005, p. 862). The first belief, that the body belongs to God, results in a mandate for Jewish people to maintain their health and well-being both proactively (through preventative means) and retroactively (through treatment means) (Dorff, 2005).

Health and well-being decisions may be made based on religious tradition or cultural tradition (Dorff, 2005). For example, Orthodox, Conservative, and Reform individuals—including older adults—may make radically different decisions about their health care based on the particular interpretations of their tradition. Those Jews who are Orthodox or Conservative may consult with their rabbis—whose opinions they may consider binding—in determining a course of action regarding health; Reform Jews, too, might consult with their rabbi, but his or her opinion might not be considered binding, given Reform Judaism's emphasis on personal autonomy (Dorff, 2005). In a like manner, Jewish people come from many different cultures (e.g., American and Canadian, North African, Italian, French, Russian), each with its particular understandings of Jewish beliefs and customs (Dorff, 2005).

There is a Jewish prohibition on suicide and assisted suicide—the result of the belief that one does not own one's body; rather it "belongs to God" (Dorff, 2005, p. 862). Although suicide is prohibited, it is not prohibited to pray that one be delivered from this life (Dorff, 2005). As parallel beliefs, the process of dying does not need to be unnecessarily prolonged, and questions of medical interventions should be answered in favor of the benefit of the one who is suffering (Dorff, 2005).

Once someone has been diagnosed with a terminal condition, Dorff (2005) stated that it is permissible "to withhold or withdraw drugs and machines if it is in the [person's] best interest" (p. 863). However, this is not required, and indeed "heroic measures" may be taken, considering the pros and cons of the potential treatment, what is in that person's best interest, and his or her preferences (Dorff, 2005, p. 863). When a condition is terminal, a cure is impossible, and medical treatment is no longer a reasonable option, Dorff (2005) indicated that palliative care may be prescribed, so that the dying person may be comfortable in his or her last days; in the same line of thinking, medications to reduce pain may be prescribed.

Death in Judaism traditionally is understood to occur when breathing and heartbeat both stop (Dorff, 2005). In recent years, however, the concept of brain death is being accepted by Reform, Conservative, and some Orthodox communities. Dorff (2005) indicated that even after death, Jews are to honor "the dead body as God's property," and any autopsy performed must be conducted "with due reverence for the dead" and, upon completion, the remains allowed to be interred (p. 863).

Dorff (2005) stressed the importance of supporting the sick through visits to them and recommended that one "sit on the same plane as the patient, enable the patient to talk about the illness ... engage the patient in discussion of the usual topics ... and pray with and for the patient" (p. 864). These practical guidelines may be useful not only for friends and family of an ill elder person but also for counselors and other health care professionals.

Primal Religions

Primal religions are those of ancient origin and practiced by aboriginal peoples throughout the world—in Australia, the Americas, Southeast Asia, Africa, and the Arctic (Smith, 1991). These religious and spiritual traditions are diverse and complex. In this section, we will briefly examine some of the characteristics that, in general, these traditions share, and we will discuss a specific example of primal religion, that of the First Nations people of North America.

Smith (1991) identified several characteristics that generally are shared by primal religions. He noted that primal traditions are marked by unique understandings of the value of oral tradition, the sense of place, and the sense of time. Primal religions value the oral tradition as a way of keeping the religious and spiritual animate and alive (Smith, 1991). They value the sense of place, the sense that the sacred cannot be disengaged from its place (Smith, 1991). The sense of time is neither linear (progressing from past to present to future) nor circular; rather, it is the eternal now (Smith, 1991).

In primal religions, the meaning of past is not temporal; rather, past is defined proximally and means being closer to the essential source, the preeminent, the sacred. Those who came before, including animals as well as human elders and ancestors, are respected because they are "closer-to-the-source" (Smith, 1991, p. 374).

Primal religions understand the world-universe and all within it as fundamentally unified and a place in which humans and all other beings and elements—sentient and nonsentient, animate and inanimate—participate (Smith, 1991). In this primal world humans are embedded within their tribe or community, which is itself embedded within nature and connected totemically to animals, plants, and rocks (Smith, 1991). Because of this, "everything is, in its way, religious" (Smith, 1991, p. 376). Primal religions tend to view the world through a "symbolist" perspective; that is, when viewing the ordinary world, primal peoples see the sacred, the "superior reality" that " 'contain[s]' the physical reality" (p. 377). One relatively common feature of primal religions is the existence of shamans, whom Smith called "spiritual savants," capable of engaging both good and bad spirits, healing others, predicting the future, and finding missing items (p. 380). To an older adult practicing a primal spiritual tradition, a counselor might be perceived as comparable to a shaman, as a complement to a shaman, or as contrary to a shaman.

Overview of First Nations Spirituality. By First Nations, we mean the peoples who predated the European colonization of North America. In general, First Nations peoples do not distinguish between native spiritual tradition and native culture. That is, culture and spirituality not only coexist but are each other. Culture is expressed through spirituality, and spirituality is expressed through the culture. Garrett and Garrett (1994) stated that traditional First Nations values include "sharing, cooperation, being, the group and extended family, noninterference, harmony with nature, a time orientation toward living in the present, preference for explanation of natural phenomena according to the supernatural, and a deep respect for elders." In general, for First Nations peoples, what belongs to one belongs to all, and the activity of sharing one's wealth and good fortune is highly valued (Garrett & Garrett, 1994). First Nations people, too, place more value on being over doing; one's intrinsic worth is more valuable than what one has achieved through work, power, or wealth (Garrett & Garrett, 1994). The relationship of First Nations people to time is different from that of the dominant culture. For First Nations people, there is an emphasis on being and living in the present (Garrett & Garrett, 1994). In this way of being, there is much similarity with Eastern beliefs that emphasize mindfulness and a present-orientation to life. This similarity suggests the possibility of using, for example, Buddhist-inspired treatments for First Nations clients, including mindfulness training and other interventions.

For First Nations people, there is a sense of belonging—to one's family, one's community, one's Nation, and one's history. With First Nations people, "who you are is where you come from" (Garrett & Garrett, 1994). Family comprises not only biological relatives but also fictive kin, one's community, all beings, the natural world, and the whole of creation (Garrett & Garrett, 1994). With this perspective, all of creation is sacred, as is one's relationship with it (Garrett & Garrett, 1994).

A hallmark of First Nations spirituality is the belief in the interconnectedness and interdependence of all of creation (Garrett & Garrett, 1994). Creation, then, comprises balance among all things that exist. First Nations peoples have a great reverence for all of creation and believe in the sacred relationship that exists between every part of the universe (Garrett & Garrett, 1994). Garrett and Garrett (1994) stated eloquently,

"All things are connected, all things have life, and all things are worthy of respect and reverence." Spirituality, then, is an experience of balance and connection with everything else—not only other people but also animals and indeed all of the natural world (Garrett & Garrett, 1994). For one to express one's spirituality, one needs only to fulfill one's "place in the universe; everything else will follow" (Garrett & Garrett, 1994).

The Medicine Wheel is used by some First Nations peoples to represent the interconnected, interdependent, and cyclic nature of reality. Garrett and Garrett (1994) connected the four components of the circle of life to the four directions of the Medicine Wheel: Mental-North, Natural-South, Spiritual-East, and Physical-West. Health and well-being requires, then, a realization of the connection between North, South, East, and West—between mental, natural, spiritual, and physical—and a striving toward balance between the four components/directions (Garrett & Garrett, 1994). Through balance and harmony, we realize our rightful place in creation (Garrett & Garrett, 1994).

First Nations Spirituality and Aging. In First Nations cultures, older adults are considered the holders of wisdom and, as such, are to be honored and shown respect (Garrett & Garrett, 1994). This differs from the dominant culture's relationship to older adults, which is often marked by devaluation and neglect. In First Nations communities, older adults are the holders of tradition, the spiritual and practical teachers, leaders, and guides for the community (Garrett & Garrett, 1994). Very commonly, grandparents raise children, while parents provide financial support (Garrett & Garrett, 1994). To the extent that younger First Nations people fall under the influence of the dominant culture, their elders may find themselves increasingly marginalized (Garrett & Garrett, 1994). Conflict between generations with different levels of acculturation and different values may be a source of distress within a family.

Illness is seen as being out of balance, in some way, with creation. As such, healing arises through finding "wholeness, balance, harmony, beauty, and meaning" within oneself, one's family and community, and all of creation (Cohen, 1998). If everything is interconnected, then health and illness, too, are matters not merely of the physical body but also of the spiritual (see Cohen, 1998).

Not all illness, though, is to be treated, for illness may be a means of learning a life lesson (Cohen, 1998). Other illnesses may be considered " 'callings,' or diseases of initiation" in which one is identified to become a healer, especially for those conditions that one experienced oneself (Cohen, 1998). First Nations peoples may believe that diseases arise from internal or external sources (Cohen, 1998). Internal sources include negative thinking—about oneself or about others. External sources include stress, negative thoughts that others have, environmental poisons, and physical and emotional trauma. First Nations treatments often take place through prayer and chanting, music, smudging,[6] herbal treatment, "laying on of hands," counseling, and the use of ceremony (Cohen, 1998). Furthermore, First Nations people look to nature as a source of healing, and "natural elements, such as earth, water, mountain, and sun, are considered elder healers" (Cohen, 1998). Counseling, when it is used, should be positive and strengths based and may utilize humor, kindness, and wisdom (Cohen, 1998). Counselors, too, may consider collaborating with shamans in their work with First Nations elders.

Shinto

Overview. **Shinto** is the ancient, animist religion of Japan (Cortese, 1999). It is a religion centered on deity worship expressed through three basic principles: vitalism, priestism, and particularism (Hansen, 2007, cited in Mizuno & Slingsby, 2007). *Vitalism* is belief in the power of deities, *priestism* is the utilization of religious intermediaries to contact a deity to intercede in illnesses, and *particularism* is the concept that a deity confers blessings on its "immediate community in accordance with that community's particular needs" (Mizuno & Slingsby, 2007, p. 115). Deities in Shinto, however, are not entities that exist outside the natural world; rather, they are the spirits that exist within nature itself (Cortese, 1999). For example, in Shinto, there is the Sun Goddess. The Sun Goddess's direct descendent was the emperor, and her indirect descendents were the Japanese people (Smith, 1991).

Shinto tends to be nondogmatic and among adherents allows considerable room for meaning-making (Cortese, 1999). One core concept, though, is that of **kami**—the spiritual power that exists within all of nature as well as in the deceased (Cortese, 1999). When honored, kami is benign; when slighted, it may become enraged (Cortese, 1999). Through honoring and showing respect and regard for nature, kami is soothed; by honoring and showing respect and regard for the deceased, kami is soothed.

Shinto and Aging. There is little written in English on Shintoism and aging or Shintoism and death. Mizuno and Slingsby (2007) noted that Shinto focuses on purity, to which sickness and mortality are the antithesis. In the Shinto tradition, full and complete death is recognized only after it has been verified by the religion; prior to that, an individual may be considered temporarily dead (Mizuno & Slingsby, 2007). One who is temporarily dead is one whose soul has separated from the body but who has the potential to "be revived through spiritual methods" (Mizuno & Slingsby, 2007).

Considering again kami, respect can be shown through keeping an altar for honoring deceased loved ones. Cortese (1999) stated that Shinto adherents who keep these traditions find it easier to adjust to the death of a beloved family member. Furthermore, not only does Shinto encourage one to honor the deceased, it encourages adherents to "continued loyalty, support and nonabandonment even after the death of a family member"; as such, "the death of a loved one may not be viewed as such a sorrowful catastrophe" (Cortese, 1999, p. 47). Even in death, loved ones need continued support from the living (Cortese, 1999), so the bonds between the living and the dead may be experienced differently from those in other religious traditions.

Taoism

Overview. **Taoism** is a Chinese philosophical system, traditionally believed to have been developed by Lao Tze and expressed in the *Tao Te Ching*, that evolved into a state religion around 440 BCE and remained so until 1911, when the Ch'ing Dynasty ended ("Taoism," 2008). Today, it has about 20 million adherents, mostly in Taiwan, though also in North America and around the world. North Americans are likely to encounter Taoist ideas through martial arts such as tai chi, acupuncture, and meditation traditions such as qigong.

Unlike Buddhism, Taoism deals more with cosmology than psychology; unlike Christianity, Taoism focus more on philosophy than religion (Ai, 2006). There are a number of fundamental ideas in Taoism including oneness, dynamic balance, cyclical growth, and harmonious action (Mason, 2008). Oneness means that all of reality is an expression of the Tao; dynamic balance means that from the Tao comes yin and yang, the balance of all opposites; cyclical growth means that yin and yang qualities complement each other in a cyclical fashion, just as night follows day; and harmonious action means that opposites exist within and arise from each other, just as solids form from liquids or liquids turn to gas (see Mason, 2008).

Some major Taoist concepts include *Tao, te, ch'i, ming,* and *wu wei* (Hansen, 2007). *Tao* is a somewhat elusive concept meaning the universal principle, "the way of ultimate reality," "the way of the universe," and "the way of human life" (Ai, 2006; Smith, 1991, pp. 198–199). Not only is it the guide or the path, it is the transcendent itself. *Te* is performance of the Tao; it is a virtue and power in action that flows from the Tao, what Hansen (2007) referred to as virtuosity. *Ch'i* is the essential energy that flows throughout the entire universe. *Ming* refers to the idea that all things have a name, and within that name is the understanding of what the thing is as well as what it is not; in other words, all named things contain within that name both the thing and its complement (Hansen, 2007). Smith (1991) defined **wu wei** as a "suppleness," a flow that comfortably and naturally occurs when we yield and bend (p. 208).

Smith (1991) distinguished three strains of Taoism that coexist and overlap with one another: *philosophical* Taoism, *vitalizing* Taoism, and *religious* Taoism. Philosophical Taoism tries to conserve te by being conscientious in its use; vitalizing Taoism tries to increase te through various means such as nutrition, movement, and meditation; and religious Taoism tries to utilize te to make life better for the community.

Taoism and Aging. Tai and Lin (2001) suggested that the bioethical principles developed in the West may be problematic when applied to Asia and recommended that bioethicists in Asia develop an ethics sensitive to its cultural contexts—in this instance, the context of Taoism. We can consider aging from the perspectives of oneness, dynamic balance, cyclical growth, and harmonious action. Old age may be a time of recognizing the fundamental oneness that underlies all of reality and a realization that one has a transcendent connection to all of reality. Considering aging from the perspective of dynamic balance, one may consider that the Tao by its very nature balances youth with old age, birth with death. If we look at aging from a cyclical perspective, we can appreciate the cyclical nature of birth, development, dying, and death, which is manifest within humanity (and indeed all of life). Harmonious action suggests, too, that within the living of life there exists death, within death there is an understanding of life, and we cannot have one without the other.

Philosophical Taoism might suggest that, in aging, we further learn to conserve *te*. Vitalizing Taoism would recommend practices such as tai chi or qigong or treatments such as acupuncture to increase te and extend life. Religious Taoism might focus on older adult's development as practitioners who use te for the good of the community. When working with an older Taoist client, we should try to understand if our client ascribes to philosophical, vitalizing, or religious Tao (or, more likely, combinations of these) and how their understanding of old age, illness, dying, and death are informed by their beliefs.

Humanism

Overview. Let us define **humanism** not as a religion but as a nontheistic philosophy of life. Baggini and Pym (2005) defined a humanist not as a person who is religious but as one who seeks to live a moral life. In their definition, a humanist focuses on this one life that we know we have; a humanist does not focus on transcendental concerns or profess a belief in the supernatural. Baggini and Pym (2005) clarified that humanists are not amoral; rather they seek the moral life as an end in and of itself, not derived from a god or gods or religion but derived from reason and experience. Humanists deem that moral principles are not based on religious beliefs and that humans must depend on themselves and themselves alone to determine what is a moral life (Baggini & Pym, 2005). Humanists, then, are atheists or agnostics who live their lives in accord with a rationally determined code of ethics and morality. It is not likely that an older client who is a humanist would describe him- or herself as such; hence, the counselor should clarify in his or her own mind the philosophical perspective of the client. It is possible (and perhaps desirable) for a counselor to do so without labeling the client as a humanist or the follower of any other organized system of thought.

Humanism and Aging. A humanist might consider aging to be a natural part of life, neither good nor bad but an inevitable reality of human existence. A humanist, furthermore, might not fear death, for it simply means the cessation of existence (Baggini & Pym, 2005).

This does not mean, however, that humanist clients do not talk about religion or spirituality; after all, many—perhaps most—humanist clients were raised in a religious tradition, including those previously discussed. Furthermore, this does not mean that humanist clients do not need to talk about concerns related to aging or death. In fact, humanist clients may come into counseling with concerns about aging; they, too, might want to discuss their fears about death (see Baggini & Pym, 2005). Other than atheism or agnosticism coupled with a reliance on human reason as a source of ethics and the moral life, humanists do not share other tenets in common. As such, any given client who is a humanist will have developed his or her own formulation for interpreting and applying to his or her life a humanistic perspective.

If you are a counselor who is religious, it would be incumbent on you to respect your clients' nontheistic beliefs, to not impose your belief system onto your clients, to support their belief systems, and to respect their wishes in terms of responses to aging and their mortality. To do this means that you as a counselor recognize that "people can live happy, full and moral lives without recourse to religious dogma and rituals" (Baggini & Pym, 2005, p. 1236), even if your personal beliefs differ from those of your client. Baggini and Pym (2005) wisely reminded us that in counseling the needs of a humanist are no less important to consider than the needs of a religionist and that sensitivity to the philosophical perspective of a humanist client is no less important than is sensitivity to the religious or spiritual perspective of a religious client.

CHAPTER SUMMARY

In this chapter, we undertook an initial review of many of the world's major religions. We discussed Hinduism, Buddhism, Taoism, Shintoism, Confucianism, Judaism, Islam, Christianity, and primal religions. We also discussed humanism. Some of the religions we discussed focus on dogma—including Christianity and Islam—whereas others allow for considerable diversity of thought—such as Hinduism or the secular philosophy of humanism. Yet other religions—among them Shintoism and primal traditions—emphasize connection to the natural world. In addition to learning a little about each of these traditions, the most important thing you can take away from this chapter is to understand that your client exists within a larger context—a context that includes his or her religious, spiritual, or philosophical community, beliefs, and behaviors. Learn to appreciate how this larger context influences what your client thinks about aging, old age, sickness, dying, and death; what he or she feels; and what he or she does in response to these experiences. Do not impose your values on your clients; rather seek to understand their values and where their values come from and try to determine how best to use your clients' values and beliefs in their service. In Chapter 9, we will turn our attention to the topic of multiculturalism and aging.

CASE STUDY

Devi, who works as a midlevel manager at a local company, is a 60-year-old Indo-Canadian woman. She comes to counseling concerned that her father, now 80 years old and suffering from a rapid decline in health, is no longer interested in Western medical treatments. She states, in fact, that as her father's health has deteriorated, he has become more and more focused on Ayurvedic interventions and spiritual issues and balks at seeing his doctor. Furthermore, her father increasingly speaks of a longing to return to India to live in an ashram. It has been 10 years since he was last able to visit.

Devi was born and raised in Canada. Her father and mother were born in India, though they immigrated with their parents and siblings to Canada when they were children. Devi states that unlike many of her peers, she feels less connected to her cultural heritage than she would like to be. Devi indicates that her parents always wanted to ensure that she and her sibling (a younger sister) were integrated into Canadian society, so her parents spoke primarily English in the home. Because of that, she feels she does not have as good a command of Hindi as she would like. She states that she has always felt different from other Canadians, too. Unlike her

Euro-Canadian friends, she practices Hinduism. As a child, she says she was oftentimes the object of racist comments by other students. Since her mother's death 5 years ago, Devi has been her father's caretaker. She complains that although on the one hand she understands her father's interest in the spiritual, on the other hand, she cannot understand "why he would not do all within his power" to extend his life for as long as possible. She is concerned that if he were to move to India, he would die.

Questions

1. Discuss the role and impact of spirituality and religion in this case.
2. At what stage of ashrama is Devi's father? Why do you say that? Would you bring up the concept of ashrama to Devi if she did not mention it? Why or why not?
3. Discuss at least two intergenerational or cultural factors influencing this case.
4. In counseling, what more would you like to learn from or about Devi?
5. Would you conduct a spiritual assessment of Devi? Why or why not? If so, what specifically do you want to know? What specific questions would you ask?
6. Is the real issue Devi's father's stated desire to move to India? If not, what do you believe the real issue to be?

CHAPTER QUESTIONS

1. Name and describe the basic beliefs of at least five of the major world religions.
2. Consider your or your family's religious or spiritual background. Where would you place it within the context of the world's major religious traditions?
3. Do your religious or spiritual background and beliefs influence your work in counseling? (Hint: They do!) Describe how they influence your work in both positive and negative ways. Be specific.
4. Visit a church, temple, congregation, or other religious community different from your own. If you can, speak with a religious leader from that community about his or her faith and its view of aging and end of life.

5. Choose a religious or spiritual tradition different from your own and compare and contrast with your own tradition its beliefs as well as its attitudes toward aging and death and dying.
6. Write the story of your religious or spiritual development or evolution. Start with your childhood and continue up through the present.

GLOSSARY

Anatman: is the Buddhist concept of no-self, the belief that there is no substantial nature to the self.

Ashrama: is the Hindu term for the four stages of life through which humans progress: student, householder, forest dweller, and ascetic.

Atman: is a Hindu concept most closely translated as "the soul"; it is that timeless, ageless part of each of us that will be united with the divine.

Ayurvedic medicine: is the traditional Indian medicine that seeks to rebalance the system of those who are out of balance (hence, suffering from various symptoms).

Buddhism: is a religio-philosophical system based on the teachings of Siddhartha Gautama (the Buddha) that posits Four Noble Truths as well as belief in karma, rebirth, and liberation through enlightenment.

Ch'i: is the Taoist concept of spirit or breath that infuses the world.

Christianity: though diverse, in general holds that redemption occurs through the death and resurrection of Jesus and a belief in a judgment day when the righteous will enjoy everlasting life with God in heaven.

Chun-tze: is the Confucian concept of an individual who exists within the context of his or her relationship to others.

Confucianism: is a philosophical system that is based on the teachings of Confucius and that emphasizes familial responsibility, social responsibility, right behavior, morality, honesty, and compassion.

Dharma: refers to the rules of appropriate behavior.

Hinduism: the dominant religious tradition of India, posits the existence within each of us of a reality that—through various practices—can be united with the ultimate divine reality.

Humanism: is not a religion per se but a philosophy that states that a moral life can be based on reason and without reference to a god or gods.

Islam: is a religion in which one professes belief in one God, Allah, and Muhammad as his prophet; prays; practices charity; fasts during Ramadan; and makes a pilgrimage to Mecca, if possible.

Judaism: is a cultural and religious tradition with considerable diversity of thought and belief; in general, though, Judaism posits the existence of a single, universal God who created the universe and all in it and who is the only appropriate object of worship.

Kami: is the spiritual power in Shintoism that exists within all of nature as well as in the deceased.

Karma: is the law that every action has consequences: Actions in past lives have consequences in the present life, and actions in this present life have consequences in future lives.

Li: refers to the social rules and understanding of one's place in society, learning how to resolve the conflicts between personal wants and needs.

Ming: is the Taoist belief that all named things contain within that name both the thing and its complement.

Moksha: is liberation from the cycle of rebirth and full realization of union with the divine reality.

Monotheism: is the belief that there exists only one God.

Primal religions: are religions of the native peoples of various lands as well as traditions that do not necessarily subscribe to the notion of a formal, structured institution.

Rebirth: is a Buddhist belief that the karmic forces in a previous being's life will influence the life into which that force takes new form.

Ren: is the Confucian concept of compassion for others.

Resurrection: refers to the Christian belief that three days after Jesus died, he arose from the dead and entered heaven.

Samsara: is the endless cycle of birth, death, and rebirth to which all beings are subjected until they obtain enlightenment.

Shinto: is the ancient, animist religion of Japan and focuses on reverence for kami.

Taoism: is a spiritual-philosophical system that developed in China and focuses on the cyclical nature of all of reality.

Wu wei: is the Taoist concept of things progressing as they are meant to be.

FURTHER INFORMATION

1. A brilliant introduction to the world's religion is Huston Smith's *The World's Religions: Our Great Wisdom Traditions* (San Francisco: HarperSanFrancisco, 1991).

2. Although the primary texts of your clients' spiritual traditions can sometimes be challenging to read and comprehend without commentaries, it may be invaluable to familiarize yourself with them. These texts include the *Dhammapada* (Buddhist), the *New Testament* (Christian), the *Analects* (Confucian), the *Bhagavad-Gita* (Hindu), the *Qur'an* (Muslim), the *Torah* (Jewish), and the *Tao Te Ching* (Taoist). Primal and indigenous religions do not have a common core text, but you might consult such books as John G. Neihardt's *Black Elk Speaks* (Lincoln, NE: Bison Books, 2004) or Marta Moreno Vega's *The Altar of My Soul* (New York: Ballantine, 2001) to gain a deeper understanding of some of these traditions. Likewise, humanists do not have a core text, but you might be interested in reading Richard Dawkins's provocative *The God Delusion* (Boston: Houghton Mifflin, 2006). English translations of many of the religious texts are available online through the Massachusetts Institute of Technology's Internet Classics Archive at http://classics.mit.edu.

3. An interesting book bridging Chinese thought (Buddhist, Taoist, and Confucian) and counseling is Robert Santee's *An Integrative Approach to Counseling* (Thousand Oaks, CA: Sage, 2007).

NOTES

1. Following Huston Smith (1991).
2. *BCE* means before the common era; that is, before the beginning of the Christian calendar. *CE* means common era; that is, the era subsequent to the beginning of the Christian calendar.
3. Huston Smith's book is a must-read.
4. God, in the Christian tradition, typically is referred to as masculine.
5. The four principles of biomedical ethics were introduced in our discussion of Confucianism and aging.
6. Smudging comprises the bundling and drying of a set of herbs or plant material that is subsequently lit in a purification or prayer ceremony.

CHAPTER 9

Multicultural Gerontological Counseling

Judge not by the eye but from the heart.

—Cheyenne proverb

Life for me ain't been no crystal stair.

—Langston Hughes (1902–1967)

CHAPTER OVERVIEW

In this chapter, we will use a cultural competence and cultural humility perspective to look at some of the issues present in the culturally diverse world of older adults. We will explore some issues facing older African Americans, Latino/a Americans, Asian and Pacific Islander Americans, First Nations elders (Native Americans), and lesbian, gay, bisexual, and transgender Americans.

CULTURAL COMPETENCE AND CULTURAL HUMILITY

An effective, competent gerontological counseling will demonstrate cultural competence and humility. In this chapter, we will define cultural competence and cultural humility and introduce you to information to begin to develop a stronger understanding of the cultural experiences of different groups of older adults, including those from different races and ethnicities, sexual orientations, gender identities, and other groups.

There are inequalities in health care provisions in the United States based on race and ethnicity, sexual orientation, gender identity, socioeconomic status, and other factors. European Americans, for example, are more likely to receive more—and more culturally appropriate—care than other racial or ethnic groups. This inequality is due in part to the behaviors of practitioners (Smedley, 2002, cited in Capitman & Reynoso-Vallejo, 2007). Specifically, individuals lacking in knowledge of cultural traditions other than their own "may ask clients fewer and less relevant questions in interracial or inter-ethnic encounters" (Capitman & Reynoso-Vallejo, 2007). Other challenges in working with older adults who are from disenfranchised groups come about through stereotyping, collecting information that is limited in quality and/or quantity, and misinterpreting information because of a lack of cultural knowledge (Capitman & Reynoso-Vallejo, 2007).

One way to reduce health inequities in work with older adults is through development of cultural competence. By **cultural competence** we mean acquisition of multicultural awareness, knowledge, and skills (see Sue et al., 1982). Cultural competence means the ability to provide elders with appropriate care, based in part on their cultural experiences, beliefs, and values. It means acquiring the specific skills that allow us to include cultural issues within the context of the counseling relationship. Through cultural competence, we can reduce the biases and stereotypes we hold that result in older adults not receiving the services they need; we can develop cultural competence by further learning about and understanding individuals and groups and integrating that understanding into our practices (Capitman & Reynoso-Vallejo, 2007). Cultural competence can reduce health care inequities and improve the communication between providers and consumers of health services (Capitman & Reynoso-Vallejo, 2007).

Cultural Humility

The world of elders comprises a tremendously diverse group of older adults. These diversities take many forms: culture, race and ethnicity, socioeconomic status, gender identity, sexual orientation identity, religion, immigration experience, and age itself. (A 65-year-old, for example, may be very different from a 95-year-old.) The list goes on.

Furthermore, any given older client will identify him- or herself, or be identified by others, in more than one way. For example, you may work with an older client who identifies as Black, Catholic, male, and heterosexual. Or you may work with an older client who identifies as female, African American, nonreligious, and middle class. Your perceptions of your client may be similar to those of your client, or they may differ radically from those of your client.

It is important to have an understanding of one's clients' background, traditions, and life events in order to provide multiculturally sensitive care (Capitman & Reynoso-Vallejo, 2007). In the recent past, it has been understood that counselors need to demonstrate multicultural competence when working with older adults—that is, we need to be sensitive to our clients' cultures (conventionally defined in terms of race or ethnicity, though now embracing many dimensions). Yet having knowledge of an older client's cultural background is not enough. Given that each client is unique, the care we provide needs to be sensitive to the uniqueness of the client.

In other words, although it is important to be sensitive to cultural experience, there is more to consider (Capitman & Reynoso-Vallejo, 2007). Not only do older clients have some common cultural experiences, each client also has unique experiences, and these unique experiences help form or define his or her way of being in the world—his or her values, attitudes, beliefs, feelings, and behaviors. Furthermore, this is as true for counselors as it is for clients or for any person. A counselor's thoughts, feelings, and behaviors are shaped by his or her unique experiences and are reflected in thoughts, feelings, and behaviors about the counseling relationship, counseling goals, and what is considered appropriate counseling behaviors. Knowledge of others' cultures is not sufficient for providing a high level of care; counselors also need self-awareness regarding how their experiences influence what they think, feel, and do.

Tervalon and Murray-Garcia (1998, cited in Capitman & Reynoso-Vallejo, 2007) discussed physician competence in terms of cultural humility versus cultural competence. Much of what they wrote about is relevant to counseling. Unique characteristics of **cultural humility** include intercultural exchange (such as service provider self-reflection and critique) and incorporation of service provider and client characteristics into a relationship that is "mutually beneficial and balanced" (Tervalon & Murray-Garcia, 1998, cited in Capitman & Reynoso-Vallejo, 2007). A defining characteristic of cultural humility is the importance placed on individual assessment; that is, looking at each client as unique. Individual assessment calls on our ability to demonstrate cultural humility in approaching each client by seeking to understand how he or she sees him- or herself and how he or she understands from where his or her thoughts, feelings, and actions arise (Capitman & Reynoso-Vallejo, 2007).

In other words, we as counselors do not need to be expert cultural anthropologists; we do not need to know every detail of every culture's values, beliefs, or code of behaviors. What we do need is to be receptive to gaining knowledge from our clients, insight from ourselves, and wisdom from the world around us. This openness requires that we be honest with ourselves about our own values, prejudices, preconceived notions, and beliefs about our clients. If we open ourselves to others, in humility, we demonstrate a willingness to understand that other person's experience. If we let others know that we are open to them, in humility, we demonstrate our sincere desire to know the other. If we design our counseling experience—the setting, the process, the techniques—to be universally sensitive, we demonstrate, in humility, a true desire to help.

Increasingly, there is recognition of a large inequity in access to quality health care for some older adults—namely, those from socially disenfranchised groups, including ethnic and racial minorities and the poor. Capitman and Reynoso-Vallejo (2007) believed it is essential to transcend cultural barriers to successfully develop community partnerships and to provide support services to disenfranchised elders. John Capitman offered five recommendations:

1. *Recognize your own biases.* Become self-aware of your experiences, attitudes, and motivations. Work with the range of stakeholders, even those who have beliefs and backgrounds different from yours.
2. *Acknowledge your inability to know another person's experience.* Do not assume that you can understand another's experience of discrimination—ageism, racism, sexism, heterosexism, or any other "ism." Ask the other person about his or her experience, even when this feels uncomfortable. Humbly accept the various ways in which others differ—culturally, in terms of life experience, and in terms of attitudes, problem solving, and other ways.
3. *Acknowledge that it is hard to work through barriers.* This requires acknowledging that histories of discrimination are not going to be overcome in a day or two of being culturally sensitive. Focus on what can be done in the present that will move society to a more inclusive place.
4. *Acknowledge that there is much to learn.* Be aware that you can obtain a tremendous amount of information about diversity— whether it is related to age, race and ethnicity, or other dimensions. Consider your growth in knowledge about diversity and inclusion to be a matter of lifelong learning.
5. *Be willing to share power.* Acknowledge that all relevant parties—especially those who historically have been marginalized—should have a stake in sharing power. When this happens, people feel a part of the process and take responsibility for its outcomes (Community Partnerships for Older Adults, 2007b).

Although John Capitman's comments were within the context of community partnerships, they are equally relevant to counselors, who might be encouraged to develop more collaborative ways of working with clients.

OLDER ADULTS, CULTURAL EXPERIENCES, AND EXPRESSION OF DIVERSITY

Older adults come from varied backgrounds and have varied experiences influenced by racial or ethnic, economic, sexual orientation, gender, and other factors. Historically, classifications of people have been the result of dominant sociopolitical-economic groups imposing their categories on others, with the categories subsequently used in lawmaking, customs, and cultural beliefs (Capitman & Reynoso-Vallejo, 2007).

One might argue that many of these diversities are cultural artifacts created by society. Whether this is the case, and whether we are part of the dominant group or the disenfranchised, we do internalize beliefs, the end result being an experiential impression that perceived differences are real (Capitman & Reynoso-Vallejo, 2007). The ways in which we are defined by others (or define ourselves) impact our life experiences, including our experiences of aging. For example, we may define ourselves as belonging to a particular gender. Yet our experience may be radically different from that of other people who define themselves as that same gender because of the community in which we live or our socioeconomic status, our religion, or our level of education (Capitman & Reynoso-Vallejo, 2007).

A client might define herself as female. That tells you something about her, but not much. Although she will share some experiences common to most women, she also will have life experiences that differ from those of many women because she, for example, lives in a college town in Iowa (unlike most women), is decidedly upper-middle class (unlike many women), is Unitarian Universalist (like some women), has a degree in medicine (like some women), is older (like some women), and is retired (like some women). An older, retired, female physician in small-town Iowa, who is a member of a liberal church congregation, likely has different life experiences than those of a young, underemployed or unemployed woman in a rural community who has a high school education, is poor, and belongs to no church congregation. These differences may indeed influence the kinds of issues, resources, and deficits brought to a counselor.

Diversity is identified and expressed in many ways. Race and ethnicity are common ways to categorize people. Other common ways of categorizing people include gender identity, sexual orientation identity, socioeconomic status, immigration status, religion, and place of residence (Capitman & Reynoso-Vallejo, 2007), as well as age, weight/size, language, and ability/disability. In this section, we will differentiate race and ethnicity and discuss two emerging topics in multicultural counseling: spirituality/religion and social class.

Race and Ethnicity. In North America, we commonly consider race and ethnicity to be fundamental ways in which to group people. In everyday parlance, people oftentimes confound the terms *race* and *ethnicity*, have different understandings of these terms, or change their perceptions of these terms (Capitman & Reynoso-Vallejo, 2007).

Ethnicity is an understanding of a common identity, history, and/or experience that transcends specific characteristics such as race, religion, or geography (McGoldrick, Pearce, & Giordano, 1982) or is a belief in a common ancestry (Shibutani & Kwan, 1965). **Race** is a social categorization based on skin color or other physical characteristics, even though research has demonstrated greater variability within rather than between racial groups (Lee, Blando, Mizelle, & Orozco, 2007). Whether classified in terms of ethnicity or race, these simplistic ways of categorizing people do not reveal the true varieties of experiences (whether cultural, historical, or socioeconomic) of the range of people captured by their inclusion in a particular racial or ethnic group (Capitman & Reynoso-Vallejo, 2007).

Spirituality and Religion

Until very recently, spirituality and religion were believed to be inappropriate topics within the counseling relationship. However, counselors increasingly are sensitive to the spiritual and religious dimensions of older clients and—although not providing spiritual direction or recommendations regarding religion—can help a client explore the interactions between a client's spiritual and religious life and beliefs and his or her issues.[1]

Spirituality/religion is but one facet of culture, and it frequently is confounded (whether intentionally or unintentionally) with culture.[2] An older adult client may identify him- or herself with a particular cultural or racial group (e.g., Asian American) but may belong to a Protestant, Catholic, Muslim, or Jewish congregation or have other or no religious affiliations. Counselors should take a cultural humility perspective, attend to the particular spiritual or religious beliefs and affiliations of each client, and not assume that identification with a particular cultural group indicates affiliation with a particular spiritual or religious tradition or that affiliation with a particular spiritual or religious tradition indicates any particular set of beliefs or activities (Lee et al., 2007).

Socioeconomic Status

Another way of thinking about culture is in terms of socioeconomic status or social class. There is a culture of the poor, a culture of the rich, and a culture of the middle class. The issues, concerns, and resources of older clients from each of these cultures are likely to vary. Poor older adults may be concerned about housing, food, basic medical care, and how to pay for these things; poor older adults may look to a counselor as resource for care management or connection to social services. Rich older adults may be concerned about receiving the best medical care, passing their financial wealth on to their progeny, and other issues; given these different concerns, rich older adults may perceive a counselor differently. Social class issues are playing an increasingly important role in the lives of older people, given the rapidly increasing disparity between the rich and the poor.[3] This is evident not only internationally (between nations or continents)[4] but also within nations.

Wealth inequality influences elders' income security, access to housing and food, access to medical and mental health resources, and other issues. We know that wealth is disproportionally distributed by race and ethnicity, and poverty oftentimes is confounded with race or ethnicity (Lee et al., 2007).[5] Furthermore, we know that income is unequally distributed by gender, with women earning only about 80% of what men earn (U.S. General Accounting Office, 2003).

Particularly salient to our discussion is the fact that wealth is disproportionally distributed by age. Poverty measures based on National Academy of Sciences recommendations showed that whereas 13.5% of the overall U.S. population lives in poverty, 15.2% of older adults live in poverty, a percentage equivalent to the number of children who live in poverty (Zedlewski, 2009). In other words, the percentage of older adults who live in poverty is higher than that of the general population and is roughly equivalent to the percentage of children who live in poverty. The poverty rate of older adults, too, varies geographically; conservative estimates range from a low of about 7% in Iowa, Alaska, Minnesota, and New Hampshire to a high of over 20% in the District of Columbia and Mississippi (Henry J. Kaiser Family Foundation, 2009). The poverty rate among older adults could be reduced by investment in skills building and job placement (Zedlewski, 2009), activities highly relevant to the field of counseling, especially rehabilitation and career counseling.

Although there are differences in wealth associated with race and ethnicity, with gender, and with age, it is important to take a cultural humility approach and understand the socioeconomic status of one's clients and its interaction with race or ethnicity, gender, and age, as well as our own socioeconomic status, social class, gender, and race/ethnicity biases and how they impact our work as counselors.

CULTURAL IDENTITY DEVELOPMENT

Cultural identity development refers to the degree to which a person integrates culture (broadly defined, including race and ethnicity, gender identity, sexual orientation, ability, age, etc.) into his or her sense of being and sense of self (Lee et al., 2007). Most models of cultural identity development are stage based; that is, they posit that people move from less healthy to more healthy stages and that they do this at different rates (Lee et al., 2007). A critique of stage-based models is that they rely on a linear (i.e., first-order cybernetic) understanding of change, when in fact people may be in more than one stage simultaneously, may return to earlier stages (which in itself may not be unhealthy), and may really represent a broadening of responses to the world rather than a replacement of a less mature responding with a more mature responding (Lee et al., 2007). Given these caveats, stage-based models have value in that they help counselors understand how a client experiences culture and how a client's attitudes about self are related to attitudes about others, both in and outside of his or her cultural group (Lee et al., 2007). We will briefly review two models of cultural identity development: Atkinson, Morten, and Sue's (1989) Racial/Cultural Identity Development Model and Troiden's (1989) four-stage model of sexual orientation identity development.

Atkinson et al.'s (1989) Racial/Cultural Identity Development Model comprises five stages: (a) conformity, (b) dissonance, (c) resistance and immersion, (d) introspection, and (e) integrative awareness (see Lee et al., 2007). In the first stage, conformity, the individual's values mirror those of the dominant culture, and he or she is likely to have a negative view of his or her racial/cultural group or that of other minorities; a person at this stage is likely to prefer a counselor from the dominant racial/cultural group (Lee et al., 2007). In the second stage, dissonance, the individual experiences intrapsychic conflict, begins to become more fully aware of how culture influences his or her life, and begins to dispute his or her cultural identity; a person at this stage may find a culturally sensitive counselor to be beneficial. As a person moves into the third stage, resistance and immersion, he or she rejects stereotyping by the dominant racial/cultural group and embraces a minority cultural group identity; a person at this stage may be distrustful of counselors from the dominant group and may prefer a counselor from his or her cultural group. In the fourth stage, introspection, the person will begin to challenge his or her ethnocentrism as a basis for judgment of self or others; a counselor who has an expansive understanding of culture and the relationship between culture, self, and others may be most helpful in supporting client exploration of differentiation. In the final stage, integrative awareness, the individual learns to value him- or herself and value others (whether they are similar or dissimilar); a counselor who understands and appreciates cultural differences might be most helpful to the client (Lee et al., 2007). When a counselor is working with an older racial/cultural minority client, an understanding of the client's stage of identity development may be valuable in determining client–counselor match and in helping a client explore the relationship between race/culture and his or her presentation in counseling.

Another model—one focused on sexual orientation identity development—is Troiden's (1989) four-stage model. Like other theories of identity development, the focus of Troiden's model is on elaborating the evolution of a minority individual's understanding of his or her self as different from that of individuals from the dominant culture. Like other theories of identity development, it assumes that the understanding of a dominant culture individual's identity development may evolve in a different way, given his or her de facto membership in the dominant culture.

Troiden's model comprises the stages of (a) sensitization, (b) identity confusion, (c) identity assumption, and (d) commitment (see Lee et al., 2007). In the sensitization stage (generally, though not always, occurring in prepubescence), the child has a sense of being different from his or her peers and has concerns about gender identity more than sexual orientation identity. In the identity confusion stage (generally occurring around ages 17–18), the adolescent begins to come face-to-face with his or her same-sex feelings and behaviors; this stage marks an increased risk for self-destructive behaviors, including suicide. In the identity assumption phase (roughly ages 19–23), the individual moves more and more into a social sphere marked by same-sex community, becomes less isolated, and begins to more effectively handle the stigma of same-sex attraction. In the final stage, commitment, the individual accepts his or her same-sex attraction, feelings, and behaviors and incorporates them into a sense of self; the individual also develops committed relationships, has fewer inner struggles, and may find his or her sexual orientation identity to be a less important part of his or her life (see Lee et al., 2007). Although not without its limitations and critics, this and other stage models can act as templates for the counselor to better understand potential issues and presentations of the client.

Unlike racial/cultural identity development models that assume that an individual at an earlier age understands him- or herself as different from others, sexual orientation identity models oftentimes assume a stage at which an individual identifies with the dominant (i.e., heteronormative) culture—an understanding that can lead to intrapsychic conflict.[6] Challenges may arise in counseling older gay or lesbian (or other sexual minority) clients who are at earlier stages of sexual orientation identity development or, because of cohort or cultural influence, believe that one's sexual orientation should be hidden, even if it results in pain and distress.

ETHNIC MINORITY OLDER ADULTS

In the United States, ethnic and racial minority older adults are increasing at a rate far higher than the general population (Lee et al., 2007). Furthermore, ethnic and racial minority older adults are more likely than their European American counterparts to have had less education, to be poorer, and to have a shorter life span (Administration on Aging, 2001), as well as to have fewer options for housing, an increased risk for illnesses, and overall a poorer quality of life (Baruth & Manning, 1991). In the following sections, we will take a brief look at older African American, Latino/a, Asian and Pacific Islander, and First Nations people.

African American Elders

A report by the American Association of Retired Persons (AARP) (1995) has identified African American elders as the fastest growing segment of the African American population. The Administration on Aging (2001) expects that by 2030, the number of African American elders will increase by 131% (see Table 9.1). African American elders differ from the general population of elders in terms of whom they live with, where they live, whom they tend to rely on, medical issues, communication styles, and coping mechanisms (Lee et al., 2007).

African American elders are more likely than European American elders to not live with their spouses (either because of separation, divorce, or other factors) (AARP, 1995). African American elders are more likely than European American elders to live in urban environments and with an adult child (Baruth & Manning, 1991; Myers & Schwiebert, 1996). In general, African American elders rely on informal support networks, including family and church. African American elders are more likely than European American elders to be hospitalized and for longer periods

TABLE 9.1   Percentage Increase of U.S. Older Adults by 2030, by Race/Ethnicity and Lesbian, Gay, Bisexual, and Transgender (LGBT) Status

Race/Ethnicity or LGBT Status	Percentage Increase in Population
African American	131[a]
Latino/a	328[a]
Asian and Pacific Islander	285[a]
First Nations	147[a]
LGBT	Unknown

[a] Administration on Aging, *Achieving Cultural Competence: A Guidebook for Providers of Services to Older Americans and Their Families*, U.S. Department of Health and Human Services, Washington, DC, 2001.

of time. This may be the result of higher chronic disease rates, including diabetes, heart disease, and stroke (AARP, 1995; Pouliot, 1996). In terms of communication styles, Vontress (1976) found that African American elders may be more vocal in verbalizing feelings contrary to their real feelings, or they may be verbally restrained and not reveal their true emotions. This may manifest as an **ethic of toughness** coping mechanism (Rooks & Whitfield, 2004).

African Americans represent the only cultural group to come to the United States as slaves (Lee et al., 2007). Although slavery was abolished in the 1800s, lingering racism has remained and is manifest in many ways—in hate groups and hate crimes, overt and covert racism, and economic, religious, and social discrimination. In the counseling setting, attention must be paid to the potential for counselor bias (recall the importance of cultural humility), as African American clients are more likely than European American clients to be rated as impaired, less verbal, and in families with poor relations (Jordan, 1993).

Latino/a Elders

Latino/a[7] elders come from a variety of North, Central, and South American and Caribbean cultural backgrounds and have varying levels of acculturation. Latinos/as may have a long family history in the United States or may be immigrants or descendents of immigrants from one or a number of nations or regions, including Mexico, Puerto Rico, Cuba, El Salvador, the Dominican Republic, and others (see Pew Hispanic Center, 2005). Latino/a elders differ based on communities of origin and differ from the general population of older adults on measures of education, job/career, employment, perception of old age, life satisfaction, health and hospitalization, support networks, and medical problems (Lee et al., 2007). Among Latinos/as, Puerto Ricans tend to have among the lowest levels of education, the highest rates of unemployment, and the highest rates of depression (Moscicki, Rae, Regier, & Locke, 1987; Sue & Sue, 2003; Zapata, 1995), whereas Cubans tend to have the highest levels of education, the most economic clout, and the highest percentage of home-ownership (Trueba, 1999; Zapata, 1995).

The Administration on Aging (2001) expects the number of older Latinos/as to increase 328% by 2030. Latinos/as are among the least educated elders; slightly more than one in four older Latinos/as have completed high school (AARP, 1995). Older Latinos/as oftentimes have been employed in jobs that did not offer retirement benefits—such as farm work or unskilled labor—and have remained working when other elders would have retired. Furthermore, older Latinos/as have higher rates of unemployment (AARP, 1995) and are more likely to be look-ing for work than are African American or European American elders. This is complicated by the fact that Latinos/as tend to identify old age as beginning earlier in life—around age 60—relative to African Americans (age 65) or European Americans (age 70) (Baruth & Manning, 1991). Possibly because of this, older Latinos/as report less life satisfaction than older African Americans or European Americans (Johnson et al., 1988). Compared to the general population of older adults, older Latinos/as are more likely to have poorer health (including chronic issues such as hypertension, diabetes, arthritis, cancer, and high cholesterol), to have limitations in activities, to spend days bedridden (AARP, 1995; Baruth & Manning, 1991), and to be cared for at home.

Cultural values important to Latinos/as include commitment to family (familism), male honor and loyalty (**machismo**), and, for females, self-sacrifice, chasteness, and duty (**marianismo**). In general, Latinos/as tend to prefer social relationships marked by personal, individual con-tact (**personalismo**). In counseling, this may translate into a preference for more personal small talk, self-disclosure, warmth, and genuineness within the counseling relationship (see Lee et al., 2007).

Asian and Pacific Islander Elders

Asian American and Pacific Islander elders are among America's most linguistically and culturally diverse groups. They include older adults whose cultural backgrounds are Asian (e.g., Chinese, Japanese, Korean, or Tibetan), Southeast Asian (e.g., Cambodian, Laotian, Thai, Hmong, or Vietnamese), South Asian (e.g., Indian, Sri Lankan), and Pacific

Islander (e.g., Samoan, Hawaiian, or Fijian). The Education and economic clout vary within Asian and Pacific Islanders, with Asian Indians tending to be the most educated and to have the highest occupational prestige scores and Cambodians, Laotians, and Hmong tending to be the least educated and to have the lowest occupational prestige scores (Le, 2006). Asian and Pacific Island families may embrace or be influenced by Hinduism (India), Buddhism (Asia, Southeast Asia), Confucianism (China), Daoism (China), Catholicism (Philippines, Vietnam), and/or Protestantism (South Korea) (Le, 2006).

The Administration on Aging (2001) anticipates that by 2030 there will be a 285% increase in the number of older Asian and Pacific Islanders. Asian elders differ from the general population of older adults on a number of factors including work, linguistic isolation, poverty, health, intergenerational family issues, cultural expectations, and suicide (Lee et al., 2007). Older Asian Americans are more likely than older European Americans to remain in the workforce (AARP, 1995). About 30% are linguistically isolated because they do not speak English, and about 13% live in poverty (AARP, 1995; Yeo & Hikoyeda, 2000; Young & Gu, 1995). Common medical problems include cancer, diabetes, and hypertension (Yee, 2004).

Intergenerational challenges are the most frequent reason that older Asian Americans seek counseling (Baruth & Manning, 1991). Many older Asian Americans expect that family members will care for them; stress occurs in the family system, then, when this is not the case (Baruth & Manning, 1991). Also, older Asian Americans are at three times the risk of suicide than the general population and should be assessed for suicide potential; older Chinese women and older Asian American men without families may be among the most vulnerable (see Shi, 2005).

When counseling Asian American elders, the counselor should attend to the values of family, shame and guilt, respect for others, restraint in interpersonal style, a strong stigma attached to mental illness, a group rather than individual orientation, focus on achievement, a sense of duty, and specific role expectations (Uba, 1994). Further recommendations include the use of bilingual or bicultural counselors, attention to psychological difficulties expressed somatically, and the use of psychoeducational interventions or approaches (Homma-True, 1990).

First Nations (Native American) Elders

First Nations elders include people who identify as American Indians, Native Americans, and Alaska Natives (Lee et al., 2007). The population of First Nations elders is expected to increase by 147% by 2030

(Administration on Aging, 2001) and may be more likely to live in urban settings than in rural communities or on tribal lands. As we discussed in Chapter 7, First Nations elders may share one or more of a number of common cohort experiences. Nearly 50% of First Nations people living on or near reservations are unemployed and live in poverty (Herring, 1991). Furthermore, First Nations people have lower life expectancies than European Americans (AARP, 1986), with fewer graduates from school and higher histories of teen pregnancy—all existing within the context of one half of a millennium of cultural oppression by the dominant society, especially through government policy (Sutton & Broken Nose, 1996). The result has been an understandable distrust of government and, by extension, those—including counselors—associated with government agencies (see Lee et al., 2007).

Values held by First Nations people include an appreciation of spirituality in one's life and reverence for the earth, harmony with nature (Baruth & Manning, 1991), attention to dreams and visions (Matheson, 1986), and dance as spiritual expression (Richardson, 1981). Other values include elevation of tribe and family over self (Anderson & Ellis, 1995), cooperation, sharing (Axelson, 1993), working collectively to solve problems (Sutton & Broken Nose, 1996), the importance of grandparents in child rearing (Garrett & Garrett, 1994), the use of oral rather than written tradition (Sage, 1991), focus on the present (Baruth & Manning, 1991), and tolerance of behaviors (LaFromboise, Berman, & Sohi, 1994).

Communication Styles. When counseling First Nations elders, one should be attentive to potential client–counselor differences in communication styles (Lee et al., 2007). First Nations patterns of communication may differ significantly from dominant culture patterns. These differences include the showing of respect by avoiding eye contact, using few words when speaking, valuing listening over speaking, emphasizing nonverbal communication, and being indirect when criticizing (Hendrix, 2001). When counseling First Nations elders, then, it is incumbent upon the counselor to be aware of and sensitive to the above behavioral patterns (Lee et al., 2007).

OLDER ADULTS, SEXUAL ORIENTATION, AND GENDER IDENTITY

Older lesbian, gay, bisexual, and transgender (LGBT) people are the most invisible of an invisible minority (Blando, 2001). Because of pervasive institutional discrimination, it is difficult to estimate the number of LGBT Americans and, thus, the number of older LGBT Americans.

Some factors that make estimation more difficult are differences of definitions of LGBT—for example, whether LGBT people are those who have LGBT fantasies, who self-identify as LGBT, or who engage in LGBT behavior—and survey techniques that mask accurate reporting—for example, whether responses are confidential.

Sexual orientations and gender identities are complex and involve biological, social, and psychological dimensions. Sexual orientation, whether heterosexual or lesbian, gay, bisexual, or something else, may have a foundation in hormonal or genetic factors (see LeVay & Valente, 2006), possibly interacting with sociological factors. Heterosexual and nonheterosexual identities and behaviors are present throughout the world.

Gender identity, too—whether male, female, a third gender, or something else—may have foundations in hormonal, genetic, and sociological factors. Transgender identities exist in many different cultures. In some cultures and subcultures, including but not limited to those in India and among First Nations peoples, transgender identities not only are recognized but may be embraced as special or sacred (Istar Lev, 2004).

In North America, prejudice against lesbian, gay, and bisexual people (homoprejudice) or against transgender people (transprejudice) tends to be associated with right-wing political entities or with extremist religious groups (see Lee et al., 2007). Though these prejudices are quickly disappearing, the long history of discrimination by particular sociopolitical and religious groups continues to have a strong, negative impact on the well-being of older LGBT people.

For this section we will define LGBT people as follows:

- *Lesbian:* women who self-identify as lesbian and/or express sexual or romantic fantasies or behaviors primarily involving other women.
- *Gay men:* men who self-identify as gay and/or express sexual or romantic fantasies or behaviors primarily involving other men.
- *Bisexual:* persons who self-identify as bisexual and/or express sexual or romantic fantasies or behaviors involving men and women.
- *Transgender:* persons who self-identify as transgender and/or persons born with culturally sanctioned characteristics of one gender (male or female) and self-identify with—and have the psychological experience of—the other gender and/or self-identity or cultural-identity of belonging to a third gender. Transgender individuals may have other definitions. An adept counselor will utilize the client's way of identifying. Transgender identity is different from sexual orientation identity; transgender persons

also may identify as gay, lesbian, straight, queer, or bisexual, or they may identify in some other way (Lee et al., 2007).

One estimate puts the number of older LGBT Americans at between 1 million and 3 million; although this is a sizable number, little is known about this population (Cahill, South, & Spade, 2000). Touched on in Chapter 7, major cohort differences between younger and older LGBT individuals include pre- versus post-World War II generations, pre- versus post-Stonewall generations, pre- versus postadvent of AIDS generations (Shankle, Maxwell, Katzman, & Landers, 2003), and pre- versus postfeminism generations.

Shankle et al.'s (2003) discussion of issues of the older LGBT community focused on the following:

- transgender aging, transphobia, or lack of knowledge of transgender issues among health care workers, transgender health (e.g., about the long-term effects of hormone usage), and social issues (e.g., about the need for transgender culturally sensitive long-term care);
- ethnic, racial, and religious issues for LGBT elders, including affiliating with LGBT-hostile ethnic, racial, or religious groups or returning to family-of-origin for long-term care in later life;
- isolation: as people grow older, their social circles shrink because of death or chronic illness; furthermore, ageism both within and outside of the LGBT communities contributes to isolation;
- legislation, especially as it relates to long-term care, subsidized housing, and, in many states, no laws against sexual orientation and/or gender identity discrimination;
- LGBT-specific communities; that is, housing communities that cater to LGBT elders;
- LGBT housing options, including retirement communities, naturally occurring retirement communities, assisted living facilities, and nursing homes;
- financial concerns, including poverty in late life and lack of legal and financial protections because of state and/or federal denial of equal rights to marry for same-sex couples;
- elder abuse, notably homophobic elder abuse;
- mental health and substance abuse issues and the relative lack of specifically LGBT elder research and interventions; and
- HIV/AIDS among older LGBT persons (Shankle et al., 2003).

In this chapter, we will look at the LGBT elder issues of victimization by/survivorship of hate crimes, coming out in later life, relationship issues, and spirituality issues (see Lee et al., 2007), as well as loneliness, health issues (which may manifest differently in LGBT elders than in the general population of elders) (Jones, 2001), and issues specific to transgender elders.

Hate Crimes

A large percentage of LGBT people have been the object of hate crimes (Herek, 1989), including verbal and physical assaults, insults, threats, vandalism, arson, rape, and murder. In response to hate crimes, survivors may have feelings of acquiescence, humiliation, self-recrimination, guilt, lack of feeling, desperation, sadness, and anger (see Bohn, 1983/1984, cited in Bridgewater, 1992).

Coming Out

Living what historically has been termed a closeted life (i.e., one in which one's sexual orientation or gender identity is hidden) means that one is part of an invisible minority, which can lead to strong feelings of isolation. When working with an older LGBT individual, the counselor may want to consider the degree to which the client is out, to whom, and under what circumstances, if any. A client may not be out because he or she fears the loss of important relationships, job loss, or discrimination (Lee et al., 2007). Coming out, though, is associated with good mental health and more satisfying relationships (Berger, 1990; DeAngelis, 1994) and so may be an important task in later life for those who have not done so.

Relationships

There are relationship issues that are unique to same-gender couples, given the lack of equivalence in legal, religious, economic, and social benefits afforded mixed-gender couples (Murphy, 1992). As of the writing of this book, marriage was available for same-sex couples in the United States only in New England, Iowa, and Washington, D.C., and outside the United States in Canada, the Netherlands, Belgium, Norway, South Africa, Spain, Sweden, Argentina, and several municipalities.

Though this is changing rapidly and for the better, with more communities, states/provinces, and nations performing and/or recognizing marriage, civil partnerships, and registered or unregistered cohabitation between same-gender people, the denial of marriage rights may still have negative mental health implications for lesbian and gay people (Herdt & Kerzner, 2006), including older lesbian and gay people who may be in very long-term relationships and who desire the social recognition and benefits of such. Working with older lesbian and gay people around relationships may include issues related to bereavement, affective and physical correlates of aging, and legal planning (Donahue & McDonald, 2005), as well as the emotional impact of marriage discrimination and financial and estate planning.

Another relationship issue is related to the degree to which one partner is out compared to the other partner, and this may impact displays of affection in public (and concomitant conflict over this between the members of the couple), as well as relationships with coworkers or family members (Blando, 2001).

Additional stressors common to LGBT people include changes in health, retirement, social support, and ageism (common stressors in the lives of older adults generally), coupled with being of minority status and being the object of familial, social service, religious, and government discrimination (see Cahill et al., 2000).

Spirituality

Given the diversity of beliefs about LGBT people found in various churches, congregations, and other religious institutions, and given the importance that spirituality oftentimes plays in the lives of older adults, issues related to religion and spirituality may be brought into the consulting room, especially by those LGBT older adults from traditions that are extremist in their beliefs and condemnatory rather than inclusive and supportive. Older LGBT people who were raised in or now associate with liberal traditions may express a healthy sense of self in relation to the divine, God, nature, the universe, or whatever the tradition embraces. Those who were raised in or now associate with extremist conservative traditions may present with feelings of confusion, self-hatred, alienation, isolation, depression, suicidal thoughts, and other negative social and psychological concerns. These latter clients require counseling that acknowledges the potential strengths of spirituality while emphasizing the right to full civil and social rights for all people, including LGBT people. This may require challenging the belief that sexual orientation or gender identity issues are moral or cultural issues (as right-wing political and extremist religious groups try to define them) and instead emphasizing that they are basic human/civil rights issues.

Other Issues

Loneliness may manifest differently in LGBT elders than in the general population (Jones, 2001). Specifically, LGBT people may not be able to rely on family, church, and legal systems to ameliorate loneliness. Because of loss of friends from AIDS, older gay people may have fewer friends remaining in their network. Though Jones (2001) posited that older gay people who do not have children may not have the support that comes from intergenerational interaction (Jones, 2001), in reality, older LGBT people may have intergenerational interaction with nieces and nephews, fictive kin, and other nonbiological progeny. A relative lack of intergenerational interaction, though, may be exacerbated by age stereotypes and linguistic differences (e.g., identification as a homosexual among older individuals and as queer among younger individuals) (Fox, 2007).

Poor health is another factor that may differentially affect LGBT people (Jones, 2001). Lack of health care access, especially culturally sensitive health care, will contribute to poor health outcomes. An additional psychosocial issue faced by older LGBT people is the lack of access to housing and social services. This is due to institutionalized discrimination against LGBT people by federal, state, and local governments and communities (Cahill et al., 2000), fueled by extremist political and religious organizations and their oftentimes-successful attempts to inject religious prejudices into state policy. Social isolation among older LGBT people and ageism are further barriers to access and present additional problems.

Transgender Issues

Some transgender people have faced negative experiences in trying to seek employment (leading to a lack of financial security in later life) and housing and have experienced difficulties in receiving appropriate medical care (see, e.g., Donovan, 2002). In fact, joblessness and poverty are prevalent among transgender people (Xavier et al., 2004, Clement-Nolle, Marx, Guzman, & Katz, 2001, both cited in Williams & Freeman, 2007).

Discrimination, whether on individual, corporate, and/or public levels, results in isolation of transgender older adults, with concomitant negative effects on health, as well as on length and quality of life (Williams & Freeman, 2007). Thirty percent to 40% of transgender people do not have a regular medical doctor and rely on emergency rooms and urgent care for health care treatment, suggesting that transgender people's health care needs are untreated or undertreated (Feldman & Bockting, 2003, cited in Williams & Freeman, 2007) and that access to health care and health insurance is inadequate (Xavier et al., 2004, and Cahill et al., 2000, both cited in Williams & Freeman, 2007). Although gains have been made, it remains the case that some insurance companies refuse medical care (including medical care not related to sex reassignment or hormone therapy), and some physicians refuse to treat transgender patients (see Hong, 2003, and Drabble, Keatley, & Marcelle, 2003, both cited in Williams & Freeman, 2007). Treatment for mental health issues also may be a challenge for older transgender people (Williams & Freeman, 2007). There may be discrimination against transgender elders in nursing care and retirement facilities (Cahill et al., 2000, and Johnson & Jackson, 2005, both cited in Williams & Freeman, 2007). Challenges may be present in terms of caring for an elder transgender person; examples include a lack of familial support in later life or conflicts when a transgender elder needs assistance with personal activities such as bathing and toileting (see Williams & Freeman, 2007).

Strengths

Although LGBT older adults may experience unique difficulties in later life, these same groups may approach later life with unique strengths, including an ability to manage stigma, crisis management, role flexibility, and community/friendship/social support (see Anetzberger, Ishler, Mostade, & Blair, 2004). LGBT elders may have worked through the challenges of being a stigmatized other (related to LGBT status) earlier in their lives; this experience may help them work through the stigma of age (i.e., ageism) in later life. Likewise, LGBT elders earlier in life may have had experience in crisis management related to hate crimes, police raids, the AIDS crisis, and other health or social issues; the experience of surviving these crises may better prepare LGBT people for the crises of later life, including chronic or terminal illness. Kimmel (2002) suggested that older LGBT people may have both crisis competence and accumulated stress. In addition, LGBT people may have a lifetime of role flexibility and feel greater comfort in taking on more roles other than those that are stereotypical of their gender; this comfort in atypical sex-role activities may serve older LGBT people in later life.

Treatment, including counseling, may be most effective when it takes into consideration the importance of the LGBT community in the life of LGBT older adults. Even though fewer gay men and lesbians live with a life partner than do heterosexuals, they are likely to have stronger nonfamily social networks (Cahill et al., 2000), networks that may be utilized in treatment interventions. Older LGBT clients may be encouraged to nurture friendships to increase life satisfaction (Cahill et al.,

2000). There are a number of examples of successful LGBT community interventions, from the AIDS epidemic and HIV prevention work (see Logan, 1997) to programs that serve lesbians with life-threatening ill- nesses (see AssistHers, n.d.; Logan, 1997). Because of this community orientation, however, counselors from within the community may need to be particularly sensitive to potential issues related to boundaries and dual relationships (Lee et al., 2007).

Advocacy

There are a number of issues on which counselors can advocate on behalf of older LGBT people. These include advocating for the inclusion of LGBT people in census counts and in academic research; lesbian health issues; aging in place; government-funded social services that do not discrimi- nate against LGBT elders; religion-based social services that do not dis- criminate against LGBT elders; Social Security, Medicare, and Medicaid policies that impact older LGBT people; and future authorizations of the Older Americans Act to include LGBT elder issues (Apuzzo, 2001). Further advocacy should address the relative lack of older LGBT representation in the LGBT press and media, lack of diverse LGBT representation in the general media, and advocacy with corporations and businesses (Apuzzo, 2001) to provide services, products, and support to LGBT elders.

CHAPTER SUMMARY

This chapter began with a discussion of cultural competence and cultural humility and the differences between them. We looked at two theories of identity development—one of racial/cultural identity development and the other of sexual orientation identity development. We also explored some of the counseling issues of Asian and Pacific Islander, African American, First Nations, and Latino/a elders. We ended our chapter with a discussion of lesbian, gay, bisexual, and transgender identities and issues often present in LGBT elders. In Chapter 10, we will address the later life issues of grandparents as primary caregivers for grandchil- dren, older adult reentry students, and retirement.

CASE STUDY

Maria self-identifies as an older, lesbian Latina. She married when she was in her 20s and had and raised five children. Her husband died 10 years ago. She says the older she gets, the more she appreciates both the strengths and the limitations of Latino/a culture, as well as the strengths and the limitations of the dominant culture. She also states that it is only in the past few years that she has begun to socialize more with other lesbian women and has begun to date other women. She states that she still feels some discomfort about this—like she is at some level shaming her family by her involvement with other women. In addition to this psychological discomfort, Maria is experiencing health problems but does not have a regular physician. From time to time over her life, she has been treated by traditional folk healers (known as *curanderas*).

Questions

1. At which stage of Atkinson, Morten, and Sue's (1989) Racial/ Cultural Identity Development Model would you place Maria? Why?
2. At which stage of Troiden's (1989) four-stage model of sexual orientation identity development would you place Maria? Why?
3. What is your perception of and thoughts and feelings about Maria in terms of her age and sexual orientation identity? Her ethnicity and sexual orientation identity?
4. Why might Maria not have a regular physician? Should you encourage her to see a physician or other licensed health professional?

CHAPTER QUESTIONS

1. Define cultural humility, and give an example. How does cultural humility differ from cultural competence?
2. Describe Capitman's five recommendations for transcending cultural barriers. Give an example of how each of these is relevant in counseling older adults.
3. How do you define race and ethnicity? How is this similar to or different from that of your colleagues?
4. What are examples (other than race and ethnicity) of "cultures" (broadly defined) of which older adult clients are a part?
5. Discuss why it is important to consider issues of spirituality and religion when working with older adults.
6. Discuss changes in the distribution of wealth over time and how this has an impact on older adults.

7. Describe Atkinson, Morten, and Sue's Racial/Cultural Identity Development Model. If you identify with a racial or ethnic minority, is it congruent with your experience of racial and/ or ethnic identity development? What is one criticism of this model? How do you think this model would differ if applied to a dominant racial or ethnic group?

8. Describe Troiden's model of sexual orientation identity development. If you identify as a sexual orientation minority, is it congruent with your experience of sexual orientation identity development? From an aging perspective, what is one criticism of this model? How do you think this model would differ if applied to the dominant sexual orientation group?

9. What is the role of spirituality, religion, and/or church in the psychosocial well-being of African American elders?

10. How would you address the cultural and spiritual differences that may exist between yourself and an Asian American elder who is of a different cultural or spiritual tradition than yourself?

11. Describe some of the cultural values held by Latinas/os and how those values may impact counseling.

12. What are your perceptions of and thoughts and feelings about older LGBT people? Define *homoprejudice* and *transprejudice*. To what degree are you aware of your homoprejucide and transprejudice? How might this affect your ability to work effectively with an LGBT older adult?

13. What are some common concerns of older LGBT people? What are some strengths that LGBT people may bring to aging? Give a concrete example of one thing you might do to advocate for LGBT elders.

GLOSSARY

Cultural competence: comprises awareness of one's biases and perspectives, knowledge of other cultures, and counseling skills informed by this knowledge.

Cultural humility: comprises cultural exchange between oneself and one's client: intercultural exchange, counselor self-reflection and critique regarding cultural understanding, and the development of an egalitarian relationship that honors the individuality of the client within the context of the various cultures in which he or she resides.

Cultural identity development: refers to the degree and rate at which a person integrates into and identifies with a culture in his or her life.

Ethic of toughness: is a coping mechanism found among some older African Americans that manifests through verbalizing feelings contrary to their real feelings or verbal restraint and not revealing their true emotions.

Ethnicity: is an understanding of a common identity, history, and/or experience that transcends specific characteristics such as race, religion, or geography.

Machismo: is the set of qualities of male honor and loyalty as the Latino ideal.

Marianismo: is the set of qualities of self-sacrifice, chasteness, duty, and enduringness as the Latina ideal.

Personalismo: is the preference by many Latinas/os for personalized interpersonal interactions.

Race: commonly is a social categorization based on skin color or other physical characteristics.

FURTHER INFORMATION

1. For an excellent discussion of older adults, diversity, and cultural humility, although not specifically addressed to counselors, see *Inclusion and Diversity* (Portland, ME: Community Partnerships for Older Adults, 2007) at http://www.partnershipsforolderadults. org/resources/levelone.aspx?sectionGUID=8da7bbe9-2d4b-4c2e-8a49-ff12b211ae54. Community Partnerships for Older Adults is a national program of the Robert Wood Johnson Foundation within the University of Southern Maine.

2. G. William Domoff presents a discussion of wealth and power in America on his Web site *Who Rules America?* (Santa Cruz, CA: Author, 2009) at http://sociology.ucsc.edu/whorulesamerica/power/wealth.html.

3. See Lee, Blando, Mizelle, and Orozco's chapter "Cultural Identity Development," in *Introduction to Multicultural Counseling for Helping Professionals* (2nd ed., pp. 89–100) (New York: Routledge, 2007) for a concise introduction to the topic of cultural identity development.

4. Excellent discussions of LGBT aging issues are to be found in Herdt and de Vries's *Gay and Lesbian Aging: Research and Future Directions* (New York: Springer, 2003) as well as in Kimmel, Rose,

and David's (Eds.) *Lesbian, Gay, Bisexual, and Transgender Aging: Research and Clinical Perspectives* (New York: Columbia University Press, 2006).

NOTES

1. As we learned in Chapter 8, spirituality and religion can influence an older client's beliefs about aging, sickness, dying, and death.
2. For example, a small but vocal subset of Americans speaks of the United States as a Christian nation even though this is contrary to historical fact, given that the First Amendment of the U.S. Constitution states, "Congress shall make no law respecting an establishment of religion, or prohibiting the free exercise thereof" (National Records and Archive Administration, 2010).
3. In the United States in 2004, for example, the upper class (i.e., the top 1% of households) owned about 42% of the nation's financial wealth; the management, professionals, and small business owners class (i.e., the next 19%) owned about 50% of the financial wealth; the wage and salaried class (i.e., the remaining 80% of households) owned the remaining 8% of the financial wealth (see Wolf, 2007, cited in Domhoff, 2009). Moreover, the top 1/10 of the top 1% of households had more "combined pre-tax income than the poorest 120 million people" (Johnson, 2006, cited in Domhoff, 2009). Between 1983 and 2004, this concentration of wealth in the top 1% of households was the result of tax policies that were biased in favor of the wealthy as well as a social and government environment that contributed to a weakening of labor unions (Domhoff, 2009). When one compares the American CEO average annual pay to the American factory worker average annual pay, for example, this wealth disparity becomes even more clear. In 1960, the ratio of American CEO pay to American factory worker pay was 42:1. By 2005, it was 411:1 (Domoff, 2009). That is, for every $1 made by a factory worker, a CEO made $411.
4. Consider the economic wealth of Europe or North America in comparison to the economic poverty of Africa.
5. In 2004, for every dollar held by an average European American household, the average African American household held 10 cents, whereas the average Latino/a household held about 5 cents (Domoff, 2009).
6. A Latino/a child, for example, may understand that he or she is Latino/a because his or her family and community identify as Latino/a, is told that he or she is Latino/a, and understands that the dominant

culture is not Latino/a. A gay or lesbian child, for example, may not understand that he or she is gay or lesbian because he or she lives in a heterosexual family, itself embedded in a heteronormative community, and is assumed by others to be heterosexual.

7. I use the term *Latino/a* to designate this cultural group, rather than the term *Hispanic* (a federal government term used to designate people of Spanish cultural or linguistic origin, including those from Central America, South America, and some Caribbean nations as well as Spain). See Lee, Blando, Mizelle, and Orozco (2007) for a discussion of terms used to identify Latino/a Americans.

CHAPTER 10

School, College, and Career Counseling and Older Adults

Grandparenting, Reentry Students, and Retirement

To the world you may be one person, but to one person you may be the world.

—Attributed to Bill Wilson, Taylor Hanson, and others (n.d.)

You can learn new things at any time in your life if you're willing to be a beginner.

—Barbara Sher (1995)

CHAPTER OVERVIEW

There is a growing body of older adults who take on the role of primary caregiver for their grandchildren. Some older adults involve themselves in education by taking courses or receiving college degrees. Others continue working or engage in volunteering. In this chapter, we will explore those aspects of aging that are most salient to school, college, and career counseling. For school counseling we will explore issues of grandparenting, for college counseling we will address issues of reentry of older students in colleges and universities, and for career counseling we will look at particular issues of retirement.

GRANDPARENTING

Counselors who work in school settings or work with children may have occasion to interact with older adults. This is likely to occur when an older adult—a grandparent—is a custodian, guardian, or primary care-giver for a grandchild. In this section, we will explore grandparents and child rearing.

Who Are Grandparents?

About 94% of older adults are grandparents (Hooyman & Kiyak, 1988, cited in Pruchno & Johnson, 1996), nearly one half of whom are less than 60 years old, and one third of whom are less than 55 years old (Schwartz & Waldrop, 1992, cited in Pruchno & Johnson, 1996). Grandparents often are drawn into the caregiver role for grandchildren after parental alcohol or other drug abuse, imprisonment (Armas, 2003), HIV/AIDS, psychiatric problems, or the death of a parent; in cases of teen pregnancy (see Fuller-Thomson, Minkler, & Driver, 1997); or when their own children are single or divorced. These factors result in multiple stressors for the grandparents, who not only care for their grandchildren but also witness psychosocial problems in their children (Lumpkin, 2008).

   The role of grandparents may be one filled with meaning for elders—a role that allows older adults to engage and be involved socially with their grandchildren (Hayslip, Henderson, & Shore, 2003). Kivnick (1982, 1983, cited in Hayslip et al., 2003) suggested that the meaning of grand-parenthood had five qualities. These are (a) centrality, (b) valued elder, (c) immortality through clan, (d) reinvolvement with personal past, and (e) indulgence. *Centrality* refers to finding the role of being a grandpar-ent highly personally relevant. *Valued elder* refers to admiration by—and advice-seeking and help sought by—grandchildren. *Immortality through clan* refers to the belief that one will live on through one's grandchildren. *Reinvolvement with personal past* refers to reliving ear-lier life experiences through one's grandchildren, and *indulgence* refers to leniency with and spoiling of one's grandchildren (Kivnick, 1982, 1983, cited in Hayslip et al., 2003).

Custodial and Near-Custodial Grandparents

About 4.5 million minors live with **custodial or near-custodial grand-parents** (U.S. Census Bureau, 2000, cited in Ross & Aday, 2006). By custodial or near-custodial grandparents, we mean those grandparents who assume the role of guardian to a grandchild or to grandchildren. About 2.5 million grandparents (about 11% of all grandparents) are caregivers for their grandchildren (see Fuller-Thomson et al., 1997; Lumpkin, 2008), often for a long time—88% for at least 6 months and 38% for at least 5 years (U.S. Census Bureau, 2000, cited in Lumpkin, 2008) (see Table 10.1).[1]

Custodial grandparents comprise males and females, the wealthy and the poor, and all ethnic/racial groups. Custodial grandparents are more likely than noncustodial grandparents to have had more children themselves, to have at least one of their children living with them, and to have children living within 20 miles of their home (see Fuller-Thomson et al., 1997). Being female, having an offspring die in the previous 5 years, being African American, and being a younger grandparent are all associated with an increased likelihood of being a custodial grandparent (see Fuller-Thomson et al., 1997).

Around 5% of children live in households that include their grandparents or other relatives, and in about one third of these households, neither parent is present—that is, these are **skipped-generation** families (see Fuller-Thomson et al., 1997). In these households, then, grandparents are the de facto primary (and in many cases the only) caregivers (see Fuller-Thomson et al., 1997). The fact that almost three in four custodial grandparents begin their responsibilities prior to their grandchild turning 5 years of age suggests that these grandparents are involved in caregiving for the long haul.

Custodial and near-custodial grandparents suffer more stresses than noncustodial grandparents (Lumpkin, 2008). They more generally have higher rates of poverty than families with children (19% versus 14%) (Armas, 2003), reduced physical health and restricted mobility,

TABLE 10.1   Custodial Grandparenting Facts and Figures

Number of grandparents in the United States	22.7 million
Number who are custodial	2.5 million[a]
Number of minors who live with custodial (or near-custodial) grandparents	4.5 million[b]

[a] U.S. Census Bureau, 2000, cited in Lumpkin, J. R., "Grandparents in a Parental or Near-parental Role: Sources of Stress and Coping Mechanisms," *Journal of Family Issues*, 29(3), 2008.

[b] U.S. Census Bureau, 2000, cited in Ross, M. E. T., and Aday, L. A., "Stress and Coping in African American Grandparents Who Are Raising Their Grandchildren," *Journal of Family Issues*, 27(7), 2006.

interpersonal problems with spouses, and neurological difficulties (see Lumpkin, 2008), and they may suffer from depression, social isolation, and less satisfaction in the role of grandparent (see Fuller-Thomson et al., 1997).

In addition to these stresses, additional stresses may result from problems common in grandchildren raised by grandparents (Harrison, Richman, & Vittimberga, 2000, cited in Lumpkin, 2008). Specifically, near-custodial grandparents may have greater difficulties than custodial grandparents, with parental presence limiting grandparental freedom to exercise control over their grandchildren (Lumpkin, 2008).

How Well Do Children Raised by Custodial Grandparents Fare?

There is no clear-cut answer to the question of how well children who are raised by custodial grandparents fare. On the one hand, these children have been reported to fare better than those raised by grandparents and one parent (Thomas, Sperry, & Yarbrough, 2000). On the other hand, children raised in kinship foster care (i.e., care by a family member other than their parents) are more likely to exhibit behavior problems than those children not raised in kinship foster care.

One study of teacher ratings of children demonstrated that although more than one half of those raised in kinship care were rated average or good in classroom behavior, slightly over one half were rated as having poor study habits, and nearly one half were rated as having poor attention and concentration (Dubowitz & Sawyer, 1994, cited in Thomas et al., 2000). Furthermore, children cared for by older relatives were more likely to exhibit behavior problems than those cared for by younger relatives (Dubowitz & Sawyer, 1994, cited in Thomas et al., 2000), which may be the result of older relatives' greater willingness or ability to care for children with behavior problems (Thomas et al., 2000). That is, these children may not have behavior problems because they are cared for by older relatives but are cared for by older relatives because they have behavior problems.

How Well Do Custodial Grandparents Fare?

From a strictly theoretical perspective, grandparenting has the potential to be beneficial to the grandparent. Erikson's theory of life span development suggests that older adults' conflicts revolve around generativity versus self-absorption (Thomas et al., 2000).[2] Grandparenting can be a role that contributes to generativity as grandparents contribute to their grandchildren's well-being. Even disengagement theory, which posits that aging is marked by withdrawal from social engagement, suggests that as elders disengage socially from extrafamilial contexts, they turn their focus toward grandparenting (Thomas et al., 2000).

Whereas grandmothers report "biological renewal" in grandparenting, grandfathers report "emotional fulfillment" (Neugarten & Weinstein, 1968, cited in Thomas et al., 2000, p. 6). For grandmothers, an increase in problems in old age has been associated with an increase in investment in the role of grandparenthood and the benefits it bestows; for grandfathers, a decrease in problems in old age has been associated with "indulgence and a sense of immortality" brought about through grandparenthood (Kivnick, 1982, cited in Thomas et al., 2000, p. 6). There are gender differences in the subjective experience of grandparenting, and grandparents are not immune to gender-role stereotyping. In fact, they tend to purchase gender-role stereotypical gifts and to engage in gender-role stereotypical behaviors with their grandchildren (Thomas et al., 2000). Furthermore, grandparent behaviors may differ based on age. Being older than 65 years is associated with formal grandparenting (i.e., delineating grandparenting from parenting), whereas being under 65 years is associated with fun-seeking grandparenting (i.e., being playful and informal) or distant grandparenting (i.e., being kind but remote) (Neugarten & Weinstein, 1968, cited in Thomas et al., 2000).

Custodial grandparents face stresses, including financial problems, as well as physical health decline and depression, especially in grandmothers (Kelly, 1993, Roe et al., 1995, and Minkler & Roe, 1993, all cited in Thomas et al., 2000). Common stressful *situations* that grandparents deal with include the illness of children, caring for grandchildren, grandchildren's problems in school, and problems in disciplining grandchildren (Lumpkin, 2008). Custodial grandparents are more likely than others to report less satisfaction with their role as grandparent, are more likely to perceive a poorer relationship with their grandchildren, and are more likely to express lesser well-being (Shore & Hayslip, 1990, cited in Pruchno & Johnson, 1996).

Grandparents in near-custodial roles are more likely to report more coping (therein suggesting they experience more stress), and they utilize emotion- or problem-focused coping strategies to deal with this stress (Lumpkin, 2008). Emotion-focused coping strategies are those that attempt to manage stressful emotions; problem-focused coping strategies are those that attempt to manage a stressful environment (see Folkman & Lazarus, 1980, 1985, cited in Lumpkin, 2008). Common coping mechanisms include the emotion-focused strategies of positive reappraisal and escape-avoidance and the problem-focused strategy of planful problem solving (Lumpkin, 2008). Grandparents may put a positive spin on stress and try to see the benefits of the situation (positive reappraisal) while also hoping that the stressful situation will disappear (escape-avoidance). Grandparents also are likely to take direct action to try to manage a problem (planful problem solving) (Lumpkin, 2008).

Grandfather Caregivers. Grandfathers are at lesser risk of depression than are grandmothers, possibly because of the fact that they are more likely to have a spouse, own their home, be employed outside the home, and have more connections to formal resources (Kolomer & McCallion, 2005). However, grandfathers have reported "the feeling of missing freedom, experiencing child rearing differently than they had with their own children, and fear of what would happen to the grandchildren should the grandfather's health fail" (Kolomer & McCallion, 2005, p. 289). More specifically, at least some grandfathers see their plans for retirement change, including a reduction of their investment in travel or hobbies. Some contrast their relatively minor hand in raising their children to their greater satisfaction in being involved in the lives of their grandchildren. Others worry about their health and how a decline in health would affect who would care for their grandchildren (Kolomer & McCallion, 2005).

Noncustodial Grandparents

Grandparenting, although an increasingly common experience, is an experience marked by ambivalence (Mason, May, & Clarke, 2007). *Ambivalence,* here, means that grandparents have conflicting positive and negative feelings and behaviors about their role and relationships. Mason et al. (2007) explained it this way: There are two cultural standards for grandparents, *being there* and *not interfering.* On the one hand, grandparents should be there for their progeny, whereas on the other hand, grandparents should not interfere in the life of their progeny. For these elders, to be a good parent means to allow their adult children to be independent, but this may conflict at times with their sense of responsibility toward their grandchildren. In other words, there may be conflict between *not interfering* in one's adult children's families and having the desire to *intervene* when one sees problems that can be remedied. There also can be conflict between *being there* for one's progeny and having the desire to support *self-determination* in one's adult children.

Ambivalence, then, arises from elders parenting their children and grandparenting their grandchildren, especially when the norms for each of these roles conflict with one another. In Mason et al.'s (2007) study of grandparents, there was a consensus that grandparents should not interfere, coupled with a belief that there are exceptions to this norm. These exceptions to the rule included times of extreme circumstances, crisis, or being privy to certain information the parents did not have or the experience that the parents were mistaken in their behaviors with their children (Mason et al., 2007). The problem with exceptions is that in breaching norms, grandparents may have self-perceptions that they may no longer be good parents because they are interfering and not letting their children have the autonomy they should enjoy or because of self-perceptions that they (the grandparents) were poor at parenting (Mason et al., 2007).

Ambivalence, too, may be felt in the pull between *being there* for one's family and *having time for oneself* (Mason et al., 2007). Whereas *being there* is a quality in which a grandparent is available on an as-needed or as-desired basis, *self-determination* requires having time for oneself, being autonomous, and creating and maintaining one's own social network. Intrapersonal conflict arises when the expectations of being available when needed interfere with the desire for agency and self-determination. Intrapersonal conflict arises when "obligation" collides with "independence" (Mason et al., 2007, p. 697). Managing this conflict requires—at some level—finding a balance between enmeshment and independence—a movement toward what Bowen (1978) referred to as individuation.

Multicultural Considerations

African American Grandparents. About 12% of African American grandchildren live with their grandparents, whereas about 4% of European American grandchildren live with their grandparents. African American grandmothers are more likely to act as parental or near-parental figures in their grandchildren's lives and report more peer support and less burden than do European American grandmothers (Watson & Koblinsky, 1997, and Pruchno, 1999, cited in Thomas et al., 2000). African American grandfathers more often state that they are involved in teaching their grandchildren than do European American grandfathers (Watson & Koblinsky, 1997, cited in Thomas et al., 2000).

A high percentage (92%) of African American custodial grandparents experience stress (Ross & Aday, 2006). Higher levels of stress have been found in grandparents who have higher incomes, possibly because these grandparents are working as well as raising grandchildren or possibly because those with higher incomes expect more freedom than they find when they take on the role as custodian (Ross & Aday, 2006). Higher levels of stress, too, are found in those grandparents who have spent less than 5 years raising their grandchildren, possibly because they have not established routines, have not yet adapted to their role as caregivers, or have not yet accepted that they will be caregivers for their grandchildren for an extended length of time (Ross & Aday, 2006). Stress is higher for married grandparents than for those not married, possibly because time and energies have to be shared between caring for one's grandchildren and attending to one's spouse (Ross & Aday, 2006).

Stress is lower for those grandparents who utilize counseling, possibly because counseling helps them cope with their caregiving situation (Ross & Aday, 2006). Stress is lower, too, for those whose grandchildren use tutors, special education, or other school programs, possibly because these programs allow the child to access academic assistance that will then not have to be provided by the grandparent caregiver (Ross & Aday, 2006).

Counterintuitively, those grandparent caregivers who come into the role because of parental substance abuse resulting in child neglect report less stress than those who come into the role for any other reason (Ross & Aday, 2006). Those grandparents who assume the caregiving role because of death of their grandchildren's parents report more stress than those who assume the role for any other reason (Ross & Aday, 2006).

As one might predict, the greater the use of coping strategies, the lower the stress. Specifically, the use of positive reappraisal, accepting responsibility, confrontive coping, self-control, planful problem solving, and distancing are associated with lower levels of stress (Ross & Aday, 2006). Interestingly, too, there is among some families a "role reversal" in which the grandchildren's parents take on the roles normally assumed by the grandparents, and the grandparents take on the roles normally assumed by the parents (Ross & Aday, 2006).

Latino/a American Grandparents. Latino/a grandparents are the family members who are likely to pass along family history to grandchildren, show pride in their ethnic heritage, offer support in times of crisis, and influence family decisions (Thomas et al., 2000). A study of Latina grandmothers (*abuelas*) found that positive emotions are associated with family factors, particularly emotional closeness to the grandchild (Goodman & Silverstein, 2005). Negative emotions are also predicted by family factors, particularly behavior problems in the grandchild and more conflict with and distance from the parent (Goodman & Silverstein, 2005). Among Latina grandmothers, isolation from the dominant culture institutions is associated with lower positive affect, whereas the presence of a less dysfunctional family and closer relationships is associated with higher levels of well-being (Goodman & Silverstein, 2005).

First Nations Grandparents. First Nations grandparents who reside with grandchildren are more likely than European American grandparents to be caregivers (Armas, 2003). Fuller-Thomson (2005) studied Canadian First Nations custodial grandparents in skipped-generation households and found high levels of poverty and disability. In skipped-generation households, First Nations grandparents are more likely than grandparents more generally to be caregivers and are more likely to be raising at least two (and sometimes more) grandchildren. Compared to grandparent caregivers overall, First Nations grandparents are more likely to be female, unmarried, and unemployed; to not have completed high school; and to have a language in addition to those of the dominant cultures (in Canada, these are English and French). Furthermore, relative to other grandparents, First Nations grandparents are more likely to be providing care for an elder, to spend more than 30 hours per week on child care, and to spend more than 30 hours per week on housework. Although recognizing that First Nations cultures offer to grandparents a significant and important role in caregiving for children, the large issue of poverty among First Nations grandparent caregivers must be addressed, including issues specifically related to eliminating barriers to participation in the labor force, improving access to health care, and improving resources to deal with multiple caregiving demands (i.e., those of raising grandchildren while concurrently providing care to elders) (Fuller-Thomson, 2005). Each of these issues calls for advocacy on the part of counselors.

Counseling and Advocacy Issues

Counseling interventions for custodial and near-custodial grandparents typically include training in parenting skills, especially for those grandparents who have grandchildren with behavior problems, as well as provision of emotional support (Thomas et al., 2000). These interventions may comprise teaching grandparents how to use child-centered play with their grandchildren as a vehicle for communicating support and limit-setting (Bratton, Ray, & Moffit, 1998, cited in Thomas et al., 2000). Custodial grandparents who "attach a high level of meaning to grandparenthood may be more amenable to counseling or other professional or non-professional help in maintaining meaning" (Hayslip et al., 2003, p. 10).

Other interventions may be more comprehensive and include combinations of medical treatment, social services, and psychotherapy to maximize grandparent and/or grandchild functioning (Grant, Gorden, & Cohen, 1997, and Whitley, White, Kelley, & Yorke, 1999, both cited in Thomas et al., 2000; Kelly, Yorker, Whitley, & Sipe, 2001, cited in Lumpkin, 2008). Interventions, too, may comprise coping skills-training, as well as information provision about social services and how to gain social support (Jones & Kennedy, 1996, Burnette, 1998, and Szinovacz & Roberts, 1998, each cited in Thomas et al., 2000).

Results of these interventions have included changes in grandparents on a number of dimensions—including improved psychological well-being, decreased distress, increased social support, and increased public benefits but not increased physical health (Kelly, Yorker, Whitley, & Sipe, 2001, cited in Lumpkin, 2008). Counselors to school-aged children would benefit from becoming familiar with agencies that provide case-management or other social services in order to be able to offer appropriate referrals to custodial grandparents when needed. Counselors also might assist grandparents in finding resources that can support them in devising and implementing plans of action that directly address sources of stress.

In addition, counselors should act as advocates for custodial grandparent families, especially those involved in the child welfare system because of financial constraints or need for formal support services. Because of child welfare policies, custodial grandparents may be put in a position of being required either to legally adopt their grandchildren or to witness extrafamilial placement of their grandchildren (Murphy, Hunter, & Johnson, 2008).

Murphy et al. (2008), in their study of African American custodial grandmothers, found that although grandmothers had pride and a sense of fulfillment in their role as caretaker, they also felt that "their sacrifices went unacknowledged by the child welfare system" (pp. 77–78). Although the grandmothers did not like state intrusion into their family when state support was limited, disliked that child welfare ignored their role as formal caregivers, disliked child welfare's expectations that they would take on the role of mother rather than that of grandmother, and resented expectations that they monitor for the state the status of their adult children, they did engage in advocacy—especially in terms of "social justice, social action, and involvement in child welfare policy efforts" (Murphy et al., 2008, p. 84). Counselors can support these advocacy efforts and engage in advocacy themselves for reduced state intrusion, increased state support, nonimposition of parental roles, non-monitoring of adult child status, and other efforts that would improve the lives of custodial grandparents and the children for whom they care.

REENTRY OLDER STUDENTS

Demographics

What is the fastest growing population in higher education? If you guessed older students, you would be right. Since the 1970s, the percentage of students who are older (often placed in a group labeled *nontraditional students*) has increased more than that for other age groups (see Silverstein, Choi, & Bulot, 2002), and the rate at which older adults are participating in higher education is increasing (see Kim & Merriam, 2004). In 1999, nearly one third of adults age 65 and older were involved in an educational program (U.S. Department of Education, 2001, cited in Kim & Merriam, 2004).

In general, the more education one has had, the more likely one is to participate in educational programs (Kim & Merriam, 2004). Today's older adults are better educated than their parents or grandparents and are more likely than their predecessors to want to be involved in educational programs (American Council on Education, 2007). Older adults express a variety of motives for higher education, yet there is limited information about older learners (American Council on Education, 2007).

Nearly three out of four (71%) adults expect to continue working past retirement age (Merrill Lynch, 2006, cited in American Council on Education, 2007). Many older adults are looking for education to continue their work lives. About 30% expect to work part-time for enjoyment, 25% expect to work part-time for financial gain, 15% expect to become entrepreneurs, and 7% expect to start a new career (American Association of Retired Persons [AARP], 2004, cited in American Council on Education, 2007).

Some older adults are looking to higher education to help them maintain, expand, or change their careers; they desire "prior learning assessment, accelerated program formats, improved career counseling, and job placement" (American Council on Education, 2007, p. 3). Other older adults are looking to higher education to fulfill social needs. No matter the motivation, older adults face obstacles: There is limited outreach to this population, course choice and availability oftentimes is limited, transit to and from educational institutions may be difficult, and paying for education may be financially prohibitive (American Council on Education, 2007).

Let's look at three factors common to older students: motivation for enrolling, obstacles faced, and expectations posteducation (American Council on Education, 2007; Silverstein et al., 2002).

Motivation

Motivation for learning can be conceptualized in several different ways, with adult learners identified as goal-, activity-, or learning-oriented learners (Houle, 1961, cited in Kim & Merriam, 2004, and in Michie, Glachan, & Bray, 2001). *Goal-oriented* learners engage in education for specific purposes, typically related to employment, whereas *activity-*

oriented learners do so for the purposes of socializing, and *learning-oriented* learners for the sake of education (Houle, 1961, cited in Kim & Merriam, 2004, and in Michie et al., 2001). Learning for younger adults tends to be more activity oriented; in addition, men are more externally motivated, and women are more motivated by intellectual interest (Boshier, 1971, cited in Kim & Merriam, 2004). Furthermore, socioeconomic status (SES) influences adult participation in education; lower SES people use education to meet needs of survival, whereas higher SES people utilize education for self-development and understanding (Miller, 1967, cited in Kim & Merriam, 2004).

We can characterize motivation for education as either instrumental or expressive (Parsons, 1951, and others, cited in Kim & Merriam, 2004; Hiemstra, 1976, and others, cited in Silverstein et al., 2002). Instrumental motivators essentially refer to attending school, getting trained, or learning because of job or career needs or desires. An older student may want to get trained in the use of new technologies for business, for example, so that he or she may explore job opportunities that require proficiency in the use of new technologies. Expressive motivators essentially refer to attending school, getting trained, or learning for the sake of interest.[3] An older student may take literature or philosophy courses, for example, because he or she is interested in these. Older adults enroll in higher education in some circumstances for instrumental reasons and in other circumstances for expressive purposes (Silverstein et al., 2002). One common instrumental reason for enrolling is for social contact and sociability (Manheimer, 2005, Lamb & Brady, 2005, both cited in American Council on Education, 2007; see also Kim & Merriam, 2004). That is, some older adults enroll in higher education to expand their social network. Also, given the erosion of older adults' financial stability, elders increasingly are enrolling for instrumental, work-related reasons (see Scala, 1996, cited in Silverstein et al., 2002), including skills enhancement (Manheimer, 2005, cited in American Council on Education, 2007).[4]

Kim and Merriam (2004), in their study of older adults enrolled in an Institute for Learning in Retirement, found that those with higher levels of education were less likely to be enrolled for the purpose of social stimulation; likewise, those who had resided longer in the community were less likely to enroll for social contact. Finally, those who were married were less likely to enroll for social contact reasons.

It is clear that there is a relationship between level of education and likelihood in enrolling in higher education: Older adults who are more educated are more likely to take part in higher education activities. Given that the level of education continues to increase, it is likely that in the future the demands will increase for elder-relevant and elder-friendly higher education programs (see Kim & Merriam, 2004). Furthermore, many older adults are engaged in education for cognitive stimulation (Kim & Merriam, 2004). This, too, suggests that institutions of higher learning need to address the intellectual stimulation wants and needs of older learners.

Michie et al. (2001) reported that reentry students (in their study, those over age 22 who had not gone directly into college from high school) who were in school for cognitive stimulation reported higher academic self-concept, greater congruence between the work they did and the grades they received, higher confidence that their academic abilities were rated high by peers, higher confidence in their self-ratings of academic ability, and greater satisfaction with life in college. Students who were in school for the purpose of career advancement indicated they had more academic stress, and students who were in school solely for social contact reported more academic self-doubt (Michie et al., 2001). The more doubt one has, the lower one's self-esteem; the higher one's self-esteem, the higher one's confidence in one's academic abilities.

Reentry students reported more negative past education experiences than *direct* students (Michie et al., 2001). Furthermore, reentry women had a more negative academic self-concept than did reentry males (Michie et al., 2001). Academic stress was highest for those students who went back to school to further their careers, whereas a positive academic self-concept and the highest levels of satisfaction with education were found among those students who attended school for cognitive stimulation (Michie et al., 2001). Reentry students are more likely to lack confidence in their academic abilities and underestimate themselves, to be more anxious, and to try to avoid making mistakes (Daines, 1992, cited in Michie et al., 2001). They oftentimes are not happy with their previous ventures in education (Krager & Wrenn, 1990, cited in Michie et al., 2001) but are motivated to learn and achieve (Hopper & Osbourne, 1975, cited in Michie et al., 2001). It remains to be seen whether these findings apply to older reentry students, yet they do provide some insight into issues that potentially may be of relevance to older reentry students.

Barriers

There are particular demographics, attitudes, and structures—including age, race/ethnicity, and geographic factors—that act as barriers to education for older adults (American Council on Education, 2007). Older adults often have illnesses, family responsibilities (including caregiving), or work responsibilities that contribute to a general lack of time for other activities, which in turn inhibit them from engaging in lifelong learning opportunities (American Council on Education, 2007). Racial/ethnic minorities tend to suffer from lower incomes, poorer health, less access to medical care, lower education levels, and lower levels of participation in the workforce (Federal Interagency Forum on Aging-Related Statistics, 2006, cited in American Council on Education, 2007). Geographic factors, too, may act as obstacles to education: Educational programs are more readily found in urban settings than in rural settings (Roberson, 2004, cited in American Council on Education, 2007), and communities with educated older adults are more likely to cater to that group than to other groups (e.g., immigrants and refugees with lesser education levels) (Brady, 2007, cited in American Council on Education, 2007). Counselors can act as social justice advocates for greater access to education for older adults with disabilities or medical issues, access to caregiving support for older adults who want to return to school, and immigrant and refugee education programs.

Attitudes, too, can present obstacles to education. Ageism (whether overt or covert) at educational institutions may act as a disincentive to enrollment. Those elders who have incorporated ageist attitudes into their sense of self may find it hard to participate in educational activities, believing that they are too old, too set in their ways, or not desirous of being with other old people (see Lamb & Brady, 2005, Lamdin & Fugate, 1997, both cited in American Council on Education, 2007). For older clients who have incorporated ageist biases into their sense of self, counselors may provide psychoeducational interventions focused on agency and ability of older adults, or they may refer older clients to support groups where they can work through biases and interact with other elders who are working or have worked through ageist beliefs.

Finally, there are structural barriers to participation in education. These include commuting/transit issues, support issues (including lack of access to culturally sensitive counseling and availability of informal learning options), and problems in financing one's education (see American Council on Education, 2007).

Economic barriers include high tuition costs (especially for those on fixed incomes) and supplemental costs (e.g., transit and books), whereas physical barriers include lack of elder-friendly campus design, limited parking, and limited ability to meet the needs of elders with disabilities (Silverstein et al., 2002). Some barriers are those specific to an individual and may be classified as situational or dispositional (see Cross, 1977, cited in Silverstein et al., 2002). Examples of situational factors include caregiving, family obligations, course offering time conflicts, personal health problems, unsupportive family, or paid employment responsibilities (see

Cross, 1977, cited in Silverstein et al., 2002; Silverstein et al., 2002). Dispositional factors include, for example, having the disposition—that is, belief—that one is too old, too sick, or too set in one's ways to learn (see Cross, 1977, cited in Silverstein et al., 2002; Silverstein et al., 2002). Although some of these factors may be amenable to remediation through counseling—for example, dispositional factors may require, as mentioned earlier, psychoeducation on ageism and how to fight it—other factors may require referral to other resources—for example, to a clinic for the treatment of health problems or to a financial aid counselor for information about financing studies.

Intentions

What do older adults *intend* to do with their learning? Intentions are for either full-time work (more likely for those 50–59) or part-time work/volunteering (for those 60 and older) (see Silverstein et al., 2002). Some elders may work part-time for enjoyment, whereas others will do so for income; some plan to start a new business, whereas others plan to be full-time employees (see Table 10.2).

Overall, about 66% of older workers plan to work during their retirement years (American Council on Education, 2007). About 50% of those want a paying job in a nonprofit organization (MetLife Foundation/Civic Ventures New Face of Work Study, 2005, cited in American Council on Education, 2007). Many older adults, though, anticipate ageism in the workplace to interfere with their acquiring the employment they

TABLE 10.2   Intentions of 50- to 59-Year-Olds Who Plan to Work in Later Life

Intention	Percentage With Intention
Work part-time for enjoyment	25
Work part-time for income	15
Start own business	8
Work full-time in a new job	3
Plan to never retire	14
Plan to not work at all	17
Have other plans or do not know how they will spend retirement	17

Note: MetLife Foundation/Civic Ventures New Face of Work Study, 2005, cited in American Council on Education, *Framing New Terrain: Older Adults and Higher Education*, Author, Washington, DC, 2007.

want (PCC Task Force on Aging, 2007, cited in American Council on Education, 2007).

Learning Outside of School

An AARP (2000) survey found that people age 50 and older used newspapers, magazines, books, and journals for learning. This was true regardless of gender, age, economic status, or educational background. This survey also found that an overwhelming percentage of adults age 50 and older felt that they learned by (a) first watching or listening and then thinking and/or by (b) touching something and then physically "manipulating it or figuring it out" (AARP, 2000, p. 1).

Counseling and Advocacy

In terms of counseling, one may focus on the motivations, barriers, and intentions of the older adult client in continued learning, whether at an institution of higher education or at some other venue. Specific issues addressed will vary based on the client and may include those of demographics, attitudes, social structures, motivations, barriers, and post-education intentions.

The most common educational topics of interest to older adults are hobbies or pastimes, "advanced skills," learning in order to enjoy more or get more pleasure from life, health and nutrition, and stress management (AARP, 2000, p. 2). These adults tend to prefer learning in "loosely-structured" groups or in workshops or being self-taught (AARP, 2000, p. 2). Furthermore, these adults want to use what they have learned, they desire at least some control over their learning, and they show a willingness to spend small amounts of money to learn (AARP, 2000).

All of this suggests that educational institutions should look at ways of offering options that are interesting and meaningful to this age group. They should consider learning options composed of fairly unstructured groups or classes, workshops, or options for being self-taught—that is, options that offer older adults more control over the learning process—and they should find ways to be sensitive to the economic issues facing older adults when considering cost options and financial assistance (see AARP, 2000).

There are a number of model education programs for older adults, including Institutes for Learning in Retirement, Elderhostels, and Osher Lifelong Learning Institutes (American Council on Education, 2007). In terms of counselor advocacy, it is imperative to press colleges and universities to become older-learner friendly. Silverstein et al. (2002) recommended the development of a standing committee on older learners to increase awareness of older learners' needs; increase older learners' awareness of programs of tuition and fee reductions and waivers; identify motivations, barriers, and expectations; provide job and volunteer placement; increase older learners' awareness of support services; and address issues related to physical barriers and disability. The American Council on Education (2007) recommended encouraging outreach to elders from the full range of educational backgrounds (dropout through PhD) and from underrepresented groups, developing programming that is welcoming and available to elders, and providing options for funding of elders' education. Counselors working in college settings may take a lead on committees that address these concerns, on the development of outreach programs, and on informing the higher education community about the needs of older students.

RETIREMENT

Many people, when reflecting on old age and work, think in terms of full retirement. Full retirement, though, is but one option in later life. Older adults may bring to career counseling a number of concerns, such as the following:

- Should I retire? If so, when?
- What will retirement look like?
- Will I need to continue working for economic or other reasons?
- What is the meaning of my work and my work life?
- Can I find meaning in activities other than work?
- What is the place of further education in my life?
- Should I gradually cut down on my work hours as a move toward full retirement?
- Should I keep a job but just work less?

Older Adults In and Out of the Workforce

Demographics. The workforce continues to become more diverse in many ways, including gender, race/ethnicity, and age (see, e.g., Burr & Mutchler, 2007). In 2002, women and men were in the workforce in nearly equal proportion (48% to 52%); from 1977 to 2002, the percentage of the labor force that was people of color increased from 12% to 21% (Galinsky, 2007).

Furthermore, the workforce is becoming older (Galinsky, 2007; Nyce, 2007). Currently, about 12% of the workforce is 55 years old or older; this percentage will nearly double by 2020, with about 20% of the workforce being 55 or older (Nyce, 2007; see also Burr & Mutchler, 2007). Looked at from another angle, whereas in 1950 there were about 7 working-age adults for each adult not working (a ratio of 7-to-1), today that ratio is 5-to-1; by 2030 the ratio may be as low as 2.7-to-1 (Nyce, 2007).

Age. Of those age 55 and older in the workforce, approximately 63% are between the ages of 55 and 64, 28% are between the ages of 65 and 69, 16% are between the ages of 70 and 74, and 6% are age 75 and older (AARP, 2006, cited in American Council on Education, 2007). The general trend regarding age is that the older the age bracket, the smaller the percentage of the workforce.

Multicultural Considerations. The racial/ethnic composition of older adults is anticipated to undergo a substantial change. Although the numbers of African Americans, Latino/a Americans, Asian Americans, and European Americans will all increase between 2004 and 2050, the percentage of European Americans is anticipated to drop from 81% to 57% of the population; meanwhile, African Americans will increase from 9% to 14%, Latino/a Americans from 7% to 20%, and Asian Americans from 3% to 9% (U.S. Census Bureau, 2004c, cited in American Council on Education, 2007). Stated another way, the general population of the United States will continue to increase, but European Americans will comprise a smaller percentage of the population, and racial/ethnic minorities will comprise a larger percentage of the population. In 2006, the percentage of adults 55 and older who held a bachelor's degree or higher was as follows: Asian American, 37%; European American, 26%; African American, 14%; and Latino/a American, 11% (U.S. Census Bureau, 2004c, cited in American Council on Education, 2007).

Gender. The percentages of older women participating in the workforce are increasing, whereas those of older men are decreasing. Whereas in 1950 87% of men age 55 to 64 were in the workforce, by 2004 this percentage had dropped to 70%. In 1950, 46% of men age 65 and older were in the workforce; by 2004 this had dropped to 19%. In contrast, 27% of women age 55 to 64 were in the workforce in 1950; by 2004 it had increased to 57%. In 1950, 10% of women age 65 and older were in the workforce; by 2004 it had increased slightly—to 12% (Fullerton, 1999, and U.S. Census Bureau, 2004a, both cited in American Council on Education, 2007).

Income. Older adults tend to be better educated today than in the past, and those with more education benefit in the form of higher yearly incomes. Those age 55 to 64 have a median income of $52,200 yearly, whereas those 65 and older have a median income of $26,036 yearly

(DeNavas-Walt, Proctor, & Lee, 2006, cited in American Council on Education, 2007). Yet there increasingly is a polarization of wealth among older adults (as in other age groups), with growth at the high and low ends, leaving a shrinking older adult middle class.

Geography. The states with the largest numbers of adults age 55 and older are California (7.2 million), Florida (5 million), New York (4.6 million), Texas (4.3 million), and Pennsylvania (3.3 million) (U.S. Census Bureau, 2007, cited in American Council on Education, 2007). In Florida, Pennsylvania, West Virginia, Maine, Montana, Hawaii, Iowa, North Dakota, and Vermont, those age 55 and older compose 25% or more of the population (U.S. Census Bureau, 2007, cited in American Council on Education, 2007). Furthermore, the median ages of the population of a number of states are increasing, due to people not moving as they get older (preferring to adapt their homes) or people moving to certain states (notably in the South Atlantic and the mountain West) (U.S. Census Bureau, 2007, He & Schachter, 2003, both cited in American Council on Education, 2007).

Burr and Mutchler (2007) detailed some of the basic demographics of older workers by race/ethnicity and gender. For older workers (i.e., age 55 and older) Asian Americans have the highest level of being in the workforce (40.6%), and African Americans have the lowest (34.3%). European Americans have the highest median income ($19,409), and Latino/a Americans have the lowest ($11,729). More than one quarter of African Americans and Latino/a Americans live in households around or below the federal poverty level. Women have the highest levels of poverty, especially African American, Latina American, and Asian American women. European Americans are more likely than Latino/a Americans and African Americans to report stress related to work. Although African American and Latino/a American workers are more likely to expect to fully retire (i.e., no longer work at all) at some point in their life, European Americans are more likely to expect to reduce their work hours, change their jobs, or become self-employed. More women and more racial/ethnic minorities report not having "given much thought to retirement" or having plans in regard to retirement (Burr & Mutchler, 2007, p. 42).

Job Security. Older workers are more likely than younger workers to lose their jobs. Sweet (2007) suggested that jobs are less secure for older workers because, compared to younger workers, they tend to be more highly compensated, and it is economical for companies to cut them from the workforce as a cost-savings measure; they are less likely to have the technological skills they need for work in emerging industries; and they are victims of ageism. Sweet (2007) pointed out that older workers' human capital and social capital tend to be devalued, older workers are less able to make job-related geographical moves because of the fact that their spouses work, they tend to remain in insecure jobs because of economic needs (including having economic inability to retire or acting as a caregiver to a family member), and they continue to want stable, secure employment (even in the face of the disintegration of this aspect of the employer–employee social contract).

Ageism. Ageism—whether personal or institutional, whether intentional or unintentional—is a problem in the workplace (Dennis & Thomas, 2007). Ageism in the workplace most often manifests as hiring bias (i.e., older adults may not be hired because of their relatively old age). Furthermore, enforcement of equal employment law—at least in cases of age discrimination—is weak, and there is limited social support for viewing age discrimination as a matter of fundamental civil rights (McCann, 2003, cited in Dennis & Thomas, 2007). Although older workers are seen as having experience, good judgment, commitment, and other positive qualities, these qualities are not particularly valued by employers; older workers also are seen as lacking flexibility, being unable to use new technologies, being unable to acquire new skills and having physical limitations, and being incompetent or slow (see AARP, 1989, 1992, 1995, 2000, cited in Dennis & Thomas, 2007; Ething, 1997, cited in Ranzijn, 2002). These negative perceptions, though false (Remeny, 1994, cited in Ranzijn, 2002), result in fewer chances for promotion, additional training, or raises (see Sterns & McDaniel, 1994, cited in Dennis & Thomas, 2007).

To fight ageism in the workplace, Dennis and Thomas (2007) recommended that diversity training include age as a category, training manuals that address ageism be created, increased prosecution of cases of age discrimination be made a priority, research into cases of ageism that are dismissed because of "no reasonable cause" be conducted, and intergenerational training be provided in the workplace.

Trainability. Although some research has suggested that older adults do not benefit from training to the extent that younger adults do (see Baltes et al., 1996, cited in Ranzijn, 2002), other research has demonstrated that older adults improve their cognitive functioning more than younger adults after they engage in complex work (Schooler, Mulatu, & Oates, 1999, cited in Ranzijn, 2002). Schooler et al. suggested that older adults may actually be superior to younger adults on workplace tasks that require judgment and decision making around ambiguous issues.

Baby Boomers. Baby boomers have been a major force in the labor market during their working age, and they will be a major force in their retirement (Galinsky, 2007). There likely will be a reduction in the labor supply in the coming years (Nyce, 2007). Namely, there will be fewer people available to enter the labor market. In rich countries such as

Germany, Japan, and Italy, the workforce is projected to shrink by one half to 1% per annum (Nyce, 2007); in Finland, a low birth rate and an aging population already are contributing to labor shortages (Bezaitis, 2008).[5] One way to mitigate this labor reduction is to encourage older workers to remain in the workforce—encouragement that is not difficult given the substantial reduction in financial security in later life, most notably in reductions in health care benefits, disincentives from Social Security to retire early, and loss or reductions of pensions and other sources of economic security (Nyce, 2007; see also Bezaitis, 2008).[6]

In fact, only 24% of older adults report that they have enough financial resources to function comfortably in retirement (Galinsky, 2007). To attract and keep older employees, employers would do well to provide health care benefits, financial incentives, and financial planning. Recruitment of older workers requires employers to be attractive to older workers, whereas retention requires sensitivity to overt or covert ageism in the workplace, with one technique for successful replacement of older works being through phased retirement (Wiener, 2008, cited in Bezaitis, 2008).

People in the workforce are working *greater hours*. In 2002, men worked in employment on average 48.2 hours per week (paid and unpaid hours), and women worked in employment on average 41.4 hours per week (paid and unpaid hours), offering clear evidence contrary to the fiction of the 40-hour workweek (Galinsky, 2007). Today, workers aged 50 and older work on average 44.7 hours per week (Galinsky, 2007). People, too, are finding that the demands of their jobs are increasing, with people more likely to be working faster and harder and not having enough time to complete their job responsibilities (Galinsky, 2007). On the upside, workers report having more opportunities to learn, as well as being creative, autonomous, and responsible and finding work meaningful (Galinsky, 2007). Workers, however, continue to report discrimination based on gender, race, national origin, and/or age (Galinsky, 2007).

Older workers report positive relationships with their supervisors equal to or higher than those reported by younger workers, and they report more satisfaction with their jobs than do younger workers (Galinsky, 2007). In fact, they are more likely than younger workers to plan to stay in their current jobs (Galinksy, 2007).

Smyer and Pitt-Catsouphes (2007) posited that as workers age, there is a shift from a work "goal orientation" to "the amount of time left at work" (p. 23). As one ages, there are changes in one's behavioral, psychological, and social dimensions, as well as changes in perceptions of time (Smyer & Pitt-Catsouphes, 2007). All of these occur within sociological contexts of occupation, family, and leisure (Rapoport & Rapoport,

1980, and White, 1995, both cited in Smyer & Pitt-Catsouphes, 2007) or of education, work, and leisure (Riely, Kahn, & Fonder, 1994, and others, cited in Smyer & Pitt-Catsouphes, 2007). These items—occupation, family, and leisure or education, work, and leisure—are referred to as the triple helixes or the three boxes of life (Smyer & Pitt-Catsouphes, 2007). These *triple helixes* or *three boxes* used to be more discrete (Smyer & Pitt-Catsouphes, 2007). For example, in the past, some people considered the ages of 5 to 18 those for schooling, 18 to 65 those for work, and 65 and later those for retirement. Today, however, these triple helixes or three boxes are more amorphous, resulting in fluidity in the relationship between work and retirement (Smyer & Pitt-Catsouphes, 2007). In fact, workers increasingly are working in bridge employment or working part-time as a stepping-stone to full retirement (Cahill, Giandrea, & Quinn, 2006, cited in Smyer & Pitt-Catsouphes, 2007).

Work and Meaning. Older workers' decisions regarding work and retirement—including the meaning of work and retirement—are influenced by economics, physical and mental health issues, job satisfaction, and familial issues (Smyer & Pitt-Catsouphes, 2007). For older adults, work and life satisfaction are positively correlated, whereas job loss is correlated with physical and mental health problems (Gallo et al., 2000, cited in Smyer & Pitt-Catsouphes, 2007). Older workers who are healthy are more likely to continue working into their retirement years (Kosloski, Ekerdt, & DeViney, 2001, cited in Smyer & Pitt-Catsouphes, 2007). Older workers who experience job dissatisfaction are more likely to move into retirement (Kosloski, Ekerdt, & DeViney, 2001, cited in Smyer & Pitt-Catsouphes, 2007), whereas those who experience job satisfaction want to continue to work (Smyer & Pitt-Catsouphes, 2007). Those older workers who also are caregivers or are responsible for a dependent—whether a parent, spouse, child, or someone else—are more likely to remain in the workforce (Szinovacz, DeViney, & Davey, 2001, cited in Smyer & Pitt-Catsouphes, 2007). Women spend more time caregiving and are more likely to indicate that they face a conflict between their work and caregiving responsibilities (Anastas, Gibeau, & Larson, 1990). Counselors of working caregivers can advocate by promoting workplace policies and community eldercare programs so that caregivers who are in the paid workforce can use employee benefits and community services to help sustain their work and caregiving responsibilities (Anastas et al., 1990).

Nuttman-Shwartz's (2007) study of Israeli pre- and postretirement older adults found that over 96% of the participants in the study referred to work in their life stories, which suggests the large influence of work on one's life and identity. Nuttman-Shwartz (2007) uncovered common themes, including the beliefs of life as work, work as a defense against fear and stagnation, retirement as freedom from work, and retirement as the converse of work. Interestingly, those retirees who referred more to work in their life stories also expressed higher levels of well-being and lower levels of distress (Nuttman-Shwartz, 2007).

Partial Retirement. U.S. workers have tended to have a conventional perspective on work and retirement. They have seen work as being full-time for their work life (roughly 20s through mid-60s), culminating in full retirement (Moen, 2007). This conventional perspective functions less well for older adults, who may desire part-time work with flexibility, control, and meaning coupled with part-time retirement and leisure. Moen (2007) referred to this alternative perspective as one of "Not So Big Jobs and Not So Big Retirements" (p. 34) and made the point that these not so big jobs should be ones that offer challenge and opportunities for growth, as well as meaning in working for the greater good. Her challenge then is to encourage employers to shape jobs that fit these needs and to encourage worker-retirees to seek out these jobs.

Encore Careers. Encore careers are jobs taken in later life for financial, meaning, and social responsibility reasons. One half of workers aged 44 to 70 would like to engage in work as educators or in health care or with a not-for-profit venture (Civic Ventures, 2008, cited in Bezaitis, 2008). These encore careers can be attractive alternatives to phased retirement and can be seen as the capstone to one's life's work (Wiener, 2008, cited in Bezaitis, 2008).

Volunteering. One alternative to continued employment, whether full- or part-time, or to full retirement is volunteering (Morrow-Howell, 2007). Older adults are rich in life experience and can contribute socially and economically, not only in paid employment but also in unpaid volunteering. Volunteer work, too, may be of benefit to the volunteer. Older adults are working in paid employment longer, but they are expecting to work fewer hours, to have more flexibility in their schedules, and to engage in job sharing. About 25% of older adults are involved in volunteer work, typically with churches or other religious organizations, and they tend to work more hours as volunteers than do younger adults (U.S. Department of Labor, 2005, cited in Morrow-Howell, 2007). Older adults who are better educated, physically healthier, and better connected socially are more likely to volunteer than those who are less educated, ill, and more socially isolated. Barriers to volunteering include increased caregiving responsibilities, limited finances requiring continued paid employment, and disability and other health problems. The baby boom generation is more likely to volunteer than the generation of their parents or grandparents (see Corporation for National and Community Service, 2007, cited in Morrow-Howell, 2007). Older adults who continue to work part-time volunteer more than those who are completely retired. This suggests that a component of reduced work hours can be increased involvement in volunteer activities. This may be especially true for those employees who volunteer through their workplace. Employers may want to establish volunteer programs that involve workers. In fact, a valuable objective for many older adults may be a combination of paid employment and unpaid volunteer work (Morrow-Howell, 2007).

Bridge Employment

Bridge employment is a job in which one engages between one's full-time career and one's complete retirement from employment (Ulrich & Brott, 2005). Bridge employment includes the options of part-time, temporary, or self-employment; typical features include reduced hours worked and lesser responsibilities, greater flexibility with the job, and lesser physical demands (Feldman, 1994, cited in Ulrich & Brott, 2005). Bridge employment may be an attractive option for older adults, who are living longer and have fewer financial resources.

Transitioning to bridge employment may pose challenges (Ulrich & Brott, 2005), however. Career counselors can assist by helping older clients "identify retirement options, determine the best retirement direction, achieve goals, and develop strategies to overcome possible barriers (Ulrich & Brott, 2005, p. 159). Ulrich and Brott (2005) found that older adults who look for bridge employment do so because they see themselves and their careers as changing, they want to exercise control in their lives, and they want to find meaning in their lives. Factors that influence success in bridge employment include planning, resource utilization, and compensation in career changes. Although many older adults engage in financial planning, they frequently do not plan their retirement lives. Oftentimes, they do not use community resources that could assist them in career changes. Others involved in bridge employment need to compensate for reduced paychecks, limited opportunity for career advancement, isolation in the workplace, loss of ties to their previous careers, and lack of responsibilities in their new jobs (Ulrich & Brott, 2005). The consequences of moving into bridge employment include reduced financial compensation, problems in moving into a new job (such as changes in job status/prestige, having limited job skills, and the need to retrain), ageism, and personal challenges (including personal limitations, issues with time management, or physical problems). Benefits of bridge employment include an increase in self-esteem, a more balanced life—one with work and leisure—and an enjoyment of working. In later life, there is often no longer the option between working and not working, and increasingly older adults are choosing bridge jobs (Ulrich & Brott, 2005).

Ulrich and Brott (2005) believed that the challenge for career counselors of older adults is how to support them in using career counseling services and how to help them with career decision making around retirement (including options of full retirement, bridge employment, and even continued full employment). Brewington and Nassar-McMillan (2000, cited in Ulrich & Brott, 2005) suggested that career counselors utilize both individual and group counseling for information dissemination, offer support—both emotional and social—and be aware of any signs of psychopathology (including depression or anxiety). Career counselors should help clients clarify how they want to use counseling; they should value the work experiences of the client, focus on client strengths, offer a variety of employment/retirement options, identify skills, and make a connection between those skills and potential jobs. Career counselors should also recognize ageism, as well as particular financial planning needs (Ulrich & Brott, 2005).

Research indicates that bridge employment is associated with retirement and overall life satisfaction; volunteering or engaging in leisure activities, too, are associated with retirement adjustment (Kim & Feldman, 2000, cited in Nuttman-Shwartz, 2007).

Counseling and Advocacy

Older adults remaining in the workforce or reentering the workforce may benefit from "later life planning" (Hansen, 1993, cited in Canaff, 1997). Canaff (1997) pointed out the need for career counselors to candidly explore their perceptions of aging as well as their perceptions of work and the role of work in one's life—especially in later life. Given that for many older adults counseling is not the norm, the counselor should help the client become comfortable and safe in the relationship and clarify the objective of counseling (and differentiate it from friendship). The counselor, too, should be sensitive to and adapt to any auditory or visual disabilities the client may bring in. Canaff (1997) pointed to the importance of focusing on the present and not the future (given many older adults' here-and-now orientation) and working with the client toward a collaborative relationship in the career decision-making process. Canaff (1997) also recommended deemphasizing formal testing and instead suggested assessment through interview. She reminded us of the importance of a financial assessment, the potential inclusion of the client's spouse or partner (if applicable), concerns about reentry into the workforce (if currently not employed), and the provision of information about job opportunities as well as about training options. She further suggested that counselors advocate for the older worker, providing information about older workers and reducing ageism and its deleterious effects (Canaff, 1997).

Counselors need to be sensitive to the particular developmental and social challenges facing older workers, including the importance of remaining generative and of retaining integrity (Erikson, Erikson, & Kivnik, 1986, cited in Harper & Shoffner, 2004). Older adults must consider physical, mental, and family issues. Physical health and cognitive functioning issues may be more salient in later life. Caregiving for family members, friends, or others may have an impact on workplace demands. Ageism and negative social attitudes toward aging can impact career options. For those older people no longer in the workforce, lack of contact with coworkers and lack of work activity can exact a toll. One way to remedy this is by the older adult remaining in or rejoining the workforce—whether full-time or part-time, whether in his or her old career or in a new career. Career counselors can assist in this by identifying an older adult's skills, abilities, needs, values, and personality and matching it with a job's requirements, reinforcers, and work environment (see Dawis & Lofquist, 1984, cited in Harper & Shoffner, 2004). Congruence should result in satisfaction both on the part of the employee with the job and on the part of the employer with the employee.

Premature Retirement

In later life, not all retirement is planned or desired. Ranzijn (2002) used the term **premature retirement** to refer to the loss of employment before a worker wants to or even needs to retire[7] and posited that it is result of workplace ageism. Negative effects on the individual of premature retirement include reduced self-esteem, increased mental illness, and alcohol abuse (Gallo, Bradley, Siegel, & Kasl, 2000, 2001, cited in Ranzijn, 2002).

CHAPTER SUMMARY

Counselors working in schools, colleges, or career settings may have occasion to interact with older adults. Many grandparents are primary caregivers for their grandchildren. Some older adults are returning to school, whether in a degree or nondegree program. Yet others are working or volunteering during their retirement years. In this chapter, we discussed custodial and noncustodial grandparenting and how well children in such households fare. We looked at some issues faced by African American, Latino/a, and First Nations grandparents. We discussed reentry older students, including their motivation for returning to school, barriers to education, and their plans postgraduation. We considered retirement, age, multicultural considerations, gender, income, and geography. We reviewed ageism in the workplace, partial retirement, encore careers, volunteering, and bridge employment. For grandparenting, reentry older students, and retirement, we considered counseling, social justice, and advocacy. In Chapter 11, we will consider health and rehabilitation counseling needs of older adults.

CASE STUDY

Ahnah is a 55-year-old First Nations grandmother who is caregiver for her two preteen granddaughters. Her husband died 15 years ago, and she is underemployed (working as a housecleaner just 5 hours per week) and poor. She attended grade school but not high school. She speaks a First Nations language (her first language) as well as English. In addition to caring for her two granddaughters, Ahnah is also caregiver for her brother, who has multiple medical problems. Between caring for her granddaughters and her brother and taking care of the house, Ahnah reports working almost continuously during her waking hours. She has high blood pressure and is borderline diabetic, but she receives medical care only on an intermittent basis. She has expressed a desire to receive further education or training so that she may find better paying work. She was referred to you because she needs assistance.

Questions

1. What are the primary problems in this family?
2. Describe how you would address each of these problems.
3. What specific steps would you take in terms of education and work or retirement issues for Ahnah?
4. Compare and contrast Ahnah's profile with First Nations custodial caregivers as well as custodial caregivers more generally.
5. Describe advocacy activities in which you might engage, given the particulars of this situation.

CHAPTER QUESTIONS

1. What are common motivators for older adults to become involved in education?
2. What are some common barriers to older adults' participation in education?
3. Contrast goal-, activity-, and learning-oriented learners.
4. What is the difference between instrumental motivation and expressive motivation for learning?
5. Define premature retirement, and describe its effects on the individual.
6. Discuss the issue of ageism in the workplace.
7. What are some negative stereotypes of older workers? How might you work to fight these stereotypes?
8. What is the difference between a custodial, near-custodial, and noncustodial grandparent?
9. How are the experiences of custodial grandfathers similar to and different from the experiences of custodial grandmothers?
10. What are some of the stressors present in custodial grandparenting? In a clinical setting, how would you address these stressors?
11. How do grandchildren raised by grandparents fare in comparison to those not raised by grandparents?

GLOSSARY

Bridge employment: is a job in which one engages between one's full-time career and one's complete retirement from employment.

Custodial or near-custodial grandparent: is a grandparent who is caring for a grandchild, without the presence of the parent.

Expressive motivators: for learning refer to learning for the sake of interest or learning for its own sake.

Instrumental motivators: for learning are concrete reasons often related to work or skills-building.

Premature retirement: (also known as pseudoretirement) is the loss of employment before a worker wants to or even needs to retire.

Skipped-generation households: are those households that include grandparents and grandchildren but not parents.

Stress and coping model: states that stress results from demands that outstrip a person's resources, whereas coping comprises the strategies a person uses to try to manage those very demands.

FURTHER INFORMATION

Grandparenting

American Association of Retired Persons, Grandparent Information Center, 601 E. Street NW, Washington, DC 20049, (202) 434-2296, www.aarp.org.
Child Welfare League of America, 440 First Street NW, Washington, DC 20001, (202) 638-2952, www.cwla.org.
Generations United, 440 First Street NW, 4th Floor, Washington, DC 20001, (202) 662-4283, www.gu.org.

Reentry Students

American Association of Retired Persons, Lifelong Learning, 601 E. Street NW, Washington, DC 20049, (202) 434-2296, www.aarp.org/learntech/lifelong.
American Council on Education, One Dupont Circle NW, Washington, DC 20036-1193, (202) 939-9300, www.acenet.edu.
American Council on Education, Center for Lifelong Learning, One Dupont Circle NW, Washington, DC 20036-1193, (202) 939-9300, www.acenet.edu/Content/NavigationMenu/ProgramsServices/CLLL/index.htm.
Osher Lifelong Learning Institutes, The Bernard Osher Foundation, One Ferry Building, Suite 255, San Francisco, CA 94111, (415) 861-5587, www.osherfoundation.org/index.php?olli.

Retirement

American Association of Retired Persons, 601 E. Street NW, Washington, DC 20049, (202) 434-2296, www.aarp.org.
U.S. Department of Labor, Bureau of Labor Statistics, 2 Massachusetts Avenue NE, Washington, DC 20212-0001, www.bls.gov.
U.S. Equal Employment Opportunity Commission, 131 M Street NE, Washington, DC 20507, (202) 663-4900, TTY (202) 663-4494, www.eeoc.gov.

NOTES

1. Of *custodial grandparents*, 44% began caring for an *infant* grand-child, and 72% began their caregiving responsibilities before their grandchild turned 5 (see Fuller-Thomson, Minkler, & Driver, 1997).
2. Recall that *generativity* refers to leaving a legacy, creating something for others, or giving something to a future generation, whereas *self-absorption* refers to self-centeredness or a concern with oneself to the exclusion of others.
3. An AARP (2000) survey found that more than 90% of adults age 50 and older stated that they wanted to learn in order "to keep up with what's going on in the world ... for their own spiritual or personal growth" and "for the simple joy of learning something new" (p. 2).
4. The National Center on Education Statistics (2007, cited in American Council on Education, 2007) reported that among 55- to 64-year-olds, 27% take work-related courses (instrumental), and 21% take personal interest (expressive) courses. Among those 65 and older, 5% take work-related courses, and 19% take personal interest courses.
5. In the United States, this reduction in the labor force is mitigated by the presence of legal immigrants and undocumented workers, the result being a likely diversification in the ethnic/racial composition of the workforce (Nyce, 2007).
6. Other ways to mitigate the reduction in labor supply are by increasing immigration, increasing productivity and production per worker, or outsourcing business overseas (Nyce, 2007).
7. Encel (1995, cited in Ranzijn, 2002) referred to this as *pseudoretirement*.

CHAPTER 11

Health and Rehabilitation Counseling With Older Adults

Not everything that is faced can be changed, but nothing can be
changed until it is faced.

—Attributed to James Baldwin (1924–1987)

CHAPTER OVERVIEW

Aging is associated with varying degrees of changes in the body. These
changes often result in differing abilities for some older adults that
can impact their personal, social, and work lives. In this chapter, we
will look at vocational rehabilitation issues with older adults. We will
consider health and disability and the specific issues of hearing impairment, vision impairment, and dual sensory impairment and their
impact on older clients.

REHABILITATION AND AGING

Older Adults' Vocational Rehabilitation Needs and Objectives

A major objective of rehabilitation counseling is to help people become
reengaged in the workforce. A central question is whether this objective
is congruent with the intentions of older adults involved in rehabilitation counseling.

The Veterans Health Administration runs the Compensated Work Therapy program, for example, which has as its goal increasing participants' levels of vocational functioning, preparation for return to the competitive workforce, or preparation for long-term work placement (i.e., in a sheltered workshop setting) (Drebing et al., 2002). As a whole, over one half of those in the program plan on moving into the competitive workforce, whereas only 1 in 20 states that this is his or her primary reason for being in rehabilitation (Drebing et al., 2002). The participants in Drebing et al.'s (2002) study identified other reasons for being in vocational rehabilitation, such as the desire to supplement their psychiatric treatment (including substance abuse), the desire to work in the program because it is better adapted to their disabilities and more supportive than the competitive workforce, and the desire to remain active or have more income (Drebing et al., 2002).

Confusing Older adults (55 years and older) participating in rehabilitation through the Compensated Work Therapy program are found to have lower levels of education, are more likely to receive disability payments, are more likely to suffer from a disability related to a medical condition, and are less likely to suffer from psychiatric (including substance use) disorders (Drebing et al., 2002). Older participants are less likely to work, hence less likely to receive compensation from working, and are more likely to receive compensation from retirement income and from disability income (up to age 74) (Drebing et al., 2002). Furthermore, older adults are less likely than younger adults to be in the Compensated Work Therapy program with the intention of gaining competitive employment. A higher percentage of the older adults work in sheltered workshop settings, and a lower percentage of the older adults are employed in competitive work at the time of their discharge (Drebing et al., 2002).

The fact that participants over age 55 are less likely than younger participants to look for competitive employment suggests that older adults participate in vocational rehabilitation for reasons different from those of younger adults (Drebing et al., 2002). This may be—at least in part—due to greater medical problems in older adults and/or their having available Social Security or other retirement benefits (Drebing et al., 2002). Although about 9% of participants in this program are 55 and older, there continues to be increases in both the number and the percentage of older participants. This increase is congruent with the evidence that older adults more and more are remaining in the workforce or are intending to reenter the workforce because of economic needs. In addition to gaining economic benefits, older adults who are in the paid workforce demonstrate a range of social, physical, and mental benefits (Drebing et al., 2002).

In sum, older adults involved in vocational rehabilitation through the Compensated Work Therapy program have different intentions and different needs than younger adults (Drebing et al., 2002). Specifically, they are not as likely as younger adults to use vocational rehabilitation to move into the competitive workforce, and they are more likely than younger adults to use it as a venue of financial compensation in jobs whose demands do not exceed their disabling medical conditions (Drebing et al., 2002). Older adults are more likely than younger adults to have retirement income and/or disability income, which may act as disincentives to returning to the competitive workforce (Drebing et al., 2002).

Drebing et al. (2002) believed that older adults in the Compensated Work Therapy program are misusing vocational rehabilitation; namely, they are in the program for the internal benefits it provides and not for the objective of moving into the competitive workforce. Drebing et al. (2002) tempered their position and noted that older adults *do* work toward clinically appropriate and vocationally relevant goals, including remaining in treatment, maintaining sobriety, and working in settings that are adapted to their disabilities. Drebing et al. (2002) argued, though, that programs should be developed that address the particular vocational rehabilitation needs of older adults, recognizing that older adults have different needs and objectives than their younger counterparts.

Rehabilitation Counselor Domain Knowledge

Given that older adults have different rehabilitation needs and objectives, what should a counselor of older adults know about rehabilitation? A recent study analyzed the frequency of, importance of, and recommendation for the stage of professional development in which rehabilitation counselors should acquire rehabilitation domain knowledge (Leahy, Muenzen, Saunders, & Strauser, 2009). Twelve domains (comprising 81 subdomains) were grouped into three factors—counseling knowledge, vocational knowledge, and core rehabilitation knowledge.

1. *Counseling knowledge* comprised four domains:
   a. individual counseling,
   b. group and family counseling,
   c. mental health counseling, and
   d. psychosocial and cultural issues in counseling.
2. *Vocational knowledge* comprised three domains:
   a. career counseling and assessment,
   b. job development and placement services, and
   c. vocational consultation and services for employers.

3. *Core rehabilitation knowledge* comprised five domains:
   a. case and caseload management;
   b. medical, functional, and environmental aspects of disabilities;
   c. foundations, ethics, and professional issues;
   d. rehabilitation services and resources; and
   e. health care and disability systems.

For example, certified rehabilitation counselors (CRCs) who work in state or federal rehabilitation agencies, private nonprofits, colleges and universities, mental health centers and psychiatric hospitals, and K-12 schools rate mental health knowledge as more important than did those who work for private rehabilitation companies (Leahy et al., 2009). The two domains rated as most important and most frequently used (as reported by their participants) are (a) medical, functional, and environmental aspects of disabilities and (b) case and caseload management (Leahy et al., 2009). The least frequently used domain is group and family counseling.[1]

There is, however, variation by work setting in ratings of importance or of frequency of use of particular domains. That is, rehabilitation counselors' responses to the importance of (or frequency of use of) various domains differ based on whether the rehabilitation counselors work in state or federal rehabilitation agencies, private rehabilitation companies, private practice, private nonprofit rehabilitation facilities, colleges or universities, insurance companies, K-12 schools, or other settings (Leahy et al., 2009).

The subdomains rated as most important are those related to the functional capacities of persons with disabilities and vocational issues for those with functional limitations, medical aspects/implications of disabilities, ethical standards, professional roles and responsibilities, and case management (Leahy et al., 2009). The subdomains rated as least important are knowledge of group counseling theories and interpretation/application of research findings (Leahy et al., 2009).

The subdomains used most frequently are principles of caseload management, functional capacities of persons with disabilities, medical aspects/implications, professional roles and responsibilities, and case management; the subdomain used least frequently is that of forensic rehabilitation services (Leahy et al., 2009).

Given variations in ratings of importance or frequency of use of various domains and subdomains, it is appropriate for rehabilitation counselors working with older adults to consider the particular knowledge domains most important in their work and the domains they use most frequently. Counselors, too, should understand that domains that are relevant particularly to their work with older clients may differ from domains used by rehabilitation counselors more generally or by those who work with younger populations or in settings less likely to be utilized by older adults. Furthermore, gerontological counselors should receive education and training specific to older-client-relevant domains.

AGING AND HEALTH

By 2030, the U.S. population of those age 65 and older is expected to grow from 35 million to 72 million, that is, from 12% to 20% of the total population (Federal Interagency Forum on Aging-Related Statistics, 2008). Although older Americans are living longer, they are at increased risk of certain illnesses. Furthermore, life expectancy of older Americans is less than that of older adults in many other rich nations. Chronic conditions differ by gender: Women are more likely to suffer from arthritis, whereas men are more likely to suffer from heart disease or cancer. Some health risks can be reduced by changes in behaviors, such as screenings for diseases, vaccinations, improvements in diet, increased physical activity, reductions in obesity, and quitting smoking (Federal Interagency Forum on Aging-Related Statistics, 2008). Further reductions in health risks can be accomplished by improving air quality and increasing socialization and social interaction (Federal Interagency Forum on Aging-Related Statistics, 2008).

Quality of Life

A recent report by the Centers for Disease Control and Prevention and the Merck Company Foundation (2007) identified three areas that can contribute to elders' increased quality of life: cognitive health, end-of-life care, and reducing falls. Better medical care can assist those four out of five older adults who live with one or more chronic health problems (Centers for Disease Control and Prevention and the Merck Company Foundation, 2007) and can directly or indirectly improve quality of life. Illnesses due to smoking, poor diet, and lack of physical activity accounted for over one out of three deaths in the United States in 2000 (Centers for Disease Control and Prevention and the Merck Company Foundation, 2007). Supporting older adults in quitting smoking, improving their diets, and engaging in physical activity may reduce chronic illnesses that are associated with mortality, including some of the leading causes of death: "heart disease, cancer, stroke, and diabetes" (Centers for Disease Control and Prevention and the Merck Company Foundation, 2007, p. III). Chronic illnesses—in addition to causing pain and suffering—contribute to disability, increased health care expenditures, and decreased quality of life. Cognitive problems and the rate of cognitive decline may be reduced, arrested, or reversed through the use of cognitive training, medication, or other health interventions. Physical and psychological pain and suffering present at end of life may be reduced through attending to end-of-life wishes of the loved one or offering appropriate pain-reducing medications.

Falls. Falls account for the majority of injuries and trauma-related hospitalizations in older adults and are the leading causes of injury-related deaths (Centers for Disease Control and Prevention and the Merck Company Foundation, 2007). Falls are associated with increased "mortality, disability, loss of independence, and admission to nursing homes" (Centers for Disease Control and Prevention and the Merck Company Foundation, 2007, p. V). The likelihood of falls increases with age, especially in those 80 years old and older. Many older adults who have fallen acquire anxiety around falling and may reduce or limit the physical activities in which they engage. This reduction in physical activity subsequently may result in poorer health, poorer physical functioning, lesser sociability, and increased likelihood of nursing home admission.

Risk factors for falls are categorized as either personal or environmental. Personal risk factors include one's functional ability and health, age, history of falls, female gender, multiple or psychiatric medications, weakness in the lower body, some chronic diseases, balance and gait problems, and vision impairment (Centers for Disease Control and Prevention and the Merck Company Foundation, 2007).[2] Environmental risk factors include "tripping hazards ... lack of stair railings or grab bars, slippery surfaces, unstable furniture, and poor lighting" (Centers for Disease Control and Prevention and the Merck Company Foundation, 2007, p. 29). A counselor might reduce the likelihood of client falls by addressing personal and environmental risk factors—for example, by encouraging exercise, better management of medications, and elimination of hazardous environmental conditions.

Health Improvement

Health issues in aging need not be gloomy, and in fact there is evidence that health can improve in later life. Ranzijn (2002) noted that elders—with training—can actually become stronger and more flexible and improve their balance, contrary to physical decline. Strength training is correlated with improved physical strength and quality of life in women (Damush & Damush, 1999, cited in Ranzijn, 2002); physical fitness is correlated with decreased mortality in men (Erikssen et al., 1998, cited in Ranzijn, 2002). This ability to improve health in later life presents a strong argument against the ageist belief that older workers are more likely to become ill or injured than younger workers (see Remenyi, 1994, cited in Ranzijn, 2002), and in fact, older employees are just as likely as younger employees to benefit from rehabilitation (see Jacobs, 1997, cited in Ranzijn, 2002).

Ranzijn (2002) rightly stated that there are nuanced associations between "physical activity, social interaction, cognitive function, and physical and mental health." The complexity of these subtle relationships is hinted at in findings that self-ratings of health better forecast illness and death than do physician or pathology measures (Helmer et al., 1999, and others, cited in Ranzijn, 2002). Similarly, positive affect and pleasurable activities are associated with more positive self-ratings of health than are *objectively measured* "functional ability and medical indicators" (Benyamini et al., 2000, cited in Ranzijn, 2002).

Vaillant (2000, cited in Ranzijn, 2002) found that physically healthy men with higher levels of positive cognitive qualities (e.g., altruism, sense of humor) are more likely to be physically healthy 15 years later than are men with lower levels of these qualities. On the flip side, explicitly angry people with coronary artery disease are more likely to experience disease progression than people who are less explicitly angry (Reuters Health, 2000, cited in Ranzijn, 2002). Evidence suggests that psychological health can have a positive impact on physical health and that elders can improve their physical health (Ranzijn, 2002).

Chronic Conditions

Many chronic conditions are found in older adults and tend to "require more care, are more disabling, and are more difficult and costly to treat" (National Academy on an Aging Society, 1999a, p. 1) than those chronic conditions found in midlife or youth. The most common chronic conditions in midlife (45 years and older) to old age (74 years and younger)[3] are arthritis, hypertension, and orthopedic impairments; for men, this list further includes hearing impairment and heart disease, whereas for women it includes sinusitis and hay fever (National Academy on an Aging Society, 1999a). The most common chronic conditions in the old-old and oldest-old (75 years or older) are arthritis, hypertension, hearing impairments, heart disease, and cataracts (National Academy on an Aging Society, 1999a).

People who are of lower socioeconomic status tend to have costlier or more difficult-to-treat chronic conditions. Twenty-three percent of middle-aged adults (ages 45–64) are limited in activities because of a chronic condition, and this jumps to 34% in the young-old (ages 65–74) and 45% in the old-old/oldest-old (ages 75 years and older) (National Academy on an Aging Society, 1999a). Furthermore, older adults with chronic conditions are more likely to be hospitalized (10% of those ages 45–74 and 20% of those ages 75 and older) (National Academy on an Aging Society, 1999a). In other words, if you are 75 years or older, you have a one-in-five chance of being hospitalized within the year.

Cigolle, Langa, Kabeto, Tian, and Blaum's (2007) review of data from the Health and Retirement Study found *nondisease conditions* often associated with aging that contribute to disability. These include cognitive impairment, falls, incontinence, low body mass index, dizziness, vision impairment, and hearing impairment. They found that nearly 50% of older adults (65 years of age or older) had at least one and sometimes more of these **geriatric conditions.** They also found that as the number of geriatric conditions increases, the greater the likelihood that the participant is older, a woman, a member of an ethnic/racial minority group, and unmarried; has lower education; and has lower net financial assets. Overall, the number of geriatric conditions increases with age, as does the rate of every condition, and these conditions are associated with at least one activity of daily living. *Activities of daily living* (ADLs) are the essential self-care actions that allow an older adult to function on a day-to-day basis; these include such actions as the ability to bathe, to dress, and to toilet oneself. *Instrumental activities of daily living* (IADLs), a parallel set of actions, are not as essential to biological survival, yet they allow an older adult to live independently; some common IADLs include the ability to handle money, to shop, and to prepare meals.

Cigolle et al. (2007) found that geriatric conditions are associated with lesser ability to engage independently in 5 of 14 ADLs (bathing, dressing, eating, transferring, and toileting). They concluded that non-medical geriatric conditions may be as common as chronic diseases (including heart disease, chronic lung disease, diabetes, cancer, musculoskeletal conditions, stroke, and psychiatric conditions) in older people and may have a correlation with ADL dependencies. Furthermore, they pointed out that geriatric conditions are less likely than medical conditions to be recognized and subsequently addressed.

Cigolle et al. (2007) described the Institute of Medicine model, which clarifies that diseases may or may not be associated with physical disability. Briefly stated, disease may result in impairment, which may result in functional limitations, which may result in disability. Geriatric conditions interact with various segments of this model such that these conditions may result in dependency in ADLs; conversely, dependency in ADLs may contribute to geriatric conditions; furthermore, geriatric conditions may themselves be impairments that are the result of disease.

Let us look at two common geriatric conditions, hearing impairment and vision impairment, as well as dual sensory impairment.

HEARING IMPAIRMENT

Hearing impairment is found in about 33% of the young-old (i.e., age 65 through 74) and about 50% of the oldest-old (i.e., age 85 and older) (National Institute on Aging, 2008). Overall, more than 4 out of 10 people age 65 and older report hearing loss, more than for any other age group (National Academy on an Aging Society, 1999b). Hearing loss can affect an older adult's well-being, including his or her feelings, physical functioning, and social interactions. Those with hearing loss report more depression and dissatisfaction, poorer functional health, and increased isolation. Older adults with hearing loss are more likely to report dissatisfaction with their financial situation, their physical health, their handling of problems, their family life, their friendships, and their life overall. Older men more than older women and older European Americans more than older African Americans are likely to have hearing loss. People with household incomes less than $20,000 are more likely to have hearing loss than people with household incomes of at least $50,000. Those aged 51 to 61 with hearing loss are about 50% more likely to be retired than are those without hearing loss; retirees with hearing loss are over 50% more likely to report that poor health was a major factor in their retirement decision than those retirees without hearing loss. Furthermore, retirees with hearing loss are less likely to report being satisfied with their retirement than those without hearing loss. Hearing aids can be effective with the majority of people with hearing loss; however, approximately two thirds of older adults with hearing loss are not using hearing aids, because of cost, vanity/stigma, and/or denial of the severity of their hearing loss.

Symptoms

Hearing loss may be marked by one or several symptoms (National Institute on Aging, 2008). These symptoms include having difficulty hearing television or radio shows or telephone conversations, criticizing others for mumbling when they speak, asking others to speak more loudly, leaning forward and putting one's hand around one's ear to try to hear better, having problems hearing others in noisy public settings, having greater difficulty hearing higher frequency voices (typically, voices of women or children) than lower frequency voices (typically, voices of men), and making improper responses in conversations or misunder-standing conversations (National Institute on Aging, 2008; Wallhagen, Pettengill, & Whiteside, 2006).

Types

Hearing loss can be classified as one of five types: conductive, sen-sorineural, mixed, central, and presbycusis (Wallhagen et al., 2006) (see Table 11.1). **Conductive hearing loss** is a result of sound not being able to be transmitted to the middle ear. A common cause of conductive hear-ing loss in later life is the buildup of cerumen (earwax). Other causes of conductive hearing loss are otosclerosis, infections, or cholesteatoma. **Sensorineural hearing loss** is a result of damage to the inner ear or to the neural conduits connecting the ear to the brain. Common causes of sensorineural hearing loss include disease, ototoxic substances, and extended exposure to loud noise. **Mixed hearing loss** is simply concur-rent conductive and sensorineural hearing loss. **Central hearing loss** is the result of damage to the auditory processing component of the brain. In central hearing loss, a person's ear functioning may remain, but the brain may lose the capacity to understand speech.

Presbycusis is hearing loss associated with aging; it is insidious, occurs in both ears, and is marked by high-frequency hearing loss. The loss of ability to hear high frequencies results in difficulties in speech comprehension. Common causes of presbycusis are exposure to loud noise, infections and illnesses, some specific prescription medications, and problems in the circulatory system (National Institute on Aging, 2008). Furthermore, presbycusis may be hereditary (National Institute on Deafness and Other Communication Disorders, 2008). A common comorbid disorder in aging-related hearing loss is tinnitus. Tinnitus is

TABLE 11.1   Types of Hearing Loss

Type	Description
Conductive	Sound is not transferred from outer ear to middle ear
Sensorineural	Damage to inner ear or neural conduits
Mixed	Concurrent conductive and sensorineural hearing loss
Central	Auditory processing disability; person hears but does not understand speech
Presbycusis	Hearing loss associated with aging

Note: Wallhagen, M. I., Pettengill, E., & Whiteside, M., "Sensory Impairment in Older Adults Part 1: Hearing Loss," *American Journal of Nursing, 106*(10), 40–48, 2006.

marked by ringing or other sounds in the ears. Tinnitus may be treated by medications, use of a hearing aid, or use of a masking device where listening to music can soothe the symptom and mask the sound.

Interventions

There are a number of interventions for hearing loss, among them adaptive, environmental, and assistive interventions (National Institute on Aging, 2008; Wallhagen et al., 2006). *Adaptive* interventions are those practical steps one can take to increase the likelihood of communication between a person with hearing loss and another. These practical steps include

- facing the person;
- getting his or her attention and speaking clearly;
- speaking at a normal volume (neither too loud nor too soft) while enunciating;
- standing or sitting in good lighting;
- using gestures or facial expressions;
- ensuring that your mouth is not covered by your hand (or paper or other items);
- rephrasing (and not repeating) what you say;
- ensuring that, if the person has a hearing aid, he or she is wearing it, and it is functioning; and
- if the person has a visual impairment and has glasses, that he or she is wearing them (National Institute on Aging, 2008; Wallhagen et al., 2006).

Environmental interventions include strategies to reduce background noise such as moving a conversation away from a more public space and into a more private (hence, quieter) space (National Institute on Aging, 2008; Wallhagen et al., 2006) or turning off the television or radio while conversing (National Institute on Deafness and Other Communication Disorders, 2008).

Assistive interventions include the use of hearing aids, assistive devices, and assistive services (National Institute on Aging, 2008; National Institute on Deafness and Other Communication Disorders, 2008; Wallhagen et al., 2006). *Hearing aids* are composed of a microphone, an amplifier, and a speaker. The function of a hearing aid is to amplify sound; it does not heal medical causes of hearing impairment. Private and public health insurance rarely pay for the cost of a hearing aid, which may range in price from hundreds to thousands of dollars.

Other **assistive devices** include cochlear implants (composed of a head-piece, speech processor, and receiver), pocket talkers, and such items as telephone and mobile telephone amplifying devices, television and radio listening systems, auditorium-type assistive listening systems, teletype devices, captioning for video, and alerting systems that utilize vibrations or lights.

Hearing loss clearly has an impact on an elder's quality of life. One study of older adults with hearing loss found that the more severe the hearing loss, the greater the likelihood of a hearing disability and the greater the likelihood of communication problems (Dalton et al., 2003). Furthermore, the more severe the hearing loss, the more likely the need for ADL and IADL assistance and the greater the likelihood of lower quality of life, vitality, sociability, mental health, and physical functioning.

Though hearing loss is a common problem in later life, it often-times is seen as relatively unimportant or merely a sign that one is aging. Given that hearing loss is associated with quality of life, it is incumbent upon counseling professionals to identify those who may be suffering from hearing loss, refer them to appropriate resources, and support them in acquiring hearing assistance devices and engaging in the auditory rehabilitation. Furthermore, gerontological counseling professionals should attend to the interaction between hearing loss and clients' presenting problems. For example, a counselor may work with an older couple to resolve conflict in their relationship; the particulars of their conflict, however, may be exacerbated by the fact that one or both of them may have undiagnosed, untreated, or unrecognized hear-ing impairments.

Coping

How does one cope with hearing loss? Gomez and Madey (2001) explored the relationship between hearing loss, related psychosocial fac-tors, and the perceived effectiveness of strategies for improved communi-cation (i.e., adaptive strategies), contrasting them with those that do not improve communication (i.e., maladaptive strategies). Adaptive strate-gies include wearing hearing aids, facing the person who is speaking, asking others to repeat what is said, sitting in a place that allows one to hear the speaker better, asking the speaker to talk louder, using devices for amplification, asking the speaker to talk slower, asking the speaker to face you, and asking the speaker to get one's attention before speak-ing. Maladaptive strategies include pretending to comprehend what is said, interrupting a dialogue, not talking to strangers, avoiding social situations, dominating a dialogue, and ignoring the speaker.

Coping strategies may be more influenced by nonaudiological factors than by the hearing loss itself (Gomez & Madey, 2001). Specific nonaudiological factors include one's subjective self-perception of hearing loss, anxiety around getting older, individual adjustment in the face of hearing loss, perceived social support, and perceived success of a coping strategy. Perceived coping strategy effectiveness is more likely to be associated with the use of adaptive strategies; likewise subjective perception of hearing loss is more likely to result in the use of adaptive strategies. The perception of a lack of social support, as well as having poor adjustment in the face of hearing loss, is more likely to be associated with the use of maladaptive strategies. In sum, nonaudiological factors are more likely to be associated with adaptive or maladaptive coping strategies than the objective hearing loss itself (Gomez & Madey, 2001). The more individuals with hearing loss believe that the strategy they are using is effective—independent of whether it actually is—the more likely they are to continue using it.

An astute counselor may utilize psychoeducation to help an older client who uses a maladaptive strategy—for example, pretending to understand what is being said—to recognize the limited utility of that strategy and to help that client replace it with an adaptive strategy—for example, asking someone to repeat what he or she said.

VISION IMPAIRMENT

The older one gets, the more one is likely to suffer from a vision impairment. Vision impairment is present in about 17% of adults age 45 and older, and it increases to over 26% by age 75 (American Association of Retired Persons [AARP], 1995–2008; Horowitz, Brennan, & Reinhardt, 2005). One is more likely to suffer vision impairment if, in addition to increased age, one has a lower education level, is in poorer health, and has limited informal social support (Horowitz et al., 2005).[4] Vision impairment is associated with functional disability, decreased psychological well-being, increased falls, increased hospital stays, and increased visits to a physician (Horowitz et al., 2005). Those older adults with poor vision are more likely to have an ADL disability or an IADL disability (Berger & Porell, 2008). Older adults with vision loss may suffer from adjustment disorder or from depression, they may feel like they are losing their independence and control, they may have lower self-esteem, and their relationships with friends and family may be marked by tension (Watson, 2001). As such, counselors may treat clients suffering from vision-loss-associated adjustment to disability, depression, low self-esteem, and interpersonal conflicts.

Symptoms

Some of the symptoms of vision impairment include needing to move forward to focus, having problems recognizing faces or objects, having problems with finding things, hesitating when reaching for objects, having problems identifying colors, having difficulties writing, needing brighter light to read, bumping into things, or stumbling when there is no identifiable physical problem with balance (AARP, 1995–2008).

Types

The three most common types of vision impairment in later life are age-related macular degeneration, glaucoma, and cataracts (AARP, 1995–2008). **Age-related macular degeneration** is insidious and results in loss of central vision. Although there is no cure, a person with age-related macular degeneration has, with early diagnosis, greater treatment options, including the use of medications, surgery, or lifestyle changes (Family Caregiver Alliance, 2008). *Glaucoma* is the buildup of fluid resulting in eye pressure and loss of peripheral vision. There is no cure, but there are treatments to arrest vision loss, including the use of eye drops that reduce pressure (Family Caregiver Alliance, 2008). *Cataracts* is a clouding of the lens of the eye and results in blurring of vision. The most successful treatment is surgery, which replaces the clouded lens with a plastic one (Family Caregiver Alliance, 2008).

Interventions

Some changes in vision related to aging are common. These include difficulty focusing (especially close up), problems in night vision, and problems in reading under low-light conditions (AARP, 1995–2008).

The likelihood of other types of vision impairment may be reduced through behavioral changes, such as eating a balanced diet, getting regular exercise, ceasing smoking, wearing UV sunglasses when outdoors, and wearing eye protection as necessary (AARP, 1995–2008).

There are rehabilitation services, alterations to the home, and assistive devices that may help compensate for vision impairment (Family Caregiver Alliance, 2008). *Rehabilitation services* include training in adaptive living, mobility training, vision training, and training in the use of assistive devices. Typical rehabilitation services include the development of a vision rehabilitation plan, with objectives that are sensitive to the older client's feelings and thoughts and recommendations for low-vision devices that would be useful to the client (see Watson, 2001). Older adults need to be taught how to effectively utilize compensatory devices to reduce safety concerns (such as falls, dizziness, or nausea), use ergonomic devices, and adjust illumination (Watson, 2001).

Alterations to the home to compensate for vision impairment include adding more or higher quality lights that reduce glare, emphasizing dark and light contrasts throughout the house so that important items can be easily identified, and organizing the house so that there are specific locations for specific items as well as ensuring that there are no obstacles throughout the house (Family Caregiver Alliance, 2008). Other strategies include using bright, clear colors for discrimination of objects and using senses other than vision as alternatives for successfully performing tasks (Watson, 2001).

Assistive devices include magnifying lenses, penlights, closed-circuit televisions (comprising a camera and a screen) for magnifying objects, telephones with large buttons, and audio products such as talking clocks, audio books, and voice-activated software (Family Caregiver Alliance, 2008). They also include large-print books, newspapers, and manuscripts and field-expansion devices such as reverse telescopes, field-expansion prisms, and hemianoptic mirrors (Watson, 2001).

DUAL SENSORY IMPAIRMENT

Dual sensory impairment—that is, co-occurring visual and auditory impairment—is not an uncommon problem in later life; it is estimated to affect between 5% and 9% of the older adult population (see Campbell et al., 1999, Crews & Campbell, 2004, Raina, Wong, Dukeshire, Chambers, & Lindsay, 2000, all cited in Brennan, Horowitz, & Su, 2005). The National Health Interview Survey found a relationship between dual sensory impairment and risk of death (Lam, Lee, Gomez-Marin, Zheng, & Caban, 2006). In both genders, and in all ethnic/racial groups except African Americans, those with dual sensory impairment were at increased risk of death. In other words, one may predict a greater likelihood of death if one knows that individuals suffer from concurrent visual and auditory impairment.

Why is this the case? We know that the older one gets, the more likely one is to suffer from impairments in vision, audition, or both vision and audition (Lam et al., 2006). We know that vision and hearing loss each are associated with increased risk of death. Furthermore, we know that those who have dual sensory impairment in vision and audition have a lower quality of life, have poorer balance, and have an increased likelihood of falling (Lam et al., 2006). Furthermore, those with concurrent visual and auditory impairments suffer from lower functional abilities including reduced ADLs and IADLs. The more of these factors that are present, the greater is the likelihood of mortality.

Brennan et al. (2005) studied dual sensory impairment and its relationship to everyday competence. One out of five participants in their study suffered from dual sensory impairment. This dual sensory impairment, when compared with single sensory impairment, further was associated with greater problems with IADLs than with ADLs. If the levels of dual sensory impairment are higher, there is a greater likelihood of IADL problems than of ADL problems. Dual sensory loss appears to have a greater negative impact on the more complex activities of IADLs than on the relatively simpler activities of ADLs. Elimination of, or reductions in, dual sensory impairment through visual or auditory rehabilitation may promote everyday competence in older adults.

CHAPTER SUMMARY

In this chapter, we looked at older clients' rehabilitation needs and objectives and how they differ from those of younger adults. We considered the various types of rehabilitation counselor domain knowledge and how specific domains may be more relevant to work with older clients. We explored aging and health, including quality of life, health improvement, and chronic conditions. We looked at the common experiences in later life of hearing impairment, vision impairment, and dual sensory impairment and identified symptoms, types, and interventions. In Chapter 12 we will turn to the issue of Alzheimer's disease and other dementias.

CASE STUDY

Mr. Smith is a 60-year-old European American man who is seeing you for vocational rehabilitation. He recently lost his job after an economic downturn. He has worked for many years as a salesperson in high-end men's retail clothing. He is motivated to return to work but is worried that he will have difficulties in retail given his poor eyesight. He has poor eyesight because of glaucoma; as he states, "I have bluffed my way for several years. No one has really known how bad my eyesight is. I can't see worth a damn anymore. On top of that, I can't hear anymore. Who would hire me?" He states that his poor vision is a "downer; it's like I'm an old man or something" and that he vacillates between being anxious and depressed because he does not feel he will be able to interview well or to get a job offer.

Questions

1. What is the relationship, if there is one, between Mr. Smith's physical health and psychological health?
2. What is he most in need of? Information? Interviewing practice? Supportive counseling? Medical referral? Why?
3. What steps would you engage in to help Mr. Smith?

CHAPTER QUESTIONS

1. What are the three major sets of vocational rehabilitation knowledge, and what do they comprise?
2. What is the relationship between physical health and psychological health?
3. What are the most common chronic conditions in later life?
4. How do "geriatric conditions" differ from medical conditions? What are the implications for rehabilitation counseling?
5. What are the differences between conductive, sensorineural, mixed, central, and presbycusis hearing losses?
6. Describe signs of hearing loss.
7. Define and describe adaptive, environmental, and assistive interventions.
8. Describe age-related macular degeneration, glaucoma, and cataracts.
9. Describe signs of vision loss.
10. What are the risk factors for vision loss in later life?
11. Describe rehabilitation services, alterations to homes, and assistive devices that can help one compensate for vision loss.
12. Identify some chronic conditions that differ by gender. Speculate why there are differences in chronic condition by gender.
13. Discuss falls and the personal and environmental risk factors that contribute to them.
14. What is the relationship of dual sensory impairment to everyday competence?

GLOSSARY

Age-related macular degeneration: is marked by the loss of central vision.
Assistive devices: are objects such as sound-amplifying devices, magnifying lenses, or talking clocks that allow one to compensate for a sensory loss.

Central hearing loss: is the result of damage to the auditory processing component of the brain.

Conductive hearing loss: is a result of sound not being able to be transmitted to the middle ear.

Dual sensory impairment: is impairment in two or more senses (e.g., impairment in vision and in hearing).

Everyday competence: refers to one's capacity to function autonomously within one's milieu.

Geriatric conditions: are nondisease conditions that may be associated with aging.

Mixed hearing loss: is simply concurrent conductive hearing loss and sensorineural hearing loss.

Presbycusis: is hearing loss associated with aging.

Sensorineural hearing loss: is a result of damage to the inner ear or to the neural conduits connecting the ear to the brain.

FURTHER INFORMATION

Hearing Impairment

National Institute on Deafness and Other Communication Disorders, NIDCD Information Clearinghouse, National Institutes of Health, 31 Center Drive, MSC 2320, Bethesda, MD 20892, www.nidcd.nih.gov.

American Speech-Language-Hearing Association, 10801 Rockville Pike, Rockville, MD 20852, www.asha.org.

American Tinnitus Association, P.O. Box 5, Portland, OR 97207, www.ata.org.

Laurent Clerc National Death Education Center, Gallaudet University, 800 Florida Ave. NE, Washington, DC 20002, voice and TTY: (202) 651-5000.

Vision Impairment

Lighthouse International, 111 East 59th St., New York, NY 10022, www.lighthouse.org.

American Foundation for the Blind, 11 Penn Plaza, Suite 300, New York, NY 10001, www.afb.org.

Lions Clubs International, 300 W. 22nd St., Oak Brook, IL 60523, www.lionsclubs.org.

American Academy of Ophthalmology, P.O. Box 7424, San Francisco, CA 94120, www.aao.org.

NOTES

1. In fact, group and family counseling is the only domain that is not rated at least moderately important.
2. In one study, vision impairment coupled with hearing impairment (or poor standing balance) predicted falls, probably because the other impairments did not allow older adults to receive the compensatory information they needed about their posture or their environment (Kulmala et al., 2008).
3. That is, excluding the old-old (75–84) and the oldest-old (85 and older).
4. Poorer health and limited informal social support may be linked in that those with lesser informal social support may find it more difficult to connect with appropriate health care and social services (see Horowitz, Brennan, & Reinhardt, 2005).

CHAPTER 12

Alzheimer's Disease and Other Dementias

We tend to forget that life can only be defined in the present tense.

—Dennis Potter (1935–1994)

All things change; nothing perishes.

—Ovid (43 BCE–circa 17 CE)

CHAPTER OVERVIEW

We will begin our discussion with the demographics of dementia and look at the particulars of Alzheimer's disease and vascular dementia. We will review dementia classifications and differentiate dementia from other disorders. We will discuss risk factors for dementia, symptoms of dementia, and common behavioral challenges found in persons with dementia. We will end our discussion with treatment considerations for dementia.

Dementia results from destruction of brain cells and produces cognitive, behavioral and emotional, or personality changes in an individual. Dementia comes from the Latin *demens,* meaning deprived of mind (National Institute of Neurological Disorders and Stroke, 2007), and indeed people suffering from dementia show deficits in learning, in remembering, and in communicating (American Academy of Family Physicians, 2007b). Dementia itself is not a disease but a collection of symptoms that can be caused by one or more of a number of disorders (National Institute of Neurological Disorders and Stroke, 2007). Independent of the cause, three elements are common to all dementias: progressive decline, cognitive impairment, and intact consciousness in early to mid stages (Kennedy, 2000). Dementia is positively correlated with age; in other words, the older one gets, the greater the likelihood of dementia (Kennedy, 2000). Although the most common dementia in later life is Alzheimer's disease, dementia can also result from stroke, head injuries, or trauma to the brain.

Worldwide, roughly 24 million people have dementia; each year, nearly 5 million people are newly diagnosed. Dementia is not limited to the West nor is it found primarily in rich nations; in fact, nearly two thirds of people with dementing illnesses live in developing nations. Though rich nations expect a doubling of the rate of dementia by 2040, in the world's most populous nations—India and China—the rate is expected to triple (Ferri et al., 2005, cited in Alzheimer's Research Trust, 2006). In the United States, nearly 7 million people suffer from dementia, and almost 2 million cases are severe (National Institute of Neurological Disorders and Stroke, 2007). Below, we will address Alzheimer's disease and vascular dementia. Alzheimer's disease, vascular dementia, and other dementing illnesses, however, are not a normal part of aging, and in fact many adults live full lives without symptoms of dementia (National Institute of Neurological Disorders and Stroke, 2007).

ALZHEIMER'S DISEASE

About four and a half million Americans suffer from **Alzheimer's disease** (Hebert et al., 2003, cited in National Institute of Mental Health, 2007). The number of people in the United States diagnosed with Alzheimer's disease has increased more than twofold since 1980 (Hebert et al., 2003, cited in National Institute of Mental Health, 2007), and today about 10% of persons older than 65 and about 50% of persons older than 85 have Alzheimer's disease (Evans et al., 1989, cited in National Institute of Mental Health, 2007). People with Alzheimer's disease will live an average of about 8 to 10 years after receiving the diagnosis—roughly about half as long as those who are same aged and without Alzheimer's disease—though some may live as long as 20 years (National Institute of Mental Health, 2007; National Institute of Neurological Disorders and Stroke, 2007). Alzheimer's disease is marked by gradual decline in memory and in bodily functioning. A common cause of death in Alzheimer's disease is, in advanced cases, aspiration pneumonia because of a loss of ability to swallow (National Institute of Neurological Disorders and Stroke, 2007).

VASCULAR DEMENTIA

The second most common dementia in late life is **vascular dementia**, which is the result of brain damage from cerebrovascular or cardiovascular problems, typically stroke (National Institute of Neurological Disorders and Stroke, 2007). Unlike the symptoms of Alzheimer's disease, which are insidious, symptoms of vascular dementia may occur acutely (National Institute of Neurological Disorders and Stroke, 2007). With vascular dementias, the symptoms can get better or worse. In some cases vascular dementia mimics Alzheimer's disease in that the deterioration in cognitive and other abilities happens gradually over time (National Institute of Neurological Disorders and Stroke, 2007).

DEMENTIA CLASSIFICATIONS

Dementia disorders can be classified as cortical, subcortical, progressive, primary, or secondary (National Institute of Neurological Disorders and Stroke, 2007). **Cortical dementia** is marked by damage to the cortex (the outer layer) of the brain and results in memory impairment, communication problems (including aphasia, the inability to understand or produce speech), cognitive difficulties (including an inability to recall words), and interpersonal behavior problems (Cleveland Clinic, 2007; National Institute of Neurological Disorders and Stroke, 2007). **Subcortical dementia** is the result of damage to the brain beneath the cortex (hence, *sub*cortical) and tends to result in memory, movement, and emotional changes (National Institute of Neurological Disorders and Stroke, 2007), as well as personality and attention-span changes (Cleveland Clinic, 2007). **Progressive dementia** is a dementia that results in greater impairment over time (National Institute of Neurological Disorders and Stroke, 2007).

Primary dementia is a dementia that does not result from a secondary illness or disease; Alzheimer's disease is an example of a primary dementia (National Institute of Neurological Disorders and Stroke, 2007). **Secondary dementia** results from a physical illness or injury (National Institute of Neurological Disorders and Stroke, 2007), such as advanced Parkinson's disease, multiple sclerosis, or head injury.

Differential Diagnosis

Dementia is differentiated from age-related cognitive decline, mild cognitive impairment, depression, and delirium (National Institute of Neurological Disorders and Stroke, 2007). **Age-related cognitive decline** is the typical slowing of information processing and memory that is common in later life (National Institute of Neurological Disorders and Stroke, 2007). **Mild cognitive impairment** comprises cognitive problems and memory difficulties more intense than age-related cognitive decline but not severe enough to warrant a diagnosis of dementia (National Institute of Neurological Disorders and Stroke, 2007). Depressed older adults oftentimes demonstrate symptoms that mimic dementia, such as passivity, confusion, and forgetfulness (National Institute of Neurological Disorders and Stroke, 2007); this phenomenon is called pseudodementia.

Delirium is marked by confusion, disorientation, incoherence, altered mental states, changes in personality, and/or drowsiness and is usually caused by a treatable underlying illness (National Institute of Neurological Disorders and Stroke, 2007). For the remainder of our discussion, our primary focus will be on Alzheimer's disease because it is the most common form of dementia in older adults, though much of our discussion is relevant to other types of dementia.

RISK FACTORS

Risk factors for dementia include aging, genetics/family history, smoking and alcohol use, medical conditions (including atherosclerosis, cholesterol, plasma homcysteine, and diabetes), mild cognitive impairment, Down syndrome (National Institute of Neurological Disorders and Stroke, 2007), and race/ethnicity (Gallo & Lebowitz, 1999).

Aging is the single greatest risk factor for dementia. That is, the older one gets, the more likely one is to suffer from dementia. Aging, for example, is a major risk factor for Alzheimer's disease (Evans et al., 1989, cited in National Institute of Mental Health, 2007), and symptoms of Alzheimer's disease typically first appear after a person is 65 years old (Evans et al., 1989, cited in National Institute of Mental Health, 2007).

Genetics/family history is another risk factor. There are a number of genes that are associated with an increased risk of developing Alzheimer's disease, though none are definitive, and a family history of Alzheimer's disease puts one at increased risk for developing the disease, but not definitively (National Institute of Neurological Disorders and Stroke, 2007). That is, some people with a family history of Alzheimer's disease also will develop the disease, whereas others will not; furthermore, people without a family history of Alzheimer's disease still may develop the disease (National Institute of Neurological Disorders and Stroke, 2007).

People who *smoke* are more likely than nonsmokers to show mental decline and dementia. This may be in part due to the greater likelihood of atherosclerosis and other vascular diseases in smokers (National Institute of Neurological Disorders and Stroke, 2007). Heavy *drinking,* too, is associated with increased risk of dementia (National Institute of Neurological Disorders and Stroke, 2007). Medical conditions such as atherosclerosis, high levels of cholesterol, high levels of plasma homocysteine, and diabetes have been linked to dementia (National Institute of Neurological Disorders and Stroke, 2007). Atherosclerosis, the buildup of fatty substances in the inner lining of the arteries, may result in vascular dementia by reducing blood flow to the brain, resulting in stroke (National Institute of Neurological Disorders and Stroke, 2007). Atherosclerosis also has been linked to an increased risk for Alzheimer's disease (National Institute of Neurological Disorders and Stroke, 2007). High levels of bad cholesterol (LDL) are associated with an increased risk of vascular dementia and possibly Alzheimer's disease (National Institute of Neurological Disorders and Stroke, 2007). Homocysteine, an amino acid, if present in higher than average levels in the blood, puts a person at increased risk for developing vascular dementia or Alzheimer's disease (National Institute of Neurological Disorders and Stroke, 2007). Diabetes, too, puts one at increased risk for vascular or Alzheimer's dementia.

People with *mild cognitive impairment* may be at increased risk of dementia. Not everyone with mild cognitive impairment will develop dementia, but up to 40% of older adults with mild cognitive impairment may develop dementia within 3 years of the initial diagnosis of mild cognitive impairment. People who have *Down syndrome* are likely to develop damage to the brain structure that oftentimes characterizes Alzheimer's disease (National Institute of Neurological Disorders and Stroke, 2007). Many people with Down syndrome eventually develop dementia (National Institute of Neurological Disorders and Stroke, 2007).

There are *racial/ethnic* differences in Alzheimer's disease and other dementias. African Americans and Latino Americans suffer from Alzheimer's disease and other dementias at far higher rates than do European Americans (Gallo & Lebowitz, 1999). Research is needed to understand the disparity in the prevalence of dementia disorders between European Americans, African Americans, and Latino Americans.

PROTECTIVE FACTORS

Lifestyle and pharmacologic factors have been posited to act as protective factors against dementia, though—because of dementia's likely multidimensional nature and methodological difficulties in experimental design—research has not been definitive (Coley et al., 2008). Physical exercise, for example, has been found to be a protective factor associated with less risk of cognitive decline, Alzheimer's disease, or other dementias (Laurin, Verreault, Lindsay, MacPherson, & Rockwood, 2001). Other protective lifestyle factors for Alzheimer's disease may be higher socioeconomic status, healthy diet, higher levels of education, more mental activity (Bandelow & Hogervorst, 2010), and social contact (Coley et al., 2008). Protective pharmacologic interventions may include hormone replacement therapy (HRT), prophylactic use of nonsteroidal anti-inflammatory drugs (NSAIDs), and the use of the herb ginkgo biloba (Coley et al., 2008).

SYMPTOMS

Symptoms of dementia are numerous and may include changes in memory, language, behavior, judgment, and emotions (American Academy of Family Physicians, 2007b; National Institute on Aging, 2007; Torpy, 2007). Some common symptoms include

- memory loss,
- difficulties when trying to perform common household tasks,
- language impairments,
- disorientation to time and/or place,
- impoverished judgment,
- inability to think abstractly,
- forgetting where one has left things,
- mood swings,
- changes in personality,
- passivity,
- repeatedly asking the same questions over and over,
- becoming lost in familiar surroundings,
- inability to follow directions,
- self-neglect (e.g., decline in personal hygiene, forgetting to eat, disregarding personal safety), and
- agitation or delusions (American Academy of Family Physicians, 2007b; National Institute on Aging, 2007; Torpy, 2007).

If your client displays one or more of the above symptoms or if a family member reports them to you, you might suspect dementia and should make a referral to a physician for diagnosis. Diagnosis is made subsequent to symptom review, medical history (including medications), neurological exam, laboratory tests, brain imaging, and neuropsychological testing (Family Caregiver Alliance, 2007a). Dementia-like symptoms may be the result of medication side effects, metabolic problems, nutritional deficiencies, emotional difficulties, infections, and normal-pressure hydrocephalus (Mayo Foundation for Medical Education and Research, 2007a).

COMMON PROBLEMS IN DEMENTIA

Sometimes family members of a person with dementia are hesitant to talk about their impaired loved one in front of him or her, fearing embarrassing their loved one (American Academy of Family Physicians, 2007b). For this reason, if you are working with a family dealing with dementia, in addition to conjoint counseling, you also may wish to work with family members separately from the impaired loved one. Certainly, you should encourage family caregivers of persons with dementia to share their concerns, not only about their loved one but also about themselves. Common problems addressed by families include driving cessation, sundowning, agitation, wandering, sleeplessness, intimate relationship changes, and legal and financial matters.

Cessation of driving may be particularly difficult for the impaired adult, as it is a concrete reminder of a loss of independence. To ease the transition to not driving, encourage family members to include the impaired loved one in discussions about driving, help them brainstorm ways to reduce the need for the impaired loved one to drive, and work with them to arrange for alternate means of transit for the loved one (Family Caregiver Alliance, 2007b).

One difficulty sometimes seen in a loved one with dementia is **sundowning, which is confusion by the impaired older adult that occurs at the end of the day and toward evening.** Some recommendations for helping a loved one who demonstrates sundowning is encouraging naps or quiet time in the afternoon, keeping on a night-light, and, if he or she is in a hospital, decorating the room with familiar items from home (Mayo Foundation for Medical Education and Research, 2007b).

Agitation frequently is seen in persons with dementia. This may be particularly stressful for the family. To reduce agitation, you might recommend the family members make it easier for the impaired loved one to engage in the tasks of daily living with a minimum of frustration (American Academy of Family Physicians, 2007a). For example, for impaired older adults who are not able to fully dress themselves, just give them a single item of clothing to put on by themselves and help them with the remaining articles; if bathing is difficult, consider scheduling it every other day instead of daily (American Academy of Family Physicians, 2007a).

If *wandering* is a problem, provide a safe place for it, such as an entirely fenced and secure backyard, put a message stating "stop" on the doors the impaired loved one uses or in some other way secure the doors, or use an alarm system that lets you know when a loved one strays from a particular place (American Academy of Family Physicians, 2007a).

Persons with dementia may have problems *sleeping.* Family members can assist sleep by letting the impaired loved one know when it is night, keeping the blinds open during the day, reducing caffeine intake by the impaired loved one, helping the loved one get some exercise daily, discouraging daytime napping, ensuring that the loved one's bedroom is quiet, leaving on a night-light at night to reduce confusion, and, if the impaired loved one is suffering from pain that interferes with sleep, consulting with a physician about pain medications at bedtime (American Academy of Family Physicians, 2007a).

Caring for a loved one with dementia may cause tremendous psychic (as well as physical) strain (National Institute of Neurological Disorders and Stroke, 2007). In addition, spouses or partners of a person with dementia will experience changes in their *intimate relationship* with their loved one (Family Caregiver Alliance, 2007d).

Family caregivers, too, will need to attend to *legal and financial matters* related to their loved one (Family Caregiver Alliance, 2007a); these may include durable power of attorney for health care, trusteeship, and other issues.

In terms of problematic behaviors in adults with dementia, you might encourage caregivers to follow a six-step problem-solving model:

1. Define the problem (the behavior that is problematic).
2. Discover the triggers (i.e., those factors that precede and contribute to the problem, which might include medication side effects or inability to communicate).
3. Determine if the problem is associated with a time of day (as might be the case of sundowning).
4. Identify warning signs (such as facial expressions or physical movements).
5. Determine what makes it worse (e.g., overstimulation or confrontation).
6. Determine what makes it better (e.g., distracting the impaired loved one, exercising, following a routine) (Association for Frontotemporal Dementias, 2003).

TREATMENT

Treatment for Alzheimer's disease (and other dementias) sometimes takes the form of medications as well as cognitive training (National Institute of Neurological Disorders and Stroke, 2007). *Medications* can slow progression and cause symptom improvement, which subsequently improve the quality of life for the impaired older adult, ease caregiver burden, and delay the necessity of admitting the impaired loved one to nursing care (National Institute of Neurological Disorders and Stroke, 2007). Medications may include drugs that delay the progression of symptoms as well as prescriptions to reduce agitation, anxiety, or depression or to help a person sleep (National Institute on Aging, 2007).

Furthermore, people with dementia may be helped by engaging in *cognitive training*, such as using memory aids, or may benefit from modifications in their environment (National Institute of Neurological Disorders and Stroke, 2007). Although physicians prescribe medications, a counselor may be involved in cognitive training and/or behavior modification, working directly either with the impaired older adult and/or with his or her caregivers, whether they are family or employed caregivers.

People with moderate to severe dementia will need *supervision and monitoring* to prevent self-harm through either commission or omission (National Institute of Neurological Disorders and Stroke, 2007). They may need assistance with basic functions such as eating, bathing, and dressing (National Institute of Neurological Disorders and Stroke, 2007). The provision of this supervision and assistance oftentimes requires considerable sensitivity and patience by the caregiver (National Institute of Neurological Disorders and Stroke, 2007). In inpatient or day care settings, you as a counselor may work directly with a person with dementia or with staff on cognitive training and behavior modification issues. You also are likely to work with family caregivers of persons with dementia, providing supportive counseling, supporting systemic change, and offering psychoeducation and direct training of caregivers in how to assist the impaired loved one through cognitive training and behavior modification.

CHAPTER SUMMARY

The chapter opened with a definition of dementia and demographics, followed by a discussion of Alzheimer's disease and vascular dementia. We looked at dementia classifications, including cortical, subcortical, progressive, primary, and secondary. We differentiated dementia from age-related cognitive decline, mild cognitive impairment, depression, and delirium. We looked at risk factors for dementia, including aging, genetics/family history, smoking and alcohol use, medical conditions, mild cognitive impairment, Down syndrome, and race/ethnicity. Furthermore, we discussed the symptoms of dementia. We also looked at common problems in clients with dementia—driving cessation, sun-downing, agitation, wandering, sleeplessness, intimate relationship changes, and legal and financial matters. We ended the chapter with treatment considerations, including medication, cognitive training, and supervision and monitoring. In Chapter 13, we will address counseling families around the issues of caregiving and bereavement.

CASE STUDY

George is an 85-year-old European American male with a lifelong history of depression. He lives with his 80-year-old wife, Wilma, in an indepen-dent living apartment in a continuing care facility. Once a vibrant, active professor, he increasingly is passive, confused, and forgetful. There is no history of diagnosed dementia in George's family, though Wilma notes that George's father had to have his car keys taken from him when he was in his 80s after an incident where he got lost driving and went miss-ing overnight. Wilma also mentions a serious automobile accident in midlife in which George hit his head on the windshield and suffered a mild concussion. Wilma reports that George seems more "with it" dur-ing the day but more confused as nighttime approaches and that he has trouble sleeping.

George and Wilma have two children, Thom, 60, and Mindy, 58. Thom lives in a town about a 4-hour drive away. After years of estrange-ment from Thom, George and Wilma have reached a cordial though not particularly warm relationship with him. Mindy lives nearby and is the de facto caregiver for George and Wilma. Mindy's daughter and son-in-law just had their first baby, making Mindy a grandmother. Mindy increasingly feels pulled in two directions: caring for her aging mother and father and wanting to spend more time with her children and her grandchild. Thom expresses a lack of understanding and states that it is Mindy's place as daughter to be caregiver.

Questions

1. Is George suffering from dementia, depression, or some other disorder? How do you differentiate?
2. What factors related to George are consistent with dementia? What factors are not consistent with dementia?
3. What do you make of George's increasing confusion at the end of the day?

4. What are the issues this family is facing or will face if George indeed is suffering from dementia?
5. Is there a problem in this family? If so, where does it lie? With George? With Wilma? With Mindy? With Thom?

CHAPTER QUESTIONS

1. Name one factor that may suggest a person is suffering from vascular dementia and not Alzheimer's disease.
2. Describe the three elements common to all dementias.
3. In what parts of the world is the diagnosis of dementia increasing most rapidly? Why do you think this might be the case?
4. Describe how the manifestation of cortical dementia differs from that of subcortical dementia.
5. Define primary dementia and secondary dementia.
6. What is pseudodementia?
7. Describe five risk factors for dementia. What, if anything, can be done to reduce the risk factors?
8. Describe sundowning. How is it treated?
9. Name six steps for dealing with problematic behaviors of persons with dementia.
10. What would you do with a family that, after receiving information that their elder loved one suffers from dementia, remains in denial?

GLOSSARY

Age-related cognitive decline: is the typical slowing of information processing and memory that is common in later life.

Alzheimer's disease: the most common primary dementia, is a progressive disease marked by increasing cognitive, memory, communication, and physical impairment.

Cortical dementia: is marked by damage to the cortex (the outer layer) of the brain and results in memory impairment, communication problems (including aphasia), difficulty understanding language, cognitive difficulties (including an inability to recall words), and interpersonal behavior problems.

Delirium: is marked by confusion, disorientation, incoherence, altered mental states, changes in personality, and/or drowsiness and is usually caused by a treatable underlying illness.

Dementia: is a set of symptoms such as deficits in learning, in remembering, and in communicating, indicating mind-brain impairment.

Mild cognitive impairment: comprises cognitive problems and memory difficulties more intense than age-related cognitive decline but not severe enough to warrant a diagnosis of dementia.

Primary dementia: such as Alzheimer's disease, refers to dementia that does not result from some other illness or disease.

Progressive dementia: is a dementia that results in greater impairment over time.

Pseudodementia: is the presence of symptoms in depression that mimic dementia, such as passivity, confusion, and forgetfulness.

Secondary dementia: results from a physical illness or injury, such as advanced Parkinson's disease, multiple sclerosis, or head injury.

Subcortical dementia: is the result of damage to the brain beneath the cortex and tends to result in memory, movement, emotional, personality, and attention-span changes.

Sundowning: is confusion experienced by an impaired older adult that occurs at the end of the day and toward evening.

Vascular dementia: is the result of brain damage from cerebrovascular or cardiovascular problems, typically stroke.

FURTHER INFORMATION

1. One of the best resources for learning more about Alzheimer's disease is the Alzheimer's Association, 225 N. Michigan Ave., Fl. 17, Chicago, IL 60601-7633, www.alz.org.
2. Accessible information about aging and the brain is found at the American Association of Retired Persons Healthy Brain Web site, www.aarp.org/health/brain.
3. A very good source of information about healthy aging, including information on maintaining a healthy brain, is found at the Centers for Disease Control and Prevention Healthy Aging program Web site, www.cdc.gov/aging.

CHAPTER 13

Family Issues in Counseling Older Adults

In every conceivable manner, the family is link to our past, bridge to our future.

—**Alex Haley (1921–1992)**

The Child is father of the Man.

—**William Wordsworth (1770–1850)**

CHAPTER OVERVIEW

In this chapter we will consider two specific family issues faced by clients who interact with community and mental health counselors. These are caregiving issues and bereavement. We will review what is known about families with older adults. We will discuss psycheducational and family systems approaches to working with families with older adults and discuss these within the context of caregiving and bereavement in families.

FAMILIES WITH OLDER ADULTS

Family members (especially women) are the sources of day-to-day care for the most frail (see Dwyer & Coward, 1992, cited in Bedford & Blieszner, 2000) and dependent older adults (see Brody, 1985, cited in Richardson, Gilleard, Lieberman, & Peeler, 1994). For this reason, we will explore the dynamics of families with older adults and then discuss caregiving and bereavement issues.

Nearly every extended family has older adult members, yet there is limited scholarly information about the families of older adults (Bedford

& Blieszner, 2000). Older adults may be in poor health or in good health; they may live independently or with other family members; they may be cut off or enmeshed or have psychologically healthy relations with younger family members; they may comprise blood relations or fictive kin relations. Older adults generally are not isolated from family, and many elders have weekly face-to-face, telephone, mail, or Internet contact with adult children (Qualls, 1999a). A high rate of interaction between elders and their adult children is due to the many social, emotional, and financial needs that are met within families (Qualls, 1999a). Clearly, older family members interact with younger family members, influencing and being influenced by each other (Bedford & Blieszner, 2000). Also, **collateral kin** (i.e., brothers and sisters as well as nieces and nephews and great-nieces and great-nephews) can and do interact with older relatives (Bedford & Blieszner, 2000).[1]

Just as children are a part of their parents' family, older adults are a part of their children's families (see Bedford & Blieszner, 2000). As such, there is the potential for much give-and-take across generations: Older and younger members of a family both give to the other and receive from the other (Bedford & Blieszner, 2000).

Family Life Cycle. One way of conceptualizing families is from the perspective of the *family life cycle* (Carter & McGoldrick, 1989, cited in Benbow et al., 1990). Carter and McGoldrick (1989, cited in Benbow et al., 1990) conceptualized a six-stage life cycle—the final stage being from retirement to death. This final stage has been increasing in length as people are living longer and spending a greater portion of their lives in retirement.[2] Successful adjustment to life cycle changes in one generation may assist members of another generation in adjusting to their particular life cycle changes and can reduce the likelihood that a family will be unable to successfully negotiate change in the future (Benbow et al., 1990).

Life Event Web. Another way of conceptualizing the life of families is as a *life event web* (Pruchnow et al., 1979, cited in Qualls, 1999a, p. 978). A life event web means that the major events of one's life affect the lives of other family members and vice versa (Qualls, 1999a). If this is so, then a family's interdependence requires individual family members to routinely renegotiate their roles in the family as life events unfold (Qualls, 1999a). Older adult family members may become less autonomous (e.g., because of illness or disability) and may require a shift toward greater reliance on other family members (Qualls, 1999a).[3]

CAREGIVING

Family therapy often is called for when the family's presenting problem relates to caregiving (Kennedy, 2000). The first task is to understand that in families with elders, a central task may revolve around the dialectic between an older adult's desire to maintain independence and his or her dependence on family members for caregiving (Kennedy, 2000). There are five essential points to understand about caregiving: It is stressful, the stress comes from numerous sources, families vary in the ability to adapt to the stressful situation, some parts of the situation may be changeable, and caregiving entails both change and continuity (Zarit & Zarit, 1998, cited in Kennedy, 2000).

In caregiving families, there are three main transitions: movement into the role of caregiving, movement from dependence on family and community care to social service agencies and institutionalization, and eventually grief and bereavement (Kennedy, 2000). Each of these transitions may result in anxiety and stress and also may present opportunities for growth. The counselor's job is to assist a family in successfully navigating these transitions.

Older adult care recipients who are in good health, who believe in living close to family members, and who believe in family support are more likely to be satisfied with being cared for by their adult children, whereas those who do not want to live close to other family members and want to receive help from nonfamily are not happy with being cared for by their adult children (Thomas, 1988, cited in Richardson et al., 1994). Of course the older adult care recipient is only half of the caregiving equation; the adult child care provider composes the other half.

Caregiving for an older impaired loved one can be stressful, and caregivers report financial difficulties, physical and emotional problems, social isolation, clashes between responsibilities, and reduced social and recreational pursuits (see Brody et al., 1989, cited in Richardson et al., 1994). You may wish to provide supportive counseling or even refer caregivers to support groups to help them manage feelings of isolation, guilt, frustration, and anger, as well as to share stories of joy and peace. To reduce the stress of caregiving, you might recommend that caregivers learn to recognize when they are feeling stressed and frustrated, learn to calm themselves, learn to challenge their negative self-talk, learn to be more assertive, and learn to ask for help (Family Caregiver Alliance, 2007c). One promising approach to reducing stress is **mindfulness-based stress reduction,** which focuses on the development of awareness of the present moment (Kabat-Zinn, 2005). Caregivers, too, benefit tremendously from **respite** (i.e., time off) from their caregiving responsibilities (National Institute of Neurological Disorders and Stroke, 2007). We will address in more depth two general therapeutic approaches to working with caregiving families: psychoeducation interventions and family systems interventions.

Psychoeducation Interventions

Most counseling interventions with families with older adults have as their focus the caregiver and primarily utilize psychoeducation to reduce caregiver distress (Richardson et al., 1994). Psychoeducation interventions revolve around increasing information about caregiving, improving caregiver skills, and connecting caregivers to community resources (Shellenberger et al., 1989, cited in Richardson et al., 1994). Psychoeducation groups for families, which provide moderate benefits, typically comprise instruction, education, and the dissemination of information about aging, as well as peer support so that families can share feelings, information about community resources, and a focus on problem solving (Lazarus et al., 1981, cited in Richardson et al., 1994). Psychoeducation family therapy may be useful in counseling individual families, especially in identifying stressors, helping client families become more aware of stress, problem solving to reduce stress, and identifying strategies for coping (Banks et al., 1986, cited in Richardson et al., 1994). Particularly helpful may be those family counseling groups that help caregivers identify stressors and conflicts in their families (Sheehan & Nuttall, 1988, cited in Richardson et al., 1994).

Psychoeducation includes providing to the family not only basic information about dementia or other conditions and age-related phenomena but also practical information that may improve quality of life and decrease risk. In cases of dementia, for example, information about in-home improvements can reduce dependence and improve quality of life. These improvements include such basic things as adding bed rails and bathroom safety rails, removing locks from bedrooms and bathroom doors, reducing the maximum hot water temperature, ensuring that the impaired loved one is always carrying or wearing identification, and making sure there are readable calendars and clocks around the house (National Institute of Neurological Disorders and Stroke, 2007). Psychoeducation may be provided about the importance of reducing unnecessary activities and noise in the environment, reducing clutter, removing the car or car keys so that the impaired adult no longer drives, and following a predictable daily routine (National Institute of Neurological Disorders and Stroke, 2007).

Family Systems Interventions

A complementary approach to psychoeducation counseling with families with older adults is systems-based (or systemic) family counseling. Systems-based family counseling has as its goals improved relationships

TABLE 13.1   Family Subsystems

Subsystem	Composition
Spousal	The spousal subsystem arises by the decision to *join* with another person: husband and wife, partner and partner (or in the case of lesbian and gay married couples, wife and wife or husband and husband).
Parental	The parental subsystem arises with the arrival of a child; it comprises the parents, parent, or guardian in the family.
Sibling	The children in the family.

Note: Adapted from Minuchin, S., & Fishman, H. C., *Family Therapy Techniques*, Harvard University Press, Cambridge, MA, 2004.

between the various generations of family members and greater independence for the elder members of the family; techniques include understanding the family's rules, structure, alignments, and power relationships and exploring communication patterns, altering the rules, and having the family engage in self-observation (Richardson et al., 1994).

Structural Family Systems. Structural theory conceptualizes families as systems composed of hierarchies and subsystems (see Table 13.1): specifically spousal, parental, and sibling subsystems (Minuchin & Fishman, 2004). The spousal subsystem is composed of a husband–wife, domestic partner–domestic partner, or, in the case of married gay or lesbian households, husband–husband or wife–wife. The parental subsystem is that of the mother(s) and/or father(s), and the sibling subsystem is that of the children. Through these roles, individuals—within the context of family—learn to negotiate, to accommodate, and to complement one another. Any given individual may have more than one role in the family. For example, one may be a spouse to one's partner, a parent to one's children, a child to one's parent(s), and a sibling to one's brothers or sisters. In families with older adults, hierarchical relationships between these subsystems may need to be renegotiated for caregiving to succeed. If a spouse dies, an older adult must adapt to the role of bereft spouse, which may include greater dependence on adult children. An impaired older parent may need to be cared for by his or her adult children—a reversal of the roles present in the early life of the family—and this may be a challenge to the family.

Bowenian Family Systems. Another way of thinking about families is from the perspective of how well their members are differentiated (Bowen, 1994). A family member may be well **differentiated**, meaning he or she has a clear sense of self, is sensitive to others, and is able to make independent decisions.[4] A poorly differentiated family member has a weak sense of self and depends on conformity to the ideals of others to prop up the sense of self. Families with well-differentiated members should be able to weather the challenges of caregiving more readily than those with poorly differentiated members.

Family Systems Assumptions. The family systems model has several assumptions:

- The family (and not the individual) is the unit of analysis.
- Family members communicate through their behaviors.
- Families go through identifiable stages of development.
- There may be anxiety during periods of family transition.
- In families with older adults, elders may indeed be less able to function autonomously.
- Some life events occur off-time, resulting in increased anxiety.
- Periods of family transition may offer occasions for change.
- Families with older adults share a long history (Qualls, 1999a).

Considering the *family as the unit of analysis* means looking at the reciprocal and circular interactions between family members (Qualls, 1999a). It means not scapegoating an impaired older adult or an adult child caregiver as the problem. It means recognizing that the family as an entity may be perpetuating behaviors that are maladaptive and that the family as an entity may learn a new way of being that is more adaptive.

Family members do *communicate through their behaviors* (Qualls, 1999a). These behaviors may be verbal or nonverbal and will express thoughts and feelings present in the family. Counselors can help a family identify its communication rules (e.g., what is acceptable to talk about and what is not acceptable) as well as other rules the family uses to organize and define itself. As a counselor, you can help families identify maladaptive rules and replace them with more adaptive rules.

Family development occurs in *stages linked by periods of transition* (Qualls, 1999a). For example, the period from retirement to death represents one stage in the life of a family. The transition period will be the time of exit from the world of work and entrance into the time of retirement, and this may include choosing a date for retirement, organizing one's finances, and considering new activities for retirement. Furthermore, there may be considerable *anxiety during the period of transition* (Qualls, 1999a). For example, the family may impact, as well as be impacted by, the retiree's relative success (or lack thereof) in finding meaning in retirement.

One must be sensitive to the fact that although families share many characteristics throughout the family life cycle, families with older adults face *specific challenges*, especially those of physical or cognitive impairments and reduced independence among older adult family members (Qualls, 1999a). To successfully adapt to these realities, family members may need to redefine and adjust roles and rules.

It is a reality of family life that *some life events occur off-time*; they are unexpected and nonnormative (Qualls, 1999a). An example of this is the experience of a parent who outlives his or her children. These nonnormative events can result in intense anxiety in the family and can force the family members to adjust their roles to the new reality as well as force the family members to develop or adapt their rules.

Times of transition are times that offer an *opening for change* (Qualls, 1999a). Families tend to be homeostatic, that is, they tend to perpetuate the roles and rules that are present in the family. When you think about it, it makes sense for families to be this way. Maintaining the status quo makes it easy to maintain one's place in the family, an otherwise complex entity. But change in one part of the family (and transition *is* change) will result in changes in the family system. These changes can be met either with resistance from the family (i.e., desiring to maintain the status quo) or with openness to growth and development. As a counselor, you can assist families with older adults in resisting the tendency toward homeostasis and accepting (or even embracing) change as an opportunity for the family to grow.

Finally, families with older adults share a *long history* (Qualls, 1999a). This is in contrast to recently formed families, whose histories may be relatively brief. In families with a long history, relationships, rules, and roles may be particularly complex and have a long, complicated history. Relationships will have been created between parents and children, rules may have changed over the decades of the family's existence, and roles will have changed as family members grew (see Qualls, 1999a). It is advantageous for the family counselor to seek understanding of current family challenges in the context of family members' long history together.

Psychoeducation and Family Systems

There are clear differences between psychoeducation and systemic approaches (Richardson et al., 1994). Psychoeducation family therapy oftentimes is used *preventively* to reduce the likelihood of crisis, whereas systemic family therapy is most often used to address and remedy a crisis. Psychoeducation family therapy oftentimes identifies the elder as the client and addresses the family in its role as supporter of the client, whereas systemic family therapy takes the entire family as its client. Psychoeducation approaches believe that families need information to cope, whereas systemic approaches are more likely to hold the belief that families themselves have the knowledge they need to solve problems.

Independent of the approach, it is certain that families with older adults face real challenges. Psychoeducation approaches have dominated work with families with older adults; systems-based approaches have been less widely utilized. One limitation of psychoeducation is that by excluding direct work with the impaired older adult, psychoeducation approaches may ultimately fail these particular individuals (Richardson et al., 1994). Systems-based approaches for working with families with older adults, though less developed than systems-based approaches for working with other types of families, have been demonstrated to be of benefit to those families with older adults, including caregivers and care recipients. In fact, these systems-based approaches to working with families with older adults share much in common with systems-based approaches to working with other types of families, indicating that indeed "older people are family members too" (Richardson et al., 1994, p. 236).

Qualls (1999b) described a family systems approach to intervening with families with older adults. Families regularly adjust relationships when raising children, with parents sometimes providing protection and sometimes providing assistance to their growing child (Qualls, 1999b), and families may need to adjust these relationships when a parent becomes impaired.

According to Olsen et al. (1983, cited in Qualls, 1999b), families can be conceptualized based on their level of cohesion and their ability to adapt. Families that lie along the extremes of cohesion (either disengaged or enmeshed) and families that lie along the extremes of adaptability (either chaotic in the approach or rigidly inadaptable) are marked by higher rates of mental or behavior disorders (Qualls, 1999b). Families that are most successful are those that can and do adjust—for example, by tending to lean more toward greater protection (though not enmeshment) when children are young and less so when children get older. This suggests that families can and do adjust their ways of being in response to the developmental needs of the family. Families that cannot or do not adjust do not successfully navigate the challenges of family development.

Children grow up and become adults. Although adulthood is recognizable by society (e.g., by gaining the right to vote, to drink, and to drive), it is more ambiguous within the family (Qualls, 1999b). For example, adulthood may be hazy in families where adult children receive financial assistance from their parents or where a grown child's move to another location for work is met with disappointment in the family. Enmeshed families find it hard to let adult children differentiate (e.g., by not supporting an adult child in moving out of the home to go to school or for employment or by offering money to the adult child well into that person's life). At the opposite extreme, disengaged families offer little or no support to the adult child (e.g., by communicating that adult children are on their own the day they finish high school).

What does this have to do with aging family members? In some families, adult children may not be recognized as psychological or social equals (Williamson, 1982, 1991, cited in Qualls, 1999b). In these situations, the family has not renegotiated the roles of parent and child, making it challenging for both aged parents and adult children to adapt to a shift in responsibilities within the family.

At some point, an adult child will begin to notice that his or her aged parent is depending on others more and more (Qualls, 1999b). This awareness usually comes about because an adult child is observing and monitoring an elder loved one's behavior—and witnessing physical and/or cognitive decline (Qualls, 1999b).

Early on in this process, the adult child may deny the reality of the decline, suggesting that what he or she is witnessing is "just normal aging" (Qualls, 1999b, p. 233). Or the adult child may recognize decline but remain unaware of the degree, nature, or cause of the decline (Qualls, 1999b). Especially when the family is witnessing cognitive decline, questions arise in the family about the elder loved one's ability to be involved in decision making, as well as about how to respond to inappropriate behaviors (Boss, Caron, & Horbal, 1989, cited in Qualls, 1999b). As the older adult's health declines, the adult child becomes increasingly aware that his or her relationship with the impaired loved one will change, likely in the direction of becoming more authoritative in relation to the impaired loved one. At this point, it becomes clear, to paraphrase William Wordsworth, that adult children become parents to their older fathers and mothers.

What is the role of the counselor in all of this? Qualls (1999b) indicated that clinicians should facilitate the "realization of power, authority, and responsibility" for the impaired loved one and to do so with "minimal intervention" (p. 234). She identified several particularly useful interventions: labeling and educating, facilitating the family's taking of responsibility, and accepting power over parents (Qualls, 1999b) (see Table 13.2).

The first intervention, labeling and educating, simply entails putting a label on the challenge the family presents with and then educating the family about the challenge. A family may present with an elder who is forgetful, passive, and confused. The counselor may refer the elder for assessment, which may result, for example, in a diagnosis of Alzheimer's disease or of depression. The clinician can discuss this diagnosis with the family, describe how it manifests and its likely course, and offer suggestions for

TABLE 13.2   Qualls's Interventions for Families With Older Adults

Intervention	Description
Labeling and educating	Identifying what the problems are and educating the family about the problems and their prognosis
Taking responsibility	Family members owning the fact that they are now responsible for their impaired elder loved one
Accepting power over parents	Realizing and accepting the reality that the old family role where children were subordinate to parents has changed

Note: Adapted from Qualls, S. H., "Realizing Power in Intergenerational Family Hierarchies: Family Reorganization When Older Adults Decline," in M. Duffy (Ed.), *Handbook of Counseling and Psychotherapy With Older Adults* (pp. 228–241), Wiley, New York, 1999b.

how the family can deal with it. Oftentimes, this type of intervention is all that the family initially needs; at other times, the family members may close their eyes to the information provided (Qualls, 1999b).

The second intervention requires the clinician to facilitate a family's taking responsibility for providing assistance to the impaired loved one (Qualls, 1999b). Taking responsibility may sound straightforward, but, in practice, it may be difficult to facilitate given any of a number of factors—the general busyness of family members, conflicted relations with the impaired elder, lack of psychological equality between the adult child and the elder parent, or adult children's inability or unwillingness to address issues of their own or their parent's mortality (Qualls, 1999b).

The third intervention requires that adult children accept the fact that they do have power over their impaired parent, something they may be hesitant to do. Having power over the well-being and care of an elder may result in feelings of anxiety—especially related to concerns about the impaired elder's potential for legally or personally turning against the adult child caregiver, fears that they will be perceived as betraying the elder and having to deal then with the elder's subsequent resentment and distrust, or concerns that they will not be able to keep promises they made to their impaired loved one (e.g., a promise never to institutionalize the loved one) (Qualls, 1999b).

Jarkvik and Small (1988, cited in Kennedy, 2000) enumerated steps that can improve relations between older adult children and their aged parents: monitoring moods, identifying emotional intensity, planning and assessing the family situation, listening, and compromising. These steps can be carried out in family meetings. Zarit and Zarit (1998, cited in Kennedy, 2000) suggested that the counselor, when meeting with families, collaborate with the aged adult and caregiver on choosing whom to call to the family meeting, ideally held in the aged adult's home. At the time of the meeting, its purpose should be explicitly stated, with the goals being information and development of a stronger working relationship. The counselor should be attentive to the needs of the older adult and then to the caregiver and his or her family. Older adult needs may include issues of assessment, diagnosis, and treatment, as well as discussion of transitions related to future care (e.g., nursing care). Caregiver and family needs may include addressing stressors and supporting the family more broadly in taking responsibility for the care of the older loved one so that responsibility does not fall entirely on one individual. Through a family meeting, a family may develop an implementable and realistic care plan (see Kennedy, 2000).

BEREAVEMENT

We must recognize that the issue of death and dying exists in the larger social context of North America. Johnson (2004) suggested that there are three lessons that North Americans are taught about death and that we subsequently internalize. First, we learn that we are not to talk about death. Second, we are taught to deny to others the intensity of emotions one feels after the death of a loved one. And third, we learn that we are supposed to get over the death of the loved one and get on with life as soon as possible. We are taught to deny aging and subsequently death; society has promoted the belief that grief is a pathological state to be addressed by health care professionals (Johnson, 2004). Johnson (2004) suggested that we approach grief as a "natural reaction to loss" (p. 435) rather than a pathological state—not as something to deny or recover from or cure but instead as something to work through and find meaning in.

J. William Worden (2001) identified four tasks of grief (see Table 13.3). The first is to accept the reality of the loss. Accepting this

TABLE 13.3   Worden's Four Tasks of Grief

Task	Description
Accept	Accept the reality of the death of the loved one.
Pain	Experience the pain of grief.
Adjust	Adjust to an environment that is now without the loved one.
Reinvest	Reinvest one's energies into life.

Note: Adapted from Worden, J. W., *Grief Counseling and Grief Therapy: A Handbook for the Mental Health Professional* (3rd ed.), Springer, New York, 2001.

reality comes about through the realization that the deceased is no longer physically with the bereft. The second is to experience the pain of
grief. This is an inescapable task, a task that, no matter how hard one
tries, must ultimately be experienced. This pain may manifest itself in
feelings, thoughts, and behaviors, as well as somatically. The third task
is to adjust to an environment in which the deceased loved one is absent.
This environmental adjustment may mean that the bereft now needs
to depend on him- or herself for things for which he or she formerly
depended on the deceased spouse or loved one (e.g., cooking, finances,
or emotional support). It may mean taking on more or new responsibilities. And the fourth task is to reinvest one's energies into life. This
requires acceptance of the reality of the loved one's death while holding
the memory of the loved one close, recognizing that one need not forget
the deceased, and then utilizing one's energies in continuing to live, in
engaging with others, and in memorializing the deceased.

There is one certainty in families with older adults: At some point a
loved one will die. And when that occurs, the death will leave the family
in grief. How one grieves the death of a loved one depends on a number
of factors, including the personality characteristics of the one bereft,
the relationship between the bereft and the deceased, and the social and
community support (or lack thereof) for grieving and bereavement.

As a counselor, you may offer supportive, psychoeducation, or family systems interventions to your clients. You also should attend to the
transference issues that may arise in your client around loss more generally, especially as it may manifest when the counseling relationship
ends. Oftentimes, these endings heighten the intensity of the emotions
being felt by the client and can bring forward important material for
your client to work through. Finally, you should attend to the particular countertransference issues that arise in yourself around the specific
issues of death and dying or issues of loss more generally, especially as
they manifest in the particulars of your life. If you can be honest with
yourself and if you can directly address your personal issues around
death and dying, you will be more present to help your clients in this
period of transition.

CHAPTER SUMMARY

In this chapter we considered two family issues faced by clients who
interact with community and mental health counselors—caregiving and
bereavement. We reviewed some of what is known about families with
older adults. We then compared psychoeducation and family systems
approaches to counseling families with older adults, especially in the

context of caregiving and bereavement. In Chapter 14, we will explore some of the psychological problems that at times are part of an older adult's presentation. These include anxiety, depression, suicide, and alcohol or other drug use.

CASE STUDY

Lawrence, age 81, was married to Loraine for nearly 60 years. Loraine died 6 months ago at age 78. Rose, their daughter, a self-described "Daddy's girl," lives one mile from Lawrence. Rose has a daughter; furthermore, Rose is caregiver for her grandchild. Rich, Lawrence's son, lives in another state, though he makes frequent trips home to see his father. Rich describes his relationship with his parents as "complicated." Rich's frequent trips cause him to be out of the office, resulting in additional work stresses. Lawrence was a lawyer, and he has arranged to transfer his trust to his children upon his death. When the family is together, Rose tries to talk about Loraine, but Lawrence and Rich shy away from those conversations. When alone, Lawrence cries about the loss of his wife and privately fears living alone. Rich, meanwhile, believes that he needs to get over his mother's death and become the new patriarch of the family. As a counselor-in-training, this is the first time you have worked with a family around these issues.

Questions

1. What are some of the caregiving issues present in this case?
2. What are some of the bereavement issues present in this case?
3. Does this family need conjoint family counseling? Individual counseling?
4. What psychoeducation interventions might benefit this family?
5. What family systems interventions might benefit this family?
6. At which of Worden's four tasks of grief is each member of the family?

CHAPTER QUESTIONS

1. What is meant by collateral kin? Are they present and active in your family?
2. What is the life event web?
3. What are the three main transitions in caregiving families?

4. What is mindfulness-based stress reduction?
5. What aspects of the family are looked at in family systems interventions?
6. How does one become part of a spousal subsystem? A parental subsystem? A sibling subsystem?
7. What is meant by the statement that some family life events occur off-time? Give an example.
8. What is meant by psychoeducation interventions? Give an example.
9. Compare and contrast psychoeducation interventions with family systems interventions.
10. Discuss Qualls's three interventions for families with older adults.
11. Describe Worden's four tasks of grief.

GLOSSARY

Collateral kin: refer to an individual's brothers and sisters and their offspring (nieces and nephews, great-nieces and great-nephews, and so forth).

Differentiation: refers to the level to which a person has a clear sense of self, is sensitive to others, and is able to make independent decisions.

Mindfulness-based stress reduction: is a stress-reduction technique that focuses on the development of awareness of the present moment.

Respite: is time off from one's caregiving responsibilities.

Subsystem: refers to a smaller group within a family, either the spouses, the parents, or the siblings (children).

FURTHER INFORMATION

1. An excellent resource for caregiving is the Family Caregiver Alliance, www.caregiver.org.
2. See Ernest Becker's classic *The Denial of Death* (New York: Free Press, 1973) for an elaboration on this topic and its implications for individuals and ultimately the community.

3. For more information about bereavement and grief, see Theresa Rando's *How to Go on Living When Someone You Love Dies* (New York: Bantam, 1991) or J. William Worden's *Grief Counseling and Grief Therapy: A Handbook for the Mental Health Professional* (3rd ed.) (New York: Springer, 2001).

4. See the following resources for end-of-life issues: AARP End-of-Life Resources, www.aarp.org/relationships/grief-loss/info-08-2009/end_of_life_counseling_why_it_really_matters.html; National Hospice and Palliative Care Organization, www.nhpco.org; Robert Wood Johnson Foundation's *Means to a Better End: A Report on Dying in America Today,* www.rwjf.org/files/publications/other/meansbetterend.pdf; and the Center for Practical Bioethics's *Aging and End-of-Life Care,* www.practicalbioethics.org/cpb.aspx?pgID=885.

NOTES

1. Collateral kin are an important part of the African American family experience (Bedford & Blieszner, 2000). African Americans are more likely than European Americans to have contact with relatives, to receive support from relatives, and to have a family member available for caregiving (Johnson, 1995a, cited in Bedford & Blieszner, 2000).

2. Challenges seen at this final life stage include accommodation to retirement, adjustment to disability and illness, grandparenting and great-grandparenting issues, loss of social status, loss of friends and peers, and death of a partner (Benbow et al., 1990).

3. Of course, a focus on autonomy is at least in part culturally determined, with some cultures placing greater and others lesser emphasis on it (Qualls, 1999a).

4. In structural counseling language, a family that is marked by a healthy level of differentiation is said to have *clear* boundaries. Those who are overinvolved have *diffuse* boundaries, and those who are distant have *rigid* boundaries.

CHAPTER 14

Psychological Issues in Community and Mental Health Counseling

Though life is marked with pain,
healing with hope remains—
the dawn of a new day.

—J.B.

Expectations and beliefs of the sufferer shape their suffering.

—Ethan Watters (2010)

CHAPTER OVERVIEW

Older adults may suffer from a range of mental disorders, including but not limited to depression, anxiety disorders, and alcohol and drug (especially prescription drug) abuse. In this chapter we will consider specific mental health issues, including anxiety, depression, suicide, and drug and alcohol abuse, that may be present in older clients who interact with community and mental health counselors. After discussion of each of the mental health issues' risk factors and client symptoms and signs, we will address counselor responses to those older clients who present with these issues, as well as counselor responses to families of older adults who suffer from these issues.

ANXIETY

Introduction

Though not as prevalent as depression, anxiety and anxiety disorders are not uncommon in later life. Older adults may suffer from energy-zapping symptoms of worry or nervous tension even more than diagnosable anxiety disorders (Gallo & Lebowitz, 1999). Anxiety disorders include acute stress disorder, agoraphobia without history of panic disorder, anxiety disorder due to general medical condition, generalized anxiety disorder, obsessive-compulsive disorder, panic disorder with or without agoraphobia, post-traumatic stress disorder (PTSD), social phobia, specific phobia, and substance-induced anxiety disorder (American Psychiatric Association, 2000). Also to consider is the non–*DSM-IV-TR* classification **anxious depression** or mixed anxiety-depression disorder.[1] We will limit our comments to generalized anxiety disorder, anxiety disorder due to a general medical condition, and anxious depression.

Upward of 15% of older adults may suffer from anxiety symptoms (Manela, Katona, & Livingson, 1996, cited in Scogin, Floyd, & Forde, 2000). In addition to phobic disorders, one of the most common anxiety disorders in later life is generalized anxiety disorder (Flint, 1994, cited in Flint, 2005; Gallo & Lebowitz, 1999). Anxiety also may be present in adults suffering from specific medical disorders (anxiety disorder due to a general medical condition), may not be recognized by the older adults themselves as anxiety, and may be overlooked by health and even mental health professionals (Scogin et al., 2000).

Risk Factors

An older adult whose anxiety began earlier in life is more likely to have more severe symptoms of anxiety in later life and is more likely to have symptoms of depression (Scogin et al., 2000). Anxiety disorders are more common in women (Beekman et al., 1988, Musil, 1998, both cited in Scogin et al., 2000); in fact about 6% of women and 4% of men who are healthy, community-residing elders suffer from an anxiety disorder. Older adults who have an **external locus of control** are more likely to suffer from worry (Wisocki, 1988, cited in Scogin et al., 2000).[2] About 38% of depressed older adults also suffer from an anxiety disorder (Alexopoulos, 1990, cited in Scogin et al., 2000); many of these cases might ultimately be classified as anxious depression.

About 33% of older adults with **dementia** also suffer from anxiety; those in the earlier stages of dementia are more likely to evidence

TABLE 14.1   Symptoms of Anxiety

Symptoms	Anorexia, aches and pains, stomach upset, diarrhea, dizziness, dry mouth, faintness, fatigue, restlessness, hyperventilation, sweating, muscle tension, pallor, nausea, heart palpitations, paresthesis, sexual problems, shortness of breath, urinary problems, vomiting, insomnia, and facial flushing

Note: Adapted from Small, 1997, and Folks and Fuller, 1997, both cited in Scogin, F., Floyd, M., and Forde, J., "*Anxiety in Older Adults,*" in S. Krauss Whitbourne (Ed.), *Psychopathology in Later Adulthood* (pp. 117–140), Wiley, New York, 2000.

symptoms of anxious mood (Wands et al., 1990, cited in Scogin et al., 2000); those in later stages are more likely to present as agitated (Eisdorfer et al., 1992, cited in Scogin et al., 2000). Persons with dementia who tended to be more dominant in their dealings with others are more likely to demonstrate anxiety (Orrell & Bebbington, 1996, cited in Scogin et al., 2000), as are those whose relationships are marked by ambivalent rather than secure attachments (Magai & Cohen, 1998, cited in Scogin et al., 2000).

Older adults with more physical illnesses are more likely to suffer from anxiety (or other psychological problems) (Penninx et al., 1996, cited in Scogin et al., 2000). Particularly noteworthy is the fact that over one third of people suffering from Parkinson's disease also suffer from an anxiety disorder (Stein, Heuser, Juncos, & Uhde, 1990, cited in Scogin et al., 2000).

Client Symptoms and Signs

In later life, anxiety may manifest as a physical symptom or a cluster of physical symptoms. Common symptoms include anorexia, aches and pains, stomach upset, diarrhea, dizziness, and dry mouth (Small, 1997, Folks & Fuller, 1997, both cited in Scogin et al., 2000) (see Table 14.1).

Types of Anxiety

Generalized Anxiety Disorder. Generalized anxiety disorder is marked by daily or near-daily worry about many different things, lasting at least 6 months, as well as by at least three of the following additional symptoms: restlessness, fatigue, concentration difficulties, irritability, muscle tension, or problems sleeping (Scogin et al., 2000). For elders, the worries tend to be more about health issues (Person & Borkovec, 1995, cited in Scogin et al., 2000) and tend to begin earlier in life (Blazer, George, & Hughes, 1991, cited in Scogin et al., 2000). Older adults suffering from generalized anxiety disorder also display more "anxiety, worry, depression, and social fears" than others (Beck, Stanley, & Zebb, 1996, cited in Scogin et al., 2000, p. 121).

Anxiety Due to a General Medical Condition. Anxiety due to a general medical condition typically presents as "anxiety, panic attacks, and obsessions or compulsions" about somatic or medical problems (Scogin et al., 2000, p. 124). Common medical problems that may result in anxious symptomatology include disturbances in the endocrine, cardiovascular, and respiratory systems; problems with metabolism; neurological disorders such as hyperthyroidism; and congestive heart failure (Kennedy, 2000). Steroids, thyroid hormone, caffeine, and ephedra may also cause symptoms of anxiety (Kennedy, 2000). The following indications might suggest an underlying medical problem in a client's anxiety presentation:

- atypical age of onset,
- no history of mental disorders.
- no family history of mental disorders,
- poor response to standard treatments,
- greater severity than normally seen, and
- anomalous cognitive processing (Vickers, 1998, cited in Scogin et al., 2000).

Anxious Depression. Anxious depression (or mixed anxiety-depression disorder) is being considered for inclusion in the next version of the *DSM*. It is a combination disorder that includes components of anxiety and of depression. Comorbid anxiety and depression is a common clinical presentation (Gallo, Rabins, & Iliffe, 1997, cited in Scogin et al., 2000). It is marked by dysphoric feelings as well as at least four of the following symptoms: concentration problems, sleep problems, fatigue, irritability, worry, crying, expecting the worst, hopelessness, low self-esteem, and hypervigilance (Scogin et al., 2000).

Counselor Responses to Anxiety

Common treatments for anxiety disorders in late life include **cognitive behavioral therapy** (CBT), relaxation training, and pharmacotherapy (Scogin et al., 2000); other evidence-based approaches include supportive therapy and cognitive therapy (Ayers, Sorrell, Thorp, & Loebach Wetherell, 2007).

CBT may be a most effective treatment for anxiety in late life. With CBT, you as a counselor work with your older client to identify and change irrational thoughts, as well as to change behavioral responses to anxiety-inducing situations. Stanley and Beck (2003) found that older adults who suffer from generalized anxiety disorder benefit from CBT and report that their anxiety and worry improve, as does their quality of life (Stanley & Beck, 2003; Wetherell, Gatz, & Craske, 2003).

Relaxation training has its roots in meditation and mindfulness training. It may be a particularly efficacious and economical treatment for reducing anxiety (Ayers et al., 2007). In *progressive relaxation, a client learns to tense and relax muscles, thereby reducing feelings of tension and subsequent anxiety.* An alternative to progressive relaxation is *imaginal relaxation in which a client imagines tensing and relaxing muscles.* It is especially useful for those older clients who suffer from medical problems that prevent them from actually tensing and relaxing muscles (Scogin et al., 2000).

Pharmacotherapy may be useful for some older adults who suffer from anxiety disorders. The most common medications for treatment of anxiety include benzodiazepines, buspirone, beta-blockers, and selective serotonin reuptake inhibitors, though each of these medications or classes of medications may result in side effects or interactions with other medications in use by an older adult (Scogin et al., 2000). Antidepressants are probably most preferable in the pharmacological treatment of older adults, especially given the common comorbid finding of anxiety and depression in later life (Flint, 2005). Benzodiazepines may be particularly risky when used in older adults, and their use may increase the likelihood of side effects such as "cognitive impairments, falls, and respiratory depression" and when discontinued may lead to "rebound anxiety, recurrence of original symptoms, and withdrawal" (Gorenstein & Papp, 1995, p. 1).[3]

Families Dealing With Anxiety

Symptoms of anxiety in older adults, as is true of other psychological issues, should not be dismissed as normal or a normal part of aging. Anxiety is not normal, and it is treatable. Family members who suspect an older loved one is suffering from anxiety should encourage that person to receive a medical review to rule out medical problems, a review of medications for possible side effects or interactions, and a referral to a mental health professional for treatment.

MAJOR DEPRESSION

Introduction

Major depression is a mood disorder marked by feelings of sadness, hopelessness, and loss; changes in appetite, sleep, and interest in sex; and self-critical thoughts and beliefs. It is a common disorder in later life not only in the United States but also worldwide. In fact, major depression and dysthymia (a pervasive set of lower grade depressive symptoms) are the most common mood disorders in late life (King & Markus, 2000). Other mood disorders include Bipolar I and Bipolar II disorders and cyclothymia. In this section, our focus will be on major depression. Major depression is treatable through counseling and pharmacotherapy. In older adults, depressive symptoms oftentimes coexist with anxiety (Kennedy, 2000).

International Perspective

According to the World Health Organization (2007), about 121 million people suffer from depression. It is the leading cause of years lived with disability and is a major contributing factor in the global burden of disease (World Health Organization, 2007). Fewer than 1 in 4 (in some countries fewer than 1 in 10) people who suffer from depression have access to effective treatment, primarily because of an absence of resources and providers and the presence of social stigma (World Health Organization, 2007). Depression tends to be underdiagnosed in developing nations (BBC News, 2007); even when it is diagnosed, resources available for treatment are limited, given that only very small percentages of developing nations' health budgets are devoted to mental health treatment. In developing nations, depressed people often self-medicate by purchasing depression medications on the black market, frequently resulting in undermedication, overmedication, or the unsafe mixing of drugs (BBC News, 2007).

There is some evidence that Asian immigrant elders in North America may be at particular risk for depression (Mui & Kang, 2006). Mui and Kang (2006) found rates of depression in a sample of Asian elder immigrants (Chinese, Korean, Indian, Filipino, Vietnamese, and Japanese) to be about 40%, far higher than rates found in older people more generally or in older adult Asians in the general population in the United States or in Asia. They suggested that this high rate of depression is associated with "acculturation stress caused by elders' perception of a cultural gap between themselves and their adult children" (Mui & Kang, 2006, p. 243).

U.S. Demographics

About 20% of community-residing older adults and 50% of nursing-home-residing older adults suffer from depression (American Psychological Association, 2003). Up to 15% of community-residing older adults may suffer significant symptoms of depression (Gallo & Lebowitz, 1999). Depression is most common in the older-old (75 years and older) (Gatz et al., 1997, cited in King & Markus, 2000) and more common in older women than in older men (Gallo & Lebowitz, 1999). There is some suggestion that depression, too, is becoming more common in subsequent cohorts of older adults (Blazer, 1994, Gatz et al., 1997, both cited in King & Markus, 2000).

In spite of its high prevalence, depression is not a normal part of aging, and most older adults do not suffer from depression. Most of those who do suffer from depression want treatment. Depression is emotionally distressing, and it also results in additional physical, mental, and social impairments (American Psychological Association, 2003). Depression can result in an increase in somatic complaints, memory and concentration problems, and social isolation. Depression tends to be recurrent; for older adults, this means that they likely have suffered depression in the past, and unfortunately a history of depression places individuals at increased risk for future episodes of depression (American Psychological Association, 2003).

There is a strong relationship between depression and morbidity as well as depression and mortality (Whyte & Rovner, 2006). Older adults who are depressed use the health care system at higher rates than those who are not depressed, and they have poorer health behaviors and "excess disability" (American Psychological Association, 2003; Kennedy, 2000). Older adults oftentimes do not have access to treatment because of a limiting access to mental health services by insurers, underdiagnosis and lack of referral by primary care physicians, and a limited number of mental health professionals with expertise in late-life depression (American Psychological Association, 2003).

Risk Factors

The most common risk factors for depression in later life include becoming widowed, having somatic problems, having only grade school or lesser education, having impaired functioning, and abusing or having dependence on alcohol (American Psychological Association, 2003). Other risk factors are physical illness and disability (Kennedy, 2000). Marital discord, too, has been associated with higher levels of depression in older people (Whisman, Uebelacker, Tolejko, Chatav, & McKelvie, 2006). Depression appears to be more common among European American than minority elders (Gallo & Lebowitz, 1999).

Psychological risk factors may include disruptions of self and self-object relations that occur in early life; interpersonal difficulties including grief, role problems and transitions, and social deficit problems; cognitive distortions; few pleasant events; and family challenges and stresses (King & Markus, 2000). Biological risk factors include changes in the structures and chemistry of the aging brain, changes in sleep patterns, and changes in neuroendocrine systems (King & Markus, 2000).

Older adults who have been hospitalized for depression are at risk for rehospitalization or nursing home placement. Morrow-Howell et al. (2006) found that although over one half of older adults who have been hospitalized for depression remain in the community, 23% are readmitted to psychiatric inpatient treatment, and 10% are admitted to nursing home care.

Client Symptoms and Signs

The *DSM-IV* requires that a person evidence the symptoms of depressed affect and/or **anhedonia** (an inability to take any pleasure or delight in one's day-to-day life) daily or nearly every day for at least 2 weeks. The depressed affect and/or anhedonia need to be coupled with at least three more symptoms, totaling at least five symptoms. Depression in older adults often manifests in cognitive problems, including problems with decision making and concentration, or a decreased processing speed; as well, older adults are likely to manifest learning and memory problems (King & Markus, 2000).

Common symptoms of depression in late life include the following:

- lack of concern about self-care or following medical advice,
- disinterest in socializing,
- feelings of emptiness or anxiety or difficulty sleeping,
- concentration or memory impairment,
- inexplicable somatic complaints,
- decrease or increase in appetite and weight,
- hopelessness,
- helplessness,
- irritation, and
- feeling that one is a burden (Gallo & Katz, 2006).

Depression in late life may have one or more causes, including a person's biology, the side effects of medication, and physical illness (Gallo & Katz, 2006) or a psychological response to intrapersonal or interpersonal issues. Independent of the cause of depression, it is important not to overlook symptoms because of a bias that depression is a normal part of aging (King & Markus, 2000).

Medical Conditions and Medications. For these reasons, if your client presents with symptoms that suggest depression, it is essential that medical conditions and substance abuse be ruled out. Medical conditions can be ruled out through referral to a physician for physical exam and laboratory tests (Kennedy, 2000). Common medical conditions that may present as depression include "multiple sclerosis, Cushing's disease, Parkinson's disease, Huntington's disease, Addison's disease, cerebrovascular disease, hypothyroidism, and chronic obstructive pulmonary disease" (King & Markus, 2000, p. 144).

Oftentimes, merely reviewing the symptoms of depression does not give you enough information to suggest whether the depression is primary or the result of physical illness. Physical illnesses may result in sleep problems, somatic complaints, concentration difficulties, lack of energy, poor appetite, and thoughts of death (Kennedy, 2000). More suggestive of depression are nondementia declines in motor functioning, dressing, grooming, hygiene, and interest in leisure activities and one's family, as well as denial in the face of depressed affect and irritability (Kennedy, 2000).

Your client's medications, too, should be reviewed by a professional to determine if side effects or interactions are causing or contributing to depressive symptomatology (Kennedy, 2000). "Sedatives, hypnotics and anxiolytic[s]" are commonly used in late life and may result in depression (King & Markus, 2000, p. 146). So too can common pharmacological treatments for cardiovascular problems and hypertension and central nervous system drugs (Koenig, 1997, cited in King & Markus, 2000). For frail clients, a referral for dietary assessment may be called for (Kennedy, 2000).

In older adults, depressive symptomatology may be the result of bereavement, despair over physical decline and disability, perceived poorer health, loss of hope secondary to isolation from agoraphobia, or major depression (Kennedy, 2000). Symptoms of bereavement may mimic those of depression. Clinically, bereavement is characterized by a time-limited distress in response to loss, most often the loss of a significant other—such as a spouse, family member, or friend (King & Markus, 2000). Depression is a more likely diagnosis if the feelings have lasted longer than 2 to 3 months after the loss and if the client also feels guilty, feels that he or she is worthless and better off dead, shows signs of psychomotor retardation and/or functional impairment, and experiences extraordinary auditory or visual hallucinations of the deceased (American Psychiatric Association, 1994, cited in King & Markus, 2000).

The cognitive impairments often seen in depressed older adults may mimic those seen in persons with dementia. When this occurs, it is known as **pseudodementia**. Ironically, persons with a depressive pseudodementia actually may be at greater risk of subsequently developing dementia (King & Caine, 1996, cited in King & Markus, 2000). Depression can be differentiated from dementia by sensitivity onset and symptomatology. Depression tends to have an abrupt onset, whereas dementia's onset tends to be insidious. Older adults suffering from depression tend to have more intense feelings of depression and less intense cognitive impairments than those with dementia; those suffering from depression are more likely to notice and complain of memory problems than are those suffering from dementia (King & Markus, 2000). Depressed clients are more likely to demonstrate impaired recall but not recognition, whereas those with dementia are more likely to demonstrate both impaired recall and recognition (King & Markus, 2000). For these reasons, you should ask about onset and inquire about intensity of depressed feelings, the manifestation of memory problems, and impairment of recall and recognition.

Depression coexists with physical disorders and increases physical disability (Kennedy, 2000). Over 50% of stroke patients show symptoms of depression, and depression makes rehabilitation more difficult (Kennedy, 2000). Symptoms of depression are common, too, in people suffering from dementia (as well as in their caregivers) (Kennedy, 2000). In fact, there is some suggestion that physical illness and disability are more highly associated with depression in later life than are demographic, social, interpersonal, and life event factors (Kennedy et al., 1989, cited in Kennedy, 2000).

Counselor Responses to Depression

Depression manifests itself differently in later life. Older adults are less likely to state that they feel depressed or guilty; they are less likely to present with low self-esteem or suicidal ideation (King & Markus, 2000). They are more likely to complain of bodily problems such as constipation, cramps, weight loss, and aches and pains; to complain of feeling anxious about psychomotor retardation, cognitive problems, and somatic or persecutory delusions; or to present with suicidal behavior (King & Markus, 2000). For this reason, it is important for the counselor to be sensitive to the unique signs and symptoms that may suggest depression in late life.

Treatments for depression in later life include psychotherapy, psychosocial interventions, and pharmacological interventions (American Psychological Association, 2003). Psychotherapy has been shown to be effective in treating late-life depression (Cuijpers, van Straten, & Smit, 2006). Effective psychotherapies for depression in late life include cognitive behavioral, interpersonal, problem-solving, brief psychodynamic, and reminiscence approaches (American Psychological Association, 2003). Most effective may be the combination of psychotherapy with pharmacotherapy (Kennedy, 2000).

CBT approaches treat depression by altering thoughts and behaviors that subsequently improve the depressed person's emotions (American Psychological Association, 2003). Interpersonal psychotherapy approaches address "role disputes and transitions" and interpersonal deficits, thereby addressing loss, social isolation, and feelings of helplessness (American Psychological Association, 2003). Problem-solving approaches help clients learn social problem-solving skills (American Psychological Association, 2003). Brief psychodynamic approaches address interpersonal conflicts, loss, stress, and reconciliation between the client's real and ideal accomplishments (American Psychological Association, 2003). Reminiscence therapy was developed specifically for older adults and focuses on reflecting on the major experiences of one's life (American Psychological Association, 2003).

Pharmacological treatments, too, may help those suffering from depression, though it may take at least 2 to 4 weeks (or longer) for a medication to become effective (Gallo & Katz, 2006). Physicians may prescribe selective serotonin reuptake inhibitors, serotonin–norepinephrine reuptake inhibitors, or other antidepressant medications alone or in combinations with one another or other pharmaceuticals.

Treatment of depression in later life varies according to whether the depression is related to physical illness, disability, dementia, or some other factor (Kennedy, 2000). Depression related to physical illness, disability, or dementia can be treated through restorative (e.g., medical intervention to replace a failed organ), rehabilitative (e.g., physical therapy), or supportive (e.g., counseling for caregivers and psychoeducation) interventions (Kennedy, 2000). For depression that is not clearly related to physical illness, disability, or dementia—or when the above is not as effective as desired—depression may be treated by psychotherapy, pharmacotherapy, and, in the most resistant cases, electroconvulsive therapy; furthermore, there are cases when social and caregiver interventions are required in addition to psychotherapy and/or pharmacotherapy (Kennedy, 2000).

Address social isolation by referring the older depressed client to senior centers or a church, congregation, or religious institution; bringing in a home health aide or companion; or supporting family members in visiting the impaired older adult more frequently (Kennedy, 2000). In those cases where hygiene or nutrition are lacking, referral can be made for occupational therapy, which could help the depressed older adult develop a stronger sense of self-esteem and pride in his or her appearance (Kennedy, 2000).

Families Dealing With Depression

Families who have an older adult who they believe is suffering from depression should attend to the warning signs and symptoms (Gallo & Katz, 2006). Family member participation in the care of a depressed older adult increases the likelihood of successful treatment; those who are caregivers, though, should monitor themselves also to prevent caregiver burnout (Gallo & Katz, 2006).

SUICIDE

Introduction

Worldwide, nearly one million people annually die from suicide (DeLeo, Bertolote, & Lester, 2002), many of these older adults. Just as distressing is the fact that many, many more people attempt suicides that end up being nonfatal than attempt suicides that end up being fatal. About two to three times as many older adults attempt suicides that ultimately do not result in death than those whose attempts result in death (McInosh et al., 1994, cited in DeLeo et al., 2002).

Coupled with the difficulty of death from suicide is the aftermath in terms of distress among family, friends, and colleagues left behind. The lives of those left behind are forever changed emotionally, psychologically, and subsequently socially (DeLeo et al., 2002).

Definitions

Suicide is the intentional self-infliction of physical harm that results in death. For a death to be suicide, there must be three qualities: intent to die, the self-infliction of physical harm, and this self-infliction of physical harm must result in death (DeLeo et al., 2002). Suicidal behaviors that result in death may be called fatal suicidal behaviors; suicidal behaviors that do not result in death may be called nonfatal suicidal behaviors (Canetto & Lester, 1995, cited in DeLeo et al., 2002). In the United States, suicidal behaviors that do not result in death are known as suicide attempts; outside the United States, suicidal behaviors that do not result in death may be known as **parasuicides** or deliberate self-harm (DeLeo et al., 2002).

More common than suicidal behaviors are suicidal thoughts, also called *suicidal ideation*. Suicidal thoughts range in intensity. Some people may have feelings of being tired of life, others may feel that life is no longer worth living, and yet others may wish not to wake from sleep (Paykel et al., 1974, Kessler, Borges, & Walkers, 1999, both cited in DeLeo et al., 2002). Still others have concrete plans for ending their lives. Any of the range of these thoughts may exist in older adults contemplating suicide. About 17% of older adults have thought about suicide at some point, about 2% in the previous 2 weeks, with older women more likely to have suicidal thoughts than older men (Linden & Barnow, 1997, Scocco et al., 2001, both cited in DeLeo et al., 2002).

International Perspective

Globally, rates of suicide vary considerably. In general, the highest suicide rates are found in Eastern Europe (e.g., Belarus, Estonia, Lithuania, Russia) and Sri Lanka, whereas the lowest suicide rates are found in Latin America (especially Colombia and Paraguay) and parts of Asia (notably the Philippines and Thailand) (DeLeo et al., 2002).

Sartorius (1996, cited in Goldsmith, Pellmar, Kleinman, & Bunney, 2002) found the highest suicide rates for older people in Hungary, whereas Schweizer et al. (1988, cited in Goldsmith et al., 2002) found the lowest rates in Northern Ireland, England, and Wales. Because of lack of data, the rates of suicide in African nations are unknown (Lester, 1996, cited in DeLeo et al., 2002).

Internationally, suicidality generally increases with age, with higher rates of suicide found in older adults rather than younger adults, especially old-old through oldest-old men (age 75 and older) (Pearson et al., 1997, cited in Goldsmith et al., 2002).

There is a relationship between suicide and gender. In general, suicide rates are higher in men than in women, by about three to one, though this is not the case in China, the Philippines, or Singapore—where the rates are closer to equal—or in Belarus, Lithuania, Chile, or Puerto Rico—where the rates for men are substantially higher than for women (DeLeo et al., 2002).

Also, within a given country, race/ethnicity is related to suicide. In the United States, European Americans tend to be about twice as likely to be suicidal as minorities (Moscicki, 1985, cited in DeLeo et al., 2002). A review of the literature suggests that older Chinese American women may have higher suicide rates than the general population (Shi, 2005). People of the same ethnic group tend to have similar rates of suicide, even if they live in different countries, whereas people of different ethnic groups who live in the same country may have very different rates of suicide (DeLeo et al., 2002). Rates of suicide among indigenous peoples tend to be higher than among nonindigenous peoples in Australia, Taiwan, Canada, and the United States (Hunter, 1991, Cheng & Hsu, 1992, and Lester, 1997, all cited in DeLeo et al., 2002).

Religion, too, has an impact on suicide rates. In general, suicide rates are highest in nations where religious practices are "prohibited or severely discouraged," followed by countries where Asian religions are dominant, followed by countries that are primarily Protestant and those that are primarily Roman Catholic; in general, the lowest rates are found in countries that are primarily Muslim (DeLeo et al., 2002).

Around the world, fatal suicides are more common in older adults, whereas nonfatal suicide attempts are more common in younger adults (DeLeo & Diekstra, 1990, DeLeo et al., 2001, both cited in DeLeo et al., 2002). Even if suicidal behaviors are less common in older adults, when they are engaged in, they are more likely to be fatal (DeLeo et al., 2002). Older adults typically choose more violent methods of suicide and have higher rates of fatality (DeLeo & Ormskerk, 1991, cited in DeLeo et al., 2002). Typically, it is only fate that results in an older adult's suicide attempt to be nonfatal (DeLeo et al., 2002).

U.S. Demographics

The surgeon general has recognized that in the United States, the highest suicide rates are found among older people (U.S. Public Health Service, 1999). Older adults account for 13% of the population but 20% of deaths from suicide (U.S. Public Health Service, 1999). The suicide rate for older adults is about 27% higher than it is for the general population (about 14 per 100,000 vs. about 11 per 100,000) (American Foundation for Suicide Prevention, 2007).

A number of characteristics of older adults are associated with suicidality—depression and social isolation, lethality of means, visits to health care providers, and physical illness (U.S. Public Health Service, 1999). Older adults who are suicidal are more likely to be depressed and socially isolated than younger suicidal individuals. Older adults also are more likely than younger suicidal individuals to use lethal methods to commit suicide. That is, if an older adult attempts suicide, he or she is more likely than a younger suicidal individual to have that attempt end in death. Older suicidal adults are more likely to have had a visit with a health care professional before their attempt and are more likely to have physical illnesses than younger suicidal adults. Among suicide victims, nearly three fourths of older adults had visited their primary care physician within the previous month (U.S. Public Health Service, 1999).

Men commit about 84% of all suicides among older adults; European American males in the oldest-old age group (age 85 and older) have the highest suicide rate of any group (U.S. Public Health Service, 1999). The rate of suicides in adults age 80 to 84 has increased more than in other age groups (U.S. Public Health Service, 1999). Older adults are more likely to use guns or other firearms to commit suicide; in fact, 78% of older suicidal men and 36% of older suicidal women use firearms (U.S. Public Health Service, 1999). Among older adults, rates of suicide are higher among those who are divorced or widowed than those who are married or have never been married (U.S. Public Health Service, 1999).

In addition to overt suicide attempts, older adults are at greater risk for indirect or passive suicidal behaviors, including not eating or drinking, not complying with medical treatments, or engaging in other behaviors of self-neglect (Goldsmith et al., 2002). These covert self-destructive behaviors, which often result in death, may be more common in nursing homes or for people from religious or cultural traditions that strongly forbid suicide (Farberow, 1980, cited in Goldsmith et al., 2002).

Older adults clearly are most at risk of suicide. What is distressing is that suicide prevention programs underserve this population. With the increasing percentages of the population who are older adults—and unless there is greater social interest in their welfare and more funding for prevention programs—we can expect an increase in the number of deaths by suicide in this age group.

Suicide is a psychological issue and is also a social issue. Suicide oftentimes accompanies depression. In fact, older suicide victims are more likely to have suffered with depression than any other *DSM-IV* diagnosis (Goldsmith et al., 2002). With the social mind-set that depression is a normal part of aging, depression then becomes less likely to be treated, as do suicidal thoughts, feelings, and behaviors (American Foundation for Suicide Prevention, 2007).

Risk Factors

There are a number of risk factors—internal and external—for suicide. That is, some risk factors are intrapersonal whereas others are interpersonal or social. Risk factors are demographic, psychiatric, biological, social, environmental, and related to individuals' life events (DeLeo et al., 2002). Though none of these factors in and of themselves can be used to predict suicide with certainty, an astute counselor will keep these factors foremost in his or her mind when assessing a client. The specific risk factors associated with a client, too, may begin to suggest the appropriate treatment options, including intrapersonal, interpersonal, and social service interventions.

The National Center for Injury Prevention and Control (2007) identified the following 15 risk factors for suicide:

1. Family history of suicide
2. History of abuse in childhood
3. History of previous suicide attempts
4. History of psychiatric disorders
5. Alcohol or substance abuse or dependence
6. Feelings of hopelessness
7. Hostility/aggression/impulsivity
8. Belonging to a culture that glorifies suicide
9. Media reports of suicide
10. Social isolation
11. Lack of access to counseling
12. Loss or multiple losses
13. Physical illness
14. Use of lethal means
15. Unwillingness to seek help

For older adults, the most significant factors appear to be widowhood (Smith et al., 1988, cited in Goldsmith et al., 2002), serious medical illness, and social isolation (Draper, 1994, cited in Goldsmith et al., 2002). Complicating the picture is the fact that risk factors may interact with one another (e.g., widowhood and social isolation or depression and medical illness).

Age and Gender. Men are more likely to engage in fatal suicide acts than are women (DeLeo et al., 2002). Older adults are more likely to engage in fatal suicide acts than are younger adults (Gardner et al., 1964, cited in Goldsmith et al., 2002). The greater fatality rate may be the result of the fragile health of older adults, the fact that older adults are more likely to live alone, the long-term planning of the suicide act, the more lethal means of suicide, and/or a lesser likelihood among older adults to talk to others about their intention to harm themselves (Goldsmith et al., 2002).

Psychiatric Disorders. People who commit suicide are more likely to suffer from depression, bipolar disorder, schizophrenia, anxiety disorders, conduct disorders, personality disorders, impulsivity, and a sense of hopelessness (DeLeo et al., 2002). Among older people, depression significantly increases the risk of suicide (Conwell, 2001, cited in Scogin & Shah, 2006). Among older adults, depression often manifests itself in somatic complaints: stomachaches, dizziness, heart palpitations, and pain; furthermore, elders' depression may coexist with other medical problems such as strokes, cancer, arthritis, Parkinson's disease, or Alzheimer's disease (DeLeo et al., 2002). Alcohol abuse, too, is implicated in suicide, as it may result in depression, may be a form of self-medication for depression, or may be a response along with depression to stressors (DeLeo et al., 2002).

Family History. A family history of suicide is associated with increased risk. This may be due to a genetic predisposition to suicide or to psychiatric disorders that are passed down in families (DeLeo et al., 2002).

Pain and Physical Illness. Painful illnesses, too, are associated with increased risk for suicide, especially among older adults. In fact, 25% to 80% of older adults who commit suicide may be suffering from a medical illness (DeLeo et al., 2002).

Older clients who suffer from terminal illnesses may be at increased risk for suicide. In the United States, about 2% to 4% of older adults who are terminally ill die from suicide (Goldsmith et al., 2002). These older adults are likely also to be suffering from depression. Major factors in suicidal older adults with medical illnesses include untreated or undertreated pain, anxiety over the anticipated course of the illness, not wanting to be dependent, and not wanting to burden family (Goldsmith et al., 2002). When pain is under control and depression is reduced or eliminated through treatment, older people who formerly were suicidal state that they want to live (Hendin, 1999, cited in Goldsmith et al., 2002).

Loss, Grief, and Social Isolation. Life events such as the death of a loved one, loss through retirement of a work identity, legal problems, or interpersonal difficulties are associated with an increased risk for suicide (DeLeo et al., 2002). Social withdrawal, too, may play a role in suicidality, as those who are without friends or who are socially isolated may be at increased risk (DeLeo et al., 2002). These factors are particularly important when we consider the loss of friendships through death in later life as well as the frequent social isolation in which older adults exist in North America.

Grief over the death of a spouse is a suicide risk factor, especially in older men. Suicidal thoughts are higher in older adults who are suffering from complicated or traumatic grief—a grief that includes PTSD-like symptoms (Szanto et al., 1997, cited in Goldsmith et al., 2002).

Methods. The fatality of suicidal behaviors depends in part on the method chosen. In the United States, firearms are the most common method used in fatal suicides; in China, suicide through the use of pesticides is most common; in much of the remainder of the world, hanging is a more common method (DeLeo et al., 2002). Worldwide, older adults tend to rely on methods that require less physical strength; older adults, too, tend to choose more violent methods—death by shooting, by jumping (e.g., from a bridge), or by hanging (DeLeo et al., 2002). Older adults who live in nonurban areas are more likely to use firearms, whereas those in urban areas are more likely to use nonfirearm methods (Goldsmith et al., 2002).

Protective Factors

There are a number of protective factors for suicide. That is, some factors reduce the likelihood of suicidal thoughts, feelings, and behaviors. The U.S. Public Health Service (1999) identified the following protective factors:

- family and community support,
- treatment for mental health issues,
- treatment for physical health issues,
- treatment for alcohol and other substance abuse or dependence,
- easy access to clinical treatments and support for those willing to seek help,
- ongoing primary care and mental health provider support,
- client ability to peacefully resolve problems and conflicts, and
- cultural or religious backgrounds that discourage suicide.

Other protective factors include parenthood, self-esteem, and ego repression (DeLeo et al., 2002).

Client Symptoms and Signs

Suicidality can be thought of existing along a continuum, ranging from having thoughts, to devising a plan, to gathering the means to carry out the plan, to making an attempt, to completing the fatal act.

Warning Signs. Warning signs of suicide include depression, increased alcohol or other drug use, impulsiveness, threats of suicide or expressions of a wish to die, a plan, and unexpected rage or anger (American Foundation for Suicide Prevention, 2007).

Depression in older adults is closely linked to suicidality. The surgeon general indicated that the following symptoms are most associated with depression in older adults: having subjective feelings of nervousness or emptiness, having feelings of guilt or worthlessness, feeling fatigued, having anhedonia, feeling restlessness or irritability, feeling unloved, feeling life is not worth living, sleeping and/or eating either more or less than usual, or having chronic aches and pains (U.S. Public Health Service, 1999). Low mood, pessimism, hopelessness, desperation, anxiety, psychic pain and inner tension, withdrawal, and sleep problems may also be signs of depression (American Foundation for Suicide Prevention, 2007). Clients who exhibit these symptoms should be screened for suicide.

Alcohol abuse or dependence, or the use of or dependence on other drugs, may be a sign that your older client is suicidal. A client who engages in impulsive behaviors such as reckless driving may be at increased risk. A client who threatens suicide or expresses a wish to be dead, whether this expression is passive ("I wish I was dead") or active ("I am going to kill myself"), is at increased risk. Clients who have developed a plan for suicide are at increased risk for carrying out the plan. Signs of making a plan may include giving away possessions, purchasing firearms, or acquiring poisons or medications (American Foundation for Suicide Prevention, 2007). Intense rage or anger in a client who previously did not exhibit these strong emotions may be a sign of suicidality (American Foundation for Suicide Prevention, 2007).

Suicide Crisis. A **suicide crisis** is a time of dramatically increased likelihood of suicidal behavior (American Foundation for Suicide Prevention, 2007). It oftentimes is marked by a precipitating event such as the loss of a loved one, intensification of emotions, changes in behavior, deterioration in social functioning, increased alcohol use, self-destructive behaviors, loss of control, and explosive rage (American Foundation for Suicide Prevention, 2007).

Counselor Responses to Suicidality

Counselor Thoughts and Feelings. For the counselor, a suicidal client can result in intense feelings of anxiety, helplessness, fear, or doubt about one's clinical abilities. These feelings are normal. One effective way to address these feelings is through talking to a supervisor or to colleagues about one's feelings around suicidal clients. Oftentimes, counselors join consultation groups in which they confer with fellow counselors about challenging clinical situations, including suicide. Other ways to manage these feelings are by having a plan or by learning what steps to take when you suspect suicidality or are faced overtly with a suicidal client. The best advice is to be prepared for the eventuality of working with a suicidal older client.

General Recommendations. Any hint or suggestion of suicide must be taken seriously. Listen carefully to the individual, express your concern, and let him or her know that suicidal thoughts and feelings will pass. If your client is depressed, let him or her know that depression is treatable; if your client has personal problems, let him or her know that these problems can be resolved (American Foundation for Suicide Prevention, 2007).

Clients who are acutely suicidal should not be left alone. They may need hospitalization. Hospitalization may be voluntary (i.e., your client agrees to be hospitalized) or involuntary (i.e., your client—against his or her wishes—is hospitalized to safeguard his or her life). Involuntary hospitalization typically involves a psychiatric emergency team or the police.

Suicide Assessment. Every client should be screened for suicidality. For the counselor, this can be as easy as asking the client if he or she ever has thoughts of harming him- or herself. A more structured assessment for suicide, however, should include the following:

- *Does the client have suicidal thoughts?* If so, consider the following:
- *Does the client have a plan?* A client may respond, "No, it's just that sometimes I wish I was dead." Or a client may respond, "Yes, I am going to kill myself with a gun." If the client appears to have a concrete plan, you will want to know the following:
- *Does the client have the means to carry out the plan?* If the client has a plan (e.g., using firearms), ask specifically about the means. In the above example, you might ask, "Do you have a gun? Do you have bullets? Where is the gun? Does it have bullets in it?"

If you determine that a client is, or may become, suicidal, it is incumbent upon you to take whatever steps are necessary to preserve the life of your client. This may range anywhere from having an oral and/or written agreement with your clients that they will not harm themselves (and that they will contact you if they feel like they are going to harm themselves) to ensuring that your clients are hospitalized until the crisis passes.

Intake Interviews. Prior to a suicide crisis, or even if your client does not present as suicidal, it is valuable to be aware of potential signs or symptoms that are associated with suicidality. You can do this when you conduct your intake interview, as well as over the course of treatment of your client.

When interviewing clients, you should ask about any family history of suicide. Family history may be a predictor of lethal self-harm for your client, whether it is the result of learned behavior or it is a biological predisposition to the behavior.

You also should ask about any history of child abuse or violence, whether emotional, physical, or sexual. People who have been victims of abuse in their childhood may continue to suffer from the emotional fallout of the abuse and may act by self-harm in response to these historical events.

History of a suicide attempt by your client should be of particular concern, as past behavior is the best predictor of future behavior. An older client who has attempted suicide in the past is at increased risk for suicidality.

A history of psychological or psychiatric disorders, notably depression, may place your client at increased risk for suicide. In addition to considering depression, consider diagnoses of bipolar disorder, schizophrenia, and other serious mental illnesses.

Alcohol abuse or other substance abuse may contribute to suicidality. A client who is drinking or abusing drugs may act out through self-injury or death.

Feeling hopeless can contribute to suicidality. When a client believes his or her painful thoughts, feelings, behaviors, situation, or experiences are not going to change, he or she may consider suicide as the sole option to quell that pain.

A client who is hostile, aggressive, or impulsive may be at increased risk for suicide. Ask your client, then, about how he or she interacts with others and how he or she handles conflict. You also should be observing how your client is interacting with you: Does he or she seem to be hostile, aggressive, or impulsive?

A client from a culture (broadly defined) that glorifies suicide may be at increased risk. There is some evidence that clients from such cultures may still be at increased risk even if they move into a culture that does not glorify suicide. This is one reason that it is essential for you to be knowledgeable about the cultures from which your clients come or in which they reside—as discussed in Chapter 7 and in more detail in Chapter 9.

Social isolation, too, may contribute to suicidality. When a client does not feel connected to others, beliefs may arise that he or she has no one to turn to and no option other than suicide. Clients who have experienced a loss or multiple losses may be at increased risk. These are relationship losses that occur through divorce, estrangement, or death; social losses such as isolation through moving; work losses through retirement or a change in job or work status; or financial losses resulting in reduced financial solvency, loss of home, or trouble making ends meet.

Physical illness, so common among older adults, may place a client at increased risk. Physical illness may be acute or chronic, or it may be a singular disorder or more commonly a number of disorders (e.g., increasingly debilitating arthritis coupled with chronic obstructive pulmonary disease). You should have a medical history as part of your intake with clients.

It has long been known that a client with access to a lethal means for suicide is at increased risk for suicide. The means oftentimes are guns or other weapons or medications that have been saved with plans for overdosing.

Other Considerations. Reports of suicide through the media may prompt copycat suicides. For this reason, it is important for you to be informed and knowledgeable about your client's community and world. Older people who are exposed to media reports of older adult suicides are more at risk for suicide than are those who are exposed to media reports of younger people's suicides (Stack, 1999, cited in Goldsmith et al., 2002).

Clients who lack access to psychotherapy, counseling, or other mental health treatments are at increased risk for suicide. From the perspective of social justice, one of the things you can do is work diligently for universal access to psychotherapy, counseling, or other mental health treatments for your clients.

Clients who are unwilling to seek help because of the feelings of shame associated with mental health treatment place themselves at increased risk. You are likely at some point to interact with someone who is suicidal, whether he or she is willing or unwilling to seek help.

When working around issues of suicide in older adults, you need to consider that older people are more likely to (a) engage in fatal suicide attempts, (b) have poor adherence to treatment regimens, and (c) have comorbid conditions associated with suicide, including bereavement, depression, and terminal illness (Goldsmith et al., 2002).

Suicide Prevention. Steps to prevent suicide may include the following:

- early diagnosis and treatment of mental disorders (especially depression and other mood disorders, alcohol and other substance abuse and dependence, schizophrenia, and personality disorders);
- pharmacotherapy;
- behavioral therapies (including problem-oriented interventions);
- "green cards," which give clients information about emergency services, crisis lines, and hospitalizations;
- offer of help so clients can increase their social relationships;
- maintenance of the counselor–client professional relationship;
- the utilization of suicide prevention services;

- restriction of access to means of suicide; and
- reduction of vulgar media reports of suicide (DeLeo et al., 2002).

Also promising is the placement of depression care managers into primary care medical practices with the intent of preventing and reducing suicidal thoughts and actions, feelings of hopelessness, and other symptoms of depression in older adults. The depression care managers assess older patients; inform the physician of issues of suicidality, hopelessness, and depression; monitor patient treatment compliance; provide psychotherapy to the client; and make referrals (Reynolds et al., 2001, cited in Goldsmith et al., 2002).

Families Dealing With Loss From Suicide

One of the greatest tragedies that can strike a family is the suicidality of a loved one, especially a fatal suicide. Grief in response to suicide oftentimes includes shock, numbness, disorientation, and difficulty in concentration; depression, difficulty sleeping, loss of appetite, sadness, lack of energy; anger toward the deceased, other people, or the self; relief if the suicide followed a difficult mental illness; or guilt (American Foundation for Suicide Prevention, 2007).

In most cultures, suicide remains a taboo, so it may be difficult for families to reach out to friends or even to mental health professionals for support following suicide in the family; a family's grief may remain an internal affair (DeLeo et al., 2002). When you have a client who is a family member of an older adult who has committed suicide, it is important for you as a counselor to support that person in expressing his or her grief or whatever feelings he or she has around the deceased and the suicide. It may be useful, too, to help your client connect with a support group for family survivors of suicide; sharing the tragic common experience of suicide in the family may help your client express his or her feelings (DeLeo et al., 2002).

When working with a family member or friend of a loved one who has died from suicide, you may want to support your client in whatever decision he or she makes regarding telling other people about the loved one's death, reaching out to family and friends, or maintaining contact with other people. You should allow your client to grieve in his or her own way and at his or her own pace, being cognizant of the fact that anniversaries, birthdays, and holidays may be especially hard and understanding that children in the family may need to be reassured that they were not at fault for an adult's suicide. Clients may find comfort in community, religious, or spiritual activities; in being kind to themselves;

and in beginning to enjoy life again (American Foundation for Suicide Prevention, 2007).

ALCOHOL ABUSE

Introduction

Alcohol abuse is common among older adults. Though oftentimes difficult to identify, it is treatable (Sorocco & Ferrell, 2006). Symptoms of alcohol abuse in older adults may mimic depression or dementia, or they may be ignored or denied because of ageism, feelings of discomfort, or shame (Sorocco & Ferrell, 2006).

What constitutes problem drinking? The equivalent of 0.5 ounces of alcohol is considered one drink: This amount of alcohol is found in approximately 1.5 ounces of distilled spirits, 12 ounces of beer, or 5 ounces of wine (Rigler, 2000). It is recommended that men and women 65 years of age or older who are healthy and not taking medications that interact with alcohol have no more than one drink per day or two drinks on special occasions, with somewhat lower limits for older females (Substance Abuse and Mental Health Services Administration, 1998, cited in Sorocco & Ferrell, 2006). Older adults are less well able to tolerate alcohol, given specific physical changes that are a normal part of aging, including a reduced ratio of body water to body fat, decreased blood flow through the liver, less efficiency of liver enzymes, and an increased speed at which alcohol affects the brain (Institute of Alcohol Studies, 2007). If your older client is drinking more than one drink per day, he or she may be considered to have a higher than moderate use of alcohol. Older adults who exceed the guideline for alcohol use are more likely to have an alcohol problem (Moos, Brennan, Schutte, & Moos, 2004).

Problematic alcohol use may be categorized as substance abuse, substance dependence, binge drinking, or hazardous drinking. The *DSM-IV-TR* (American Psychiatric Association, 2000) defined **substance abuse** (including alcohol abuse) as substance use that results in impaired functioning or distress coupled in the previous year with problems at work, school, or home and/or with physical risks, legal problems, or interpersonal difficulties.

Substance dependence (including alcohol dependence) is substance use that results in impaired functioning or distress coupled in the previous year with at least three of the following symptoms:

- showing tolerance;
- having withdrawals;

- using the substance in greater amounts or over a longer time than intended;
- having a desire to curb one's use;
- spending considerable time getting hold of, using, or recovering from the use of the substance;
- abandoning or decreasing social, work, or recreational interests; and/or
- continuing to use the substance in the face of physical or psychological problems made worse by the substance use (American Psychiatric Association, 2000).

Binge drinking is the ingestion of five or more drinks during one occasion at least one time during the past month (Sorocco & Ferrell, 2006). **Hazardous drinking** is use of alcohol to the extent that there are negative consequences, even when there is the absence of abuse or dependence; hazardous drinking, in other words, is drinking that results in perilous behaviors such as violence or social problems (Rigler, 2000; World Health Organization, 2004).

International Perspective. Globally about 2 billion of the world's 6.7 billion people drink alcoholic beverages; of these, about 76 million have an alcohol-use disorder (World Health Organization, 2004). Alcohol misuse has been linked to over 60 kinds of diseases, illnesses, and injuries, including cancers, cirrhosis of the liver, homicide, epileptic seizures, and auto accidents (World Health Organization, 2002, cited in World Health Organization, 2004). Furthermore, alcoholism causes about 3% of deaths annually (World Health Organization, 2004). Internationally, alcohol use and misuse vary considerably. In general, the lowest rates of alcohol consumption per capita are found in North African and Middle Eastern nations, whereas the highest rates are found in European nations (World Health Organization, 2004).

United States. One study found that 62% of community-dwelling older adults drink alcohol; roughly 6% of these older adults were heavy drinkers (Mirand & Welte, 1996, cited in Rigler, 2000). Among older adults, rates of heavy drinkers differ significantly based on gender: 13% of older men and 2% of older women are heavy drinkers (Mirand & Welte, 1996, cited in Rigler, 2000). About 1% of all hospitalizations are alcohol related (Adams et al., 1993, cited in Rigler, 2000), and high rates of alcohol-related health care are seen in emergency rooms, hospitals, psychiatric institutions, and nursing facilities (Scott & Mitchell, 1988, cited in Rigler, 2000).

In general, alcohol use remains stable across the life course. Older adults tend to consume about as much alcohol in later life as they did earlier in life, and if there is a change, it tends to be in the reduction of alcohol consumption (Adams & Cox, 1995, cited in Rigler, 2000). Decreases in alcohol use by older adults are often the result of an increased physiological effect of alcohol on the person, medical problems, financial problems, and/or a reduction in social events that present alcohol (Stinson, Dufour, & Bertolucci, 1989, cited in Rigler, 2000).

Risk Factors

Gender is a risk factor for alcohol misuse. Older men are more likely than older women to engage in problem drinking (Laforge et al., 1993, cited in Myers, Dice, & Dew, 2000). Furthermore, older people who are married are less likely to be problem drinkers than those who are not (or are no longer) married (Moos et al., 1990, Gomberg, 1995, both cited in Myers et al., 2000). Social isolation, a common phenomenon in later life, may place a person at increased risk for problem drinking (Gurnack, 1997, cited in Myers et al., 2000).

Age of onset plays a role in alcohol abuse in later life. Among older alcohol abusers, about two thirds started using when they were young (i.e., before age 40); about one third started late in life (Barrick & Connors, 2002, cited in Sorocco & Ferrell, 2006). Early-onset abusers are more likely to be male, to be of lower socioeconomic status, to drink as a method of dealing with stress, to have come from a family that has a history of alcohol abuse, to present with more severe cognitive problems, and to be less treatment compliant (Substance Abuse and Mental Health Services Administration, 1998, cited in Sorocco & Ferrell, 2006). Early-onset abusers, too, are more at risk of death or illness related to alcohol and more likely to demonstrate antisocial behavior (Rigler, 2000). Among early-onset abusers, one frequently sees a downward spiral in socioeconomic status as well as estrangement from family (Liberto & Oslin, 1995, cited in Rigler, 2000).

Late-onset abusers typically have higher levels of income and education than early-onset abusers (American Medical Association, 1996, cited in Rigler, 2000) and may have begun drinking subsequent to common stresses in later life, including retirement and decreases in social interactions, isolation and loneliness, illness and pain, or insomnia (Institute of Alcohol Studies, 2007). People with late-onset alcohol problems tend to have more financial resources and better family support; hence, they are more likely to complete treatment and may be nearly twice as likely as early-onset abusers to successfully demonstrate remission (Liberto & Oslin, 1995, Schutte, Brennan, & Moos, 1994, both cited in Rigler, 2000).

One study found that older adults who suffer from more health problems are less likely to consume alcohol, but those with higher health burdens (defined as medical conditions, physical symptoms, medications, and negative health events) are more likely to have drinking problems (Moos, Brennan, Schutte, & Moos, 2005). Older adults who abuse alcohol report more intense pain, more interruption of day-to-day activities because of pain, and more repeated use of alcohol to manage pain than do nonabusers (Brennan, Schutte, & Moos, 2005).

Shaw (2006) reported that adults whose experience of childhood was lacking in parental support are more likely to abuse alcohol in later life. Parent support is defined as "gestures or acts of caring, acceptance, and assistance that are expressed by a parent toward a child" (Shaw, 2006, p. 51). McCarthy and Davies (2003, cited in Shaw, 2006) posited that adults who as children lacked parent support are more likely to be unable to effectively cope with the stresses of aging, because of lifelong feelings of insecurity, which render them less able to seek out or provide social support during the transition from one life stage to the next.

Client Symptoms and Signs

In later life, alcohol problems tend to be underdiagnosed (Hurt, Finlayson, Morse, & Davis, 1988, cited in Rigler, 2000). Older adults who are abusing alcohol may deny their problem; even their loved ones may be in denial (Institute for Alcohol Studies, 2007).

Symptoms of alcohol misuse in older adults include cognitive problems, falls, incontinence, hypothermia, and self-neglect (Institute for Alcohol Studies, 2007). Clinicians who utilize the Michigan Alcohol Screening Test (MAST) or the CAGE questionnaire (see Table 14.2) should supplement these with additional information about the pattern, frequency, and amount of alcohol use, as well as information about its effects on the older adult's relationships, work, leisure, and other factors.

TABLE 14.2   CAGE Questionnaire

C.	1. Have you ever felt you should **cut** down on your drinking?
A.	2. Have people **annoyed** you by criticizing your drinking?
G.	3. Have you ever felt **guilty** about your drinking?
E.	4. Have you ever had a drink first thing in the morning (**eye**-opener) to steady your nerves or get rid of a hangover?

Note: Adapted from Ewing, J. A., "Detecting Alcoholism: The CAGE Questionnaire," *JAMA: Journal of the American Medical Association, 252,* 1905–1907, 1984.

Older adults' use of alcohol tends to exacerbate physical problems, including hypertension, sleep problems, malnutrition, and falls (Substance Abuse and Mental Health Services Administration, 1998, cited in Sorocco & Ferrell, 2006) and has negative interactions with prescription medications, which are so common in later life (Sorocco & Ferrell, 2006). Older adults with alcohol problems may present with impaired balance, foot drop, cognitive and other brain disturbances (such as delirium, Wernicke's syndrome, or Korsakoff's syndrome), immunosuppression, nutritional deficiencies, insomnia, and comorbid psychiatric problems (including depression) (Rigler, 2000). Although comorbid depression is common in alcohol abusers, it is not known whether alcohol misuse causes depression, depression results in alcohol misuse, or a third factor contributes to both depression and alcohol misuse (Vaillant, 1993, cited in World Health Organization, 2004).

Counselor Responses to Alcohol Abuse

Consider the least intrusive interventions first when treating alcohol problems (Substance Abuse and Mental Health Services Administration, 1998, cited in Sorocco & Ferrell, 2006). Given their age, older alcohol abusers are more likely to suffer from additional medical problems. Though detoxification can be addressed on an outpatient basis, it may be best handled in an inpatient program. Older inpatients experiencing alcohol withdrawal may be more likely to suffer symptoms of delirium, prolonged confusion, and falls, and they may depend more on others in carrying out daily activities (Kraemer et al., 1997, cited in Rigler, 2000). Subsequent to detoxification, Rigler (2000) recommended inpatient, day, and outpatient treatment programs as well as community-based groups. In general, elders who are involved in programs specifically for older adults are more likely to complete the programs than those involved in programs that do not specifically target them (Schonfeld & Dupree, 1995, Liberto, Oslin, & Ruskin, 1992, both cited in Rigler, 2000). Older adults should be supported to engage in nondrinking social activities (Institute for Alcohol Studies, 2007). In addition to a program of treatment, referral to a 12-step or similar program, especially if the program is composed of older adults, is highly recommended (Norton, 1998).

Treatments include interventions, family interventions, motivational counseling, and CBT as potential treatment options (Sorocco & Ferrell, 2006). A **brief intervention** may consist of as few as one session in which the counselor discusses with the client change strategies;

provides psychoeducation, assessment, and feedback; and works with the client to set goals and develop a contract. The counselor, too, may use behavior modification or bibliotherapy (Substance Abuse and Mental Health Services Administration, 1998, cited in Sorocco & Ferrell, 2006).

In a **family intervention**, the counselor educates family members (broadly defined) about substance abuse and prevention, codevelops an intervention, and encourages treatment (Sorocco & Ferrell, 2006). The intervention is most effective when family members' communication is "emotionally neutral, factual and supportive" (Sorocco & Ferrell, 2006, p. 461).

Motivational counseling is an approach to clinical work with abusing clients that focuses on metacommunicative messages as a way to change client behavior. Motivational counselors allow clients "to digest information, evaluate their own risks, and take responsibility for their own change efforts" (Resincow et al., 2002, Rollnick, Mason, & Butler, 1999, both cited in Sorocco & Ferrell, 2006). Counselors can help older adults who misuse alcohol by assisting them to resolve the ambivalence they feel about their drinking and by encouraging them to develop reasons for changing their alcohol use and to make a commitment to that change (Hanson & Gutheil, 2004).

CBT for treatment of substance-use problems focuses on skills development to conquer the substance abuse; the CBT counselor may use behavior modification, self-management (Sorocco & Ferrell, 2006), self-talk disputation, and other techniques to assist the client. Norton (2000) identified some of the irrational beliefs that may be present in old age and that may contribute to alcohol misuse, including beliefs that one is too old to change or to learn something new; that one must suffer because of impaired health status; that, given old-age status, one has no control over one's life; and that, as an older adult, one is no longer important.

Families Dealing With Alcohol Abuse

Family members can help an older alcohol abuser by ensuring that their loved one receives medical care if he or she demonstrates problems in thinking or self-care (Rigler, 2000). They should confirm information about the elder's drinking, confront their loved one if called for, support their loved one during the time of detoxification and treatment, help coordinate community services, and make decisions for the loved one whose cognitive abilities are severely impaired (Rigler, 2000).

Prescription Drug Misuse

Before we end our discussion, we must make a special note of prescription drug misuse. Prescription drug misuse may be defined as use of a prescription drug in a different manner, for a different length of time, or by someone other than the intended recipient of the prescription (World Health Organization, 1994, cited in Gallo & Lebowitz, 1999). Prescription drug misuse may play a role in the development of delirium and depression; furthermore, prescription medications commonly are used in suicide attempts (Gallo & Lebowitz, 1999). The phenomenon of prescription drug misuse is not as well understood as alcohol abuse, yet clearly it is a significant issue in the well-being, quality of life, and care and treatment of older adults (Gallo & Lebowitz, 1999).

CHAPTER SUMMARY

In this chapter, we discussed some of the main issues seen by counselors who work in community or mental health settings. Specifically, we considered the mental health issues of anxiety, depression, suicide, and alcohol abuse. We discussed risk factors and client symptoms and signs. We also addressed counselor responses to older clients who present with these issues as well as their families. In Chapter 15, we will look at future trends in aging and counseling.

CASE STUDY

Mrs. Jones is a 75-year-old African American female who was brought to an outpatient clinic by her 55-year-old daughter, Mary. Mary has been increasingly concerned about her mother, stating, "My mother seems different from her usual self. She forgets to buy items she needs when she's at the grocery store, she talks more slowly, and she walks more slowly. She used to be an impeccable dresser, but now if I don't help her pick out an outfit to wear, she doesn't seem to care how she looks. She's also more irritable than she's ever been." Mary states that her mother takes medication, though not reliably, for hypertension and for high cholesterol. Mary mentions, almost in passing, that her mother usually has one or two drinks in the evening most every day. "She's always been kind of nervous, and a drink helps her calm down," Mary says. When directly asked what she drinks, Mrs. Jones smiles and replies, "Different things." Mary also shares that her father, Mr. Jones, and her mother's only sister both died this past year.

Questions

1. What are the symptoms Mrs. Jones is presenting with?
2. Are these symptoms more consistent with dementia, depression, or some other illness?
3. What diagnosis would you suspect? Justify your answer.
4. What steps would you take before working with Mrs. Jones?
5. What information would you provide to Mrs. Jones's daughter about her mother?
6. What treatment approach would you use with Mrs. Jones? Justify your answer.

CHAPTER QUESTIONS

1. What are common barriers globally to treatment of depression?
2. What are the signs and symptoms of depression in older adults? How do these differ from the common signs and symptoms found in younger populations?
3. What are common risk factors for depression in older adults? How do these risk factors differ from those for depression in the general population?
4. Name and describe three approaches to treating depression in late life.
5. Develop a mnemonic for the signs and symptoms of depression in older adults.
6. What would you recommend to family members who have an older loved one suffering from depression?
7. Among older adults, what populations are at highest risk for suicide?
8. Why might suicide rates for older adults be higher in the older parts of this population?
9. Why might suicide rates for older adults be higher for those divorced or widowed?
10. What would be some of the advantages and disadvantages of having a written no-suicide contract with a client?
11. Develop a mnemonic to help you remember suicide risk factors.
12. In which parts of the world is alcohol misuse less common? More common? Hypothesize why this is the case.
13. Identify two differences between early-onset and late-onset alcohol abusers in later life.
14. What are the differences between alcohol abuse, alcohol dependence, and heavy drinking?

GLOSSARY

Alzheimer's disease: is a progressive dementia characterized by increasingly impaired memory, thought, and speech.

Anhedonia: is the loss of pleasure in life.

Anxious depression: is a combination disorder that includes components of anxiety and depression.

Binge drinking: is the ingestion of five or more drinks during one occasion at least one time during the past month.

Brief intervention: is a treatment option in which the counselor discusses with the client change strategies; provides psychoeducation, assessment, and feedback; and works with the client to set goals and develop a contract.

Cognitive behavioral therapy: approaches treat depression by altering thoughts and behaviors that subsequently improve the depressed person's emotions.

Delirium: is a disorder marked by confusion, disorientation, incoherence, altered mental states, changes in personality, and/or drowsiness and usually caused by a treatable underlying illness.

Dementia: is a destruction of brain cells that results in cognitive, behavioral, and emotional or personality changes in an individual.

Dysthymia: refers to a pervasive set of lower grade depressive symptoms.

External locus of control: is a belief that one's behaviors are controlled by circumstances outside of oneself, for example, by others or by fate.

Family intervention: is a treatment option in which the counselor educates family members about substance abuse and prevention, codevelops an intervention, and encourages treatment.

Generalized anxiety disorder: is a disorder marked by daily or near-daily worry about many different things.

Hazardous drinking: is the misuse of alcohol to the point where it causes danger to one's health, social relationships, work, or other aspects of one's life.

Interpersonal psychotherapy: approaches address "role disputes and transitions" and interpersonal deficits, thereby addressing loss, social isolation, and feelings of helplessness.

Major depression: is a mood disorder marked by feelings of sadness, hopelessness, and loss; changes in appetite, sleep, and interest in sex; and self-critical thoughts and beliefs.

Motivational counseling: is a counseling approach that focuses on encouraging the client to take responsibility for change in his or her life.

Parasuicide: is the self-infliction of physical harm that does not result in death.

Pharmacotherapy: is the treatment of a psychiatric or psychological disorder through the use of prescription drugs or medications.

Pseudodementia: is the presentation of dementia-like symptoms, such as cognitive impairment or cognitive slowing, in an older adult actually suffering from depression.

Relaxation training: is a therapeutic approach in which the individual learns to relax through a guided process of actual or imaginary tensing and relaxing of muscles.

Reminiscence therapy: is a therapeutic approach designed specifically for older adults that focuses on reflecting on the major experiences of their life.

Substance abuse: results in impaired functioning or distress coupled in the previous year with problems at work, school, or home and physical risks, legal problems, or interpersonal difficulties.

Substance dependence: results in impaired functioning or distress coupled with numerous problems related to the use of the substance.

Suicide crisis: is a time of dramatically increased likelihood of suicidal behavior, oftentimes subsequent to a precipitating event such as the loss of a loved one.

FURTHER INFORMATION

1. For a wonderful discussion of theories of depression in later life, see King and Markus's chapter "Mood Disorders in Older Adults," in Krauss Whitbourne's *Psychopathology in Later Adulthood* (New York: Wiley, 2000).

2. A thorough and thoughtful discussion of suicide, including elder suicide, from a global perspective can be found in DeLeo, Bertolote, and Lester's chapter "Self-Directed Violence," in Krug, Dahlberg, Mercy, Zwi, and Lozano's *World Report on Violence and Health* (Geneva, Switzerland: World Health Organization, 2002), http://www.who.int/violence_injury_prevention/violence/global_campaign/en/chap7.pdf.

3. The American Foundation for Suicide Prevention has an excellent, navigable Web site: http://www.afsp.org.

4. An excellent text about motivational interviewing for substance use and other problems is Miller and Rollnick's *Motivational Interviewing* (2nd ed.) (New York: Guilford, 2002).

NOTES

1. The *DSM-IV-TR* is the *Diagnostic and Statistical Manual of Mental Disorders, Fourth Edition, Text Revision.* It is the reference work for the field of psychiatry and, by extension, most all of mental health. The next version of the *DSM*, the *DSM-V*, is scheduled to be published in 2012.

2. A person with an *external locus of control* believes that his or her behaviors are the result of external circumstances and might believe, for example, that others are responsible for his or her behaviors.

3. Though they represent about 12% of the general population, older adults consume 21% of all benzodiazepine prescriptions (Kennedy, 2000).

CHAPTER 15

Future Trends in Aging and Counseling

Happiness does not notice the passing of time.

—**Chinese proverb (cited in Andrews, Biggs, & Seidel, 1996)**

The search for happiness is one of the chief sources of unhappiness.

—**Eric Hoffer (2008)**

CHAPTER OVERVIEW

In this chapter we look to the future of counseling older adults and consider the psychosocial impact of an increasingly aging population. We will consider positive psychology as it relates to later life and healthy aging. We also will consider issues in globalization that affect older adults. We will identify some of the relationships between positive psychology, globalization, and aging.

THE PSYCHOSOCIAL IMPACT OF AN AGING POPULATION

In the Netherlands, there is the World Database of Happiness, a comprehensive collection of data about happiness throughout the world. Eric Weiner, a National Public Radio reporter, searched the database and reported in his book *The Geography of Bliss* (2008) that the happiest people tend to reside in homogeneous societies (think Iceland or Switzerland), whereas the unhappiest tend to reside in former Soviet republics, filled with "general mistrust, nepotism, corruption, and envy"

(Hoffer, 2008). This finding is similar to that of the World Values Study Group (1994, cited in Diener, 2000), which found some of the highest levels of life satisfaction among people who—at least in the early 1990s—resided in Switzerland, Denmark, and Canada and some of the lowest levels of life satisfaction among those in Bulgaria, Russia, and Belarus. The inclusion of Canada, an increasingly heterogeneous society, in the World Values Study Group list of those highest in life satisfaction suggests that it is something other than social homogeneity that results in happiness.

Is there a connection between personality, social structures, and happiness? Well, yes. In fact, happy people are more likely than unhappy people to be married, extroverts, religious, sexually active, college graduates, and wealthier (Hoffer, 2008). Is there a connection between aging and happiness? Again, the answer is yes, at least among those older adults who in their lives have been altruistic, who plan, who laugh and can see the lighter side of difficult situations, who find creative ways of dealing with life's challenges by channeling their energies into healthy activities, and who are able to put challenges aside to deal with them at more appropriate times (Vaillant, 2000).

POSITIVE PSYCHOLOGY, COUNSELING, AND HEALTHY AGING

"Positive psychology is the study of the conditions and processes that contribute to the flourishing or optimal functioning of people, groups, and institutions" (Gable & Haidt, 2005, p. 104). **Positive psychology** is driven by the fundamental belief that we humans are active agents in our lives and that we organize ourselves and adapt to life's circumstances (Seligman & Csikszentmihalyi, 2000). Rather than focusing on problems or deficits, positive psychology is strengths based and focuses on those qualities that allow people to grow and thrive. These qualities are neither rare nor unique; rather they are qualities of "ordinary human strengths and virtues" (Sheldon & King, 2001, p. 216). They are the qualities of the everyman and the everywoman. Positive psychology does not deny human problems, impairments, or deficits; rather it chooses to focus on the other end of the spectrum of human experience, the positive end, as worthy in its own right, as well as for the insights it gives us into prevention of psychological problems and difficulties. Just as there can be a positive psychology, there can also be a positive psychology of aging (Ranzijn, 2002).

Seligman and Csikszentmihalyi (2000) presented an overview of positive psychology and its evolutionary basis, psychological traits, and connection to mental and physical health. We will discuss these facets of positive psychology and will broaden our discussion, whenever possible, by considering the connection to aging of positive psychology's evolutionary basis, psychological traits, and mental and physical health.

Why consider a **positive psychology of aging**? Ranzijn (2002) identified three reasons to shift emphasis to a positive psychology of aging: (a) to identify those areas in which older adults may excel and make gains, given that so much research in later life has focused on decline; (b) to reduce the costs associated with an aging population by identifying ways of improving health in late life; and (c) to recognize older clients' capacity to react to interventions that would, when successful, result in improvements in functioning.

Psychology as we know it today has emphasized pathology and the negative, and it has neglected positive qualities and traits of humanity (Seligman & Csikszentmihalyi, 2000). Geriatrics has focused on limitations in later life more than on the potential inherent in old age. Psychological research in later life has focused on decrements rather than areas of growth. This is, at least in part, because of methodological research difficulties in operationalizing (i.e., making concrete) those attributes in which older adults excel over younger people (Ranzijn, 2002). In reality, strengths-based attributes in later life are embedded within the context of an older adult's environment (Ranzijn, 2002). The implication is that laboratory studies of late life—which generally focus on the individual and are easier and cheaper to conduct—are likely to overemphasize decline, whereas late-life research that studies older adults as they exist within their social worlds can more readily identify potential.

Focusing on decline in late life represents ageism that exists among the mental health treatment community. If clients experience this ageism, they likely will not be inclined to make use of those services that have the most potential to help them (Gridley et al., 2000, cited in Ranzijn, 2002). If clients do not experience this ageism, perhaps through counselors' stronger understanding of the positive psychology of aging, they will utilize the services they need in order to grow.

A positive psychology of aging, however, is not the same as successful aging (Ranzijn, 2002). **Successful aging** can be defined in terms of effectively adjusting to those changes common in later life (see the work of Paul Baltes et al. cited in Ranzijn, 2002). According to this view of making adaptations in response to changes in later life, successful aging calls for selective optimization with compensation (see P. Baltes & M. Baltes, 1990, cited in Ranzijn, 2002). As a quick review of selective optimization with compensation, recall that *selection* means deciding to engage in those behaviors that are within the realm of the doable, given one's limitations; *optimization* means making the selection that is most likely to result in success; and *compensation* means that the new behavior is chosen to make up for a deficit. An example for many of us—and not just older adults—of selective optimization with compensation is getting prescription glasses. Selection is choosing between the options of prescription glasses, contact lenses, and surgery; optimization is choosing the alternative that is most likely to be successful given the constraints of increasing loss of eyesight; and compensation is the payoff of improved ability to see. One criticism of selective optimization with compensation is that it suggests that choices are made and behaviors engaged in because of deficits associated with old age (see Uttal & Perlmutter, 1989, cited in Ranzijn, 2002). If this criticism is correct, then it is inherently ageist to define successful aging as selective optimization with compensation.

The history of psychology and counseling *has* included researchers who studied positive qualities, experiences, and growth, including those in later life. Consider the example of Erik Erikson (discussed in Chapter 1). Erikson viewed later life as a time of potential growth, his final developmental stage being *integrity* versus despair. We should add that counseling—as a field distinct from psychology—took and has maintained throughout its history a more optimistic view of human nature. Counseling has taken and continues to explore strengths-based approaches in working with clients.

Positive psychology has grown in influence (Seligman & Csikszentmihalyi, 2000). One of its strengths is its emphasis on prevention rather than remediation of maladaptive, painful personal experiences, traits, and social institutions. A positive psychology of aging is a psychology that focuses on growth and development rather than on the problems of loss and decline. It is a psychology of what is right, good, and healthy in later life rather than of what is wrong, bad, and unhealthy. Positive psychology, at its core, is a "nurturing what is best" (Seligman & Csikszentmihalyi, 2000, p. 7). This has important implications for gerontological counseling. If we, as counselors of older adults, focus on prevention rather than remediation, we will be communicating an understanding of later life as a time of continued growth and development, a time of potential and not limitations (Ranzijn, 2002).

Seligman and Csikszentmihalyi (2000) discussed positive psychology as it exists on three levels: the subjective, the individual, and the group levels. The *subjective level* concerns itself with what we experience inside ourselves regarding our past, future, and present—that is, the extent to which we experience "well-being, contentment, and satisfaction (past), hope and optimism (future) and flow and happiness (present)" (Seligman & Csikszentmihalyi, 2000, p. 5). The *individual level* focuses on those human traits that are affirmative, optimistic, constructive, and favorable (Seligman & Csikszentmihalyi, 2000). These traits include the ability to love others, to have a satisfying work life, to be brave, to have those skills necessary to interact comfortably with others, to appreciate beauty, to be able to commit to a course of action and follow through, to forgive, to be creative, to be future directed, to be spiritual, to foster one's talents, and to acquire wisdom (Seligman & Csikszentmihalyi, 2000).

Consider wisdom. It is, perhaps, one of the hallmarks (if not *the* hallmark) of old age. Around the world, and especially outside of North America, elders are honored, venerated, and respected for their wisdom. This is not to say that all older adults are wise,[1] but it is to say that elders generally are considered wiser than young people. But how do we define wisdom? And, once we define it, how do we measure it? This is a challenge facing a positive psychology of aging, not only in terms of wisdom but also in terms of the other positive qualities of late life.

Some of the positive qualities found in later life are the result of longevity (Ranzijn & Grbich, 2001, cited in Ranzijn, 2002). Because older adults have lived long lives, they may be better able to appreciate how fragile and beautiful life is. Furthermore, because of this appreciation, older adults may be more inclined to be actively engaged in family and community (Ranzijn & Grbich, 2001, cited in Ranzijn, 2002).

At the *group level*, positive psychology is concerned with social phenomena, human qualities concerning civic responsibility, and social institutions (e.g., government or church, broadly speaking) that help us become more capable in our abilities to contribute to the communities and societies to which we belong. Seligman and Csikszentmihalyi (2000) believed we are better able to contribute to society when we exhibit the qualities of being responsible, nurturing, altruistic, and civil, as well as demonstrate moderation, tolerance of others, and an ethic that values work. It is at the group level, too, that positive psychology may have something to say about the impact of globalization on the optimal functioning of people.

Old age is perceived as a time of decline because of our emphasis on looking at the individual rather than at the individual *in the context* of his or her social environment (Ranzijn, 2002). This bias toward individualism is endemic in Western society. The deficits model of old age so prevalent in the West exists precisely because we so often consider older adults without context and do not study late life by looking at older adults in the context of their social environment (Ranzijn, 2002).

In response to a deficits-based focus on the individual, M. Powell Lawton (1989, 1991, cited in Ranzijn, 2002) developed his **person–environment fit model**. Lawton's person–environment fit model stated that to function well we must consider the fit between a person's needs and abilities and the environment's demands and characteristics (Ranzijn,

2002). For Lawton, then, a competent elder would be an elder who can adjust to his or her social and environmental settings. If the social demands are greater than the older adult's ability to adjust, then that person is labeled incompetent (Ranzijn, 2002). However, if a person is labeled incompetent, it might not be the person but the environment that needs to change (Ranzijn, 2002). All of this is a way of saying that a positive psychology of aging cannot consist merely of the characteristics of the older adult in isolation. Rather, it must consider the older adult in the context of his or her environment—the physical, social, political, and even global environments, as we shall see below. It suggests that, at times, our job as counselors may be to change not our clients but our clients' environments; this may be a matter of working toward a more just society in which older adults' needs are recognized and attended to.

Seligman and Csikszentmihalyi (2000) focused on definitions of positive experience, positive personality traits, and the social contexts of positive social institutions. Through the choice of researchers they discussed, Seligman and Csikszentmihalyi (2000) suggested that positive experience is associated with having a subjective sense of well-being, encountering optimal experiences, being optimistic, being happy, and experiencing self-determination. Positive personality qualities include wisdom, *mature* (i.e., healthy) defenses, creativeness, and giftedness (Seligman & Csikszentmihalyi, 2000). Several researchers have taken a life span developmental approach to the maturing of these qualities, "taking into account the fact that individual strengths unfold over an entire lifespan" (Seligman & Csikszentmihalyi, 2000). Finally, they indicated the importance of considering the social contexts—the communities, cultures, and institutions—in which we exist and how they shape our positive qualities and how our positive qualities shape them. It is in this context, most appropriately, that Seligman and Csikszentmihalyi (2000) discussed evolutionary development, social relations, and cultural standards, values, and expectations.

Massimini and Delle Fave (2000, cited in Seligman & Csikszentmihalyi, 2000) took a psychosocial evolutionary perspective on positive psychology. That is, they looked at evolution from psychological and cultural perspectives. They believed that we humans have learned to adapt to our environment both through social learning and through the production and use of material or symbolic artifacts. Through these means emerges culture. The symbolic representations of the self and others (the external world) are codified into descriptions and rules stored in the individual's psyche and in external phenomena (e.g., paintings or the written word) (see Massimini & Delle Fave, 2000). In directing and managing their environment, humans develop culture. And culture subsequently influences human behaviors; distinctive cultures differentially affect human behaviors.

Massimini and Delle Fave (2000) framed their discussion around the concept of **memes**, the basic unit or building block of a culture. A meme is a piece of information—a behavior, thought, or cultural artifact—that is passed on to another nongenetically, most often through imitation, though also verbally.[2] Massimini and Delle Fave (2000) believed that memes are created in human consciousness. That is, humans create memes, which in turn influence humans. In other words, humans "are the authors of their own evolution" (Seligman & Csikszentmihalyi, 2000, p. 9). New memes can be invented or can be borrowed from other cultures. Memes, too, can be imposed onto one culture from another.

On a more personal level, a meme—whether it is an idea, a value, or an artifact—is created by a person in response to a specific problem (Massimini & Delle Fave, 2000). Furthermore, given the fact that we humans actively seek out "positive and rewarding states of consciousness" (p. 27), we look for optimal experiences—that is, those experiences that provide a sense of engagement or, in Csikszentmihalyi's (1991) term, **flow**. Massimini and Delle Fave (2000) believed that optimal experience promotes human growth and development, both of the individual and, ultimately, of the culture. People, therefore, seek out optimal experience—that experience that is complex enough to challenge one to grow and develop. Massimini and Delle Fave's (2000) belief was that "individuals are the sole authors of their developmental trend, built on the preferential reproduction of those memes that are related to optimal experiences" (p. 28). Growth in complexity through optimal experiences is expressed within a cultural context; hence, a major task for humans is to complement their individual lives with their actions within their culture.

If this is the case, then collectively we are both shaping our culture and being shaped by it. If this is the case, too, natural selection for psychological traits may not solely be in response to external forces but be the result of a desire to reproduce those experiences that are most advantageous (Seligman & Csikszentmihalyi, 2000).

The work of Massimini and Delle Fave (2000) has implications for work with older adults. To promote life satisfaction and well-being among our older clients, we as counselors may want to work with elders to increase their optimal experiences and flow. This may mean exploring with them the kinds of activities that keep them *actively* engaged (watching television, for example, is a passive activity; doing crossword puzzles is a more active endeavor; creating a crossword puzzle may be more active still) and helping them find ways to involve themselves in whatever these activities are. Different clients will require different activities to experience flow.

Their work, too, has implications for older adults with disabilities. With disabilities that occur later in life—such as vision impairment, paraplegia, or even quadriplegia—there can be a *transformation of flow*, where, if original flow activities are no longer possible, the person involves him- or herself in new endeavors that provide optimal experience (Delle Fave, 1996a, cited in Massimini & Delle Fave, 2000, p. 29). These new endeavors may be vastly different from the original flow activities (Delle Fave, 1996a, cited in Massimini & Delle Fave, 2000). The bottom line is that disability need not provide an impediment to flow.

Positive psychology suggests the importance of several traits, among the most salient "subjective well-being, optimism, happiness, and self-determination" (Seligman & Csikszentmihalyi, 2000, p. 9). Let's take a look at each of these four traits.

Subjective well-being is one's personal sense of feeling good about oneself, one's life, and one's place in the grand scheme of things; in other words, it is happiness. Diener (2000, cited in Seligman & Csikszentmihalyi, 2000) reviewed personality traits that are associated with subjective well-being (or happiness). Components of subjective well-being are overall life satisfaction, satisfaction with important areas of one's life (work, intimate relationships, friendships, and so on), the experience of many positive emotions, and the experience of few negative emotions (Diener, 2000). In other words, subjective well-being is highest in those people who "feel many pleasant and few unpleasant emotions ... are engaged in interesting activities ... experience many pleasures and few pains, and ... are satisfied with their lives" (Diener, 2000, p. 34). What these factors have in common is that they are all subjective experiences. Take, for example, the experience of retirement. Satisfying retirement for one person may consist of staying home most days and reading, an activity that may be highly unsatisfying for someone who wants to be out among friends socializing. A happy retirement is in large part the subjective experience of those activities that one finds satisfying. The key here is that each of us decides what is satisfying and what is not.

Subjective well-being, however, is influenced by one's personality (Diener, 2000). Positive or negative emotions are generally maintained by a person over time. Say, for example, after years and years of playing the lottery, an older woman who generally has negative emotions has just won a small jackpot. She likely will experience very positive emotions after her win but eventually will begin to experience negative emotions again. In other words, people, even when they move away from their baseline emotions—whether these emotions are predominantly positive or negative—tend to revert back to baseline over time (see Headey & Wearing, 1992, cited in Diener, 2000).

But even this is not the whole story, for those people who make progress on meeting their goals tend to be happier than those who do not (Diener & Fujita, 1999, cited in Diener, 2000). There are two ways to make progress on goals. First, keep striving toward the goal. Second, change to a more attainable goal (in other words, adapt). If the woman who played the lottery was in need of money because she could not otherwise afford to buy some of the little luxuries in life (her goal), then winning a jackpot brought her closer to meeting those desires; hence, she likely would be happier. If, however, social isolation was more pervasive in her life, and her goal was to develop more true friendships, then she likely would not be happier, unless of course she thought money could buy her authentic friendship.[3] An alternative way for the woman playing the lottery to be happier would be to change her goals. Instead of wanting some of the little luxuries in life, she could choose to be satisfied with having her basic needs met. This would be a change in goal.

Brickman and Campbell (1971, cited in Diener, 2000) proposed the concept of the **hedonic treadmill**, which states that as our accomplishments rise and the number of possessions we own increases, so do our expectations. That is, once we adapt to those things that made us happy, we no longer find happiness in them. Think of yourself: Perhaps you have lusted after a new car. Then you buy that car of your dreams, and you are happy with your purchase. But after a while, you habituate to having a new car and begin to notice that there are still bigger cars or fancier cars or better cars. You no longer find happiness in your doesn't-feel-as-new car. The hedonic treadmill theory also works the other way: Those things that brought unhappiness no longer bring unhappiness after a while. We adapt. Okun and George (1984, cited in Diener, 2000) found even in older adults almost no correlation between physical health and subjective well-being. One can be an elder in poor health and still be happy. We adapt.

Optimism comprises hope and positive expectations about the future, whether on a smaller, more personal scale or on a larger, more global scale (Seligman & Csikszentmihalyi, 2000). Peterson (2000, cited in Seligman & Csikszentmihalyi, 2000) posited that optimism has three components: thoughts, feelings, and motivation. That is, we may think optimistically, feel optimistic, and act in ways that indicate optimism. Peterson (2000) discussed optimism from several different perspectives, that of human nature, individual differences, dispositional style, explanatory style, and hope. As a part of *human nature*, optimism ironically has been seen as a negative, as something that promotes suffering because it denies reality. (After all, how can we be optimistic in a world filled with suffering?) From this perspective, an optimistic person is one who is out of touch with reality, hence, psychologically disturbed. In reality, though, psychologically healthy people temper their reality testing and, with all else being equal, tend toward the positive. As an *individual difference*, optimism is seen as a general orientation toward life, something that is near universal in its application over time and across situations. As a *dispositional style*, optimism is discussed as a "global expectation that good things will be plentiful in the future and bad things, scarce" (Peterson, 2000, p. 47). As an *explanatory style*, optimism is seen as one way of explaining negative events in one's life, namely, as something external to the self, not consistent, and due to particular reasons. This is in contrast to a pessimistic explanatory style, where bad things happen because of factors that are internal to oneself ("It was my fault"), constant ("This is what happens"), and universal ("This always happens"). As *hope*, optimism is the belief that what is longed for is reachable and that what is desired can be had.

Peterson (2000) noted that optimism is not just the absence of pessimism and in fact argued for optimism and pessimism to be identified as two discrete qualities, each of which a person can have in high or low volume, rather than as opposite ends in a bipolar scheme. In other words, a person can be high both in optimism and in pessimism, or low both in optimism and in pessimism, or high in one and low in the other. He stated that individuals who are high in optimism demonstrate more "positive mood and good morale ... perseverance and effective problem solving ... academic, athletic, military, occupational, and political success ... popularity ... good health; and ... long life" (Peterson, 2000, p. 44). Optimism clearly is connected to lots of positive qualities!

Peterson (2000), further, distinguished between little optimism and big optimism. **Little optimism** is a positive expectation regarding a personal situation. It may manifest in a thought such as "Medicare is going to be there for me" or "I am probably going to get an A in this course." **Big optimism** is an expectation of the good on a grand scale. On a grand scale, big optimism may manifest in an individual's thought such as "The Good Lord is on our side" or "Our nation is headed in the right direction."

Happiness is a subjective feeling or sense of joy or contentment. Myers (2000, cited in Seligman & Csikszentmihalyi, 2000) found a relationship between happiness and religious faith, economic growth and income (up to a certain point, after which there is diminishing return), and close interpersonal relations. Furthermore, Myers (2000, cited in Seligman & Csikszentmihalyi, 2000) found these relationships between happiness and religion, economics, and relationships to hold true in different cultures and times.

In four ethnically and culturally diverse studies of emotions and aging, Gross et al. (1997) found differences between older adults and younger adults. In a study with African American and European American participants, they found that older adults tend to report less intense emotional impulses, less expressed positive emotions, less expressed negative emotions, and greater emotional control than do younger adults (Gross et al., 1997). There were no race or gender differences in the findings from this study. In a second study, that of Chinese Americans and European Americans, they found that older European Americans report less emotional impulse intensity than do younger European Americans, whereas for Chinese Americans emotional impulse intensity does not vary by age; also, the older adults across these racial/ethnic groups report greater anger control than do the younger adults (Gross et al., 1997). This suggests that emotional control may vary by emotion in later life; it may be stronger for anger but not for other negative emotions (Gross et al., 1997). It further suggests racial/ethnic differences in impulse intensity (Gross et al., 1997).

In their third study, of Norwegians,[4] Gross et al. (1997) found that older women report less frequent experiences of anger than do younger women; older women also report greater internal control over their anger than do younger women. Both older men and older women report greater internal control over feelings of happiness, sadness, fear, and disgust than do younger men and younger women. Finally, in a study of American nuns, Gross et al. (1997) found that older nuns report more internal and external control of happiness and sadness and internal control of fear and anger than do younger nuns. The implication of these findings is that negative emotions decrease the older one gets, and control of inner experience and outer expression of both negative and positive emotions increases in later life (Gross et al., 1997).

Overall, what can we take away from Gross et al.'s (1997) four studies? First, older adults report fewer negative emotions than do younger adults. Second, older adults demonstrate more emotional control than do younger adults. Third, some older adults are less expressive emotionally than are their younger counterparts. Gross et al. (1997) attributed these findings to an increasing ability to regulate emotions as one gets older. Older adults develop the ability "to selectively enhance positive emotions and selectively dampen their experience of aversive negative emotions" (Gross et al., 1997, p. 597). Could it be that older adults are happier than younger adults, even if they do not express happiness as intensely as younger adults? Furthermore, is this the result of older adults choosing to experience fewer negative emotions? We can say that, unlike the many qualities that associate old age with decline, in the realm of emotional regulation, old age is a time of wonderful and considerable development.

Mroczek and Kolarz (1998) initially discovered a linear relationship between age and negative affect; in other words, older adults reported less negative affect than did middle-aged and younger adults. When they looked at the data further, Mroczek and Kolarz found that this was true of men but not of women. That is, older men report less negative affect than do middle-aged and younger men. Even further, this relationship is found only for married men. That is, older married men have less negative affect than younger married men, but older unmarried men are just as unhappy as younger unmarried men.[5] In other words, there is no relationship—with the exception of married men—between age and negative affect (Mroczek & Kolarz, 1998).

Mroczek and Kolarz (1998) found a curvilinear relationship between age and positive affect. Specifically, they found that positive affect is at its lowest point at about age 35, and then it increases at an escalating rate from ages 45 to 75. Those with the most positive affect are the oldest adults in their sample. When they looked closer at these data, they found that among women, positive affect and age are associated: the older the woman, the higher the amount of positive affect, and at an increasing rate. For men, the relationship is linear: the older the man, the more the positive affect, though not at an increasing rate. Furthermore, more extraverted men demonstrate a weaker relationship between age and positive affect than do more introverted men. Even though emotions and age are related—though maybe in more complex ways than we have previously considered—Mroczek and Kolarz (1998) found that older adults have more positive affect than do younger adults. Late life can be (and for many older adults is) a time of happiness.

Self-determination can be expressed by the belief that one is the master of one's own fate and in the actions taken to control the events and destiny of one's life. It comprises the ability to succeed in particular endeavors (**competence**) and to feel a sense of being a part of a particular group or groups (**relatedness**) and the freedom to act as one sees fit (**autonomy**) (Ryan & Deci, 2000, cited in Seligman & Csikszentmihalyi, 2000). When competence, relatedness, and autonomy are met, well-being is maximized (Ryan & Deci, 2000). Kasser and Ryan (in press, cited in Ryan & Deci, 2000) found that nursing home residents whose social environments support autonomy and relatedness show higher levels of well-being.

Ryan and Deci (2000) distinguished between intrinsic motivation and extrinsic motivation. Intrinsic motivation is engaging in an activity because one values that activity in its own right. Intrinsic motivation is increased with increasing feelings of connection to others as well as of competence coupled with autonomy. Extrinsic motivation exists along a continuum and ranges from *external regulation* (engaging in an activity to get a reward or satisfy some external demand), to *introjected regulation* (engaging in an activity to enhance the self-esteem that is gained from demonstrating an ability), to *identification* (engaging in an activity because one perceives it as personally important), and finally to *integrated regulation* (engaging in an activity because it is congruent with one's values and needs) (Ryan & Deci, 2000). People who act from intrinsic motivation demonstrate "enhanced performance, persistence, and creativity ... vitality ... self-esteem ... and general well-being" (p. 69).

How much autonomy is enough, and how much is too much? Consider the rather benign example of an older adult going to the pharmacy to purchase over-the-counter cough medicine. He or she goes to the aisle and sees shelves filled with brand-name and generic versions of cough medicine; medicine labeled for colds, for colds and congestion, for colds, congestion, and coughs, for flu; night formulas and day formulas; lemon and orange flavors; and so on. A convincing argument easily might be made that too much autonomy, resulting from too much choice, is painful. Schwartz (2000, cited in Seligman & Csikszentmihalyi, 2000) indicated that, indeed, too much autonomy can be crippling. He posited that rather than resulting in happiness, it can result in discontent and even depression (Schwartz, 2000, cited in Seligman & Csikszentmihalyi, 2000). He believed that social structures must be present to constrain autonomy, to reduce the "burden of responsibility for autonomous choices" (Seligman & Csikszentmihalyi, 2000, p. 10).

Mental and physical well-being typically are viewed through a medicalized lens, especially in the case of older clients. That is, we see mental and physical well-being in terms of minimization or absence of pathology. Older clients are mentally healthy if they are not suffering from depression, anxiety, schizophrenia, obsessive-compulsive disorder, and so forth. In a like manner, older adults are physically healthy if they are not suffering from heart disease, diabetes, high cholesterol, macular degeneration, and so forth. Seligman and Csikszentmihalyi (2000) suggested that mental health (and, by association, physical health) can be considered from a strengths-based, positive psychology perspective rather than the medical, deficits-based viewpoint.

One strength, that of using mature defense mechanisms, was studied by George Vaillant (2000), who wrote extensively about the use of mechanisms of defense in healthy coping. He promoted a life span developmental approach to positive psychology and placed defense mechanisms within the context of a threefold model of coping used across the life span (Vaillant, 2000). He believed that people cope by either (a) seeking social support (i.e., asking for and getting help from others), (b) making voluntary choices to think specific thoughts that are adaptive for a given situation, and/or (c) using defense mechanisms, those mostly unconscious phenomena that result in distortions of reality to make painful situations more manageable (Vaillant, 2000). From his perspective, maturity—that full coming into one's own that is each of our birthrights—does not appear without antecedents and should evolve and grow over the course of one's life (Seligman & Csikszentmihalyi, 2000). Although all three methods of coping can be useful, Vaillant thought that the use of mature defense mechanisms offers three specific benefits: They are not influenced by socioeconomic status, they help "regulate people's perceptions of those internal and external realities that they are powerless to change," and they can be used as agents of change in day-to-day life (Vaillant, 2000, p. 89).

Vaillant (2000) indicated that the use of mature defenses—those healthy defenses of altruism, anticipation, humor, sublimation, and suppression—exert a positive influence on one's happiness. Recall that *altruism* can be used to "transform conflict" so that one takes delight in one's altruistic actions that give "to others what people would themselves like to receive" (Vaillant, 2000, p. 92). *Anticipation* allows an individual to both think about and have identifiable feelings regarding some future event. Vaillant (2000) stated that, with *humor*, people can look at a difficult situation and express strong emotions in a way that both they and others find comfortable. *Sublimation* is taking those energies that would go into a psychic conflict or be manifest in an unacceptable drive and manifesting them into personally and socially acceptable actions. Finally, *suppression*, which Vaillant (2000) defined as stoicism, is the not entirely unconscious choice to put out of active consciousness that which is causing psychic conflict. Unlike many other defenses, suppression resides to some degree in consciousness. In a healthy person, it may manifest in a thought such as "I'm not going to think about that right now" or "I'll deal with that when I get home."

Vaillant (2000), like others, stated that it is very difficult to study positive qualities, and he believed healthy defenses need to be studied in others over the course of their lives. Yet he did just that. Vaillant (2000) described his research on defense mechanisms in three groups of people, which he called the College sample, the Core City sample, and the Terman Women sample. All of the sample groups have been studied for over 50 years. The College sample comprises a single group of former Harvard students, born around 1920, who have participated in studies since 1938; the Core City sample, born around 1930, is a single group of men who came from the poorest neighborhoods in Boston; and the Terman Women, born around 1910, were among the original participants in the famous Terman study of gifted children. The people in all three groups have aged and are in the latter portion of life.

Vaillant found that the use of adaptive defense mechanisms—altruism, anticipation, humor, sublimation, and suppression—earlier in life is associated in later life with higher "income, objective psychosocial adjustment, social supports, marital satisfaction, subjective physical functioning, and joy in living" (2000, p. 96). Psychosocial adjustment measures include "job promotions and enjoyment, marital stability, games with others, and no use of psychiatrists or tranquilizers" (Vaillant, 2000, p. 95). Social support experiences include "close relations with wives, children, siblings, and social network, as well as … strength of religious affiliation, the presence or absence of a confidante, and games with friends" (Vaillant, 2000, p. 95). Subjective physical functioning includes measures of instrumental activities of daily living. Joy in living includes measures of "satisfaction with marriage, children, job, and friends" and "hobbies, sports, community activities, or religion" (Vaillant, 2000, p. 95). Among other things, using adaptive (or mature) defenses earlier in life is associated with increased income later on. It is also associated with a better *subjective* experience of physical functioning (including climbing stairs, walking long distances, and engaging in enjoyable, spirited physical activities), though not with *objective* physical health (Vaillant, 2000). Utilizing adaptive defenses, too, is associated with being able to experience stressful life events without becoming depressed (depression and stressful life events oftentimes go hand in hand). Finally, Vaillant (2000) found a reduced association between severe combat earlier in life (among the study participants, this was battle experience in World War II) and posttraumatic stress disorder in later life. In sum, Vaillant (2000) believed that adaptive (i.e., mature) defenses work not by denying and distorting painful realities but rather by integrating and lessening the pain caused by challenging psychological and social circumstances and that the use of adaptive defenses have real, tangible benefits for intra- and interpersonal well-being.

Unrealistically optimistic beliefs may protect individuals against illness (Taylor et al., 2000, cited in Seligman & Csikszentmihalyi, 2000). Indeed, people who are unrealistically optimistic about their health tend to stave off symptoms for a longer period of time and even live longer than individuals who are more realistic. Furthermore, those who are optimistic are more likely to engage in health-improving behaviors and to seek out and receive support from others (Taylor et al., 2000, cited in Seligman & Csikszentmihalyi, 2000).

Data from the famous "Nun Study" showed that those whose writings earlier in life made more reference to positive emotions had a lower risk of mortality in later life (Danner, Snowdon, & Friesen, 2001). That is, the experience of positive emotions—happiness, interest, love, hope, gratefulness, contentment, accomplishment, relief, amusement, and other unspecified positive emotions—earlier in life was associated with greater longevity later in life. What we feel and think and do today does have an effect on our future.

Just as research on negative psychology results in knowledge about illness, a focus on positive psychology should produce knowledge about good health (Salovey et al., 2000, cited in Seligman & Csikszentmihalyi, 2000). Just as negative psychological factors generally result in worse health, positive psychological factors should result in better health. People who are optimistic are more likely to acknowledge negative information about their illness and, in doing so, are better prepared to confront what may be a negative outcome, while also maintaining an exaggerated belief in a positive outcome (Salovey et al., 2000, cited in Seligman & Csikszentmihalyi, 2000). In a population where illness is more frequent, such as in later life, there is the potential for application of knowledge about how optimism—realistic or unrealistic—impacts health, illness, longevity, and other experiences.

A positive psychology of aging addresses positive experience in late life, positive personality traits among elders, and the positive social contexts in which older adults exist. Ranzijn (2002) argued convincingly that the focus of old age should not be as a time of decline but rather be as a time of growth and development; that to identify growth and development in late life, older adults need to be considered not in isolation but in the context of their environments; that there is an emerging literature on the strengths and benefits of old age; and that older adults will best be able to express their strengths when the constraints of ageism and ignorance are removed.

GLOBALIZATION, COUNSELING, AND AGING

The world's elder population is growing by about 800,000 per month (Kinsella & Velkoff, 2001). Most of this growth is occurring in developing countries. Already, 59% of older people live in developing nations (Kinsella & Velkoff, 2001). Although Europe is the region currently with the largest percentage of older adults (as a proportion of its total population), and Africa is the region with the smallest percentage of older adults, the percentage of older adults is expected to grow fastest in East and Southeast Asia, even as the median age is expected to rise in all countries (Kinsella & Velkoff, 2001).

Furthermore, the oldest-old (i.e., age 85 and older) is the fastest growing segment of older adults in many nations, including the United States (Kinsella & Velkoff, 2001). The growth rate of the oldest-old is nearly twice that of those age 65 and older. Over 50% of the oldest-old live in just six countries—China, India, the United States, Japan, Germany, and Russia (Kinsella & Velkoff, 2001). It has been estimated that the likelihood at birth of living to age 100 has risen from 1 in 20 million to 1 in 50 (yes, 50, not 50 million) for some subsets of the population (Kinsella & Velkoff, 2001). This aging of the population is thought to result from decreases in birth rates as well as improvements in life expectancies in adulthood. The particulars of aging populations, too, are being impacted by globalization.

Globalization is the relatively unconstrained movement of people, technology, media, capital, and ideas from a particular region of the world to other regions. Though globalization typically refers to the movement of technology, capital, and ideas (notably free market capitalism) from rich nations to developing nations, it also manifests as human migration and movement of creative human culture (e.g., music) from developing nations to rich nations. Globalization, assuredly, is resulting in an increased pace of modernization throughout the world, as well as an increased push against such modernization. Most proponents and critics of globalization speak in terms of its economic impact as it appears in the form of free market capitalism. Proponents suggest that globalization produces economic improvement in the lives of people of developing nations; critics posit that globalization results in exploitation of the poor for greater benefit of the rich. In general, multinational corporations, which often act with minimal government oversight, support globalization.

It is argued that globalization results in the deterritorialization of culture (Hermans & Kempen, 1998, cited in Saraswathi, 2005). According to this view, globalization is increasing exponentially, resulting in the intermingling of cultures and challenges to the historical understandings of human thought, feelings, and behaviors by psychology (Saraswathi, 2005) and, by association, counseling. It is argued, too, that globalization does not equal universalization (Roland, 2001, cited in Saraswathi, 2005). In this perspective, we are not becoming a global village with a single set of shared values. Rather, what is evolving is a "range of psychological worlds" (Saraswathi, 2005, p. 48).[6]

Consider, for example, the increasing sense of a bicultural identity among individuals, as well as the challenges offered by this new identity in terms of beliefs about the self in the culture of origin versus the adopted culture (Saraswathi, 2005). As counselors, how do we work with bicultural identity to the benefit of our clients? Or consider the more complex bicultural identity of an older adult from a culture that values elders who migrates to a culture that values youth. What does this experience say to elders about themselves, their value to others, and their self-esteem? How do we work with our older clients who have this experience?

There are five phenomena that result in deterritorialization (see Table 15.1): ethnoscapes, technoscapes, mediascapes, financescapes, and ideoscapes (Appadurai, 1990, cited in Saraswathi, 2005).

TABLE 15.1 Precipitants of Deterritorialization

Precipitant	Description
Ethnoscapes	Groups that move across cultures and national borders
Technoscapes	Information and hard technologies
Mediascapes	Media, including TV, radio, movies, recorded music, and podcasts
Financescapes	Financial markets
Ideoscapes	Ideas and beliefs, including those that are political, religious, or philosophical

Note: Adapted from Saraswathi, T. S., "Hindu Worldview in the Development of Selfways: The 'Atman' as the Real Self," *New Directions for Child and Adolescent Development, 109,* 43–50, 2005.

Ethnoscapes are groups that move across cultures and national borders, including legal immigrants, tourists, guest workers, undocumented workers, and refugees. **Technoscapes** are the global languages of technology, including information technologies such as search engines or software and hard technologies such as automobiles, computer hardware, or factory technologies. **Mediascapes** embrace the entire range of media—newspapers, television, radio, movies, recorded music, podcasts, and so forth. **Financescapes** are financial markets, such as those for gold and other precious metals, national currencies, stock exchanges, and commodity markets. **Ideoscapes** include the entire range of "political, religious, and other philosophies, dogmas, or creeds, and the ideas and beliefs that characterize any group of peoples" (Saraswathi, 2005, p. 47). Accordingly, cultures no longer can be considered inviolate and unchanging; rather they are continuously evolving, heterogeneous organisms (Saraswathi, 2005).

In terms of ethnoscapes, there are about 200 million international migrants in the world today; they represent about 3% of the worldwide population ("Open Up: A Special Report on Migration," 2008). International migrants bring benefits to rich countries either as skilled workers needed in industry or as unskilled workers willing to take jobs left unfilled by natives. International migration of skilled workers often comes at the detriment of the poor nations they leave behind. That is, they leave their home countries with chronic shortages of skilled labor.

Relevant to older adults, international migrants from poor countries to rich countries may fill positions in nursing homes or other care facilities that otherwise would be left unfilled by natives because of low wages or poor working conditions. International migrants from poor countries to rich countries may also send monies back to relatives in poor countries that may result in an improvement in quality of life.

However, international migrants from poor to rich countries may leave behind elder loved ones who otherwise would be directly dependent on the migrant for care. It is important to remember, too, that there are substantial constraints on the mobility of the poorest of the poor, for it takes money to migrate internationally. The poorest of the poor do not migrate internationally.

Earlier in life, international migrants are motivated by economic and labor factors (i.e., they are looking for a higher and more stable standard of living), or they migrate as a dependent (child, spouse, or other relative) or as a refugee (Blakemore, 1999). Increasingly older adults are international migrants, and even those who are not may still be affected by migration of family members or through a decision to migrate even later in life (Blakemore, 1999).

Migration patterns in later life can take one of six forms:

1. Some migrants plan to stay where they are in their adopted country.
2. Some are uncertain about whether to stay or to move back to their country of origin.
3. Some are circular migrants (visiting the old country and then returning to the new, repeatedly).
4. Some plan to return to the old country.
5. Some plan to move to a third country.
6. Some plan to move within their adopted country (Blakemore, 1999).

Each of these six decisions brings with it care costs to either the old country or the adopted country and has implications for how family support for elder loved ones is manifested (Blakemore, 1999). In countries with relatively small populations (e.g., in the Caribbean), aging trends may be influenced by out-migration of working-age adults and the in-migration of retirees (who tend to be older) as well as the return of those who previously had migrated out of the country. This may put economic pressures on the nation to care for its aging population even as its working-age population decreases. For some smaller nations, globalization—at least in the form of ethnoscapes—has a direct impact on the aging population.

In terms of financescapes, economies increasingly are intermingling. Most nations today have some pension system in place for older adults. These pension systems are changing and generally not for the better. Pensions are being taxed (sometimes for the first time) or taxed at higher rates, requiring more years of work before one becomes eligible or requiring greater contributions from workers themselves (Engardio & Matlack, 2005). In rich nations, the safety net of pensions is being eroded and will leave greater numbers of older adults ill-prepared for managing later in life.

Culturally, and as an example of an ideoscape, globalization may be having an effect on the way we perceive aging, particularly in changing perceptions of youth and childhood but also in changing perceptions of growing older (Ruddick, 2003). The West is marked by declining fertility rates and an aging population, leading to fewer younger workers (Ruddick, 2003). The extension of youth and childhood puts a press on older adults to compensate: Older adult workers are pressed to be " 'youthful' in their ability to retool intellectually"; to take on new, unproven careers; to dress more youthfully; and even to make over their bodies to appear younger, whether through exercise or diet or, more radically, through plastic surgery (Ruddick, 2003, pp. 351–352).

Ethnoscapes may change through wars, territorial disputes, and conflicts between ethnic, cultural, or religious groups (see Massimini & Delle Fave, 2000). In open conflicts, the dominant group will end up imposing its memes on the subordinate group. Older adults move from one part of the world to another and may be compelled to adapt to new cultural contexts that are at times radically different from the cultures they left (Massimini & Delle Fave, 2000). Massimini and Delle Fave (2000) made the suggestion that cultures that are experiencing changes due to human migration must promote biculturalism. To support their view, they cited studies of people from the Navajo nation and people from Thailand (see Delle Fave & Inghilleri, 1996, and Inghilleri & Delle Fave, 1996, both cited in Massimini & Delle Fave, 2000). Both Navajo and Thai cultures use the strategy of biculturalism to integrate their culture of origin with Western culture. Both cultural groups report optimal experiences from traditional culture practices and from modern cultural practices in work, leisure, social relations, and religion. That is, people who use biculturalism successfully choose and integrate memes from each culture.

Massimini and Delle Fave's (2000) model may be applied to older adults in two ways. First, we may consider older adults who migrate from their culture of origin to another culture. The implication for older adults might not be any different than it is for anyone who migrates: Older adults who integrate optimal experiences from their traditional culture with those from the new culture may best adapt to their migration. It is the second application that is perhaps most intriguing. Consider that older adults belong to a particular cohort, with its own social, political, and economic histories and its own art, music, and dance. Furthermore, by way of current cultural norms, older adults exist in the culture of old age. Perhaps older adults who function best in old age are those who can choose optimal experiences from their cohort and culture of old age, as well as those from contemporary culture, integrate them, and experience the best of both worlds.

Massimini and Delle Fave (2000) believed that biculturalism is superior to assimilation and to insulation. *Assimilation* can be defined as the incorporation of the minority culture into the majority culture by the transference of majority culture beliefs, values, and behaviors en masse to the minority culture, thereby resulting in a loss of the minority culture's traditional sense. The cost of assimilation is the loss of one's culture of origin. We define *insulation* as the attempt by traditional cultures to avoid the trappings of modern culture. Massimini and Delle Fave (2000) believed that this leads to seclusion, isolation, and eventual extinction of the traditional culture.

In sum, Massimini and Delle Fave (2000) believed that there can be individual growth and global evolution, and each can complement and support the other. They posited that we can view our activities from the perspective of individuals, or we can view our activities from a more universal perspective—one that recognizes the broad, global connection that we have with each other, the earth, and indeed all of existence (Massimini & Delle Fave, 2000). They further posited that globalization—because it promotes and results in vast economic inequality—is negative, does not promote multiculturalism, does not integrate cultures, and does not promote collaboration or the give-and-take between cultures that marks authentic evolution (Massimini & Delle Fave, 2000).

Globalization does have an impact on happiness. We know that subjective well-being (i.e., happiness) is influenced by society (Diener, 2000). In general, people who live in rich nations report higher levels of subjective well-being than do people who live in developing nations (Diener, 2000). In Western European societies and in Canada, for example, most people's basic needs (enough food, potable water, health care) are met, and indeed in these societies subjective well-being is higher (Diener, 2000). To the extent that globalization brings to developing nations improvements in food production and distribution, clean water, and improved health care, populations of those developing nations should experience increasing levels of subjective well-being. To the extent that globalization robs developing nations of food production and distribution, clean water, and improved health care, populations of those developing nations likely will experience low levels of subjective well-being.

The correlation between the wealth of a nation and the subjective well-being of its citizens, though high, is not perfect (Diener, 2000). That is, some nations (e.g., Argentina, Brazil, and Chile) with lower purchasing power per person have higher levels of subjective well-being than one might predict, whereas others (e.g., Russia and other former Soviet republics) have much lower levels of subjective well-being than would be expected given their purchasing power per person (Diener, 2000). Diener (2000) suggested that in the former example, cultural influences impact subjective well-being, and in the latter example, years of political and economic unrest impact subjective well-being. Intriguingly, some of the very poorest developing nations, measured by purchasing power per person, did not have the lowest levels of subjective well-being; Diener (2000) suggested that this may be the case because of generally increasing incomes in these nations as well as lower expectations among their citizens. In rich nations where incomes are increasing, subjective well-being is not (Diener, 2000). On the one hand, the greater the wealth of a nation, the higher the subjective well-being; on the other hand, increasing income or purchasing power, if one already lives an economically comfortable life, does not result in higher subjective well-being (Diener, 2000). It may be that money really cannot buy happiness.

Diener (2000) speculated that there is a "common set of economic desires around the world" (p. 39), and the higher the purchasing power of a nation's citizens, the more likely these wants can be fulfilled. Thinking in terms of globalization, and especially in terms of technoscapes and ideoscapes, people around the world are exposed to (and subsequently want) what those in rich nations have. If subjective well-being, even in part, is influenced by one's making progress toward one's goals, there likely will be many people in developing nations who are not able to meet the goals they have learned and incorporated into their worldview (e.g., a shiny car, dining out, fancy clothes, and so forth). Subsequently, one can safely predict many unhappy people in the developing world. In rich nations, no matter how wealthy the citizens, advertisers are continuously raising the bar of what is socially desirable (e.g., not only a car but a new car; not only a new car but a new, bigger car; not only a new, bigger car but a new, bigger car loaded with the newest electronic gadgets). One cannot win, no matter how much one has; the insidious effects of materialism leave one wanting even more.

Globalization can affect subjective well-being in another way. Culture has a tremendous impact on subjective well-being. Culture influences what is seen as good and desirable as well as what is seen as bad and undesirable. The goals and values present in a culture will alter an individual's subjective well-being (Diener, 2000). If the goals are such that people in a developing nation can make progress toward them, then the result should be an increase in subjective well-being; if the goals are such that they are for the most part unattainable, then the result should be a decrease in subjective well-being. It is because of this that globalization's negative impact on developing nations may be particularly insidious. Globalization influences developing nations through mediascapes (images of a young and prosperous West) and ideoscapes (values that suggest that youth and the acquisition of material goods will make one happy). If cultures influence what one believes to be good or bad, then North Americans (and increasingly developing nations) are doomed to unhappiness because of a culture that values youth and degrades old age. We do not grow young; each of us grows older day by day. If we incorporate the valuing of youth over old age, our subjective sense of well-being is likely to decrease as we age.

Another way in which culture influences subjective well-being is through its degree of optimism, social support, coping patterns, and level of control of individual wants (Diener, 2000). More optimistic cultures may have citizens with higher levels of subjective well-being; those that have stronger social support or whose cultural coping patterns value adaptation, too, may have citizens with higher levels of subjective well-being.

Diener (2000) discussed the differences between individualistic societies and collectivist societies. The United States is often offered as an example of an individualistic culture; South Korea is an example of a collectivist culture. Self-esteem and life satisfaction are more highly correlated in individualistic cultures (Diener & Diener, 1995, cited in Diener, 2000). That is, self-esteem is connected to happiness in individualistic cultures: the higher one's self-esteem, the greater one's happiness and vice versa. This is not so much the case in collectivist cultures. Suh et al. (1998, cited in Diener, 2000) found that people who live within individualistic cultures are more likely to make decisions after taking into account their emotions; hence, a connection between pleasant emotions and life satisfaction. Those in collectivist cultures are more likely to make decisions based on consideration of social norms; hence, conformity with social norms is associated more with life satisfaction. Diener (2000) speculated that collectivism exerts a social norm that says one should be willing to forfeit individual happiness to fulfill one's obligations— a norm not shared by those immersed in an individualistic society. He believed that the forfeit of individual happiness is tempered by the level of social support found in collectivist societies (Diener, 2000). We might speculate that older adults in collectivist societies are more satisfied with their lives, even though they have sacrificed personal happiness, because they receive greater social support, typically from family members.

The hedonic treadmill theory may have something to say about the effects of globalization. As incomes rise, so do expectations and desires, and at the point of having enough financial resources, subjective well-being no longer increases (Diener, 2000). That is, we adapt to having more money, and money no longer buys the sense of subjective well-being that it once did. For people in rich nations, having more is not going to produce more happiness.

Can whole cultures be optimistic or pessimistic? Peterson (2000) argued no, that cultures, to flourish, must by necessity be optimistic—at least in terms of big optimism. That is, a culture must believe that it *can* reach its goals and that it *can* progress. The goals, however, will vary from culture to culture: Some place greater value on beauty or the arts or wisdom, and others place greater value on material well-being or sports. In other words, Peterson (2000) believed that cultures are optimistic, but the particulars of a given culture's optimism will vary depending on what it values. He pointed to American big optimism being focused on values of individualism, capitalism, and materialism and expressed in positive thinking literature. Positive thinking promotes the idea that each of us is responsible for our own well-being; that if something is going wrong, only we ourselves can right it. Through globalization, this concept of positive thinking may be seeping into historically collectivist cultures, with huge implications for aging in those cultures.

If Ryan and Deci (2000) were correct, then those cultures that support autonomy, relatedness, and competence should have residents who demonstrate greater internal motivation or external, integrated motivation, and we should expect them to show greater well-being. Cultures that promote feelings of secure connection to significant others (relatedness), feelings that one can successfully complete the tasks and activities valued by one's social group (competence), and feelings that one can choose one's activities of one's own accord and without external pressure (autonomy)[7] should result in citizens who demonstrate well-being. Ryan and Deci (2000) further proposed that these needs for autonomy, relatedness, and competence must be met across an individual's life span. That is, older adults need to have experiences of autonomy, relatedness, and competence as much as younger adults and children need these experiences. When working with older adults, you should consider the degree to which your client is in an environment that supports autonomy, relatedness, and competence and what you can do to help your client experience greater levels of these three types of experience.

In contrast, cultures that do not support feelings of competence, autonomy, and relatedness should result in individuals who do not engage in behaviors from intrinsic motivational or extrinsic, integrated motivational factors. We would predict, too, that people in these cultures would show lower levels of well-being (or, conversely, higher levels of pathology). In fact, Kasser and Ryan (1993, 1996, cited in Ryan & Deci, 2000) found that people who value intrinsic qualities of affiliation, personal growth, and community are more likely to show higher levels of well-being, whereas those who value extrinsic goals of wealth, fame, and image show lower levels of well-being. They argued that the former set of qualities helps a person meet those basic needs of autonomy, relatedness, and competence, whereas the subsequent set of goals does not. This has implications for globalization; media, particularly advertising, whets the appetite for material goods in developing nations as it does in rich nations, and it may move people who culturally and historically valued autonomy, relatedness, and competence away from these needs that promote intrinsic motivation and toward desires that promote extrinsic motivation. This, too, may result in alienation of older adults in developing nations who formerly depended on culturally congruent affiliation, autonomy, and competence.

CHAPTER SUMMARY

Looking to the future of counseling older adults, we considered the application of positive psychology principles to work with older clients. Among the concepts explored were happiness, successful aging, and wisdom. We looked at the impact of globalization on aging. We discussed the concepts of ethnoscapes, technoscapes, mediascapes, financescapes, and ideoscapes. Finally, we explored some of the relationships between positive psychology, globalization, and aging, especially in terms of globalization's effects on subjective well-being in later life.

CASE STUDY

Fatima and Ahmad are an upper-middle-class, older, Iraqi married couple. She is 75, and he is 78. They moved to the United States to live with their eldest son and his family. Fatima has been a lifelong housewife; Ahmad is a retired businessman. They had five children, three boys and two girls. Their middle son died in childhood. Both of their daughters and their youngest son live with their families in Iraq. Their eldest son was educated at a medical school in the United States, is a permanent resident, and practices medicine in the northeastern United States, where he and his family reside. Fatima and Ahmad have mixed feelings about being in the United States. They are delighted to be with their son and his family and take great delight in caring for their grandchildren, yet they long for the joys of "the old country" and their other children and grandchildren. They feel "displaced" but do not want to be called "refugees." When asked what makes them happy, Ahmad responds that he takes delight in teaching his grandchildren about their culture, history, religion, and language and that he especially likes to tell his grandchildren Iraqi jokes. Fatima smiles, rolls her eyes, and nods in agreement. Although both Fatima and Ahmad had a working knowledge of English before coming to the United States, they diligently spend 2 hours daily studying English, both reading and writing, so that they may better communicate with their grandchildren.

Questions

1. In light of positive psychology's emphasis of building on clients' strengths, what might be some of Ahmad's and Fatima's strengths? How can these strengths be brought to bear on their current circumstances?
2. Discuss Ahmad and Fatima from the perspective of M. Powell Lawton's person–environment fit model.
3. Does Ahmad or Fatima use any adaptive defense mechanisms? If so, identify the defense.
4. What is the role, if there is one, of globalization on the particulars of Ahmad's and Fatima's lives?
5. Discuss Ahmed and Fatima from the perspective of Massimini and Delle Fave's (2000) concepts of assimilation, insulation, and biculturalism. Might you help Ahmad and Fatima identify and engage in optimal experiences from an Iraqi cultural perspective and from a North American perspective? If so, how? If not, why not?

CHAPTER QUESTIONS

1. When you think about late life, do you lean more toward a positive, strengths-based view or a negative, deficits-based view? Why? (Be honest with yourself!)
2. Name and define a positive quality most often found in later life (or most often lacking in childhood). How would you measure the degree to which an older adult has this quality? How could you help an older adult strengthen this quality?
3. Explain the ageism critique of selective optimization with compensation.
4. Define flow. For you, what are the activities you engage in that represent optimal experience and flow? What feelings and thoughts do you have about these activities? (A common thought, for example, is that while one was engaged in the activity, time flew.)
5. Read one of the works of the ancient philosophers (e.g., Confucius, Aristotle, the Buddha, Plato, Lao Tzu, Seneca, or

Epictetus) on what constitutes a positive psychology (often called "the good life"), and report back on your findings.

6. What is globalization, and what is its relationship to older adults?

7. What are memes, and how do they influence our perception of aging?

8. What are the strengths and challenges of growing old in a collectivist society (such as South Korea) versus an individualistic society (such as the United States)?

9. Do you agree with Schwartz's contention that social structures necessarily should constrain autonomy? What are the implications for old age of Schwartz's view? What are the sociopolitical implications?

10. What can you do as a counselor to change or support change in social institutions (e.g., government, church, education, business, and financial institutions) so that they support a positive, strengths-based perspective of aging and late life?

GLOSSARY

Autonomy: is the feeling that one is freely choosing one's actions.

Big optimism: is an expectation of the good on a grand scale.

Competence: is the feeling of capability to engage in an activity effectively.

Ethnoscapes: refer to the changing compositions of ethnicities in various communities due to human migration patterns.

Financescapes: refer to the sphere of money and capital.

Flow: is involvement in an activity that is marked by near complete focus and concentration so that one does not feel the passing of time while engaged in that activity.

Globalization: is the relatively unconstrained movement of ideas, capital, media, people, and technology from a particular region of the world to other regions.

Hedonic treadmill: is the theory that as our accomplishments rise and the possessions we own increase, so do our expectations.

Ideoscapes: refer to ideas, particularly economic, political, social, religious, and philosophical ideas; they also refer to ideas about culture (e.g., art and music).

Little optimism: is the positive expectation regarding a personal situation.

Mediascapes: refer to media in all its manifestations, whether print, audio, or visual and whether presented using new technologies (e.g., the Internet) or traditional technologies (e.g., printed magazines, broadcast television, radio).

Memes: are the basic building blocks of a culture, pieces of information passed on to others verbally or through imitation.

Person–environment fit model: proposed by M. Powell Lawton, states that to function well, we must consider the fit between a person's needs and abilities and the environment's demands and characteristics.

Positive psychology: is a specialty that is strengths based and focuses on those qualities that allow people to grow and thrive.

Positive psychology of aging: is an approach to aging that is strengths based and not deficits based and posits that later life can continue to be a time of growth, positive development, and happiness.

Relatedness: is the feeling of belongingness, of attachment, to significant others.

Successful aging: is the ability to adapt to deficits that arise in later life.

Technoscapes: refer to technologies, including those of communication and information processing as well as manufacturing.

FURTHER INFORMATION

1. A broad range of positive psychology resources are found at the University of Pennsylvania's Positive Psychology Center Web site, http://www.ppc.sas.upenn.edu/. See also Peterson's *A Primer on Positive Psychology* (New York: Oxford University Press, 2006).
2. For further reading about positive psychology and aging, see Robert D. Hill's *Positive Aging: A Guide for Mental Health Professionals and Consumers* (New York: Norton, 2006) or George Vaillant's *Aging Well: Surprising Guideposts to a Happier Life From the Landmark Harvard Study of Adult Development* (New York: Little, Brown, 2003).

NOTES

1. My grandfather used to say that if people did not have common sense (which for him was synonymous with wisdom) by the time they were 21 years old, they would never have it.
2. An example of a meme is that of a social rule for appropriate clothing. Consider, for example, that in North America a 16-year-old girl may wear a tank top and short shorts to go shopping; an 86-year-old

woman is more likely to wear a dress or a blouse and slacks. No one told the 16-year-old or the 86-year-old what to wear, yet they learned through observation and acted through imitation in ways that society considers age appropriate. The memes, here, are the ways in which appropriate wear varies by age (and by gender, nationality, region of country, religious tradition, time of day, and so forth).

3. This lottery winner would do well to remember Billie Holiday and Arthur Herzog Jr.'s (1942) blues classic "God Bless the Child," which has the memorable lyrics regarding the relationship between money and friendship, or The Beatles' (1964) classic "Can't Buy Me Love."

4. Not Norwegian Americans.

5. In the Mroczek and Kolarz (1998) study, unmarried people comprised those who were divorced, separated, widowed, or never married.

6. Of course, not all change is the result of globalization, and in fact some changes "emerge within cultures" themselves (Saraswathi, 2005, p. 48).

7. In Ryan and Deci's (2000) view, autonomy is not synonymous with individualism; they believed that autonomy can and does exist in collectivist cultures and individualist cultures. In a collectivist culture, for example, autonomy would express itself in the feeling that one is freely choosing to contribute to the well-being of others.

References

Abeles, N., Cooley, S., Deitch, I. M., Harper, M. S., Hinnichsen, G., Lopez, M. A., et al. (1998). *What practitioners should know about working with older adults.* Washington, DC: American Psychological Association.

Academy of Achievement. (2008). *Murray Gell-Mann interview: Developer of the quark theory.* Washington, DC: Author. Retrieved November 25, 2009, from http://www.achievement.org/autodoc/page/gel0int-1

Administration on Aging. (2001). *Achieving cultural competence: A guidebook for providers of services to older Americans and their families.* Washington, DC: U.S. Department of Health and Human Services.

Ai, A. L. (2006). Daoist spirituality and philosophy: Implications for holistic health, aging, and longevity. In E. R. Mackenzie & B. Rakel (Eds.), *Complementary and alternative medicine for older adults: A guide to holistic approaches to healthy aging* (pp. 149–160). New York: Springer.

Ainsworth, M. D. (1969). Object relations, dependency, and attachment: A theoretical review of the infant–mother relationship. *Child Development, 40*(4), 969–1025.

Ainsworth, M. D. (1971). *Infancy in Uganda: Infant care and the growth of attachment.* Baltimore: Johns Hopkins.

Ainsworth, M. D., Blehar, M. C., Waters, E., & Wall, S. (1978). *Patterns of attachment: Assessed in the strange situation and at home.* Hillsdale, NJ: Lawrence Erlbaum.

Aksoy, S., & Elmai, A. (2002). The core concepts of the "four principles" of bioethics as found in Islamic tradition. *Medical Law, 21*(2), 211–224.

Aldwin, C. M., Spiro, A., & Park, C. L. (2006). Health, behavior, and optimal aging: A life span developmental perspective. In J. E. Birren & K. W. Schaie (Eds.), *Handbook of the psychology of aging* (6th ed., pp. 85–104). Burlington, MA: Elsevier.

Alzheimer's Research Trust. (2006). *Dementia statistics.* Cambridge, UK: Author. Retrieved December 9, 2007, from http://www.alzheimers-research.org.uk/contact/

American Academy of Family Physicians. (2007a). *Dementia: Info and advice for caregivers.* Shawnee Mission, KS: Author. Retrieved December 9, 2007, from http://familydoctor.org/online/famdocen/ home/seniors/mental-health/585.printerview.html

American Academy of Family Physicians. (2007b). *Dementia: What are the common signs?* Shawnee Mission, KS: Author. Retrieved December 9, 2007, from http://familydoctor.org/online/famdocen/ home/seniors/mental-health/662.printerview.html

American Association of Retired Persons. (1986). *A portrait of older minorities.* Long Beach, CA: Author.

American Association of Retired Persons. (1995). *A portrait of older minorities: Research report.* Washington, DC: Author. Retrieved October 24, 2005, from www.aarp.org/research/reference/minorities/aresearch-import-509.html

American Association of Retired Persons. (1995–2008). *Brain diseases: Vision loss.* Washington, DC: Author. Retrieved February 20, 2009, from http://www.aarp.org/health/brain/diseases/vision_loss.html

American Association of Retired Persons. (2000). *AARP survey on lifelong learning.* Washington, DC: Author.

American Council on Education. (2007). *Framing new terrain: Older adults and higher education.* Washington, DC: Author.

American Foundation for Suicide Prevention. (2007). *Facts and figures.* New York: Author. Retrieved November 29, 2007, from http:// www.afsp.org/

American Psychiatric Association. (2000). *Diagnostic and statistical manual of mental disorders (Text rev.).* Washington, DC: Author.

American Psychological Association. (2003). *Facts about depression in older adults.* Washington, DC: Author. Retrieved November 29, 2007, from http://www.apa.org/ppo/issues/olderdepressfact.html

Anastas, J. W., Gibeau, J. L., & Larson, P. J. (1990). Working families and eldercare: A national perspective in an aging America. *Social Work, 35*(5), 405–411.

Anderson, M. J., & Ellis, R. (1995). On the reservation. In N. Vacc, S. DeVaney, & J. Wittmer (Eds.), *Experiencing and counseling multicultural and diverse populations* (pp. 197–198). Bristol, PA: Accelerated Development.

Andrews, R., Biggs, M., & Seidel, M. (Eds.). (1996). *The Columbia world of quotations.* New York: Columbia University Press. Retrieved March 17, 2008, from http://www.bartleby.com/66/32/2132.html

Anetzberger, G. J., Ishler, K. J., Mostade, J., & Blair, M. (2004). Gray and gay: A community dialogue on the issues and concerns of older gays and lesbians. *Journal of Gay and Lesbian Social Services, 17*(1), 23–45.

Angelou, M. (1993). *On the pulse of morning*. New York: Random House.

Apuzzo, V. M. (2001). Keynote speeches: A call to action. *Journal of Gay and Lesbian Social Services, 13*(4), 1–11.

Araoz, D. (2006). *The symptom is not the whole story: Psychoanalysis for non-psychoanalysts*. New York: Other Press.

Arden, M. (2007). Is it too late? Key papers on psychoanalysis and ageing. *Psychodynamic Practice, 13*(3), 324–327.

Aries, P. (1974). *Western attitudes toward death: From the Middle Ages to the present*. Baltimore: Johns Hopkins University Press.

Armas, G. C. (2003, October 16). Grandparents often are primary caregivers to a grandchild because their children are in jail or on drugs. *Associated Press*. Retrieved August 1, 2008, from 0-www.lexisnexis.com.opac.sfsu.edu/us/lnacademic/delivery

Ashrama. (2008). In *Encyclopedia Britannica*. Retrieved January 8, 2008, from http://www.britannica.com/eb/article-9009845/ashrama

AssistHers. (n.d.). *AssistHers*. Houston, TX: Author. Retrieved August 13, 2006, from http://www.assisthers.org/mainwebsite_html/about.htm

Association for Frontotemporal Dementias. (2003). *Managing difficult behavior*. Philadelphia: Author. Retrieved December 10, 2007, from http://www.ftd-picks.org/features/printfriendly.php?p-caregiver.managing

Association for Spiritual, Ethical, and Religious Values in Counseling. (2006). *ASERVIC competencies for integrating spirituality into counseling*. Alexandria, VA: American Counseling Association. Retrieved August 25, 2006, from http://www.aservic.org

Atkinson, D. R., Morten, G., & Sue, D. W. (1989). *Counseling American minorities: A cross-cultural perspective* (3rd ed.). Dubuque, IA: Brown.

Axelson, J. A. (1993). *Counseling and development in a multicultural society*. Pacific Grove, CA: Brooks/Cole.

Ayers, C. R., Sorrell, J. T., Thorp, S. R., & Loebach Wetherell, J. (2007). Evidence-based psychological treatments for late-life anxiety. *Psychology and Aging, 22*(1), 8–17.

Baggini, J., & Pym, M. (2005). End of life: The humanist view. *The Lancet, 366*, 1235–1237.

Baker, H. S., & Baker, M. N. (1987). Heinz Kohut's self psychology: An overview. *American Journal of Psychiatry, 144*, 1–9.

Ball, A. (Writer) (2004). Can I come up now [Television series episode]? In A. Ball (Producer), *Six feet under*. New York: Home Box Office.

Baltes, M. M., & Carstensen, L. L. (1999). Social-psychological theories and their applications to aging: From individual to collective. In V. L. Bengtson & K. W. Schaie (Eds.), *Handbook of theories of aging* (pp. 209–226). New York: Springer.

Bandelow, F., & Hogervorst, E. (2010). *Dementia: Risk factors and early diagnosis.* Retrieved March 7, 2010, from http://bandelow.lboro.ac.uk/dementia/dementia.html

Baruth, L. G., & Manning, M. L. (1991). *Multicultural counseling and psychotherapy.* New York: Merrill.

BBC News. (2007). *Call for action over third world depression.* London: Author. Retrieved November 29, 2007, from http://news.bbc.co.uk/2/hi/health/492941.stm

Becker, E. (1973/1997). *The denial of death.* New York: Free Press/Simon & Schuster.

Bedford, V. H., & Blieszner, R. (2000). Older adults and their families. In D. H. Demo, K. R. Allen, & M. A. Fine (Eds.), *Handbook of family diversity* (pp. 216–231). New York: Oxford.

Belsky, J. (1999). *The psychology of aging: Theories, research, and interventions.* Pacific Grove, CA: Brooks/Cole.

Benbow, S., Egan, D., Marriott, A., Tregay, K., Walsh, S., Wells, J., et al. (1990). Using the family life cycle with later life families. *Journal of Family Therapy, 12,* 321–340.

Berger, R. M. (1990). Passing: Impact on the quality of same-sex couple relationships. *Social Work, 35,* 328–332.

Berger, S., & Porell, F. (2008). The association between low vision and function. *Journal of Aging and Health, 20*(5), 504–525.

Bezaitis, A. (2008). The workforce landscape: Graying but gritty. *Aging Well, 1*(4), 16–19.

Bianchi, E. (2005). Living with elder wisdom. *Journal of Gerontological Social Work, 45*(3), 319–329.

Biggs, S. (1998). Mature imaginations: Ageing and the psychodynamic tradition. *Aging and Society, 18,* 421–439.

Birren, J. E. (1988). A contribution to the theory of the psychology of aging: As a counterpart of development. In J. E. Birren & V. L. Bengtson (Eds.), *Emergent theories of aging* (pp. 153–176). New York: Springer.

Birren, J. E., & Deutchman, D. E. (1991). *Guiding autobiography groups for older adults: Exploring the fabric of life.* Baltimore: Johns Hopkins.

Birren, J. E., & Deutchman, D. E. (2005). Guided autobiography groups. In B. Haight & F. Gibson (Eds.), *Burnside's working with older adults: Group process and techniques* (4th ed., pp. 191–204). Boston: Jones & Bartlett.

Blakemore, K. (1999). International migration in later life: Social care and policy implications. *Ageing and Society, 19*, 761–774.

Blando, J. A. (2001). Twice hidden: Older gay and lesbian couples, friends, and intimacy. *Generations, XXV*(2), 87–90.

Blando, J. (2006). Spirituality, religion and counseling. *Counseling and Human Development, 39*(2), 1–16.

Bohlmeijer, E., Smit, F., & Cuijpers, P. (2003). Effects of reminiscence and life review on late-life depression: A meta-analysis. *International Journal of Geriatric Psychiatry, 18*, 1088–1094.

Bowen, M. (1978/1994). *Family therapy in clinical practice.* Northvale, NJ: Aronson.

Bowins, B. (2004). Psychological defense mechanisms: A new perspective. *American Journal of Psychoanalysis, 64*(1), 1–26.

Bowlby, J. (1988). *A secure base: Parent–child attachment and healthy human development.* New York: Basic.

Braam, A. W., Bramsen, I., van Tilburg, T. G., van der Ploeg, H. M., & Deeg, D. J. H. (2006). Cosmic transcendence and framework of meaning in life: Patterns among older adults in the Netherlands. *Journal of Gerontology: Social Sciences, 61B*(3), S121–S128.

Brennan, M., Horowitz, A., & Su, Y.-P. (2005). Dual sensory loss and its impact on everyday competence. *The Gerontologist, 45*(3), 337–346.

Brennan, P. L., Schutte, K. K., & Moos, R. H. (2005). Pain and use of alcohol to manage pain: Prevalence and 3-year outcomes among older problem and non-problem drinkers. *Addiction, 100*, 777–786.

Bridgewater, D. (1992). A gay male survivor of antigay violence. In S. H. Dworkin & F. J. Gutierrez (Eds.), *Counseling gay men and lesbians: Journey to the end of the rainbow* (pp. 219–230). Alexandria, VA: American Counseling Association.

Brooks, C. W., & Matthews, C. O. (2000). The relationship among substance abuse counselors' spiritual well-being, values, and self-actualizing characteristics and the impact on clients' well-being. *Journal of Addictions and Offender Counseling, 21*(1), 23–33.

Burnside, I., & Haight, B. K. (1992). Reminiscence and life review: Analysing each concept. *Journal of Advanced Nursing, 17*, 855–862.

Burr, J. A., & Mutchler, J. E. (2007). Employment in later life: A focus on race/ethnicity and gender. *Generations, XXXI*(1), 37–44.

Butzenberger, K., & Fedorova, M. (1989). [Interpretations of Buddhism and classical Indian medicine]. [Abstract]. *Sudhoffs Archives, 73*(1), 88–109. (Article in German)

Cahill, S., South, K., & Spade, J. (2000). *Outing age: Public policy issues affecting gay, lesbian, bisexual and transgender elders.* New York: Policy Institute of the National Gay and Lesbian Task Force Foundation.

Canaff, A. L. (1997). Later life career planning: A new challenge for career counselors. *Journal of Employment Counseling, 34,* 86–93.

Capitman, J., & Reynoso-Vallejo, H. (2007). *Cultural competence vs. cultural humility.* Portland, ME: Community Partnerships for Older Adults. Retrieved June 1, 2009, from http://www.partnershipsforolderadults.org/resources/levelthree.aspx?sectionGUID=774e17bd-fa1e-4253-8d6d-34d808334fb0

Carlson, J., & Kjos, D. (2000). *Cognitive-behavioral therapy with Dr. John Krumboltz: Psychotherapy with the experts* [Video]. Upper Saddle River, NJ: Pearson (Merrill).

Carlson, T. D., Kirkpatrick, D., Hecker, L., & Killmer, M. (2002). Religion, spirituality, and marriage and family therapy: A study of family therapists' beliefs about the appropriateness of addressing religious and spiritual issues in therapy. *American Journal of Family Therapy, 30,* 157–171.

Caro, C. M. (2007, August). *Inquiry into the dimensions and transformational potential of existential grief.* Paper presented at the 115th annual convention of the American Psychological Association, San Francisco, CA.

Center for Applied Special Technology. (2009a). *UDL guidelines.* Wakefield, MA: Author. Retrieved November 20, 2009, from http://www.cast.org/publications/UDLguidelines/index.html

Center for Applied Special Technology. (2009b). *UDL guidelines: Version 1.0.* Wakefield, MA: Author. Retrieved November 20, 2009, from http://www.udlcenter.org/aboutudl/udlguidelines

Centers for Disease Control and Prevention and the Merck Company Foundation. (2007). *The state of aging and health in America 2007.* Whitehouse Station, NJ: Merck Company Foundation.

Chao, S.-Y., Liu, H.-Y., Wu, C.-Y., Jin, S.-F., Chu, T.-L., Huang, T.-S., et al. (2006). The effects of group reminiscence therapy on depression, self esteem, and life satisfaction of elderly nursing home residents. *Journal of Nursing Research, 14*(1), 36–44.

Cheng, S. K. (1990). Understanding the culture and behaviour of East Asians—A Confucian perspective. Retrieved December 19, 2007, from http://www.ncbi.nlm.nih.gov/sites/entrez?Db=pubmed&Cmd=ShowDetailView&TermToSearch=2073227&ordinalpos=2 2&itool=EntrezSystem2.PEntrez.Pubmed.Pubmed_ResultsPanel. Pubmed_RVDocSum

Cheraghi, M. A., Payne, S., & Salsali, M. (2005). Spiritual aspects of end-of-life care for Muslim patients: Experiences from Iran. *International Journal of Palliative Nursing, 11*(9), 468–474.

Cicero. (2001). *Treatises on friendship and old age* (E. S. Shuckburgh, Trans.). Champaign, IL: Project Gutenberg.

Cigolle, C. T., Langa, K. M., Kabeto, M. U., Tian, Z., & Blaum, C. S. (2007). Geriatric conditions and disability: The Health and Retirement Study. *Annals of Internal Medicine, 147*, 156–164.

Claudel, B. (2004). Psychanalitic [*sic*] psychotherapy: Practice and indications in the aged. *Psychologie Neuropsychiatrie du Vieillissement, 2*(3), 191–195.

Cleveland Clinic. (2007). *Types of dementia.* Cleveland, OH: Author. Retrieved December 10, 2007, from http://www.clevelandclinic.org/health/health-info/docs/2300/2340.asp?index=9170

Cohen, K. B. H. (1998). Native American medicine. *Alternative Therapies in Health and Medicine, 4*(6), 45–57. Retrieved January 22, 2008, from http://0-web.ebscohost.com.opac.sfsu.edu

Coleman, P. G. (2005). Reminiscence: Developmental, social and clinical perspectives. In M. L. Johnson (Ed.), *The Cambridge handbook of age and ageing* (pp. 301–309). Cambridge, UK: Cambridge University Press.

Coley, N., Andrieu, S., Gardette, V., Gillette-Guyonnet, S., Sanz, C., Bruno Vellas, B., & Grand, A. (2008). Dementia prevention: Methodological explanations for inconsistent results. *Epidemiologic Reviews, 30*(1), 35–66. Retrieved March 7, 2010, from http://epirev.oxfordjournals.org/cgi/content/full/30/1/35

Community Partnerships for Older Adults. (2007a). *Inclusion and diversity.* Portland, ME: Author. Retrieved from http://www.partnershipsforolderadults.org/resources/levelone.aspx?sectionGUID=8da7bbe9-2d4b-4c2e-8a49-ff12b211ae54

Community Partnerships for Older Adults. (2007b). *Inclusion, diversity key to strong community partnerships.* Portland, ME: Author. Retrieved March 20, 2010, from http://www.partnershipsforolderadults.org/resources/resource.aspx?resourceGUID=8c0b3739-c049-4f19-84eb-29c6ad8caf28&sectionGUID=43caf1ac-99a7-4a32-9a67-ccca5e4ff309

Corbett, L., & Stein, M. (2005). Contemporary Jungian approaches to spiritually oriented psychotherapy. In L. Sperry & E. P. Shafranske (Eds.), *Spiritually oriented psychotherapy* (pp. 51–74). Washington, DC: American Psychological Association.

Cortese, A. J. (1999). Ethical issues in a subculturally diverse society. In T. F. Johnson (Ed.), *Handbook on ethical issues in aging* (pp. 24–58). Westport, CT: Greenwood.

Coward, H., Sidhu, T., & Singer, D. (2000). Bioethics for clinicians: 19. Hinduism and Sikhism. *CMAJ: Canadian Medical Association Journal, 163*(9), 1167–1170.

Crawford, S. C. (2003). *Hindu bioethics for the 21st century.* Albany: State University of New York Press.

Crowell, S. (2004). *Existentialism.* Retrieved March 11, 2008, from http://plato.stanford.edu/entries/existentialism/

Crowther, M. R., Parker, M. W., Achenbaum, W. A., Larimore, W. L., & Koenig, H. G. (2002). Rowe and Kahn's model of successful aging revisited: Positive spirituality—The forgotten factor. *The Gerontologist, 42*(5), 613–620.

Csikszentmihalyi, M. (1991). *Flow: The psychology of optimal experience.* New York: Harper.

Cuijpers, P., van Straten, A., & Smit, F. (2006). Psychological treatment of late-life depression: A meta-analysis of randomized controlled trials. *International Journal of Geriatric Psychiatry, 21,* 1139–1149.

Dalby, P. (2006). Is there a process of spiritual change or development associated with ageing? A critical review of research. *Aging and Mental Health, 10*(1), 4–12.

Dalton, D. S., Cruickshanks, K. J., Klein, B. E. K., Klein, R., Wiley, T. L., & Nondahl, D. M. (2003). The impact of hearing loss on quality of life in older adults. *The Gerontologist, 43*(5), 661–668.

Danner, D. D., Snowdon, D. A., & Friesen, W. V. (2001). Positive emotions in early life and longevity: Findings from the Nun Study. *Journal of Personality and Social Psychology, 80*(5), 804–813.

Dawkins, R. (2006). *The God delusion.* Boston: Houghton Mifflin.

DeAngelis, T. (1994). More research is needed on gay, lesbian concerns. *APA Monitor, 25*(9), 39.

DeLeo, D., Bertolote, J., & Lester, D. (2002). Self-directed violence. In E. G. Krug, L. L. Dahlberg, J. A. Mercy, A. Zwi, & R. Lozano (Eds.), *World report on violence and health.* Geneva, Switzerland: World Health Organization. Retrieved November 23, 2007, from http://www.who.int/violence_injury_prevention/violence/global_campaign/en/chap7.pdf

Dennis, H., & Thomas, K. (2007). Ageism in the workplace. *Generations, XXXI*(1), 84–89.

Desai, P. N. (1988). Medical ethics in India. *Journal of Medical Philosophy, 13*(3), 321–255.

De Vries, B., & Watt, D. (1996). A lifetime of events: Age and gender variations in the life story. *Journal of Aging and Human Development, 42*(2), 81–102.

Didion, J. (2006). *We tell ourselves stories in order to live: Collected nonfiction.* New York: Everyman's Library.

Diener, E. (2000). Subjective well-being: The science of happiness and a proposal for a national index. *American Psychologist, 55*(1), 34–43.

Doherty, W. J. (2003). A wake up call: Comment on "Lived religion and family therapy." *Family Process, 42*(1), 181–183.

Domoff, G. W. (2009). *Who rules America?* Santa Cruz, CA: Author. Retrieved June 3, 2009, from http://sociology.ucsc.edu/whorulesamerica/power/wealth.html

Donahue, P., & McDonald, L. (2005). Gay and lesbian aging: Current perspectives and future directions for social work practice and research. *Families in Society: The Journal of Contemporary Social Services, 86*(3), 359–366.

Donovan, T. (2002). Being transgender and older: A first person account. *Journal of Gay and Lesbian Social Services, 13*(4), 19–22.

Dorff, E. N. (2005). End-of-life: Jewish perspectives. *The Lancet, 366,* 862–865.

Drebing, C. E., Losardo, M., Van Ormer, A., Krebs, C., Penk, W., Nasser, E., et al. (2002). Vocational rehabilitation and older adults: Patterns in participation and outcome. *Journal of Rehabilitation, 68*(3), 24–32.

Duffy, R. D., & Blustein, D. L. (2005). The relationship between spirituality, religiousness, and career adaptability. *Journal of Vocational Behavior, 67*(3), 429–440.

Edwards, B. (1986). *Drawing on the artist within: How to release your hidden creativity.* London: HarperCollins.

Eisenhandler, S. A. (2005). "Religion is the finding thing": An evolving spirituality in late life. *Journal of Gerontological Social Work, 45*(1–2), 85–103.

Elkins, D. N. (2005). A humanistic approach to spiritually oriented psychotherapy. In L. Sperry & E. P. Shafranske (Eds.), *Spiritually oriented psychotherapy* (pp. 131–152). Washington, DC: American Psychological Association.

Engardio, P., & Matlack, C. (January 31, 2005). Global aging. *BusinessWeek.*

Engelhardt, H. T., & Iltis, A. S. (2005). End-of-life: The traditional Christian view. *The Lancet, 366,* 1045–1049.

Erford, B. T., Eaves, S. H., Bryant, E. M., & Young, K. A. (2010). *35 techniques every counselor should know.* Upper Saddle River, NJ: Pearson.

Erikson, E. (1963/1987). *Childhood and society* (2nd ed.). New York: Norton.

Erikson, E. (1982). *The life cycle completed.* New York: Norton.

Ewing, J. A. (1984). Detecting alcoholism: The CAGE questionnaire. *JAMA: Journal of the American Medical Association, 252,* 1905–1907.

Fallott, R. D. (2001). Spirituality and religion in psychiatric rehabilitation and recovery from mental illness. *International Review of Psychiatry, 13*, 110–116.

Family Caregiver Alliance. (2007a). *Fact sheet: Dementia.* San Francisco, CA: Author. Retrieved December 10, 2007, from http://www.caregiver.org/caregiver/jsp/print_friendly.jsp?nodeid=569

Family Caregiver Alliance. (2007b). *Fact sheet: Dementia and driving.* San Francisco, CA: Author. Retrieved December 10, 2007, from http://www.caregiver.org/caregiver/jsp/print_firnedly.jsp?nodeid=432

Family Caregiver Alliance. (2007c). *Fact sheet: Dementia, caregiving and controlling frustration.* San Francisco, CA: Author. Retrieved December 10, 2007, from http://www.caregiver.org/caregiver/jsp/print_friendly.jsp?nodeid=891

Family Caregiver Alliance. (2007d). *Sexuality and dementia.* San Francisco, CA: Author. Retrieved December 10, 2007, from http://www.caregiver.org/caregiver/jsp/print_firnedly.jsp?nodeid=677

Family Caregiver Alliance. (2008). *Vision loss.* San Francisco: Author. Retrieved February 20, 2009, from http://www.caregiver.org/caregiver/jsp/content_node.jsp?nodeid=2222

Federal Interagency Forum on Aging-Related Statistics. (2008). *Older Americans 2008: Key indicators of well-being.* Washington, DC: Author.

Firestone, R. W. (1993). Individual defenses against death anxiety. *Death Studies, 17*, 497–515.

Firth, S. (2005). End-of-life: A Hindu view. *The Lancet, 366*, 682–686.

Fitchett, G., Rybarczyk, B. D., DeMarco, G. A., & Nicholas, J. J. (1999). The role of religion in medical rehabilitation outcomes: A longitudinal study. *Rehabilitation Psychology, 44*(4), 333–353.

Flinders, S. L. (2003). The internal struggles of aging. *Journal for the Psychoanalysis of Culture and Society, 8*(2), 258–262.

Flint, A. J. (2005). Generalised anxiety disorder in elderly patients. *Drugs and Aging, 22*(2), 101–114.

Forest, P.-G. (2007). *Social justice in an aging society.* Montreal, Quebec: Pierre Elliott Trudeau Foundation. Retrieved March 21, 2009, from www.edad-vida.org/Congres2007/PonenciaPierre-GerlierForest.pdf

Fortner, B. V., & Neimeyer, R. A. (1999). Death anxiety in older adults: A quantitative review. *Death Studies, 23*, 387–411.

Fosshage, J. L. (1998). Self psychology and its contributions to psychoanalysis: An overview. *Journal of Analytic Social Work, 5*(2), 1–17.

Fox, R. C. (2007). Gay grows up: An interpretive study of aging metaphors and queer identity. *Journal of Homosexuality, 52*(3–4), 33–61.

Freud, A. (1936/1966). *The ego and the mechanisms of defense* (C. Baines, Trans., Rev. ed.). Madison, CT: International Universities Press.

Fuller-Thomson, E. (2005). Canadian First Nations grandparents raising grandchildren: A portrait in resilience. *International Journal of Aging and Human Development, 60*(4), 331–342.

Fuller-Thomson, E., Minkler, M., & Driver, D. (1997). A profile of grandparents raising grandchildren in the United States. *The Gerontologist, 37*(3), 406–412.

Gabbard, G. O. (1990). *Psychodynamic psychiatry in clinical practice.* Washington, DC: American Psychiatric Press.

Gable, S. L., & Haidt, J. (2005). What (and why) is positive psychology? *Review of General Psychology, 9*(2), 103–110.

Galinsky, E. (2007). The changing landscape of work. *Generations, XXXI*(1), 16–22.

Gallagher-Thompson, D., Thompson, L. W., & Rider, K. L. (n.d.). *California older person's pleasant events schedule.* Retrieved February 1, 2010, from http://oafc.stanford.edu/coppes.html

Gallo, J. J., & Katz, I. (2006). *Depression.* New York: American Geriatrics Society. Retrieved November 29, 2007, from http://www.american-geriatrics.org/education/forum/depression.shtml

Gallo, J. J., & Lebowitz, B. D. (1999). The epidemiology of common late-life mental disorders in the community: Themes for the new century. *Psychiatric Services, 50*(9), 1158–1166.

Garrett, J. T., & Garrett, M. W. (1994). The path of good medicine: Understanding and counseling Native American Indians. Retrieved January 22, 2008, from http://0-web.ebscohost.com.opac.sfsu.edu/ehost/detail?vid=13&hid=4&sid=2e850d10-f660-492f-b115-d656fbd446c9%40SRCSM2

Gatrad, A. R., & Sheikh, A. (2001). Medical ethics and Islam: Principles and practice. *Archives of Disease in Childhood, 84*(1), 72–75.

Gibson, F., & Burnside, I. (2005). Reminiscence group work. In B. Haight & F. Gibson (Eds.), *Burnside's working with older adults: Group process and techniques* (4th ed., pp. 175–190). Boston: Jones & Bartlett.

Goldsmith, S. K., Pellmar, T. C., Kleinman, A. M., & Bunney, W. E. (Eds.). (2002). *Reducing suicide: A national imperative.* Washington, DC: National Academy Press. Retrieved November 28, 2007, from http://www.nap.edu/books/0309083214/html/

Gomez, R. G., & Madey, S. F. (2001). Coping-with-hearing-loss model for older adults. *Journal of Gerontology: Psychological Sciences, 56B*(4), P223–P225.

Goodman, C. C., & Silverstein, M. (2005). Latina grandmothers raising grandchildren: Acculturation and psychological well-being. *International Journal of Aging and Human Development, 60*(4), 305–316.

Gorenstein, E. E., & Papp, L. A. (1995, August). *Cognitive-behavioral treatment of late-life anxiety disorders.* Paper presented at the annual meeting of the American Psychological Association, New York.

Gross, J. J., Carstensen, L. L., Pasupathi, M., Tsai, J., Skorpen, C. G., & Hsu, A. Y. C. (1997). Emotion and aging: Experience, expression and control. *Psychology and Aging, 12*(4), 590–599.

Grube, G. M. A., & Reeve, C. D. C. (1992). *Plato: Republic.* Cambridge, MA: Hackett.

Guo, Z. (1995). Chinese Confucian culture and the medical ethical tradition. *Journal of Medical Ethics, 21*(4), 239–246.

Haight, B., & Gibson, F. (2005). *Burnside's working with older adults: Group process and techniques* (4th ed.). Boston: Jones & Bartlett.

Haight, B. K., & Haight, B. S. (2007). *The handbook of structured life review.* Baltimore: Health Professions Press.

Haight, R. S. (2005). Group psychotherapy. In B. Haight & F. Gibson (Eds.), *Burnside's working with older adults: Group process and techniques* (4th ed., pp. 233–245). Boston: Jones & Bartlett.

Hall, C. R., Dixon, W. A., & Mauzey, E. D. (2004). Spirituality and religion: Implications for counselors. *Journal of Counseling and Development, 82,* 504–507.

Hansen, C. (2007). Taoism. In E. N. Zalta (Ed.), *The Stanford encyclopedia of philosophy.* Stanford, CA: Stanford University Press. Retrieved January 22, 2008, from http://plato.stanford.edu/entries/taoism/#Important

Hanson, M., & Gutheil, I. A. (2004). Motivational strategies with alcohol-involved older adults: Implications for social work practice. *Social Work, 49*(3), 364–372.

Harper, M. C., & Shoffner, M. F. (2004). Counseling for continued career development after retirement: An application of the theory of work adjustment. *Career Development Quarterly, 52,* 272–284.

Hartz, G. W. (2005). *Spirituality and mental health: Clinical applications.* Binghamton, NY: Haworth.

Hattie, J. A., Myers, J. E., & Sweeney, T. J. (2004). A factor structure of wellness: Theory, assessment, analysis, and practice. *Journal of Counseling and Development, 82,* 354–364.

Hays, J. C., Meador, K. G., Branch, P. S., & George, L. K. (2001). The Spiritual History Scale in four dimensions (SHS-4): Validity and reliability. *The Gerontologist, 41*(2), 239–249.

Hayslip, B., Henderson, C. E., & Shore, R. J. (2003). The structure of grandparental role meaning. *Journal of Adult Development, 10*(1), 1–11.

Hendrix, L. R. (2001). *Curriculum in ethnogeriatrics: Ethnic specific modules; American Indian/Alaska Native*. Stanford, CA: Collaborative on Ethnogeriatric Education, Stanford Geriatric Education Center. Retrieved July 8, 2005, from www.stanford.edu/group/ethnoger

Henry J. Kaiser Family Foundation. (2009). *Poverty rate by age, states (2006–2007), U.S. (2007)*. Menlo Park, CA: Author. Retrieved June 4, 2009, from http://statehealthfacts.org/comparetable.jsp?ind=10&cat=1

Hepple, J. (2004). Psychotherapies with older people: An overview. *Advances in Psychiatric Treatment, 10*, 371–377.

Herdt, G., & de Vries, B. (2003). *Gay and lesbian aging: Research and future directions*. New York: Springer.

Herdt, G., & Kerzner, R. (2006). I do, but I can't: The impact of marriage denial on the mental health and sexual citizenship of lesbians and gay men in the United States. *Sexuality Research and Social Policy: Journal of the NSRC, 13*(1), 33–49.

Herek, G. M. (1989). Hate crimes against lesbians and gay men: Issues for research and policy. *American Psychologist, 44*, 948–955.

Herring, R. D. (1991). Counseling Native American youth. In C. C. Lee & B. L. Richardson (Eds.), *Multicultural issues in counseling: New approaches to diversity* (pp. 37–47). Alexandria, VA: American Counseling Association.

Hill, R. D. (2006). *Positive aging: A guide for mental health professionals and consumers*. New York: Norton.

Hinterkopf, E. (2005). The experiential focusing approach. In L. Sperry & E. P. Shafranske (Eds.), *Spiritually oriented psychotherapy* (pp. 207–234). Washington, DC: American Psychological Association.

Hodge, D. R. (2003). The intrinsic spirituality scale: A new six-item instrument for assessing the salience of spirituality as a motivational construct. *Journal of Social Service Research, 30*(1), 41–61.

Hoffer, E. (2008, January 19). The secret of happiness: It's in Iceland. *The Economist*, pp. 90–91.

Homma-True, R. (1990). Psychotherapeutic issues with Asian American women. *Sex Roles, 22*(7–8), 477–486.

Hopkins, E., Woods, Z., Kelley, R., Bently, K., & Murphey, J. (1995). *Working with groups on spiritual themes*. Duluth, MN: Whole Person Associates.

Horney, K. (1992). *Our inner conflicts: A constructive theory of neurosis*. New York: Norton. (Original work published 1945)

Horowitz, A., Brennan, M., & Reinhardt, J. P. (2005). Prevalence and risk factors for self-reported visual impairment among middle-aged and older adults. *Research on Aging, 27*(3), 307–326.

Hsieh, H.-F., & Wang, J.-J. (2003). Effect of reminiscence therapy on depression in older adults: A systematic review. *International Journal of Nursing Studies, 40*, 335–345.

Ingersoll, R. E., & Bauer, A. L. (2004). An integral approach to spiritual wellness in school counseling settings. *Professional School Counseling, 7*(5), 301–308.

Institute of Alcohol Studies. (2007). *Alcohol and the elderly.* Cambridgeshire, UK: Author.

Istar Lev, A. (2004). *Transgender emergence: Therapeutic guidelines for working with gender-variant people and their families.* Binghamton, NY: Haworth.

Ivey, A., Ivey, M., Myers, J., & Sweeney, T. (2005). *Developmental counseling and therapy: Promoting wellness over the lifespan.* Boston: Houghton Mifflin/Lahaska.

Ivey, A. E., Ivey, M. B., & Zalaquett, C. P. (2009). *Intentional interviewing and counseling: Facilitating client development in a multicultural society* (7th ed.). Belmont, CA: Brooks/Cole.

Johnson, C. V., & Hayes, J. A. (2003). Troubled spirits: Prevalence and predictors of religious and spiritual concerns among university students and counseling center clients. *Journal of Counseling Psychology, 50*(4), 409–419.

Johnson, F., Foxall, M., Kelleher, E., Kentopp, E., Mannlein, E., & Cook, E. (1988). Comparison of mental health and life satisfaction of five elderly ethnic groups. *Western Journal of Nursing Research, 10*, 613–628.

Johnson, K. (2004). Grief in North America: A death denying society. *Journal of Palliative Nursing, 10*(9), 435.

Jones, B. E. (2001). Is having the luck of growing old in the gay, lesbian, bisexual, transgender community good or bad luck? *Journal of Gay and Lesbian Social Services, 13*(4), 13–14.

Jonson, H., & Magnusson, J. A. (2001). A new age of old age? Gerotranscendence and the re-enchantment of aging. *Journal of Aging Studies, 15*, 317–331.

Jordan, M. B. (1993). Diversity issues concerning therapists: Diagnosis and training. *Independent Practitioner, 13*(5), 216–218.

Judaism. (2008). In *British Broadcasting Association.* Retrieved January 23, 2008, from http://www.bbc.co.uk/schools/religion/Judaism

Kabat-Zinn, J. (2005). *Full catastrophe living: Using the wisdom of your body and mind to face stress, pain, and illness.* New York: Bantam Dell.

Kahn, M. (1997). *Between therapist and client: The new relationship* (Rev. ed.). New York: Freeman.

Kennedy, G. J. (2000). *Geriatric mental health care: A treatment guide for health professionals*. New York: Guilford.

Keown, D. (2005). End of life: The Buddhist view. *The Lancet, 366*, 952–955.

Kilpatrick, S. D., & McCullough, M. E. (1999). Religion and spirituality in rehabilitation psychology. *Rehabilitation Psychology, 44*(4), 388–402.

Kim, A., & Merriam, S. B. (2004). Motivations for learning among older adults in a learning in retirement institute. *Educational Gerontology, 30*(6), 441–455.

Kim, S. H. (2005). Confucian bioethics and cross-cultural considerations in health care decision-making [Abstract]. *Journal of Nursing Law, 10*(3), 161–166. Retrieved December 19, 2007, from http://www.ncbi.nlm.nih.gov/sites/entrez?db=pubmed&Cmd=ShowDetailView&TermToSearch=16832930&ordinalpos=1&itool=EntrezSystem2.PEntrez.Pubmed.Pubmed_ResultsPanel.Pubmed_RVDocSum

Kimmel, D. (2002). Aging and sexual orientation. In B. E. Jones & M. J. Hill (Eds.), *Mental health issues in lesbian, gay, bisexual, and transgender communities* (pp. 17–36). Washington, DC: American Psychiatric Publishing.

Kimmel, D., Rose, T., & David, S. (Eds.). (2006). *Lesbian, gay, bisexual, and transgender aging: Research and clinical perspectives*. New York: Columbia University Press.

King, D. A., & Markus, H. E. (2000). Mood disorders in older adults. In S. Krauss Whitbourne (Ed.), *Psychopathology in later adulthood (pp. 141–172)*. New York: Wiley.

King, P. H. M. (1974). Notes on the psychoanalysis of older patients: Reappraisal of the potentialities for change during the second half of life. *Journal of Analytic Psychology, 19*, 22–37.

Kinsella, K., & Velkoff, V. A. (2001). *An aging world: 2001*. Washington, DC: U.S. Census Bureau.

Knight, B. G. (2004). *Psychotherapy with older adults* (3rd ed.). Thousand Oaks, CA: Sage.

Knight, B. G., & Satre, D. D. (1999). Cognitive behavioral psychotherapy with older adults. *Clinical Psychology: Science and Practice, 6*(2), 188–203.

Kohli, M. (2006). Aging and justice. In R. H. Binstock & L. K. George (Eds.), *Handbook of aging and the social sciences* (6th ed., pp. 456–478). San Diego, CA: Academic Press. Retrieved March 20, 2009, from www.iue.it/SPS/People/Faculty/CurrentProfessors/PDFFiles/KohliPDFfiles/Aging&JusticeCh25Handbook.pdf

Kolomer, S. R., & McCallion, P. (2005). Depression and caregiver mastery in grandfathers caring for their grandchildren. *International Journal of Aging and Human Development, 60*(4), 283–294.

Kosmin, B. A., Mayer, E., & Keysar, A. (2005). *American religious identification survey.* Retrieved July 22, 2006 from http:///www.gc.cuny.edu/faculty/research_briefs/aris/religion_ethnicity.htm

Kottler, J. A. (2000). *Nuts and bolts of helping.* Needham Heights, MA: Allyn & Bacon.

Kraus, C. A., Kunik, M. E., & Stanley, M. A. (2007). Use of cognitive behavioral therapy in late-life psychiatric disorders. *Geriatrics, 62*(6), 21–26.

Kulmala, J., Viljanen, A., Sipila, S., Pajala, S., Parssinen, O., Kauppinen, M., Koskenvuo, M., Kaprio, J., & Rantanen, T. (2008, November). Poor vision accompanied with other sensory impairments as a predictor of falls in older women. *Age and Ageing,* 1–6.

LaFromboise, T. D., Berman, J. S., & Sohi, B. K. (1994). American Indian women. In L. Comas-Diaz & B. Greene (Eds.), *Women of color: Integrating ethnic and gender identities in psychotherapy.* New York: Guilford.

Laidlaw, K., Thompson, L. W., Dick-Siskin, L., & Gallagher-Thompson, D. (2003). *Cognitive behavior therapy with older people.* New York: Wiley.

Lam, B. L., Lee, D. J., Gomez-Marin, O., Zheng, D. D., & Caban, A. J. (2006). Concurrent visual and hearing impairment and risk of mortality: The national health interview survey. *Archives of Ophthalmology, 124,* 95–101.

Langer, N. (2004). Resiliency and spirituality: Foundations of strengths perspective counseling with the elderly. *Educational Gerontology, 30,* 611–617.

Laurin, D., Verreault, R., Lindsay, J., MacPherson, K., & Rockwood, K. (2001). Physical activity and risk of cognitive impairment and dementia in elderly persons. *Archives of Neurology, 58,* 498–504.

Lazarus, L. W., Cohler, B. J., & Lesser, J. (1996). Self-psychology: Its application to understanding patients with Alzheimer's disease. *International Psychogeriatrics, 8*(Suppl. 3), 253–258.

Le, C. N. (2006). Asian-nation: The landscape of Asian America. *Socioeconomic Statistics and Demographics.* Retrieved June 26, 2009, from www.asian-nation.org/demograhpics.shtml

Leahy, M. J., Muenzen, P., Saunders, J. L., & Strauser, D. (2009). Essential knowledge domains underlying effective rehabilitation counseling practice. *Rehabilitation Counseling Bulletin, 52*(2), 95–106.

Lee, W. M. L., Blando, J. A., Mizelle, N., & Orozco, G. (2007). *Introduction to multicultural counseling for helping professionals* (2nd ed.). New York: Routledge.

LeVay, S., & Valente, S. M. (2006). *Human sexuality* (2nd ed.). Sunderland, MA: Sinauer.

Levenson, M. R., Jennings, P. A., Aldwin, C. M., & Shiraishi, R. W. (2005). Self-transcendence: Conceptualization and measurement. *International Journal of Aging and Human Development, 60*(2), 127–143.

Lin, Y.-C., Dai, Y.-T., & Hwang, S.-L. (2003). The effect of reminiscence on the elderly population: A systematic review. *Public Health Nursing, 20*(4), 297–306.

Logan, C. R. (1997). It takes a village to care for a lesbian. *Counseling Today, 39*(9), 29, 35, 55.

Luborsky, L., & Barrett, M. S. (2006). The history and empirical status of key psychoanalytic concepts. In S. N. Hoeksema, T. Cannon, & T. Widiger (Eds.), *Annual review of clinical psychology* (pp. 1–19). Palo Alto, CA: Annual Reviews.

Lukoff, D., & Lu, F. (2005). A transpersonal-integrative approach to spiritually oriented psychotherapy. In L. Sperry & E. P. Shafranske (Eds.), *Spiritually oriented psychotherapy* (pp. 177–206). Washington, DC: American Psychological Association.

Lumpkin, J. R. (2008). Grandparents in a parental or near-parental role: Sources of stress and coping mechanisms. *Journal of Family Issues, 29*(3), 357–372.

MacCluskie, K. (2010). *Acquiring counseling skills: Integrating theory, multiculturalism, and self-awareness.* Upper Saddle River, NJ: Merrill.

Magnavita, J. J. (2008). Psychoanalytic psychotherapy. In J. L. Lebow (Ed.), *Twenty first century psychotherapies: Contemporary approaches to theory and practice* (pp. 206–236). New York: Wiley.

Mannan, H. M. (1996). Death as defined by Hinduism. *Saint Louis University Public Law Review, 15*(2), 423–432.

Marmot, M. (2007, February). *Health equity in an ageing world.* Paper presented at the UN Commission for Social Development, New York.

Maselko, J., & Kubzansky, L. D. (2006). Gender differences in religious practices, spiritual experiences and health: Results from the U.S. general social survey. *Social Science and Medicine, 62*(11), 2848–2860.

Mason, B. (2008). *Taoist principles.* Retrieved January 22, 2008, from http://www.taoism.net/enter.htm

Mason, J., May, V., & Clarke, L. (2007). Ambivalence and the paradoxes of grandparenting. *The Sociological Review, 55*(4), 687–706.

Massimini, F., & Delle Fave, A. (2000). Individual development in a bio-cultural perspective. *American Psychologist, 55*(1), 24–33.

Matheson, L. (1986). If you are not an Indian, how do you treat an Indian? In H. Lefley (Ed.), *Cross-cultural training for mental health professionals* (pp. 115–130). Springfield, IL: Charles C. Thomas.

Mayo Foundation for Medical Education and Research. (2007a). *Dementia: It's not always Alzheimer's.* Rochester, MN: Author. Retrieved December 10, 2007, from http://www.mayoclinic.com/print/dementia/AZ00003/METHOD=print

Mayo Foundation for Medical Education and Research. (2007b). *Sundowning: Late-day confusion.* Rochester, MN: Author. Retrieved December 10, 2007, from http://www.mayoclinic.com/print/sundowning/HQ01463/METHOD=print

McFarland, C., Ross, M., & Giltrow, M. (1992). Biased recollections in older adults: The role of implicit theories of aging. *Journal of Personality and Social Psychology, 62*(5), 837–850.

McGoldrick, M., Pearce, J. K., & Giordano, J. (Eds.). (1982). *Ethnicity and family therapy.* New York: Guilford.

McHenry, B., & McHenry, J. (2007). *What therapists say and why they say it: Effective therapeutic responses and techniques.* Boston: Allyn & Bacon.

McKee, P., & Barber, C. E. (2001). Plato's theory of aging. *Journal of Aging and Identity, 6*(2), 93–104.

Medvedev, Z. A. (1990). An attempt at a rational classification of theories of aging. *Biological Reviews of the Cambridge Philosophical Society, 65*(3), 375–398.

Mehta, K. (1997). The impact of religious beliefs and practices on aging: A cross-cultural comparison. *Journal of Aging Studies, 11*(2), 101–114.

Michie, F., Glachan, M., & Bray, D. (2001). An evaluation of factors influencing the academic self-concept, self-esteem and academic stress for direct and re-entry students in higher education. *Educational Psychology, 21*(4), 455–472.

Mijares, S. G., & Khalsa, G. S. (Eds.). (2005). *The psychospiritual clinician's handbook: Alternative methods for understanding and treating mental disorders.* Binghamton, NY: Haworth.

Mikulas, W. L. (2002). *The integrative helper: Convergence of Eastern and Western traditions.* Pacific Grove, CA: Brooks/Cole.

Mikulincer, M., Florian, V., & Hirschberger, G. (2007, August). *Existential perspective on close relationships.* Paper presented at the 115th annual convention of the American Psychological Association, San Francisco, CA.

Miller, L. (2005). Interpersonal psychotherapy from a spiritual perspective. In L. Sperry & E. P. Shafranske (Eds.), *Spiritually oriented psychotherapy* (pp. 153–175). Washington, DC: American Psychological Association.

Miller, W. R., & Rollnick, S. (2002). *Motivational interviewing* (2nd ed.). New York: Guilford.

Minuchin, S., & Fishman, H. C. (2004). *Family therapy techniques.* Cambridge, MA: Harvard University Press.

Mitchell, S. A., & Black, M. J. (1995). *Freud and beyond: A history of modern psychoanalytic thought.* New York: Basic Books.

Mizuno, T., & Slingsby, B. T. (2007). Eye on religion: Considering the influence of Buddhist and Shinto thought on contemporary Japanese bioethics. *Southern Medical Journal, 100*(1), 115–117.

Moen, P. (2007). Not so big jobs and retirements: What workers (and retirees) really want. *Generations, XXXI*(1), 31–36.

Moos, R. H., Brennan, P. L., Schutte, K. K., & Moos, B. S. (2004). High-risk alcohol consumption and late-life alcohol use problems. *American Journal of Public Health, 94*(11), 1985–1991.

Moos, R. H., Brennan, P. L., Schutte, K. K., & Moos, B. S. (2005). Older adults' health and changes in late-life drinking patterns. *Aging and Mental Health, 9*(1), 49–59.

Moraglia, G. (1994). C. G. Jung and the psychology of adult development. *Journal of Analytic Psychology, 39,* 55–75.

Moreno Vega, M. (2001). *The altar of my soul.* New York: Ballantine.

Morrow-Howell, N. (2007). A longer worklife: The new road to volunteering. *Generations, XXXI*(1), 63–67.

Morrow-Howell, N. L., Proctor, E. K., Blinne, W. R., Rubin, E. H., Saunders, J. A., & Rozario, P. A. (2006). Post-acute dispositions of older adults hospitalized for depression. *Aging and Mental Health, 10*(4), 352–361.

Moscicki, E. K., Rae, D. S., Regier, D. A., & Locke, B. Z. (1987). The Hispanic health and nutrition examination survey: Depression among Mexican Americans, Cuban Americans, Puerto Ricans. In M. Gaviria & J. D. Arana (Eds.), *Health and behavior: Research agenda for Hispanics* (pp. 145–159). Chicago: University of Illinois at Chicago.

Moursund, J., & Kenny, M. C. (2002). *The process of counseling and therapy* (4th ed.). Upper Saddle River, NJ: Prentice Hall.

Mroczek, D. K., & Kolarz, C. M. (1998). The effect of age on positive and negative affect: A developmental perspective on happiness. *Journal of Personality and Social Psychology, 75*(5), 1333–1349.

Mui, A. C., & Kang, S.-Y. (2006). Acculturation stress and depression among Asian immigrant elders. *Social Work, 51*(3), 243–255.

Murphy, B. C. (1992). Educating mental health professionals about gay and lesbian issues. *Journal of Homosexuality, 22*(3/4), 229–246.

Murphy, B. C., & Dillon, C. (2008). *Interviewing in action in a multicultural world* (3rd ed.). Belmont, CA: Thomson Brooks/Cole.

Murphy, S. Y., Hunter, A. G., & Johnson, D. J. (2008). Transforming caregiving: African American custodial grandmothers and the child welfare system. *Journal of Sociology and Social Welfare, XXXV*(2), 67–89.

Myers, J. E. (2005). Wellness in later life: Research implications. In J. E. Myers & T. J. Sweeney (Eds.), *Counseling for wellness: Theory, research, and practice* (pp. 99–104). Alexandria, VA: American Counseling Association.

Myers, J. E., Dice, C. E., & Dew, B. J. (2000). Alcohol abuse in later life: Issues and interventions for counselors. *ADULTSPAN Journal, 2*(1), 2–14.

Myers, J. E., & Schwiebert, V. L. (1996). *Competencies for gerontological counseling.* Alexandria, VA: American Counseling Association.

National Academy on an Aging Society. (1999a). Chronic conditions: A challenge for the 21st century. *Challenges for the 21st Century: Chronic and Disabling Conditions, Number 1*(November), 1–6.

National Academy on an Aging Society. (1999b). Hearing loss: A growing problem that affects quality of life. *Challenges for the 21st Century: Chronic and Disabling Conditions, Number 2*(December), 1–6.

National Center for Injury Prevention and Control. (2007). *Suicide prevention scientific information: Risk and protective factors.* Atlanta, GA: Centers for Disease Control and Prevention. Retrieved November 20, 2007, from http://www.cdc.gov/ncipc/dvp/suicide/Suicide-risk-p-factors.htm

National Institute of Mental Health. (2007). *Numbers count: Mental disorders in America.* Bethesda, MD: Author. Retrieved December 9, 2007, from http://www.nimh.nih.gov/health/publications/the-numbers-count-mental-disorders-in-america.shtml

National Institute of Neurological Disorders and Stroke. (2007). *Dementia: Hope through research.* Bethesda, MD: Author. Retrieved December 10, 2007, from http://www.ninds.nih.gov/disorders/dementias/detail_dementia.htm?css=print

National Institute on Aging. (2007). *Forgetfulness: It's not always what you think.* Bethesda, MD: Author. Retrieved December 10, 2007, from http://www.niapublications.org/agepages/forgetfulness.asp

National Institute on Aging. (2008). *Age page: Hearing loss.* Washington, DC: Author. Retrieved February 20, 2009, from http://www.nia.nih.gov/HealthInformation/Publications/hearing.htm

National Institute on Deafness and Other Communication Disorders. (2008). *Hearing loss and older adults.* Washington, DC: Author. Retrieved February 20, 2009, from http://www.nidcd.nih.gov/health/hearing/older.asp

National Records and Archive Administration. (2010). *Bill of Rights: Amendment I.* Retrieved February 19, 2010, from http://www.archives.gov/exhibits/charters/bill_of_rights_transcript.html

Neihardt, J. G. (2004). *Black Elk speaks.* Lincoln, NE: Bison Books.

Nelson-Becker, H., Nakashima, M., & Canda, E. (2007). Spiritual assessment in aging: A framework for clinicians. *Journal of Gerontological Social Work, 48*(3–4), 331–347.

Norton, E. D. (1998). Counseling substance-abusing older clients. *Educational Gerontology, 24*(4), 373–389.

Nuttman-Shwartz, O. (2007). Is there life without work? *International Journal of Aging and Human Development, 64*(2), 129–147.

Nyce, S. A. (2007). The aging workforce: Is demography destiny? *Generations, XXXI*(1), 9–13.

O'Hanlon, B. (2006). *Pathways to spirituality: Connection, wholeness, and possibility for therapist and client.* New York: Norton.

On Lok SeniorHealth & Stanford Geriatric Education Center. (2004). *Diversity, healing and health care.* San Francisco and Stanford, CA: Author. Retrieved March 25, 2009, from www.gasi.org/diversity.htm

Open up: A special report on migration. (2008, January 5). *The Economist, 386*(8561), pp. 3–5.

Ortiz, L. P. A., & Langer, N. (2002). Assessment of spirituality and religion in later life: Acknowledging clients' needs and personal resources. *Journal of Gerontological Social Work, 37*(2), 5–21.

Patton, L. (2008). *Hermann von Helmholtz.* Stanford, CA: Stanford Encyclopedia of Philosophy. Retrieved November 25, 2009, from http://plato.stanford.edu/entries/hermann-helmholtz/

Peterson, C. (2000). The future of optimism. *American Psychologist, 55*(1), 44–55.

Peterson, C. (2006). *A primer in positive psychology.* New York: Oxford University Press.

Pew Hispanic Center. (2005). *Fact sheet: Hispanic attitudes toward learning English.* Washington, DC: Author. Retrieved June 26, 2009, from www.pewhispanic.org

Pipher, M. (1999). *Another country: Navigating the emotional terrain of our elders.* New York: Riverhead.

Polcin, D. L., & Zemore, S. (2004). Psychiatric severity and spirituality, helping, and participation in Alcoholics Anonymous during recovery. *American Journal of Drug and Alcohol Abuse, 30*(3), 577–592.

Pollak, J. M. (1979–1980). Correlates of death anxiety: A review of empirical studies. *Omega: An International Journal for the Study of Dying, Death, Bereavement, Suicide, and Other Lethal Behaviors,* 10(2), 97–116.

Pouliot, J. S. (1996). Diabetes: Are you its type? *Better Homes and Gardens,* 74(6), 74, 76, 79.

Pruchno, R. A., & Johnson, K. W. (1996). Research on grandparenting: Review of current studies and future needs. *Generations,* 20(1), 65–70.

Pyszczynski, T., Greenberg, J., Solomon, S., & Maxfield, M. (2006). On the unique psychological import of the human awareness of mortality: Theme and variations. *Psychological Inquiry,* 17(4), 328–356.

Qualls, S. H. (1999a). Family therapy with older adult clients. *JCLP/In Session: Psychotherapy in Practice,* 55(8), 977–990.

Qualls, S. H. (1999b). Realizing power in intergenerational family hierarchies: Family reorganization when older adults decline. In M. Duffy (Ed.), *Handbook of counseling and psychotherapy with older adults* (pp. 228–241). New York: Wiley.

Rando, T. (1991). *How to go on living when someone you love dies.* New York: Bantam.

Ranzijn, R. (2002). Towards a positive psychology of ageing: Potentials and barriers. *Australian Psychologist,* 37(2), 79–85.

Reker, G. T., & Wong, P. T. P. (1988). Aging as an individual process: Toward a theory of personal meaning. In J. E. Birren & V. L. Bengtson (Eds.), *Emergent theories of aging* (pp. 214–246). New York: Springer.

Richardson, C. A., Gilleard, C. J., Lieberman, S., & Peeler, R. (1994). Working with older adults and their families—A review. *Journal of Family Therapy,* 16, 225–240.

Richardson, E. H. (1981). Cultural and historical perspectives in counseling Indians. In D. W. Sue (Ed.), *Counseling the culturally different* (pp. 216–255). New York: Wiley.

Riegel, J. (2006). Confucius. In E. N. Zalta (Ed.), *The Stanford encyclopedia of philosophy.* Stanford, CA: Stanford University Press. Retrieved January 23, 2008, from http://plato.stanford.edu/entries/confucius/

Rigler, S. K. (2000). Alcoholism in the elderly. *American Family Physician,* 61(6), 1710–1724. Retrieved December 5, 2007, from http://www.aafp.org/afp/20000315/1710.html

Rinpoche, S. (1994). *The Tibetan book of living and dying.* New York: HarperOne. (Audible.com version)

Rizzuto, A.-M. (2005). Psychoanalytic considerations about spiritually oriented psychotherapy. In L. Sperry & E. P. Shafranske (Eds.), *Spiritually oriented psychotherapy* (pp. 31–50). Washington, DC: American Psychological Association.

Rogers, C. (1995). *On becoming a person.* New York: Mariner. (Original work published 1961)

Rooks, R. N., & Whitfield, K. E. (2004). Health disparities among older African Americans: Past, present, and future perspectives. In K. E. Whitfield (Ed.), *Closing the gap: Improving the health of minority elders.* Washington, DC: Gerontological Society of America.

Ross, M. E. T., & Aday, L. A. (2006). Stress and coping in African American grandparents who are raising their grandchildren. *Journal of Family Issues, 27*(7), 912–932.

Roth, S. (1990). *Psychotherapy: The art of wooing nature.* Northvale, NJ: Jason Aronson.

Rowe, J. W., & Kahn, R. L. (1997). Successful aging. *The Gerontologist, 37,* 433–440.

Ruddick, S. (2003). The politics of aging: Globalization and the restructuring of youth and childhood. *Antipode, 35*(2), 334–362.

Ryan, R. M., & Deci, E. L. (2000). Self-determination theory and the facilitation of intrinsic motivation, social development, and well-being. *American Psychologist, 55*(1), 68–78.

Sachedina, A. (2005). End-of-life: The Islamic view. *The Lancet, 366,* 774–779.

Sadler, E., & Biggs, S. (2006). Exploring the links between spirituality and "successful ageing." *Journal of Social Work Practice, 20*(3), 267–280.

Safran, J. D. (Ed.). (2003). *Psychoanalysis and Buddhism: An unfolding dialogue.* Boston: Wisdom.

Sage, G. P. (1991). Counseling American Indian adults. In C. C. Lee & B. L. Richardson (Eds.), *Multicultural issues in counseling: New approaches to diversity* (pp. 23–35). Alexandria, VA: American Counseling Association.

Sandhu, D. S. (2007). Seven stages of spiritual development: A framework to solve psycho-spiritual problems. In O. J. Morgan (Ed.), *Counseling and spirituality: Views from the profession* (pp. 64–92). Boston: Lahaska.

Santee, R. (2007). *An integrative approach to counseling.* Thousand Oaks, CA: Sage.

Saraswathi, T. S. (2005). Hindu worldview in the development of self-ways: The "Atman" as the real self. *New Directions for Child and Adolescent Development, 109,* 43–50.

Schools: Hinduism. (2008). In *British Broadcasting Association*. Retrieved January 8, 2008, from http://www.bbc.co.uk/schools/religion/hinduism/

Schroots, J. J. F. (1996a). Theories of aging: Psychological. In J. E. Birren (Ed.), *Encyclopedia of gerontology* (Vol. 2, pp. 557–567). New York: Academic Press.

Schroots, J. J. F. (1996b). Theoretical developments in the psychology of aging. *The Gerontologist, 36*(6), 742–749.

Scogin, F., Floyd, M., & Forde, J. (2000). Anxiety in older adults. In S. Krauss Whitbourne (Ed.), *Psychopathology in later adulthood* (pp. 117–140). New York: Wiley.

Scogin, F., & Shah, A. (2006). Screening older adults for depression in primary care settings. *Health Psychology, 25*(6), 675–677.

Sears, R. W. (2007, August). *Contemplation of death in existential psychotherapy and Eastern wisdom traditions*. Paper presented at the 115th annual convention of the American Psychological Association, San Francisco, CA.

Segal, D. L., Coolidge, F. L., & Mizuno, H. (2007). Defense mechanism differences between younger and older adults: A cross-sectional investigation. *Aging and Mental Health, 11*(4), 415–422.

Seifert, L. S. (2002). Toward a psychology of religion, spirituality, meaning-search, and aging: Past research and practical application. *Journal of Adult Development, 9*(1), 61–70.

Seligman, M. E. P., & Csikszentmihalyi, M. (2000). Positive psychology: An introduction. *American Psychologist, 55*, 5–14. Retrieved March 16, 2008, from http://www.ppc.sas.upenn.edu/ppintroarticle.pdf

Shafranske, E. P. (2005). A psychoanalytic approach to spiritually oriented psychotherapy. In L. Sperry & E. P. Shafranske (Eds.), *Spiritually oriented psychotherapy* (pp. 105–130). Washington, DC: American Psychological Association.

Shankle, M. D., Maxwell, C. A., Katzman, E. S., & Landers, S. (2003). An invisible population: Older lesbian, gay, bisexual, and transgender individuals. *Clinical Research and Regulatory Affairs, 20*(2), 159–182.

Shaw, B. A. (2006). Lack of emotional support from parents early in life and alcohol abuse later in life. *International Journal of Aging and Human Development, 63*(1), 49–72.

Sheldon, K. M., & King, L. (2001). Why positive psychology is necessary. *American Psychologist, 56*, 216–217.

Sher, B. (1995). *I could do anything if only I knew what it was: How to discover what you really want and how to get it*. New York: Dell. Retrieved January 13, 2009, from http://www.motivationalquotes.

com/cgi-bin/db/db.cgi?db=db&uid=default&ID=&Quote=&Autho
r=&Source=&Prayer=&Affirmation=&Keywords=aging&keywor
d=&mh=25&sb=&so=asc&view_records=View+Records

Shi, Y. (2005). *Suicide among Chinese American elderly: A review of the literature.* Unpublished manuscript, San Francisco State University.

Shibutani, T., & Kwan, K. M. (1965). *Ethnic stratification.* New York: Macmillan.

Silverstein, N. M., Choi, L. H., & Bulot, J. J. (2002). Older learners on campus. *Gerontology and Geriatrics Education, 22*(1), 13–30.

Sink, C. (2004). Spirituality and comprehensive school counseling programs. *Professional School Counseling, 7*(5), 309–317.

Sink, C. A., & Richmond, L. J. (2004). Introducing spirituality to professional school counseling. *Professional School Counseling, 7*(5), 291–292.

Smith, H. (1991). *The world's religions: Our great wisdom traditions.* San Francisco: HarperSanFrancisco.

Smyer, M. A., & Pitt-Catsouphes, M. (2007). The meaning of work for older workers. *Generations, XXXI*(1), 23–30.

Solie, D. (2004). *How to say it® to seniors: Closing the communication gap with our elders.* New York: Prentice Hall.

Sorocco, K. H., & Ferrell, S. W. (2006). Alcohol use among older adults. *Journal of General Psychology, 133*(4), 453–467.

Stanley, M. A., & Beck, J. G. (2003). Cognitive-behavioral treatment of late-life generalized anxiety disorder. *Journal of Consulting and Clinical Psychology, 71*(2), 309–319.

St. Clair, M. (1986). *Object relations and self psychology: An introduction.* Belmont, CA: Brooks/Cole.

Sue, D. W., Arredondo, P., & McDavis, R. J. (1992). Multicultural counseling competencies and standards: A call to the profession. *Journal of Counseling and Development, 70,* 477–486.

Sue, D. W., Bernier, J. E., Durran, D., Feinberg, L., Pedersen, P. B., Smith, E. J., et al. (1982). Position paper: Cross-cultural counseling competencies. *Counseling Psychologist, 10,* 45–52.

Sue, D. W., & Sue, D. (2003). *Counseling the culturally diverse: Theory and practice* (4th ed.). New York: Wiley.

Sue, S., & Sue, D. M. (2008). *Foundations of counseling and psychotherapy: Evidence-based practices for a diverse society.* New York: Wiley.

Sulmasy, D. P. (2002). A biopsychosocial-spiritual model for the care of patients at the end of life [Special issue III]. *The Gerontologist, 42,* 24–33.

Sutton, C. T., & Broken Nose, M. A. (1996). American Indian families: An overview. In M. McGoldrick, J. Giordano, & J. K. Pearce (Eds.), *Ethnicity and family therapy* (2nd ed., pp. 31–44). New York: Guilford.

Sweet, S. (2007). The older worker, job insecurity, and the new economy. *Generations, XXXI*(1), 45–49.

Tai, M. C., & Lin, C. S. (2001). Developing a culturally relevant bioethics for Asian people. *Journal of Medical Ethics, 27*(1), 51–54.

Tan, S.-Y., & Johnson, W. B. (2005). Spiritually oriented cognitive-behavioral therapy: Spiritually oriented psychotherapy. In L. Sperry & E. P. Shafranske (Eds.), *Spiritually oriented psychotherapy* (pp. 77–103). Washington, DC: American Psychological Association.

Taoism. (2008). In *British Broadcasting Association*. Retrieved January 23, 2008, from http://www.bbc.co.uk/religion/religions/taoism/

Tarakeshwar, N., Pargament, K. I., & Mahoney, A. (2003). Measures of Hindu pathways: Development and preliminary evidence of reliability and validity. *Cultural Diversity and Ethnic Minority Psychology, 9*(4), 316–332.

Tervalon, M., & Murray-Garcia, J. (1998). Cultural humility versus cultural competence: A critical distinction in defining physician training outcomes in multicultural education. *Journal of Health Care for the Poor and Underserved, 9*(2), 117–125.

Teyber, E. (2005). *Interpersonal process in therapy: An integrative model* (5th ed.). Belmont, CA: Thomson Brooks/Cole.

Thomas, J. L., Sperry, L., & Yarbrough, M. S. (2000). Grandparents as parents: Research findings and policy recommendations. *Child Psychiatry and Human Development, 31*(1), 3–22.

Tilak, S. (1989). *Religion and aging in the Indian tradition*. Albany: SUNY Press.

Tornstam, L. (1994). Gero-transcendence: A theoretical and empirical exploration. In L. E. Thomas & S. A. Eisenhandler (Eds.), *Aging and the religious dimension* (pp. 203–225). London: Auburn.

Tornstam, L. (1997). Gerotranscendence: The contemplative dimension of aging. *Journal of Aging Studies, 11*(2), 143–154.

Torpy, J. M. (2007). Dementia. *Journal of the American Medical Association, 297*(21), 3436.

Torres, S. (1999). A culturally-relevant theoretical framework for the study of successful aging. *Aging and Society, 19*, 33–51.

Troiden, R. R. (1989). The formation of homosexual identities. *Journal of Homosexuality, 17*(1–2), 43–73.

Trueba, E. T. (1999). *Latinos unidos: From cultural diversity to the politics of solidarity*. Lanham, MD: Rowman & Littlefield.

Tsai, D. F. (1999). Ancient Chinese medical ethics and the four principles of biomedical ethics [Abstract]. *Journal of Medical Ethics, 25*(4), 315–321. Retrieved December 19, 2007, from http://www.ncbi.nlm. nih.gov/sites/entrez?db=pubmed&Cmd=ShowDetailView&TermT oSearch=10461594&ordinalpos=2&itool=EntrezSystem2.PEntrez. Pubmed.Pubmed_ResultsPanel.Pubmed_RVDocSum

Tsai, D. F. (2001). How should doctors approach patients? A Confucian reflection on personhood [Abstract]. *Journal of Medical Ethics, 27*(1), 44–50. Retrieved December 19, 2007, from http://www.ncbi. nlm.nih.gov/sites/entrez?Db=pubmed&Cmd=ShowDetailView& TermToSearch=11233378&ordinalpos=4&itool=EntrezSystem2. PEntrez.Pubmed.Pubmed_ResultsPanel.Pubmed_RVDocSum

Uba, L. (1994). *Asian Americans: Personality patterns, identity, and mental health.* New York: Guilford.

Ulrich, L. B., & Brott, P. E. (2005). Older workers and bridge employment: Redefining retirement. *Journal of Employment Counseling, 42,* 159–170.

U.S. General Accounting Office. (2003, October). *Women's earnings: Work patterns partially explain difference between men's and women's earnings.* Washington, DC: Author. Retrieved on February 21, 2010, from http://www.gao.gov/new.items/d0435.pdf

U.S. Public Health Service. (1999). *The surgeon general's call to action to prevent suicide.* Washington, DC: U.S. Department of Health and Human Services. Retrieved November 20, 2007, from http://www. surgeongeneral.gov/library/calltoaction/default.htm

Vaillant, G. E. (1985). An empirically derived hierarchy of adaptive mechanisms and its usefulness as a potential diagnostic axis. *Acta Psychiatrica Scandinavica Supplementum, 71*(319), 171–180.

Vaillant, G. E. (2000). Adaptive mental mechanisms: Their role in a positive psychology. *American Psychologist, 55*(1), 89–98.

Vaillant, G. E. (2003). *Aging well: Surprising guideposts to a happier life from the landmark Harvard study of adult development.* New York: Little, Brown.

Vatuk, S. (1980). Withdrawal and disengagement as a cultural response to aging in India. In C. L. Fry (Ed.), *Aging in culture and society: Comparative viewpoints and strategies* (pp. 126–148). New York: Praeger.

Vontress, C. E. (1976). Counseling middle-aged and aging cultural minorities. *Personnel and Guidance Journal, 55,* 132–135.

Wagner, K. D., & Lorion, R. P. (1984). Correlates of death anxiety in elderly persons. *Journal of Clinical Psychology, 40*(5), 1235–1241.

Wallhagen, M. I., Pettengill, E., & Whiteside, M. (2006). Sensory impairment in older adults part 1: Hearing loss. *American Journal of Nursing, 106*(10), 40–48.

Walsh, F. (1998). Beliefs, spirituality, and transcendence: Keys to family resilience. In M. McGoldrick (Ed.), *Re-visioning family therapy: Race, culture, and gender in clinical practice* (pp. 62–89). New York: Guilford.

Walsh, F. (Ed.). (1999). *Spiritual resources in family therapy*. New York: Guilford.

Wass, H., & Meyers, J. E. (1982, November). Psychosocial aspects of death among the elderly: A review of the literature. *The Personnel and Guidance Journal*, 131–137.

Watson, G. R. (2001). Low vision in the geriatric population: Rehabilitation and management. *Journal of the American Geriatrics Society, 49*(3), 317–330.

Watter, E. (2010, January 8). The Americanization of mental illness. *New York Times Magazine*. Retrieved January 12, 2010, from http://www.nytimes.com/2010/01/10/magazine/10psyche-t.html?pagewanted=2

Weaver, A. J., Flannelly, L. T., Strock, A. L., Krause, N., & Flannelly, K. J. (2005). The quantity and quality of research on religion and spirituality in four major gerontology journals between 1985 and 2002. *Research on Aging, 27*(2), 119–135.

Webster, J. D., & Gould, O. (2007). Reminiscence and vivid personal memories across adulthood. *International Journal of Aging and Human Development, 64*(2), 149–170.

Weiner, E. (2008). *The geography of bliss: One grump's search for the happiest places in the world*. New York: Twelve (Hachette).

Welfel, E. R., & Patterson, L. E. (2005). *The counseling process: A multitheoretical integrative approach* (6th ed.). Belmont, CA: Thomson Brooks/Cole.

Wetherell, J. L., Gatz, M., & Craske, M. G. (2003). Treatment of generalized anxiety disorder in older adults. *Journal of Consulting and Clinical Psychology, 71*(1), 31–40.

Whisman, M. A., Uebelacker, L. A., Tolejko, N., Chatav, Y., & McKelvie, M. (2006). Marital discord and well-being in older adults: Is the association confounded by personality? *Psychology and Aging, 21*(3), 626–631.

Whitbourne, S. K. (2005). *Adult development and aging: Biopsychosocial perspectives* (2nd ed.). New York: John Wiley.

Whitman, S. M. (2007). Pain and suffering as viewed by the Hindu religion. *Journal of Pain, 8*(8), 607–613.

Whyte, E. M., & Rovner, B. (2006). Depression in late-life: Shifting the paradigm from treatment to prevention. *International Journal of Geriatric Psychiatry, 21,* 746–751.

Williams, M. E., & Freeman, P. A. (2007). Transgender health: Implications for aging and caregiving. *Journal of Gay and Lesbian Social Work, 18*(3–4), 93–108.

Wink, P., & Dillon, M. (2003). Religiousness, spirituality, and psychosocial functioning in late adulthood: Findings from a longitudinal study. *Psychology and Aging, 18*(4), 916–924.

Wolf, C. T., & Stevens, P. (2001). Integrating religion and spirituality in marriage and family counseling. *Counseling and Values, 46,* 66–75.

Worden, J. W. (2001). *Grief counseling and grief therapy: A handbook for the mental health professional* (3rd ed.). New York: Springer.

World Health Organization. (2004). *World status report on alcohol 2004.* Geneva, Switzerland: Author.

World Health Organization. (2007). *Depression.* Geneva, Switzerland: Author. Retrieved November 29, 2007, from http://www.who.int/mental_health/management/depression/definition/en/

Worthington, E. L., Kurusu, T. A., McCullough, M. E., & Sandage, S. J. (1996). Empirical research on religion and counseling: A ten-year update and prospectus. *Psychological Bulletin, 199,* 448–487.

Yalom, I. D. (1980). *Existential psychotherapy.* New York: Basic Books.

Yalom, I. D. (2008). *Staring at the sun: Overcoming the terror of death.* San Francisco: Jossey-Bass.

Yee, D. (2004). Aging Asian Americans and health disparities. In K. Whitfield (Ed.), *Closing the gap: Improving the health of minority elders.* Washington, DC: Gerontological Society of America.

Yeo, G., & Hikoyeda, N. (2000). Asian and Pacific Island American elders. In G. Maddox (Ed.), *Encyclopedia of aging* (3rd ed.). New York: Springer.

Yeo, G., Hikoyeda, N., McBride, M., Chin, S.-Y., Edmonds, M., & Hendrix, L. (1999). *Cohort analysis as a tool in ethnogeriatrics: Historical profiles of elders from eight ethnic populations in the United States* (Working Paper Series Number 12). Stanford, CA: Stanford Geriatric Education Center, Stanford University School of Medicine.

Young, J. J., & Gu, N. (1995). *Demographic and socio-economic characteristics of elderly Asian and Pacific Island Americans.* Seattle, WA: National Asian Pacific Center on Aging.

Zapata, J. T. (1995). Counseling Hispanic children and youth. In C. C. Lee (Ed.), *Counseling for diversity: A guide for school counselors and related professionals* (pp. 85–108). Boston: Allyn & Bacon.

Zedlewski, S. R. (2009). *The economic recovery package will help poor older adults, but more could be done.* Washington, DC: Urban Institute. Retrieved June 4, 2009, from http://www.urban.org/ UploadedPDF/901221_economic_recovery_package.pdf

Zinnbauer, B. J., Pargament, I., Cole, B., Rye, M. S., Butter, E. M., Belavich, T. G., Hipp, K. M., Scott, A. B., & Kadar, J. L. (1997). Religion and spirituality: Unfuzzying the fuzzy. *Journal for the Scientific Study of Religion, 36*(4), 549–564.

Index

A

Access, universal design for, 56
Acting out, 95, 96
Activities of daily living (ADLs), 272
    and vision impairment, 277
Activity-continuity theories, 4
Activity theory, 14–15, 29
Addictive couple-bonds, 100
Administration on Aging, 220
Adulthood stage, 16
Advice-giving, 63–64, 74
Advocacy
    for custodial/near-custodial
        grandparents, 243–244
    for LGBT elders, 229
    for reentry older students,
        250–251
    for retirement, 259–260
African American elders, 218–219
    cohort experiences, 172
    as grandparents, 241–242
Age-related macular degeneration,
    278, 281
Ageism, and retirement, 254
Aging
    and dementia, 288
    globalization and, 362–371
    and health, 269–273
    lack of unified theory, 2
    medical models, 30
    psychosocial impact, 347–348
    and quality of life, 269–270
    social models, 30
    success models, 30
    suicide risk and, 328
    world religions perspectives,
        179–180
Aging countertransference, 120
Aging theories, x, 1–4
    activity-continuity theories, 4
    ancient historical, 4–10
    Atschley's continuity theory, 12,
        23–24
    Baltes' selective optimization with
        compensation, 12, 19
    case study, 27–28
    contemporary, 12, 19–27
    Costa and McCrae's personality
        traits model, 12, 20
    Cumming and Henry's
        disengagement theory, 11,
        17
    dialectic between, 4–6
    disengagement-geotranscendence
        theories, 4
    Erikson's stages of psychosocial
        development, 11, 15–17
    Gompertz' law, 11
    Hall's hill metaphor, 11
    Havinghurst's activity theory, 11,
        14–15
    Hindu, 7–10
    implicit, 2
    Jung's perspective, 11, 13–14
    Levinson's personality
        development theory, 12,
        20–21
    life review, 6

modern, 11–12, 11–18
Neugarten's personality and
    successful aging theories,
    11, 17–18
Plato, 4–7
Rowe and Kahn's successful aging
    theory, 12, 24–26
Salthouse's resource-reduction
    theory, 12, 19–20
Schroots's geodynamics theory,
    12, 23
Tornstam's geotranscendence
    theory, 12, 21–23
Agitation, in dementia, 291
Ainsworth, Mary, 110–112, 128
Alcohol abuse, 336–338
    binge drinking, 337
    counselor responses, 340–341
    and depression, 319
    families dealing with, 341
    international perspective, 337
    risk factors, 338–339
    signs and symptoms, 339–340
    and suicide, 331
    U.S. perspective, 337
Altruism, 95, 96, 98, 360
Alzheimer's disease, xii, 285–286,
    344
    self-psychology and, 85–86
American Association of Retired
    Persons (AARP), 218, 232,
    250
Anatman, 180, 206
Ancient theories of aging, 4
    Hindu-based, 7–10
    Plato, 4–7
Anger, 357
    as reaction to separation, 110
Anhedonia, 344
Animism, in Shinto belief, 200
Anticipation, 95, 96, 98, 360
Anxiety, 314. See also Existential
    anxiety
    anxious depression, 316
    counselor responses to, 316–317
    due to medical condition, 316
    families dealing with, 317

generalized anxiety disorder, 315
    imaginal relaxation for, 317
    physical manifestations, 315
    progressive relaxation training,
        317
    relaxation training for, 317
    risk factors, 314–315
    symptoms, 315
    types, 315–316
Anxious avoidant attachment, 111,
    112
Anxious depression, 344
Anxious resistant attachment, 111
Ascetic stage, 8, 9
Asceticism, 95, 96
Ashrama, 8, 9, 29, 182, 206
Asian elders, 220–221
Assessment, 65
Assimilation, 367
Assistive devices, 281
    for hearing impairment,
        275–276
    for vision impairment, 279
Atman, 180, 182, 183, 186, 206
Atschley, Robert, 12, 23–24
Attachment styles, 110–112
Attending skills. See also Listening
        skills
    for older adult counseling, 33
Attitude shift, 54, 55
Authority figure transference, 117
Autonomy, 192, 359, 373
    cultural support for, 370
Avoidance, 142
Ayurvedic medicine, 185, 206

B
Baby boomers, 254–255
Baltes, Paul, 1, 19
Barriers, working through, 212
Beginning stage
    of counseling, 56–59
    first session, 56–58
    subsequent sessions, 59
Beliefs, and implicit theories of aging,
    2–3
Beneficence, 192

Bereavement, 297, 307–308
    and depression, 321
Biases, recognizing counselor,
    212
Biculturalism, 367
Big optimism, 356, 370, 373
Binge drinking, 337, 344
Biomedical ethics, differences from
    Islamic tenets, 194
Bisexual elders, 223
Blando, John A., xvii
Blocking, 95, 96
Body language, 33, 37
Bowenian family systems, 301–302
Bowlby, John, 110–112, 128
Brahmin class, 181
Bridge employment, 258–259, 262
Brief intervention, 344
Buddhism, 206. *See also* Tibetan
    Buddhism
    Four Noble Truths, 186
    perspectives on aging, 185–187
    resources for death anxiety, 93

C
Career counseling, x, xii, 267
Caregiving, 297, 298–299
    family systems interventions,
        300–303
    psychoeducation interventions,
        300
Case studies, xiii
    aging theories, 27–28
    bereavement, 309
    caregiving, 309
    counseling approaches, 152–153
    counseling skills, 48–49
    counseling stages, 72–73
    culture and context, 176
    dementia, 294
    diversity issues, 229–230
    globalization and
        deterritorialization,
        371–372
    grandparenting, 261
    health and rehabilitation
        counseling, 280

psychodynamic foundations,
    101–102
psychological issues, 342
retirement, 261
spirituality and aging, 204–205
transference and
    countertransference,
    126–127
Cataracts, 278
Causal coherence, 151, 155
Central hearing loss, 274, 282
Centrality, 236
Ceremony, in Christianity, 188–189
Chaos theory, 29
Characterological transference, 119
Ch'i, 201, 206
Child transference, 116
Chinese American elders, cohort
    experiences, 172
Christianity
    factors influencing beliefs, 189
    perspectives on aging, 187–190
Chronic illness, 269–270
    and anxiety, 315
    as suicide risk factor, 329, 334
Chun-tze, 191, 206
Client comfort, 57
Client story, addressing from multiple
    perspectives, 33
Closed-ended questions, 40, 50
Cognitive analytic therapy, 136, 155
Cognitive behavioral therapy,
    137–139, 155, 344
    in anxiety, 317
    in major depression, 323
Cognitive health, 269, 270
Cognitive training, for dementia, 293
Cohort, 29, 155
Collateral kin, 310
Collectivist societies, 369
Coming out, 225
Communication skills, 35–36
Communication styles
    in First Nations elders, 222
    through behavior, 302
Community and mental health
    counseling, 313

Compassion, in Buddhist teachings,
187
Compassionate ageism, 177
Compensated Work Therapy
Program, 266, 267
Compensation, 349–350
Competence, 352, 373
cultural support for, 370, 371
Conductive hearing loss, 274, 282
Confucianism, 206
perspectives on aging, 190–192
Conscious, 103
Contemporary theories of aging, 12
Atschley's continuity theory, 12,
23–24
Baltes' selective optimization with
compensation, 12, 19
Costa and McCrae's personality
trait model, 12, 20
Levinson's personality
development theory, 12,
20–21
Rowe and Kahn's successful aging
theory, 12
Salthouse's resource-reduction
theory, 12, 19–20
Schroots's gerodynamics theory,
12, 23
Tornstam's geotranscendence
theory, 12, 21–23
Contextual perspective, x, 47
Continuity theory, 12, 23–24, 29
Controlling behavior, 95, 96
Core rehabilitation knowledge, 268
Cortical dementia, 287
Cosmology, in Taoist thought, 201
Costa, Paul, 12, 20
Counseling, 33
addressing older adults, 35
case study, 48–49
five-step model for organizing,
64–71
future trends, 347
grandparenting issues, 243–244
from multiple perspectives, 46–48
of older adults, 34
psychodynamic foundations, 77

spirituality and, 179
themes and communication,
35–36
Counseling approaches, xi, 131–134
case study, 152–153
cognitive behavioral therapy,
137–139
guided autobiography, 139,
148–152
interpersonal therapy, 136
life review, 139, 145–148
psychodynamic approaches,
135–136
and religion/spirituality, 165
reminiscence, 139, 140–145
Counseling parameters, 57–58
Counseling perspectives, 47. See also
Multiple perspectives
Counseling processes, x, 107–109
countertransference, 118–121
resistance, 124–125
termination, 125–126
therapeutic alliance, 123–124
transference, 109–118
working through, 121–123
Counseling skills, ix, x
advanced, 60–61
advice-giving, 63–64
feedback, 62
interpretation, 62–63
pros and cons, 61, 62
self-disclosure, 63
Counseling specialization, and
religion/spirituality, 166
Counseling stages, xi, 53, 55
advanced counseling skills, 60–64
beginning stage, 55–59, 65
Buddhist meditation stages, 55
case study, 72–73
end stage, 60, 65
five-step model, 64–71
Helmholtz's problem solving
stages, 54
middle stage, 60, 65
Counselor blindness, 122
Counselor role, 100–101
in responses to anxiety, 316–317

in working with spirituality,
    164–168
Counselor working through, 122
Countertransference, xi, 118, 128
    case study, 126–127
    characteristic responses, 119
    Kahn's four types, 118–119
    Knight's countertransference
        templates, 120–121
    obstructive, 122
    with older client/younger
        counselor, 116
    reactions to, 118
    realistic responses, 118
    responses to troubling material,
        119
    sources of, 119
Cross-sectional studies, 29
Crystallized intelligence, 132, 155
Cultural coherence, 151, 155
Cultural competence, xi, 231
Cultural humility, 210–213, 231
Cultural identity development,
    216–218, 232
Cultural perspective, 47
Culture, and memes, 353
Culture and context, 159
    case study, 176
    cohort experiences, 171–173
    multicultural gerontological
        counseling, 170–171
    social justice, 173–175
    spirituality and religion, 159–170
Cumming, Elaine, 11, 17
Curanderas, 230
Custodial grandparents, 236–238,
    262
    facts and figures, 237
    outcomes of children raised by,
        238
    welfare of, 238–240

D
Death
    dysfunctional attitudes about, 307
    Hindu views on, 184–185
    inevitability of, 93, 94

Islamic tenets, 193, 194
    in Jewish tradition, 196–197
    universality of, 93, 94
    unknown manner of, 94
    unknown time of, 93
Death anxiety, 89–94, 103
    internal and external resources,
        93–94
Death anxiety countertransference,
    120
Dedication, 54
    to enlightenment, 55
    to new narrative, 55
Defense mechanisms, 94–100, 103
    acting out, 95, 96
    adaptive, 97
    altruism, 95
    anticipation, 95
    asceticism, 95
    blocking, 95
    controlling, 95
    delusional thinking, 95
    denial, 95
    displacement, 95
    dissociation, 95
    distortion, 95
    externalization, 95
    humor, 95
    hypochondriasis, 95
    inhibition, 95
    intellectualization, 95
    introjection, 95
    mature, 95
    neurotic, 95
    passive-aggression, 95
    projection, 95
    psychotic, 95
    rationalization, 95
    reaction formation, 95
    regression, 95
    repression, 95
    schizoid fantasy, 95
    sexualization, 95
    somatization, 95
    sublimation, 95
    suppression, 92, 95
    unhealthy, 95

Vaillant's four levels, 95
Delirium, 288, 344
Delusional thinking, 95, 96
Dementia, xii, 296, 344
    agitation in, 291
    Alzheimer's disease, 285–286
    with anxiety, 314–315
    case study, 294
    cessation of driving in, 291
    and changes in intimate
        relationships, 292
    classifications, 287
    common problems in, 291–292
    cortical, 287
    and depression, 321–322
    differential diagnosis, 287–288
    genetics and, 288
    medical conditions predisposing
        to, 289
    primary, 287, 296
    progressive, 296
    protective factors, 289–290
    racial and ethnic factors, 289
    risk factors, 288–289
    secondary, 287, 296
    self psychology perspective, 85
    sleeping problems in, 292
    smoking and, 288–289
    subcortical, 296
    supervision and monitoring for,
        293
    symptoms, 290–291
    treatment, 292–293
    vascular, 286–287, 296
    wandering problems, 291–292
Denial, 95, 96, 97
    of aging and death, 307
Dependency countertransference, 120
Depression, 95, 97. See also Major
        depression
    and dementia, 322
    and morbidity, 319
    and mortality, 319
Despair, 90
    in old age, 16
Detachment, 111
    in Hindu culture, 182

Deterritorialization, 363
    case study, 371–372
    precipitants, 364
Developmental stages, in Hindu
        philosophy, 8
Devotion, path of, 180
Dharma, 181, 206
Differentiation, 310
Direction, determining in counseling,
        67
Directives, 41, 50
Disability, 56
    contributory factors, 271–272
Discrepancies, 50
    pointing out, 33, 45–46
Discrimination, against LGBT elders,
        227–228
Disengagement, through
        reminiscence, 142
Disengagement-geotranscendence
        theories, 4
Disengagement theory, 11, 17, 30
Displacement, 95, 96, 99
Dissociation, 95, 96
Distortion, 95, 96
Diversity, xii, 213–216
    as cultural artifact, 213
    and inequalities, 209
    in socioeconomic status, 215–216
    in spirituality and religion, 214–
        215 (See also Spirituality)
Drives, 103
Driving, cessation in dementia, 291
Dual sensory impairment, 279–280,
        282
Duty, in Hinduism, 181
Dysthymia, 344

E
Early childhood stage, 16
Education. See also Reentry older
        students
    among older adults, 244–245
    barriers to, 247–249
    as Confucian value, 190
Ego, 103
Ego integrity, 90

Ego psychology, 77–80, 80–81, 103
Eightfold path, 186
Elderhostel, 252
Emotional expression, 357
Emotionality changes, 138
Encore careers, 257
Encouraging, 50. *See also* Verbal encouraging techniques
End-of-life care, 269
Enlightenment, 54, 55
Entropy, 30
Environmental perspective, 47
Erikson, Erik, 1, 15–17, 90, 238
    life review based on eight stages, 146
Erotic transference, 118
Escape-avoidance, 239
Essential self, in Hindu philosophy, 10
Ethical action, path of, 180
Ethnic minority older adults, 218
    African American elders, 218–219
    Asian and Pacific Islander elders, 220–221
    First Nations elders, 221–222
    Latino elders, 219–220
Ethnicity, 214, 232
    and dementia, 289
    in LGBT elders, 224
Ethnoscapes, 363, 366, 373
    and deterritorialization, 364
Evaluation, in structured life review, 147
Everyday competence, 282
    dual sensory impairment and, 280
Existential anxiety, 77, 86–89, 103
Existential grief, 87
Exploration, in counseling, 66–67
Expressive motivators, 246, 262
Extended families, 297. *See also* Family issues
External locus of control, 344
External regulation, 358
Externalization, 95, 96

F
Falls, 270

reducing, 269
Familism, 220
Family cohesion, 304
Family development stages, 302
Family intervention, 344
Family issues, xii, 297
    accepting power over parents, 306
    adaptability, 304
    bereavement, 297, 307–308
    Bowenian family systema, 301
    caregiving, 297, 298–307
    case study, 309
    communication through behaviors, 302
    families with long history, 303
    families with older adults, 297–298
    family as unit of analysis, 302
    family life cycle, 298
    labeling and educating, 305, 306
    level of cohesion, 304
    life event web, 298
    off-time life events, 303
    and openings for change, 303
    parent-adult child relationships, 304–305
    psychoeducation and family subsystems, 303–307
    structural family systems, 301
    taking responsibility, 306
    Worden's four tasks of grief, 307
Family life cycle, 298
Family meetings, 306–307
Family perspective, 46
Family subsystems, 301, 310
Family systems assumptions, 302
Fantasy, 95, 97
Feedback, 62, 74
Feelings, acknowledging, 33, 44
Financescapes, 363, 365–366, 373
    and deterritorialization, 364
First Nations elders, 221–222
    cohort experiences, 172
    as grandparents, 242–243
First Nations spirituality, 198
Five aggregates, 186
Five pillars of Islam, 192, 193

Five-step counseling model, 64–65
    determining direction, 67
    exploration stage, 66–67
    termination, 70–71
    therapeutic alliance-building,
        65–66
    work-feedback-rework, 67–70
Flow, 350, 353, 354, 373
    transformation of, 354
Fluid intelligence, 132, 155
Forest dweller stage, 8, 9
Four Noble Truths, 186
Free association, 103
Freud, Anna, 81, 103
Freud, Sigmund, 77–78
    transference theory, 109–110
    on working through, 121
Freudian psychoanalytic concepts,
        77, 79–80
Future trends, xiii, 347
    case study, 371–372
    globalization and aging, 362–371
    healthy aging, 348–362
    positive psychology, 348–362
    psychosocial impact of aging,
        347–348

G
Gay elders, 223
    cohort experiences, 172
Gender
    and alcohol abuse, 337, 338
    and chronic health conditions, 269
    and death anxiety, 90
    discrimination based on, 255
    encouraging self-understanding
        of, 151
    and income distribution, 215
    and later-life work, 252, 253
    and risk of falls, 270
    and subjective experiences of
        grandparenting, 239
    and suicide risk, 325, 328
Gender identity, 222–225
    advocacy, 229
    case study, 229–230
    coming out, 225

    and hate crimes, 225
    miscellaneous issues, 227
    and relationships, 225–226
    and spirituality, 226
    strengths, 228–229
    transgender issues, 227–228
Generalized anxiety disorder, 315,
        344
Generation, 176
Generational equity, 174, 176
Generativity, vs. self-absorption, 238
Genetics, and dementia, 288
Geotranscendence, 12, 20–21, 30
Geriatric conditions, 282
Gerodynamics theory, 12, 23
Gerontological counseling, ix
Glaucoma, 278
Globalization, 373
    and aging, 362–371
    case study, 371–372
God helped, 168, 169
Gompertz, Benjamin, 11
Gompertz's law, 11
Good-enough parenting, 82, 103–104
Goodness, in Confucianism, 192
Grandchild transference, 116–117
Grandfather caregivers, 240
Grandparental countertransference,
        120
Grandparenting, xii, 235, 236
    case study, 261
    and centrality, 236
    counseling and advocacy issues,
        243–244
    custodial and near-custodial,
        236–238, 238–239
    and immortality through clan,
        236
    and indulgence, 236
    multicultural considerations,
        241–243
    noncustodial, 240–241
    and reinvolvement with personal
        past, 236
    as valued elders, 236
Grandparents
    African-American, 241–242

being there standard, 240, 241
First Nations elders as, 242–243
not interfering standard, 240, 241
Grief
    four tasks of, 307
    and suicide risk, 329–330
Group cognitive behavioral therapy,
    139
Group norms, 136
Group psychodynamic therapy, 135
Guided autobiography, 139, 148–152,
    155

H
Hall, G.S., 11, 13
Happiness, 347–348, 356
    impact of globalization on, 367
    and wealth, 369
Hate crimes, and gender identity, 225
Havinghurst, Robert J., 11, 14–15
Hazardous drinking, 344
Health, xii
    aging and, 269–270
    chronic conditions, 271–273
    falls and, 270
Health and rehabilitation counseling,
    265
    aging and health, 269–273
    case study, 280
    chronic conditions, 271–273
    dual sensory impairment, 279–280
    health improvement, 270–271
    hearing impairment, 273–277
    rehabilitation counselor domain
        knowledge, 267–269
    vision impairment, 277–279
    vocational rehabilitation needs,
        265–267
Health improvement, 270–271
Health inequities, and diversity,
    209–210
Healthy aging, 348–362
Hearing impairment, 273
    adaptive vs. maladaptive
        strategies, 276, 277
    assistive interventions, 275
    coping with, 276–277

environmental interventions, 275
    interventions, 275–276
    symptoms, 273–274
    types, 274–275
Hearing loss, types, 274
Hedonic treadmill, 355, 369, 373
Henry, William, 11, 17
Hill metaphor, 11, 13, 30
Hinduism, 1, 3, 4, 205, 206
    life span development stages, 7–10
    perspectives on aging, 180–185
    and success model of aging,
        183–184
Horney, Karen, 112–114, 128
    three neurotic types, 111
Hospitalization, likelihood of, 272
Householder stage, 8, 9
Humanism, 180, 206
    perspectives on aging, 202–203
Humor, 96, 97, 360
    as defense mechanism, 95
Hypochondriasis, 95, 96

I
Id, 80, 104
Ideal self, 150, 155
Idealized parental imago, 83, 84,
    114–115
Idealizing, 104
Identification, 55, 97, 359
Identity maintenance, through
    reminiscence, 142
Ideoscapes, 363, 373
    and deterritorialization, 364
    globalization and, 368–369
Illness, 120
    avoiding in success model of
        aging, 183
    CBT in, 137
    and crystallized intelligence, 132
    and depression, 139
    in First Nations spirituality, 199
    and hypochondriasis, 96
    in Islamic thought, 194, 195
    learning from, 150
    in LGBT elders, 227
    in medical model of aging, 7, 30

minimizing in successful aging, 12
as non-solvable problem, 126
and psychodynamic therapy, 78
as small death, 162
and social class, 173
and Taoism, 202
Imaginal relaxation, 317
Immortality, through clan, 236
Implicit theories of aging, 1, 2
In-depth exploration, 65
Income, and working older adults, 252–253
Individualistic societies, 369
Inequality
and diversity, 209
of wealth, 215
Infancy stage, 15
Inhibition, 95, 96, 98
Initial disclosure, 65
Insomnia, in dementia, 292
Inspiration, 54, 55
Institutionalization, 90
Instrumental activities of daily living (IADLs), 272
and vision impairment, 277
Instrumental motivators, 246, 262
Insulation, 367
Intake, 65
Integrated regulation, 359
Integrity, 90
in old age, 16
Intellectualization, 95, 96, 97
Intelligence, changes in, 138
Intentions, of reentry older students, 249
Interpersonal, 50
Interpersonal interaction types, 112–114
Interpersonal psychotherapy, 344
Interpersonal therapy, 136
Interpretation, 62–63, 74
Interviewer perspective, 47
Intrapersonal, 50
Introjected regulation, 358
Introjection, 95, 96
Inverted transference, 128
Islam, 207

Five Pillars, 193
perspectives on aging, 192–195

J
Japanese American elders, cohort experiences, 172
Job development/placement services, 267
Job security, 253–254
Judaism, 162, 207
perspectives on aging, 195–197
Jung, Carl, 1, 89
on life span development, 13–14

K
Kahn, Robert, 12, 24–26
four countertransference types, 118–119
Kami, 200, 201, 207
Karma, 180, 181, 207
Keywords, 33, 41–42, 50
Knight, Bob, 115–118
countertransference templates with older adults, 120–121
Knowledge, path of, 180
Kohut, Heinz, 82, 83, 104, 114–115
three fundamental relationships, 83
Kshatriya class, 181

L
Later life development. See also Aging theories
theories of, 1–4
Latino elders, 219–220
cohort experiences, 172
grandparenting experiences, 242
Learning. See also Reentry older students
activity-oriented, 245–246
learning-oriented, 246
outside of school, 250
Learning in Retirement, 250
Lesbian elders, 223
cohort experiences, 172
Levinson, Daniel, 12, 20–21
Li, 190, 207

Life event web, 298
Life review, 139, 145–148, 156
   based on Erikson's stages, 146
   duration, 147
   Plato's theory of, 6, 30
   structured, 146
   through reminiscence, 142
Life span development, Jung's
      perspective, 13–14
Listening skills, xi, 36
   addressing older adults, 35
   nonverbal skills, 37
   for older adult counseling, 33
   themes and communication,
      35–36
   verbal skills, 39–48
Little optimism, 356, 373
Locus of control, 344
Long-term care, meaning and, 89–90
Longitudinal studies, 30

M
Machismo, 220, 232
Macular degeneration, 278, 281
Major depression, 318, 344
   counselor response to, 322–324
   families dealing with, 324
   international perspective, 318
   risk factors, 319–320
   symptoms and signs, 320–322
   U.S. demographics, 319
Marianismo, 220, 232
Maturation, 131, 132, 156
Mature defense mechanisms, 95, 352,
      359, 360
McCrae, Robert, 12, 20
Meaning, 90
   for older workers, 256
   and placement in long-term care,
      89–90
   threats to, 92
Mediascapes, 363, 373
   and deterritorialization, 364
   and globalization, 368
Medical conditions
   anxiety due to, 316
   and dementia, 289

Medical models of aging, 7, 30, 183
Medications, for dementia, 293
Medicine Wheel, 199
Meditation stages, 54
   Tibetan Buddhist, 55
Memes, 353, 374
Memory impairment. See Dementia
Mental health counseling, x. See also
      Psychological issues
Messianism, 195
Migration patterns, 364–365
Mild cognitive impairment, 296
   and risk of dementia, 289
Mindfulness-based stress reduction,
      299, 310
Ming, 201, 207
Mirroring, 83, 104, 114–115
Mixed anxiety-depression disorder,
      316
Mixed hearing loss, 274, 282
Modern theories of aging, 10
   Cumming and Henry's
      disengagement theory, 11,
      17
   Erikson's stages of psychosocial
      development, 11, 15–17
   foundations, 11, 13
   Gompertz's law, 11
   Havinghurst's activity theory, 11,
      14–15
   Jung's perspective, 11
   Neugarten's personality and
      successful aging theories,
      11
Moksha, 181, 207
Monotheism, 207
Morality, in humanist thought, 203
Mortality salience, 91
Motivation, 54, 55
   among reentry older students,
      245–247
Motivational counseling, 344
   for alcohol abuse, 340–341
Moving against, 111, 113
Moving away from, 111, 113
Moving toward, 111, 112
Muhammad, 192

Multicultural gerontological
    counseling, 170–171, 209
  and cultural competence, 209–213
  and cultural experiences, 213–216
  and cultural humility, 209,
    210–213
  and cultural identity development,
    216–218
  and ethnic minority older adults,
    218–222
  expression of diversity, 213–216
  gender identity and, 222–229
  sexual orientation and, 222–229
  for working older adults, 252
Multiple perspectives, 46–48, 47, 50
Mutual perspective, 47

N
Narrative, 74
National Center for Injury Prevention
    and Control, 328
Native Americans. See First Nations
    elders
Natural ending, 74
Nature, in First Nations traditions,
    200
Near-custodial grandparents,
    236–238, 262
  outcomes of children raised by,
    238
  welfare of, 238–240
Negative emotions, 347, 358
Neugarten, Bernice, 11, 17–18
Neurotic defense mechanisms, 95
Neurotic types, Horney's, 111
Non-maleficence, 192
Noncustodial grandparents, 240–241
Nondisease conditions, 272
Nontheistic beliefs, 202
Nonverbal skills, 33, 37–39, 50
  body language, 37
  visual communication, 38–39
  vocalizations, 38
Nun study, 361

O
Object relations, 77–80, 81–82, 104

Obsession, 142
Obstructive countertransference,
    122. See also
    Countertransference
Off-time life events, 303
Old age
  culture and context, 159
  Erikson's view, 16
Older adults
  addressing, 35
  attending and listening skills, 33
  benefits of psychoanalysis, 78–79
  cohort experiences, 171–173
  counseling skills, 34
  cultural diversity in, 213–216
  desexualization norms, 118
  expressions of depression in, 322
  families with, 297–298
  health and rehabilitation
    counseling, 265
  in and out of workforce, 251–258
  percentage increase by race,
    ethnicity, and LGBT status,
    219
  practical counseling issues, 34–36
  school, college, and career
    counseling, 235
  spirituality and counseling for,
    179
  transference and counseling
    processes, 107–109
  wellness in, 33, 34
Oldest-old, 362
Open-ended questions, 39–40, 50
Openings for change, 303
Optimism, 355
  at cultural level, 370
  as dispositional style, 356
  as human nature, 355
  as individual difference, 356
  unrealistic, 361
Optimization, 349
  Baltes' theory of, 12, 19
Oral tradition, 197
Osher Lifelong Learning Institute,
    252
Other perspective, 46

P

Pacific Islander elders, 220–221
Paraphrasing, 33, 42–43, 50
Parasuicide, 345
Parental countertransference, 120
Parental family subsystems, 301
Parental transference, 117
Partial retirement, 257
Passive-aggression, 95, 96
Path of devotion, 180, 183
Path of ethical action, 180
Path of knowledge, 180
Path of physical restraint, 180
Person-environment fit model, 351,
        374
Personalismo, 220, 232
Personality development theory,
        Levinson's, 12, 20–21
Personality trait model of aging, 12,
        20
Pessimism, at cultural level, 370
Pharmacotherapy, 345
    in anxiety, 317
    in depression, 323
Philosophical systems, aging
        perspectives, 179–180
Physical fitness, 270
Physical restraint, path of, 180
Plato
    dialectic between theories, 4–6, 5
    life review, 5, 6
    on nature of wisdom, 5, 6–7
    theory of aging, 4–7
Play age stage, 16
Positive psychology, 348–362, 374
    group level, 351
    happiness, 356
    individual level, 350
    self-determination, 358
    subjective level, 350
Positive reappraisal, 239
Poverty, 215
Power sharing, 212–213
Preconscious, 104
Premature retirement, 260, 262
Presbycusis, 274, 282
Prescription drug misuse, 342

Pretreatment, 65
Primal religions, 207
    perspectives on aging, 197–200
Primary dementia, 287, 296
Problem perspective, 46
Problem resolution, 55
Problem solving, von Helmholtz's
        stages of, 54
Progressive dementia, 287, 296
Progressive relaxation, 317
Progressive self-denial, 100
Projection, 95, 96, 97
Propriety, 191, 192
Props, 144, 156
Pros and cons technique, 61, 74
    examples, 62
Pseudodementia, 296, 345
Pseudoproblems, preoccupation with,
        99
Psychiatric disorders, suicide risk in,
        329
Psychodynamic approaches, xi,
        135–136
Psychodynamic foundations, 77
    case study, 101–102
    counselor role and, 100–101
    death anxiety, 86, 89–94
    defense mechanisms, 86,
        94–100
    ego psychology, 77–80, 80–81
    existential anxiety, 86–89
    object relations, 77–80, 81–82
    self psychology, 77–80, 82–86
Psychodynamic therapy, 135
Psychoeducation family therapy,
        preventive use of, 303
Psychological health, impact on
        physical health, 271
Psychological issues, xii–xiii,
        313
    alcohol abuse, 336–342
    anxiety, 314–317
    case study, 342
    major depression, 318–324
    prescription drug misuse, 342
suicide, 324–336
Psychotic defenses, 95

Q

Quality of life, 269–270
  aging and, 269–270
  falls and, 270
Questions
  closed-ended, 40, 50
  open-ended, 39–40
  skills for asking, 38–39
  "why" type, 40

R

Race, 214, 232
  and dementia risk, 289
Racial/Cultural Identity Development
    Model, 215
Rationalization, 95, 96
Re-engagement, through
    reminiscence, 142
Reaction formation, 95, 96
Real self, 150, 156
Rebirth, 180, 181, 182, 183, 184,
    185, 186, 187, 207
Reentry older students, xii, 235, 244
  barriers to reentry, 247–249
  counseling and advocacy, 250–251
  demographics, 244–245
  intentions, 249–250
  learning outside of school, 250
  motivation, 245–247
Regression, 95, 97, 98
Rehabilitation, x, xii. *See also*
    Health and rehabilitation
    counseling
  and aging, 265–267
  counselor domain knowledge,
    267–269
  vocational, 265–267
Relatedness, 374
  cultural support for, 370–371
Relaxation training, 317, 345
Religion, 159–161, 178
  cost of, 169
  counseling approaches and, 165
  counseling specialization and, 166
  diversity in older adults, 214–215
  family history of, 169
  in LGBT elders, 224

  and suicide rates, 326
Reminiscence, 131, 134, 140–145,
    156
  functions, 141, 142
  group work in, 144
Reminiscence bump, 143, 156
Reminiscence therapy, 345
Ren, 190, 207
Repetition compulsion, 81, 104
  in context of transference,
    109–110
Repression, 95, 97
Resistance, 123, 124–125, 128
Resource-reduction theory, 12,
    19–20
Respite, 299, 310
Restatements, 33, 42
Resurrection, 188, 194, 207
  in Islamic thought, 194
Retirement, xii, 235, 251
  and ageism, 254
  among baby boomers, 254–255
  and bridge employment, 258–259
  case study, 261
  counseling and advocacy,
    259–260
  demographics, 251–252
  and encore careers, 257
  gender considerations, 252
  geographical considerations, 253
  greater hours of working during,
    255
  income issues, 252–253
  job security and, 253–254
  and meaning-making, 256
  multicultural considerations, 252
  and older adults in workforce,
    251–258
  partial, 257
  premature, 260
  and trainability, 254
  and volunteering, 257–258
Rights, duty *vs.*, 181
Role compliance, 122
Role-playing, 68–70
Rowe, John, 12, 24–26
Rumination, 142

S

Sacredness, in First Nations spirituality, 198
Salthouse, Timothy, 12, 19–120
Samsara, 180, 183, 186, 207
Schemas, 138
Schizoid fantasy, 95, 97
School age stage, 16
Schroots, Johannes, 1, 12, 23
Scripts, 138
Secondary dementia, 287, 296
Secure attachment, 111, 129
Selection, 349
Selective optimization, with compensation, 12, 19
Self-absorption, *vs.* generativity, 238
Self-control, in Confucianism, 190
Self-determination, 358
Self-disclosure, 63, 74
Self-identification, 210
Self-nourishing habits, 99
Self psychology, 77–80, 82–86, 104
   and Alzheimer's disease, 85–86
Sensorineural hearing loss, 274, 282
Sequential reciprocity, 175, 178
Sexual orientation, 222–225
   advocacy, 229
   case study, 229–230
   coming out, 225
   and hate crimes, 225
   miscellaneous issues, 227
   and relationships, 225–226
   and spirituality, 226
   strengths, 228–229
   transgender issues, 227–228
Sexualization, 95, 97
Shinto, 207
   perspectives on aging, 200–201
Sibling family subsystems, 301
Siddhartha Gautama, 185
Six realms of existence, 186
Skipped-generation households, 237, 262
Smoking, and dementia, 288–289
Social context, 131, 133, 138, 156
Social-image self, 150, 156
Social isolation

addressing, 323–324
   and suicide risk, 329–330, 333
Social justice, x, xii, 173–176
Social models of aging, 7, 30, 183
Social support, 361
Socioeconomic status
   and chronic health conditions, 271
   diversity in, 215–216
Somatization, 95, 97
Speed of processing, 138
Spiritual assessment, 168–170
Spiritual development, and client development, 161–164
Spiritual history dimensions, 169
Spirituality, xi, xii, 159–161, 178
   Buddhism, 185–187
   case study, 204–205
   Christianity, 187–190
   Confucianism, 190–192
   and counseling, 179
   counseling approaches and, 165
   counseling specialization and, 166
   counselor role in, 164–168
   diversity in older adults, 214–215
   in First Nations elders, 222
   Hinduism, 7–10, 180–185
   humanism, 202–203
   Islam, 192–195
   Judaism, 195–197
   major world religions, 179–180
   primal religions, 197–200
   and sexual identity/gender orientation, 226
   Shinto, 200–201
   Taoism, 201–202
Spousal family subsystems, 301
Spouse at a younger age transference, 117
Strength training, 270
Stress and coping model, 262
Structural family systems, 301
Student stage, 8, 9
Sturm und Drang, 14
Subcortical dementia, 287, 296
Subjective well-being, 354, 361
   and globalization, 368
   and national wealth, 367–368

Sublimation, 95, 97, 98, 360
Substance abuse, 336, 345. *See also*
    Alcohol abuse; Prescription
    drug misuse
  and suicide, 331
Substance dependence, 345
Subsystems, in families, 310
Success models of aging, 7, 11, 17–18,
    30, 183, 374
  congruence with Hindu tenets,
    183–184
  Neugarten and, 11
  Rowe and Kahn's, 24–26
Sudra class, 181
Suffering, 186
  causes of, 186
  cessation of, 186
Suicidal ideation, 325, 332
Suicide, 324
  and age, 328
  assessment, 332
  counselor responses, 331–335
  counselor thoughts and feelings,
    331–332
  definitions, 324–325
  and depression, 331
  families dealing with loss from,
    336–338
  family history and risk, 329
  and gender, 328
  general counselor
    recommendations, 332
  grief and, 329–330
  intake interviews, 332–334
  international perspective, 325–326
  Jewish prohibitions, 196
  loss and, 329–330
  methods, 330
  pain and physical illness risk
    factors, 329
  prevention, 334–335
  protective factors, 330
  psychiatric disorders and, 329
  risk among Asian Americans, 221
  risk factors, 327–330
  social isolation and, 329–330

  symptoms and signs, 330–331
  U.S. demographics, 326–327
  warning signs, 330–331
Suicide crisis, 345
Summarizing techniques, 33, 43, 50
Sundowning, 296
Superego, 104
Suppression, 95, 97, 98, 360
  in response to thoughts of death,
    92

T
Tabula rasa, 80, 115
Taoism, 207
  perspectives on aging, 201–202
  philosophical, vitalizing, and
    religious strains, 202
Technoscapes, 363, 374
  and deterritorialization, 364
Temporal coherence, 151, 156
Terminal illness, and suicide risk,
    329
Termination, 65, 70–71, 74, 125–
    126, 129
  natural ending, 71
  planned ending, 71
  unnatural ending, 71
  unplanned ending, 71
Terror management theory, 91, 104
Thematic coherence, 151, 155
Theme identification, 33, 35–36
Therapeutic alliance, 56, 123–124,
    129
  building, 65–66
  and resistance, 123
Tibetan Buddhism, 54, 55, 185. *See
    also* Buddhism
Tornstam, Lars, 12, 20–21
Toughness, ethic of, 232
Trainability, of older adults, 254
Transcendent quest, 9
Transference, xi, 79, 104, 107–109,
    109–118, 129
  Bowlby's and Ainsworth's
    attachment styles, 110–112
  case study, 126–127

Freud's templates and repetition
     compulsion, 109–110
Horney's three interpersonal
     interaction types, 112–114
inverted, 128
Knight's transference templates,
     115–118
mirroring, idealizing, and
     twinship types, 114–115
with older adults, 107–109
with older client and younger
     counselor, 116
Transference templates, 115–118
Transformation of flow, 354
Transgender elders, 223–224
Transmuting internalization, 115
Triggers, 144, 156
Twinship, 83, 84, 104, 114–115

U
Unconscious, 104
Unconscious influence, 122
Universal design, 56, 74
Unnatural ending, 74

V
Vaillant, George, 95
Vaishya class, 181
Valued elders, 236
Vanity-specialness, 100
Vascular dementia, 286–287, 296
Verbal encouraging techniques, 33,
     41, 50
Verbal skills, 39
     acknowledging feelings, 44
     asking questions, 39–40
     directives, 41
     keywords, 41–42
     paraphrasing, 42–43
     pointing out discrepancies, 45–46
     restatements, 42
     theme identification, 44–45
     verbal encouraging, 41
Veterans Health Administration, 266
Vision impairment, 277
     assistive devices, 279

home alterations for, 279
interventions, 278–279
rehabilitation services, 278
symptoms, 278
types, 278
Visual communication, 33, 38–39
Vocalization, 33, 38
Vocational knowledge, 267
Vocational rehabilitation needs,
     265–267
Volunteering, among older adults,
     257–258
von Helmholtz, Hermann, 54

W
Wandering, in dementia, 291–292
Wealth inequality, 215
Wellness, 33
     in older adults, 34
Wisdom, 351
     Plato and nature of, 6–7
Withdrawal, 98
Work-feedback-rework stage, 67–70
Working. See also Retirement
     among older adults, 251–258,
          266
     increased hours of, 255
     intentions in later life, 249
     and meaning-making, 256
Working memory, 132, 156
Working through, 55, 121–123, 129
World Database of Happiness, 347
World religions, and aging, 179–180
Wrong focus, 122
Wu wei, 201, 202, 207

Y
Yoga, path of, 180
Young adulthood stage, 16
Younger counselors, transference/
     countertransference with,
     116

Z
Zen Buddhism, 185. See also
     Buddhism